BOYS BE™

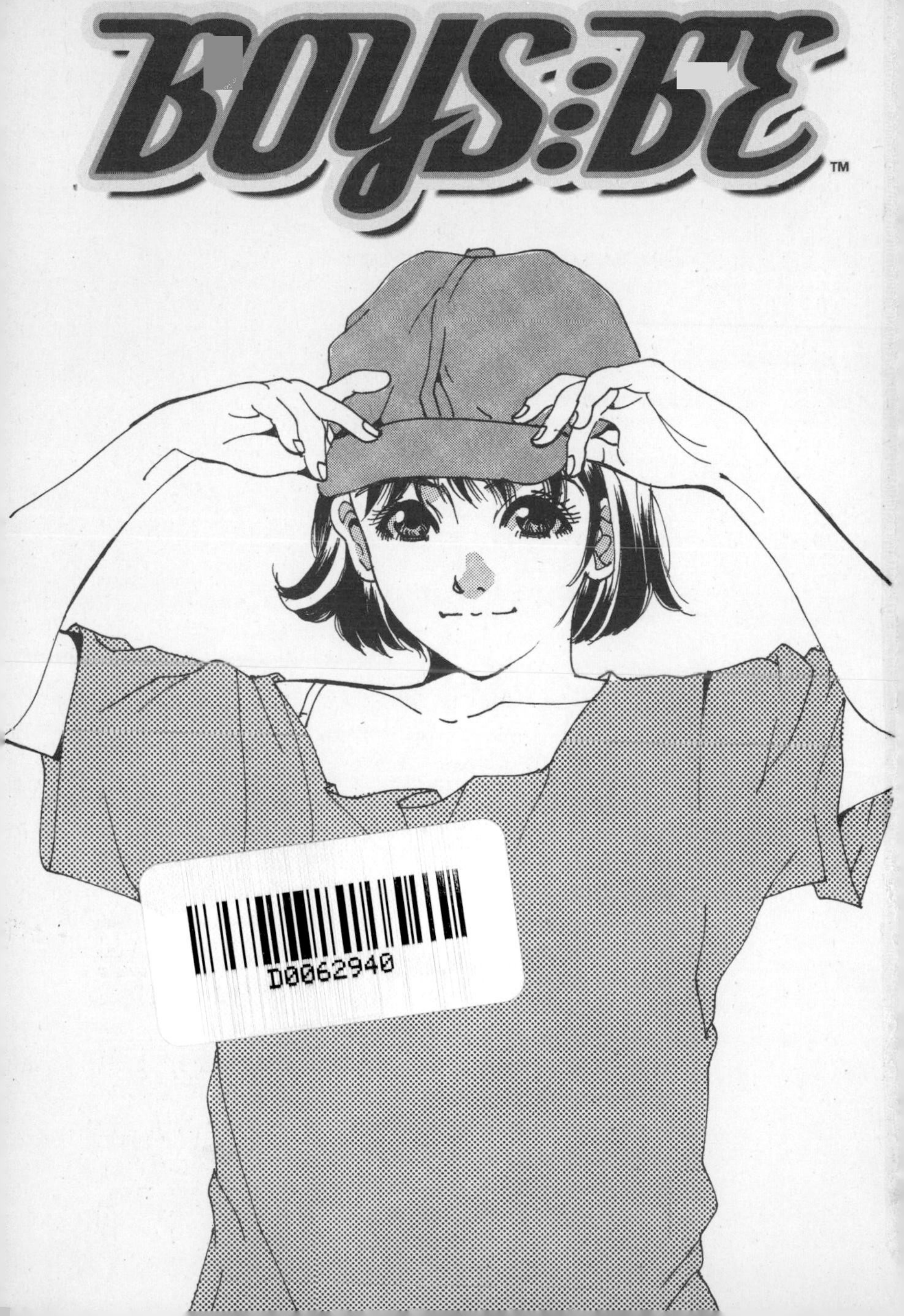

BOYS BE Second Season Vol. 2
Written by Masahiro Itabashi
Illustrated by Hiroyuki Tamakoshi

Translation - Katherine Schilling
Retouch and Lettering - Vicente Rivera Jr.
Production Artist - James Dashiell
Cover Design - Gary Shum

Editor - Carol Fox
Digital Imaging Manager - Chris Buford
Pre-Press Manager - Antonio DePietro
Production Managers - Jennifer Miller and Mutsumi Miyazaki
Art Director - Matt Alford
Managing Editor - Jill Freshney
VP of Production - Ron Klamert
President and C.O.O. - John Parker
Publisher and C.E.O. - Stuart Levy

A  Manga

TOKYOPOP Inc.
5900 Wilshire Blvd. Suite 2000
Los Angeles, CA 90036

E-mail: info@TOKYOPOP.com
Come visit us online at www.TOKYOPOP.com

ISBN: 1-59532-100-4

First TOKYOPOP printing: January 2005
10 9 8 7 6 5 4 3 2 1
Printed in the USA

BOYS BE Second Season
Vol. 2

Writer
Masahiro Itabashi

Artist
Hiroyuki Tamakoshi

HAMBURG // LONDON // LOS ANGELES // TOKYO

CONTENTS

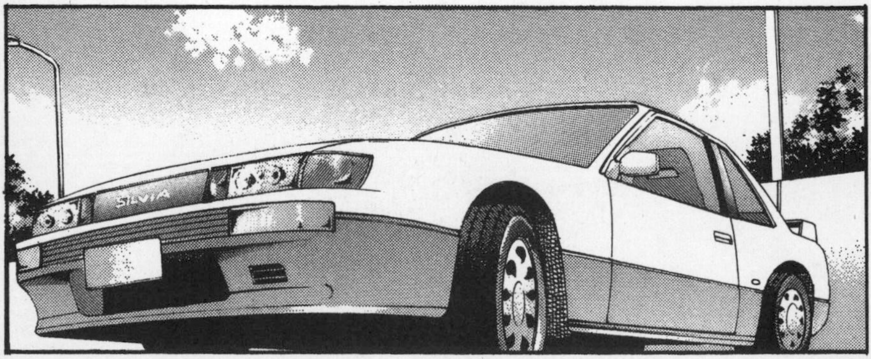

SILVIA

BOYS BE™

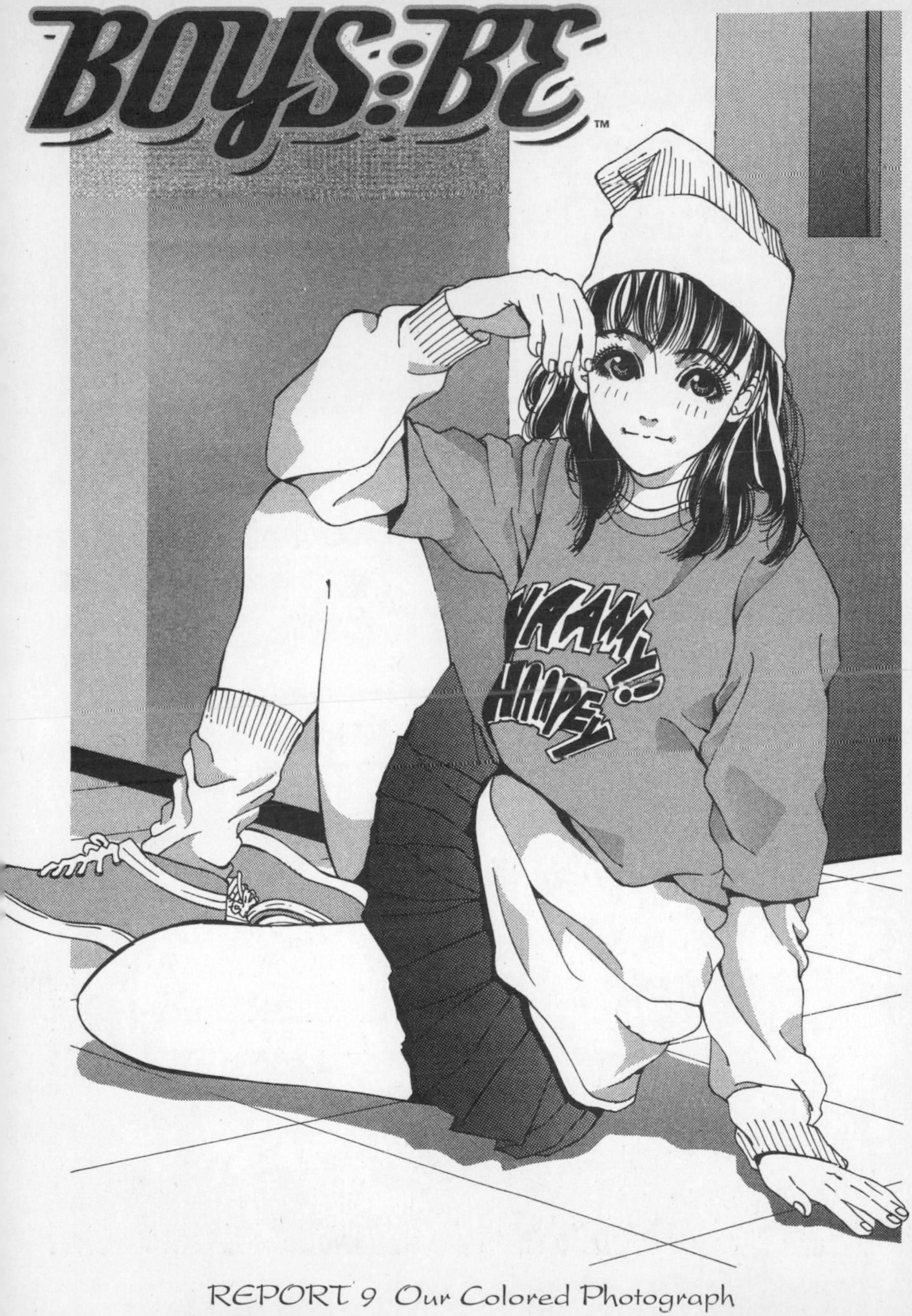

REPORT 9 Our Colored Photograph

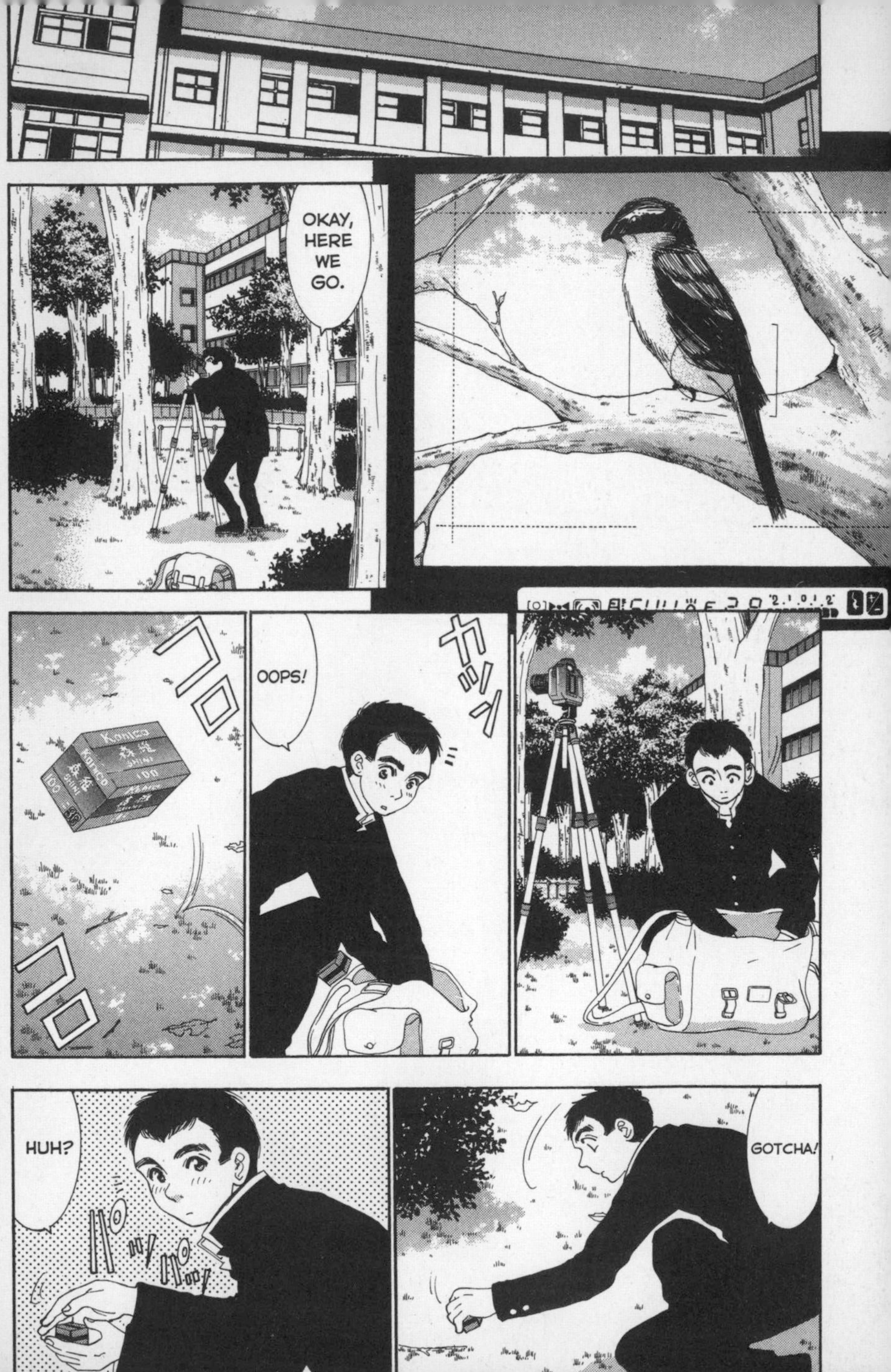
OKAY, HERE WE GO.
OOPS!
コロ
コロ
GOTCHA!
HUH?

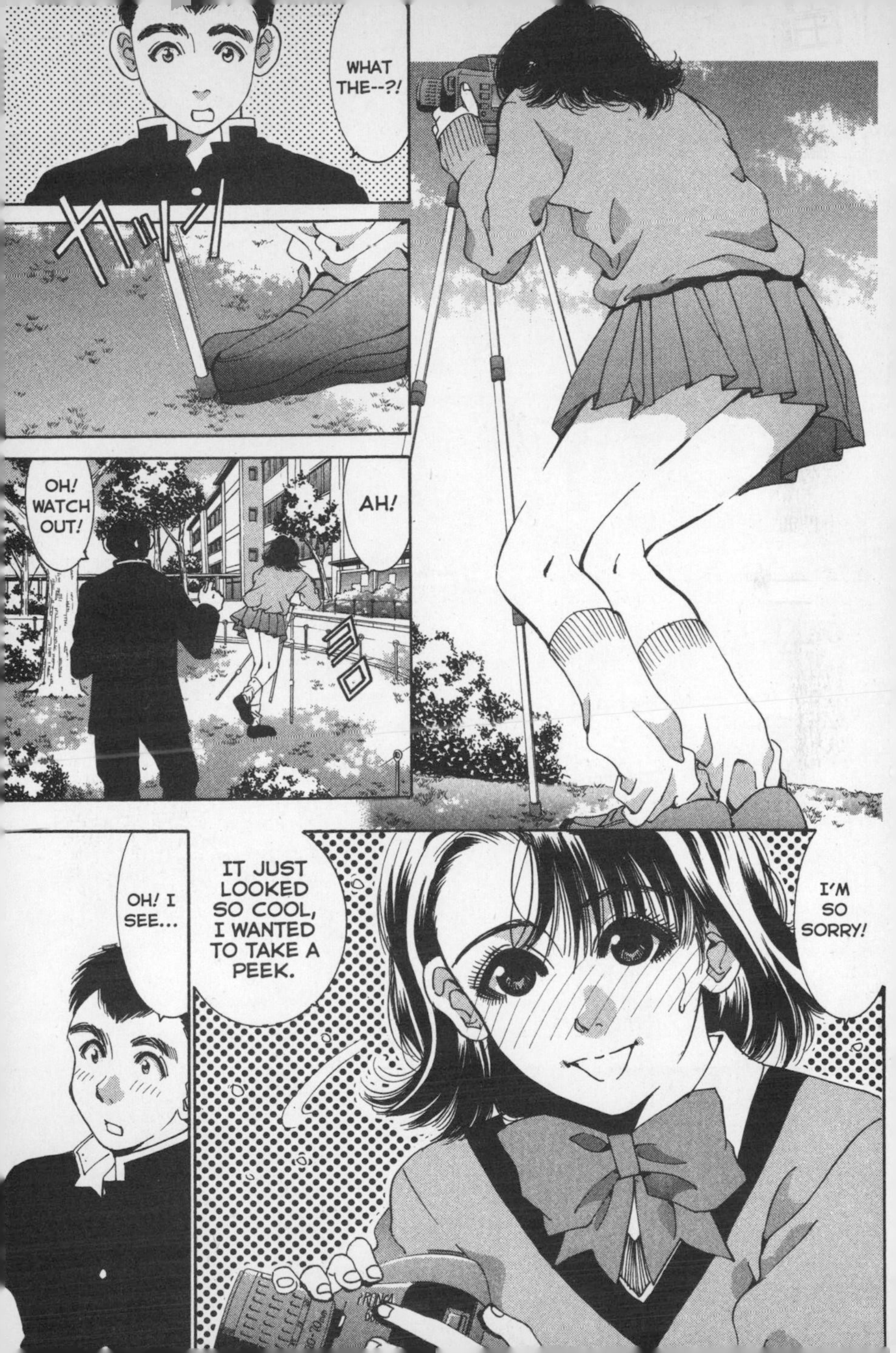
WHAT THE--?!
AH!
OH! WATCH OUT!
I'M SO SORRY!
IT JUST LOOKED SO COOL, I WANTED TO TAKE A PEEK.
OH! I SEE...

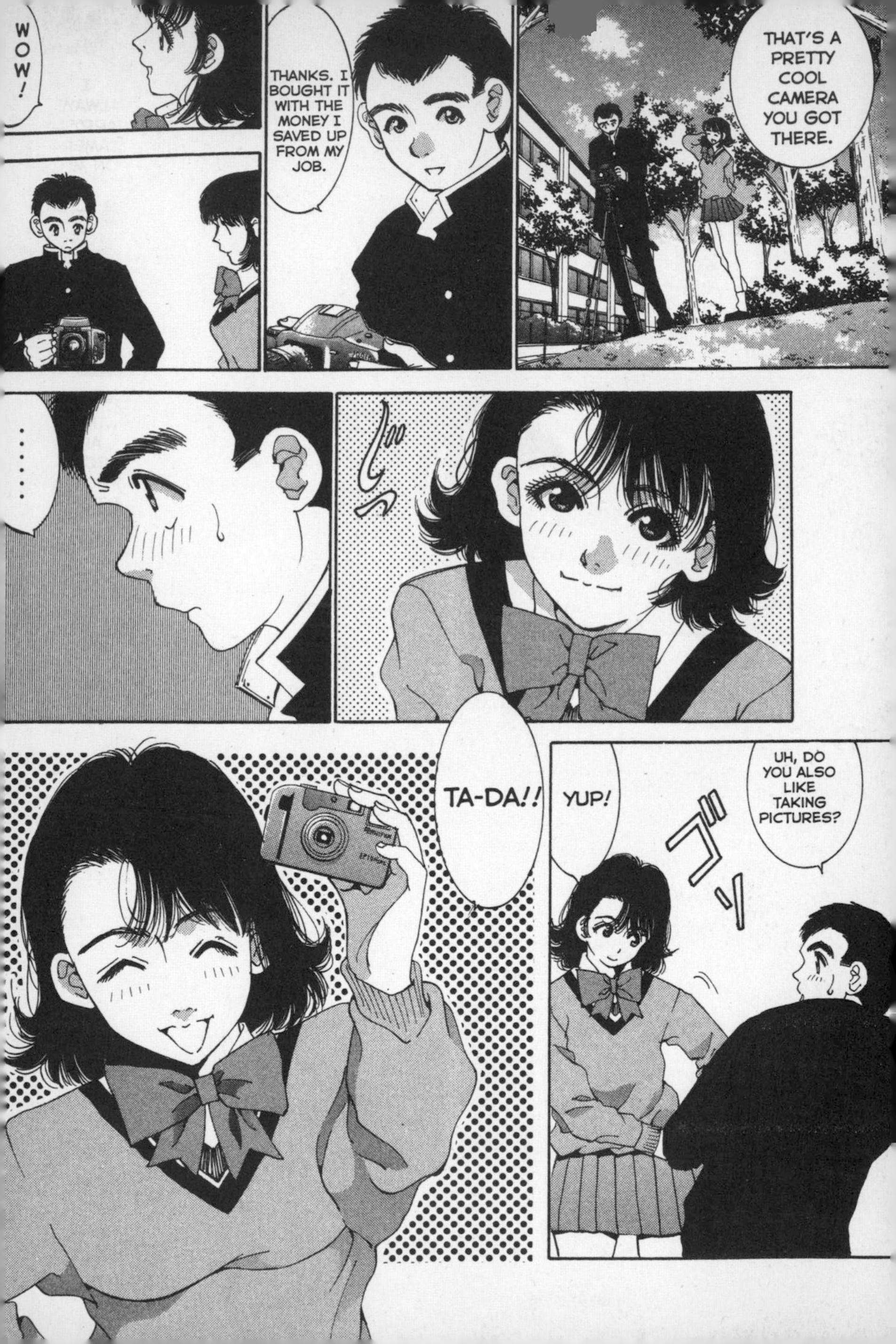
THAT'S A PRETTY COOL CAMERA YOU GOT THERE.
THANKS. I BOUGHT IT WITH THE MONEY I SAVED UP FROM MY JOB.
WOW!
......
UH, DO YOU ALSO LIKE TAKING PICTURES?
YUP!
TA-DA!!

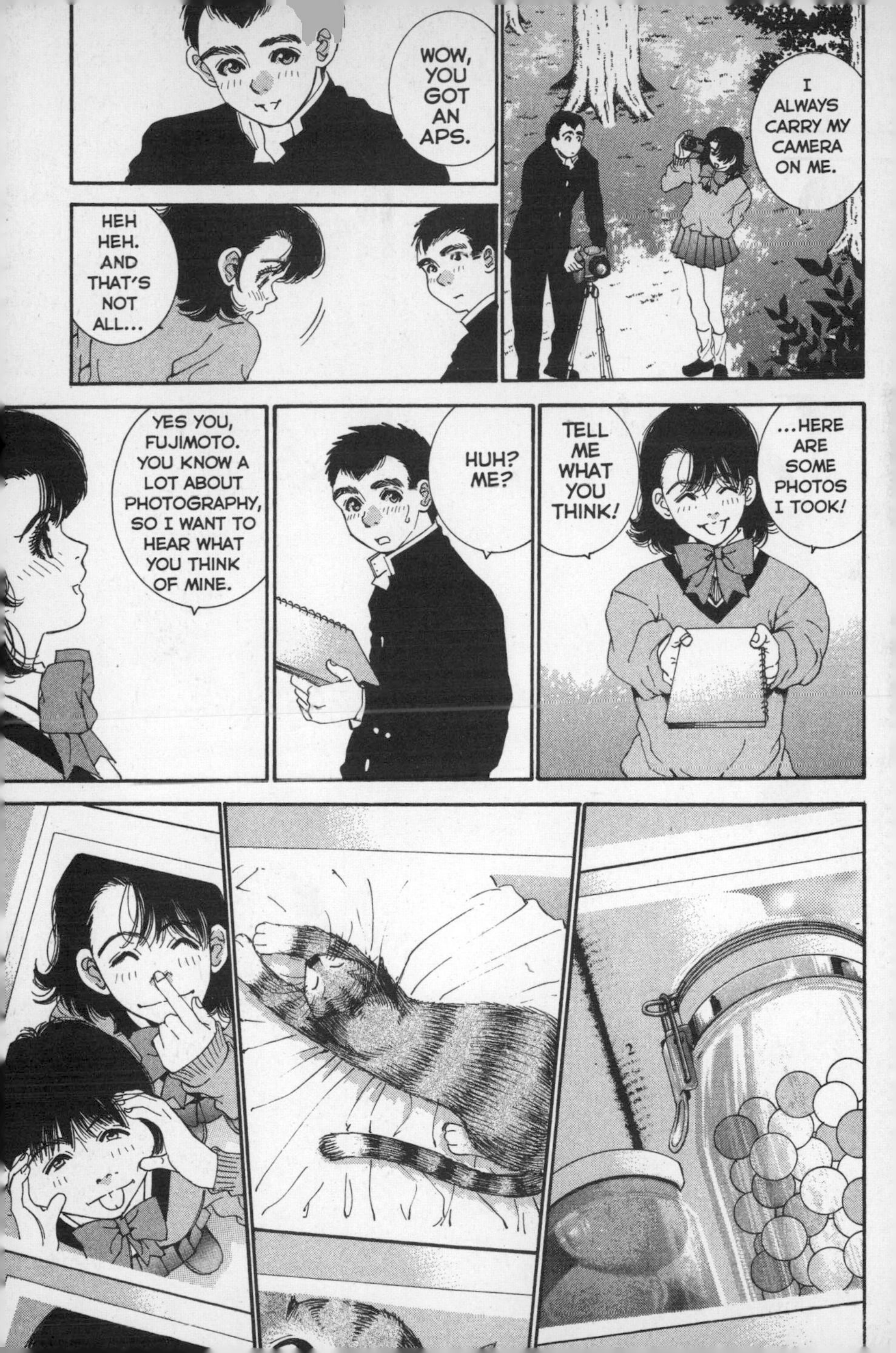
I ALWAYS CARRY MY CAMERA ON ME.
WOW, YOU GOT AN APS.
HEH HEH. AND THAT'S NOT ALL...
...HERE ARE SOME PHOTOS I TOOK!
TELL ME WHAT YOU THINK!
HUH? ME?
YES YOU, FUJIMOTO. YOU KNOW A LOT ABOUT PHOTOGRAPHY, SO I WANT TO HEAR WHAT YOU THINK OF MINE.

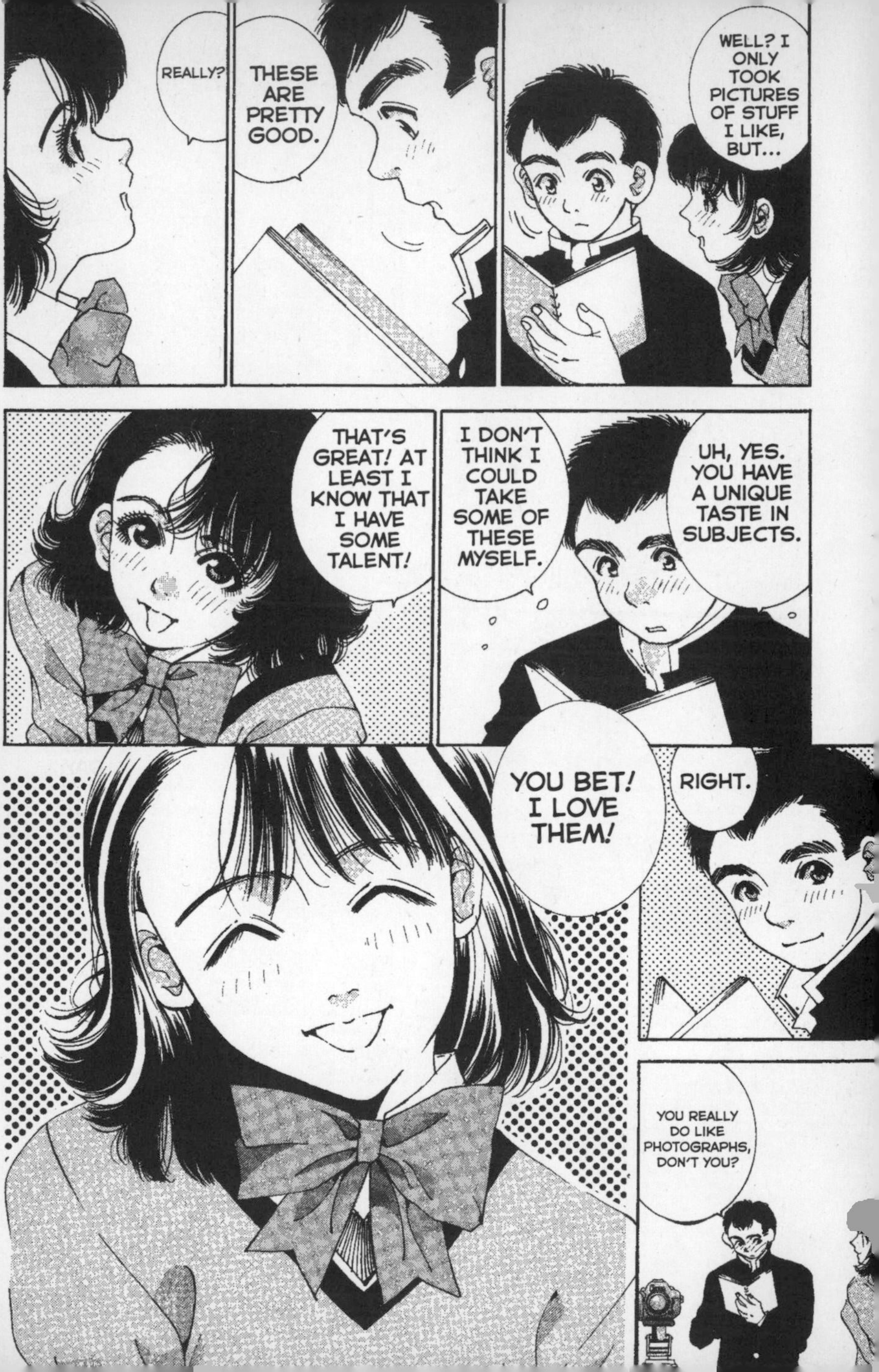
WELL? I ONLY TOOK PICTURES OF STUFF I LIKE, BUT...
THESE ARE PRETTY GOOD.
REALLY?
UH, YES. YOU HAVE A UNIQUE TASTE IN SUBJECTS.
I DON'T THINK I COULD TAKE SOME OF THESE MYSELF.
THAT'S GREAT! AT LEAST I KNOW THAT I HAVE SOME TALENT!
RIGHT.
YOU REALLY DO LIKE PHOTOGRAPHS, DON'T YOU?
YOU BET! I LOVE THEM!

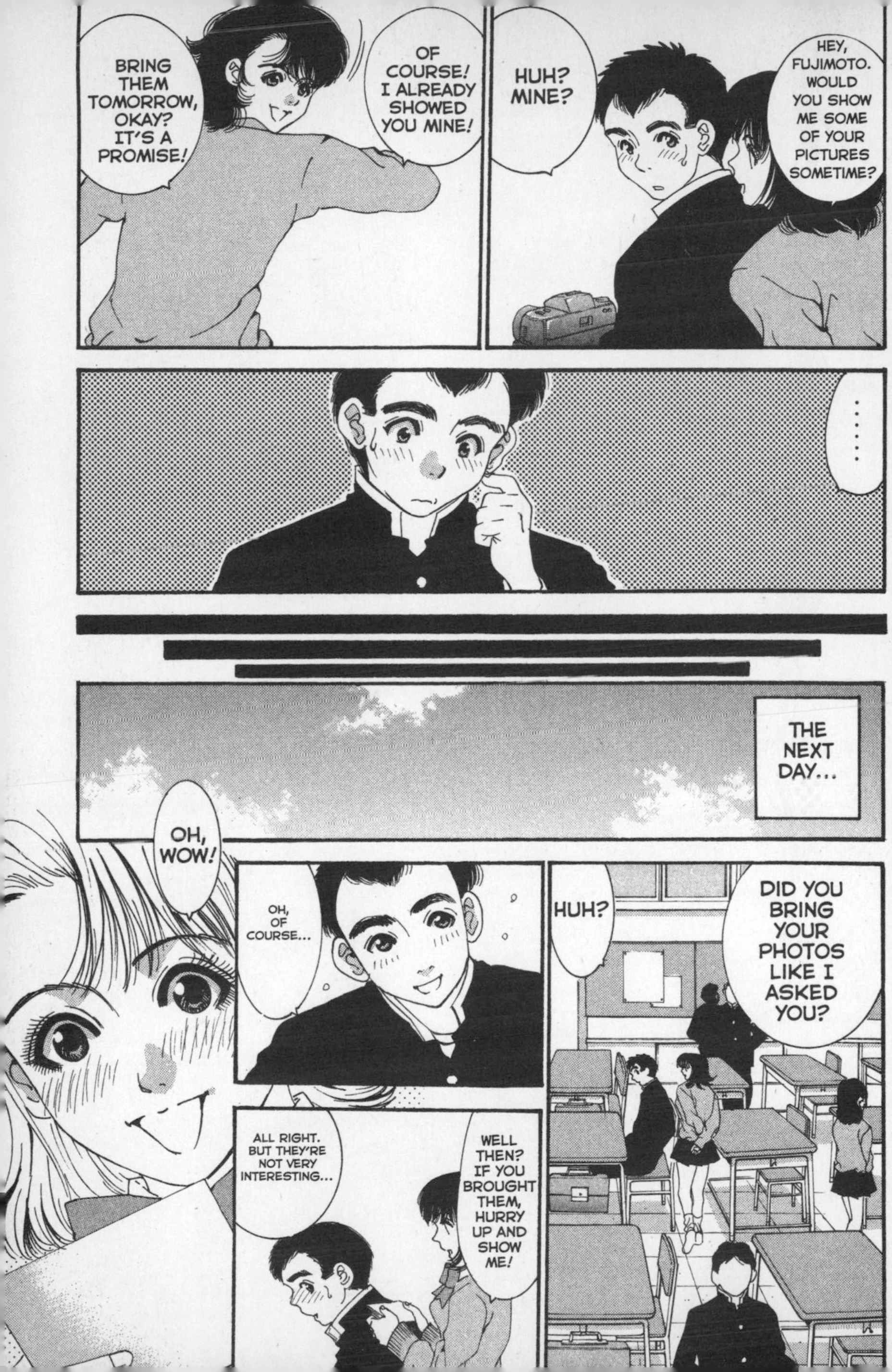
HEY, FUJIMOTO. WOULD YOU SHOW ME SOME OF YOUR PICTURES SOMETIME?
HUH? MINE?
OF COURSE! I ALREADY SHOWED YOU MINE!
BRING THEM TOMORROW, OKAY? IT'S A PROMISE!
......
THE NEXT DAY...
DID YOU BRING YOUR PHOTOS LIKE I ASKED YOU?
HUH?
OH, OF COURSE...
WELL THEN? IF YOU BROUGHT THEM, HURRY UP AND SHOW ME!
ALL RIGHT. BUT THEY'RE NOT VERY INTERESTING...
OH, WOW!

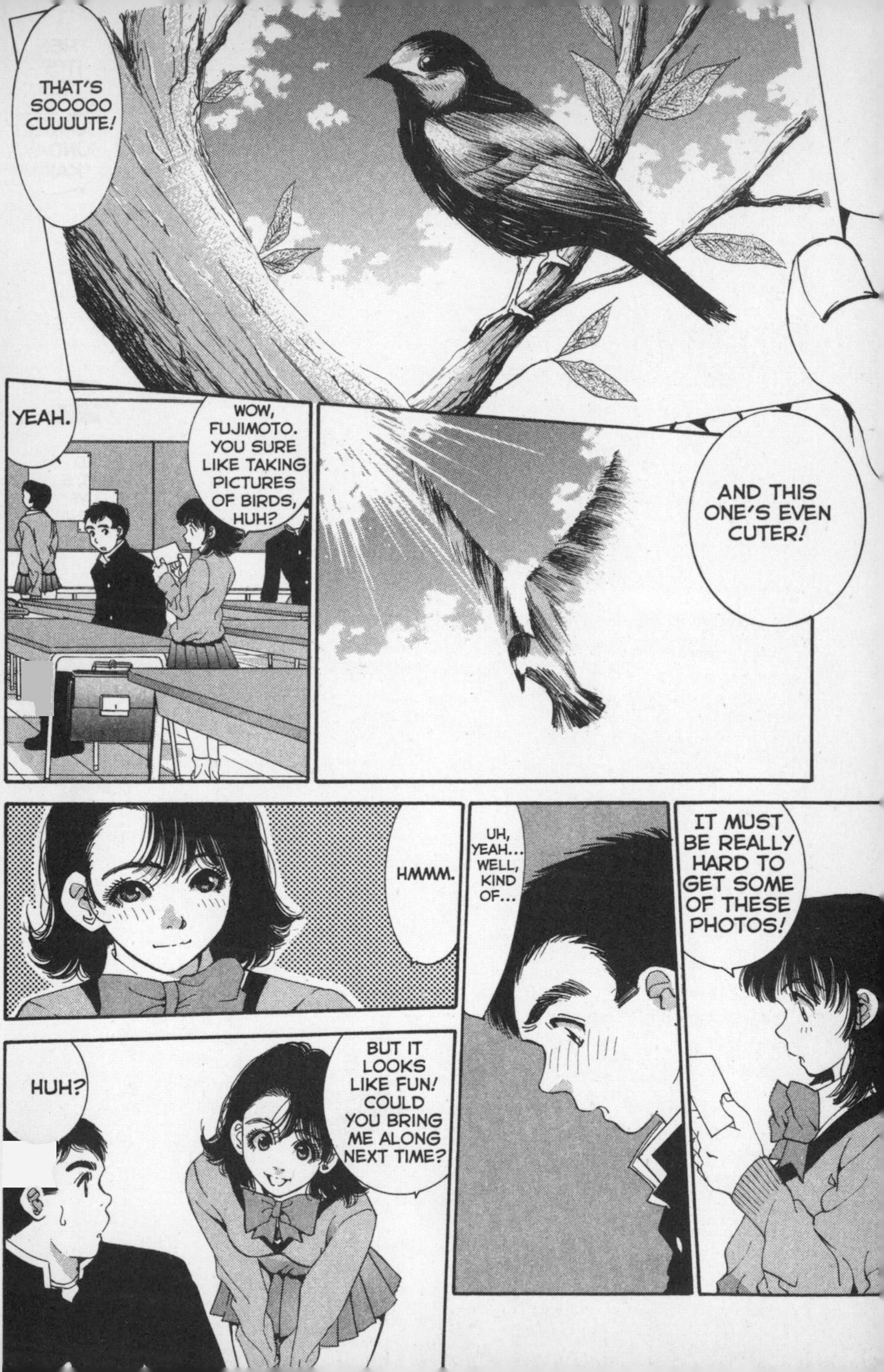
THAT'S SOOOOO CUUUUTE!
AND THIS ONE'S EVEN CUTER!
WOW, FUJIMOTO. YOU SURE LIKE TAKING PICTURES OF BIRDS, HUH?
YEAH.
IT MUST BE REALLY HARD TO GET SOME OF THESE PHOTOS!
UH, YEAH... WELL, KIND OF...
HMMM.
BUT IT LOOKS LIKE FUN! COULD YOU BRING ME ALONG NEXT TIME?
HUH?

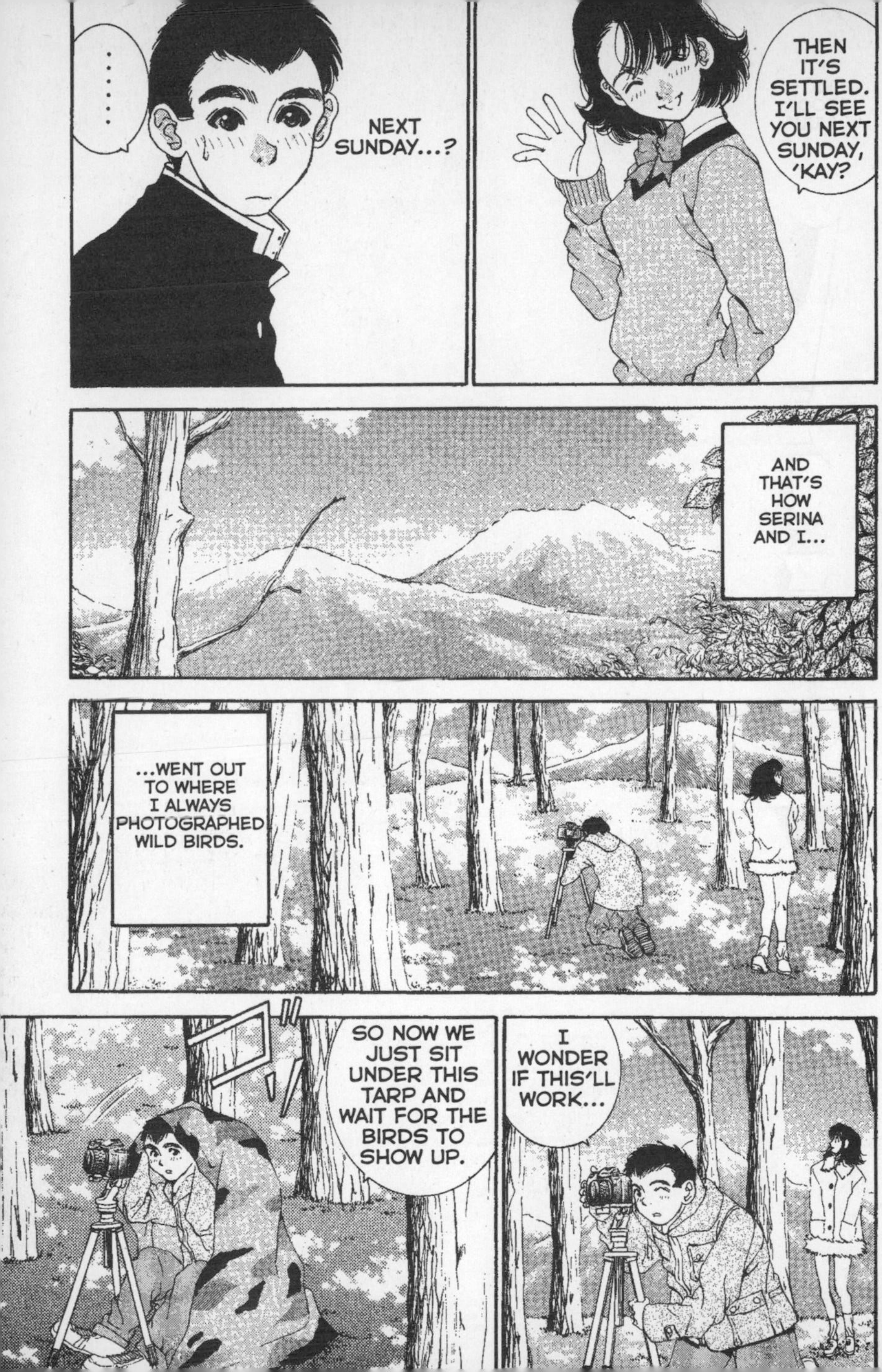
THEN IT'S SETTLED. I'LL SEE YOU NEXT SUNDAY, 'KAY?
......
NEXT SUNDAY...?
AND THAT'S HOW SERINA AND I...
...WENT OUT TO WHERE I ALWAYS PHOTOGRAPHED WILD BIRDS.
I WONDER IF THIS'LL WORK...
SO NOW WE JUST SIT UNDER THIS TARP AND WAIT FOR THE BIRDS TO SHOW UP.

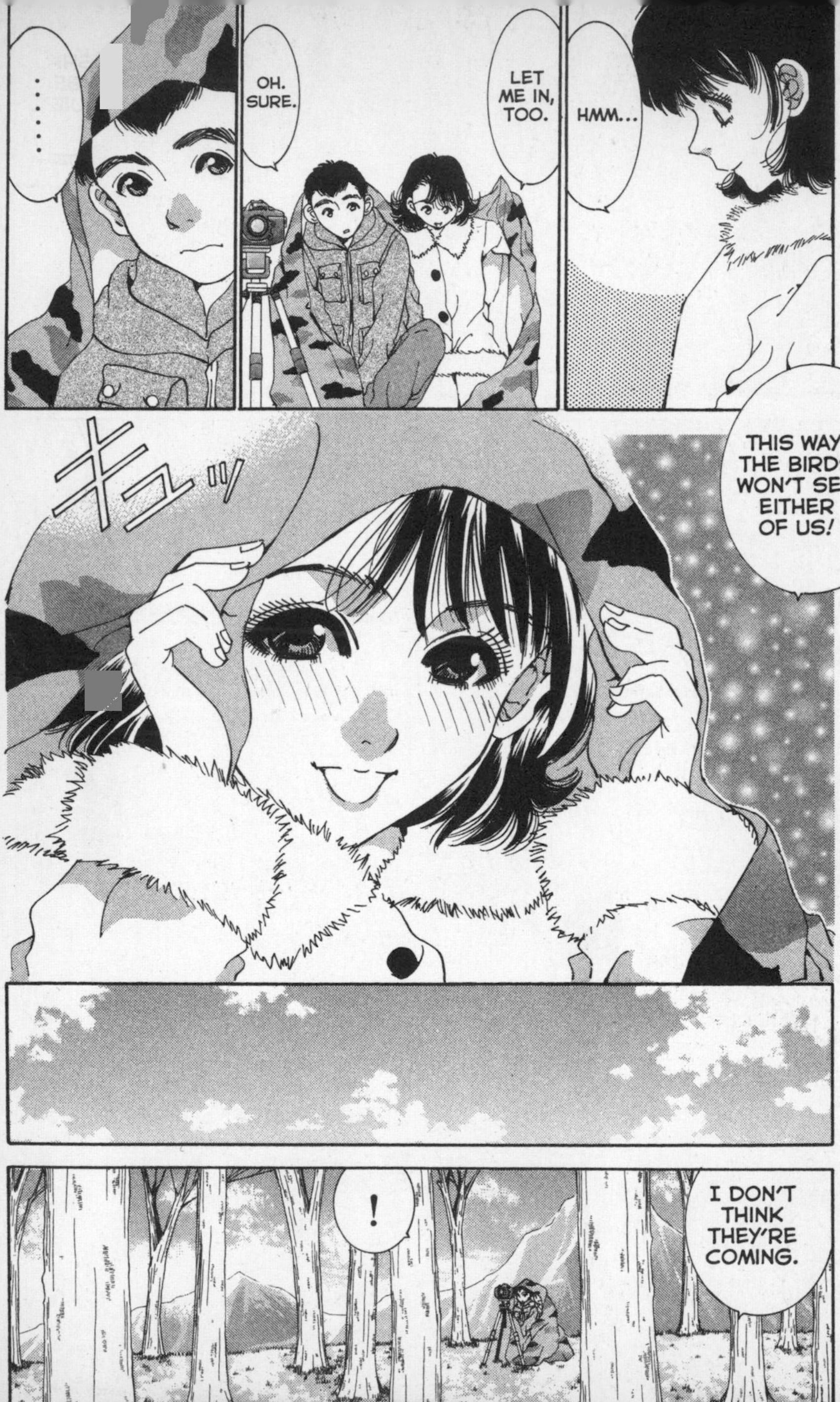
HMM...
LET ME IN, TOO.
OH. SURE.
......
THIS WAY, THE BIRDS WON'T SEE EITHER OF US!
キュッ
I DON'T THINK THEY'RE COMING.
!

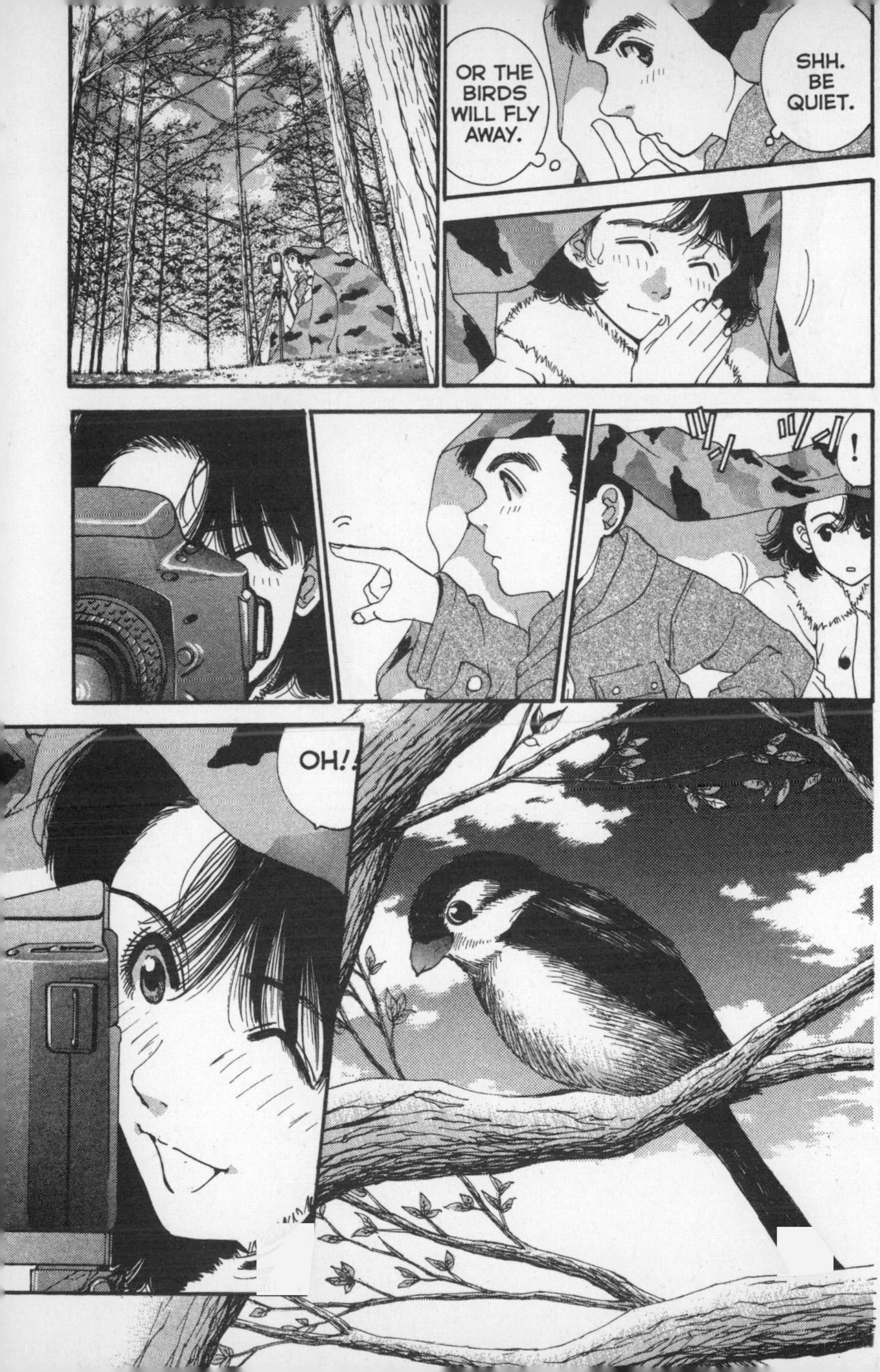
SHH. BE QUIET.
OR THE BIRDS WILL FLY AWAY.
!
OH!!

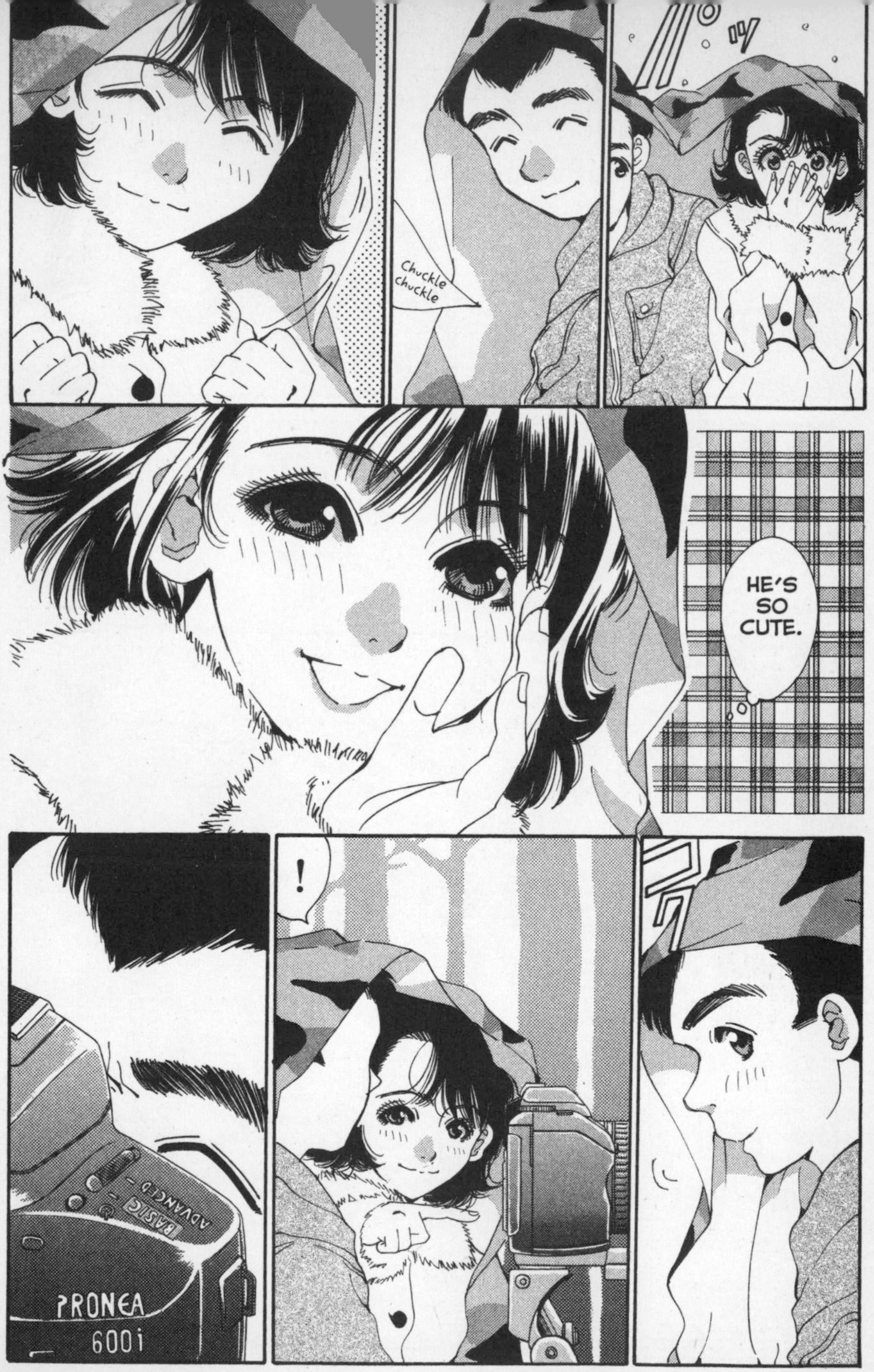
Chuckle chuckle
HE'S SO CUTE.
!
BASIC
ADVANCED
PRONEA
600i

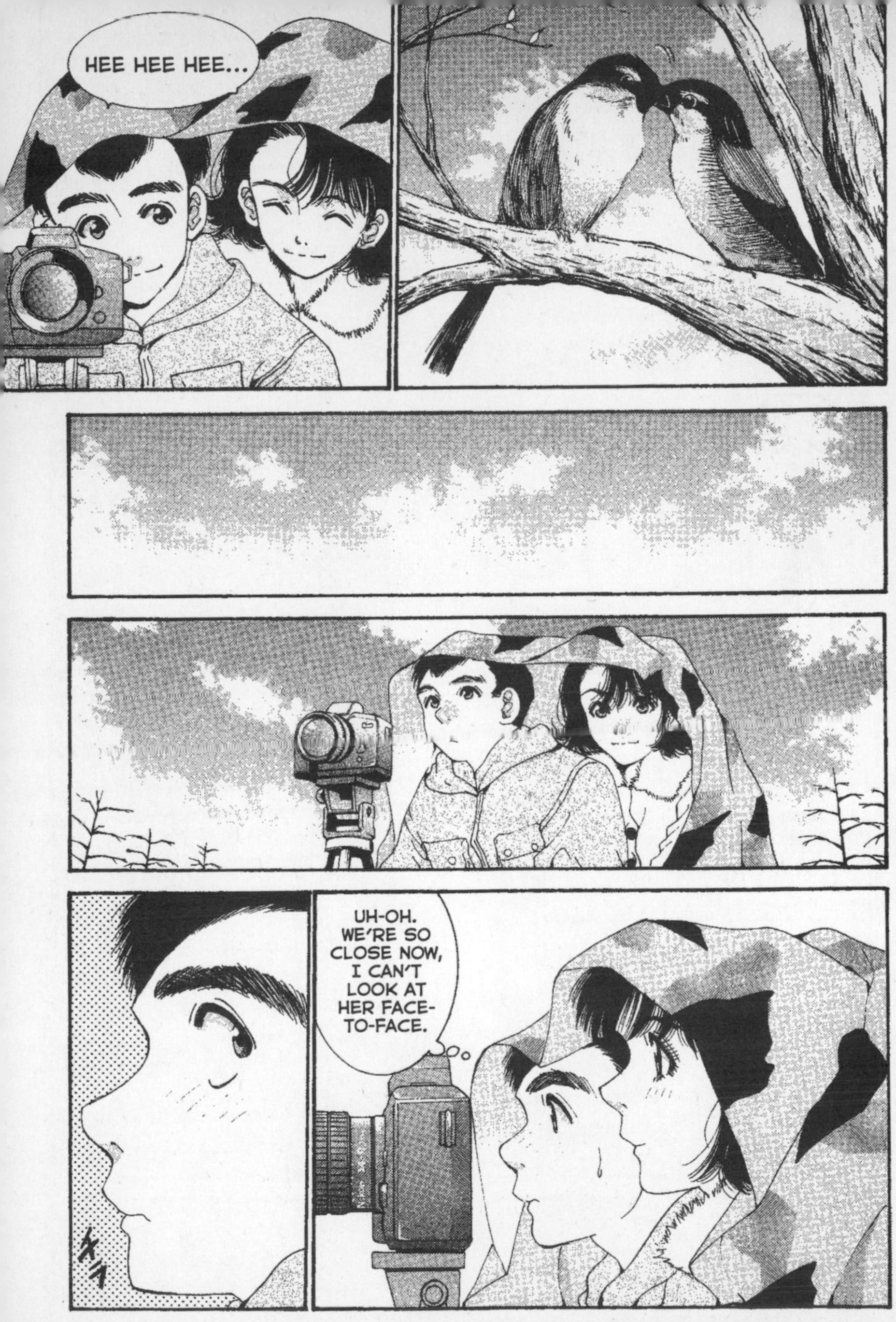
HEE HEE HEE...
UH-OH. WE'RE SO CLOSE NOW, I CAN'T LOOK AT HER FACE-TO-FACE.

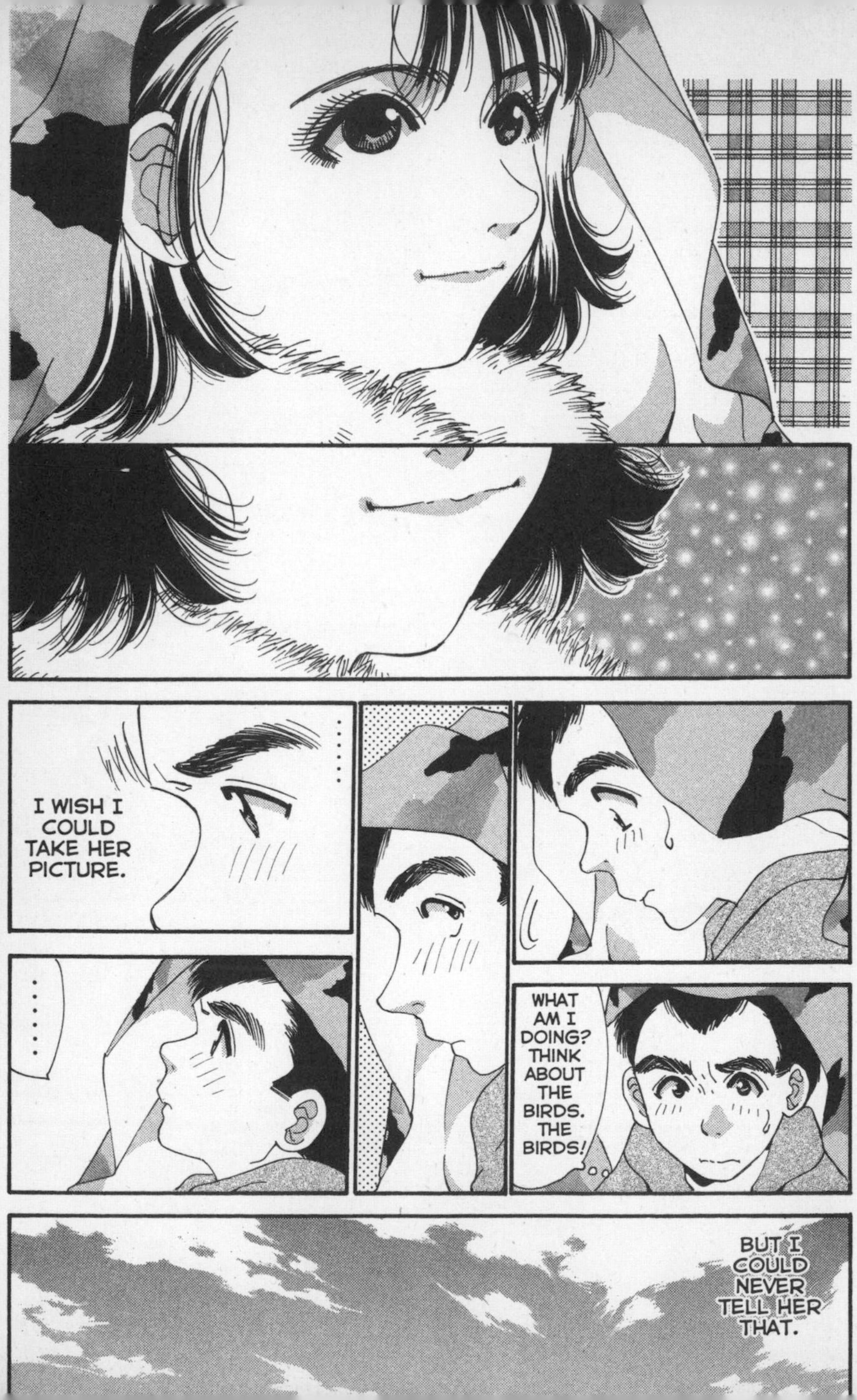
WHAT AM I DOING? THINK ABOUT THE BIRDS. THE BIRDS!
......
I WISH I COULD TAKE HER PICTURE.
......
BUT I COULD NEVER TELL HER THAT.

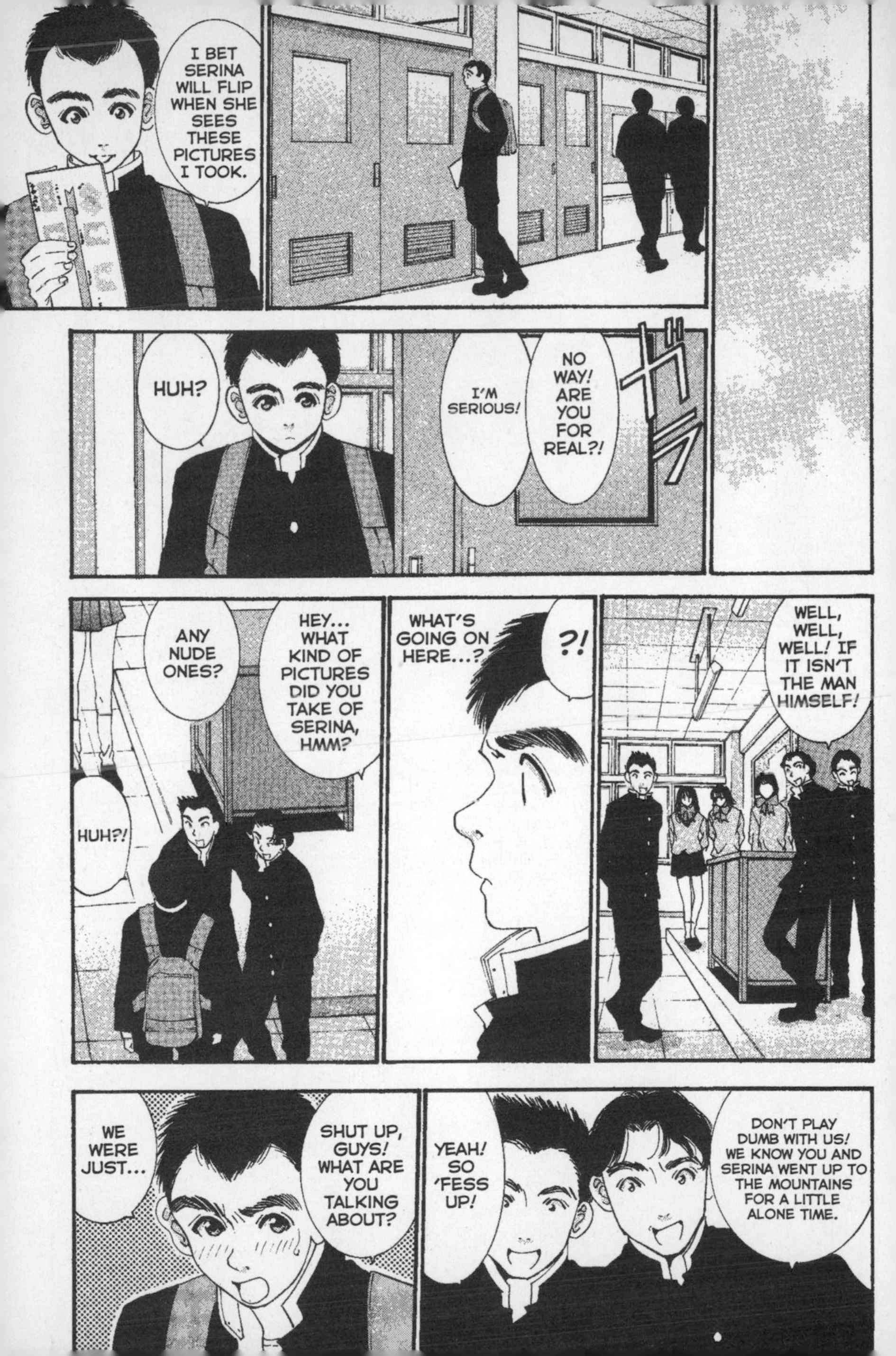
I BET SERINA WILL FLIP WHEN SHE SEES THESE PICTURES I TOOK.
ガラ
NO WAY! ARE YOU FOR REAL?!
I'M SERIOUS!
HUH?
WELL, WELL, WELL! IF IT ISN'T THE MAN HIMSELF!
?!
WHAT'S GOING ON HERE...?
HEY... WHAT KIND OF PICTURES DID YOU TAKE OF SERINA, HMM?
ANY NUDE ONES?
HUH?!
DON'T PLAY DUMB WITH US! WE KNOW YOU AND SERINA WENT UP TO THE MOUNTAINS FOR A LITTLE ALONE TIME.
YEAH! SO 'FESS UP!
SHUT UP, GUYS! WHAT ARE YOU TALKING ABOUT?
WE WERE JUST...

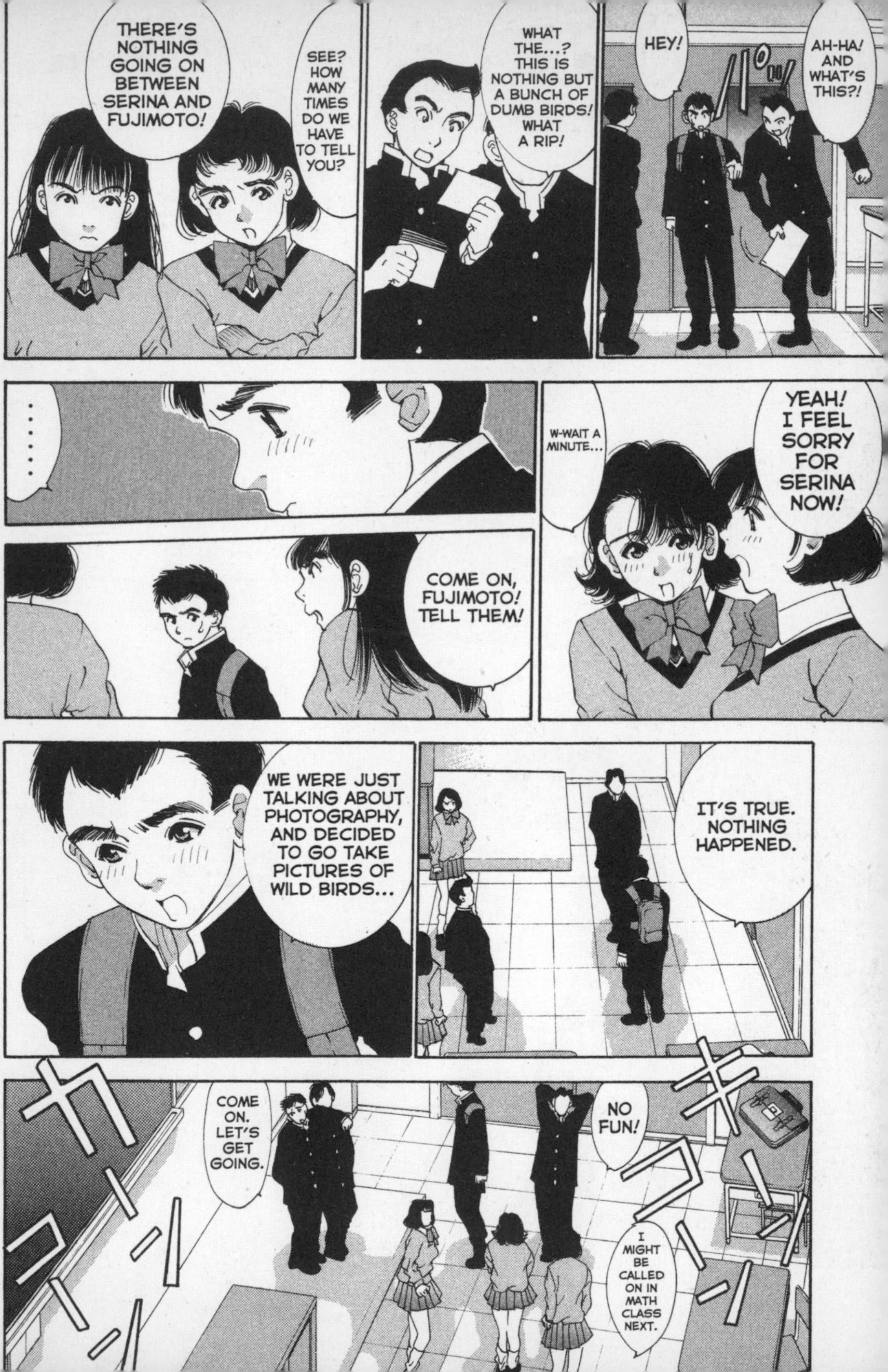
AH-HA! AND WHAT'S THIS?!
HEY!
WHAT THE...? THIS IS NOTHING BUT A BUNCH OF DUMB BIRDS! WHAT A RIP!
SEE? HOW MANY TIMES DO WE HAVE TO TELL YOU?
THERE'S NOTHING GOING ON BETWEEN SERINA AND FUJIMOTO!
YEAH! I FEEL SORRY FOR SERINA NOW!
W-WAIT A MINUTE...
......
COME ON, FUJIMOTO! TELL THEM!
IT'S TRUE. NOTHING HAPPENED.
WE WERE JUST TALKING ABOUT PHOTOGRAPHY, AND DECIDED TO GO TAKE PICTURES OF WILD BIRDS...
NO FUN!
I MIGHT BE CALLED ON IN MATH CLASS NEXT.
COME ON. LET'S GET GOING.

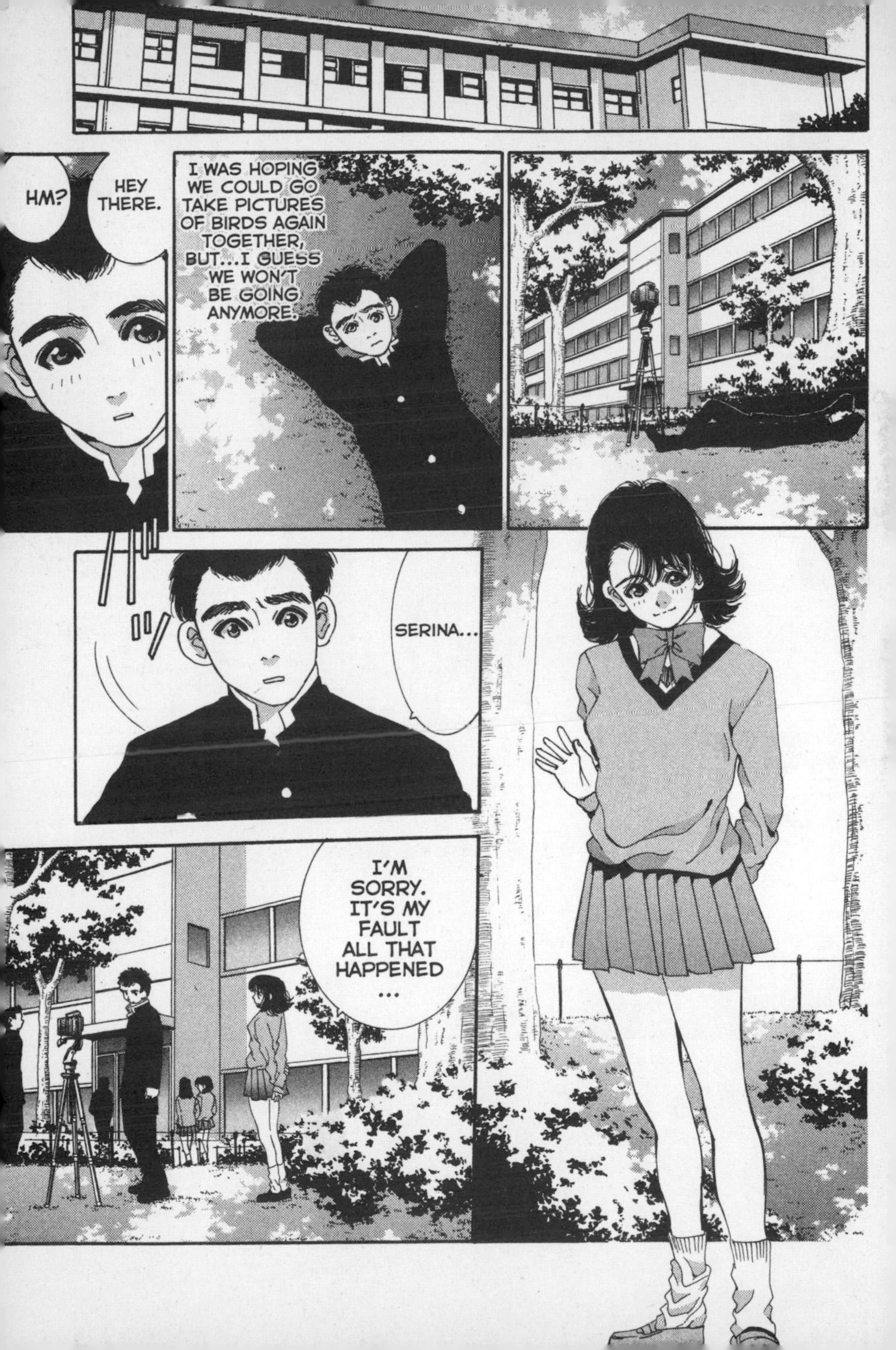
I WAS HOPING WE COULD GO TAKE PICTURES OF BIRDS AGAIN TOGETHER, BUT...I GUESS WE WON'T BE GOING ANYMORE.
HEY THERE.
HM?
SERINA...
I'M SORRY. IT'S MY FAULT ALL THAT HAPPENED ...

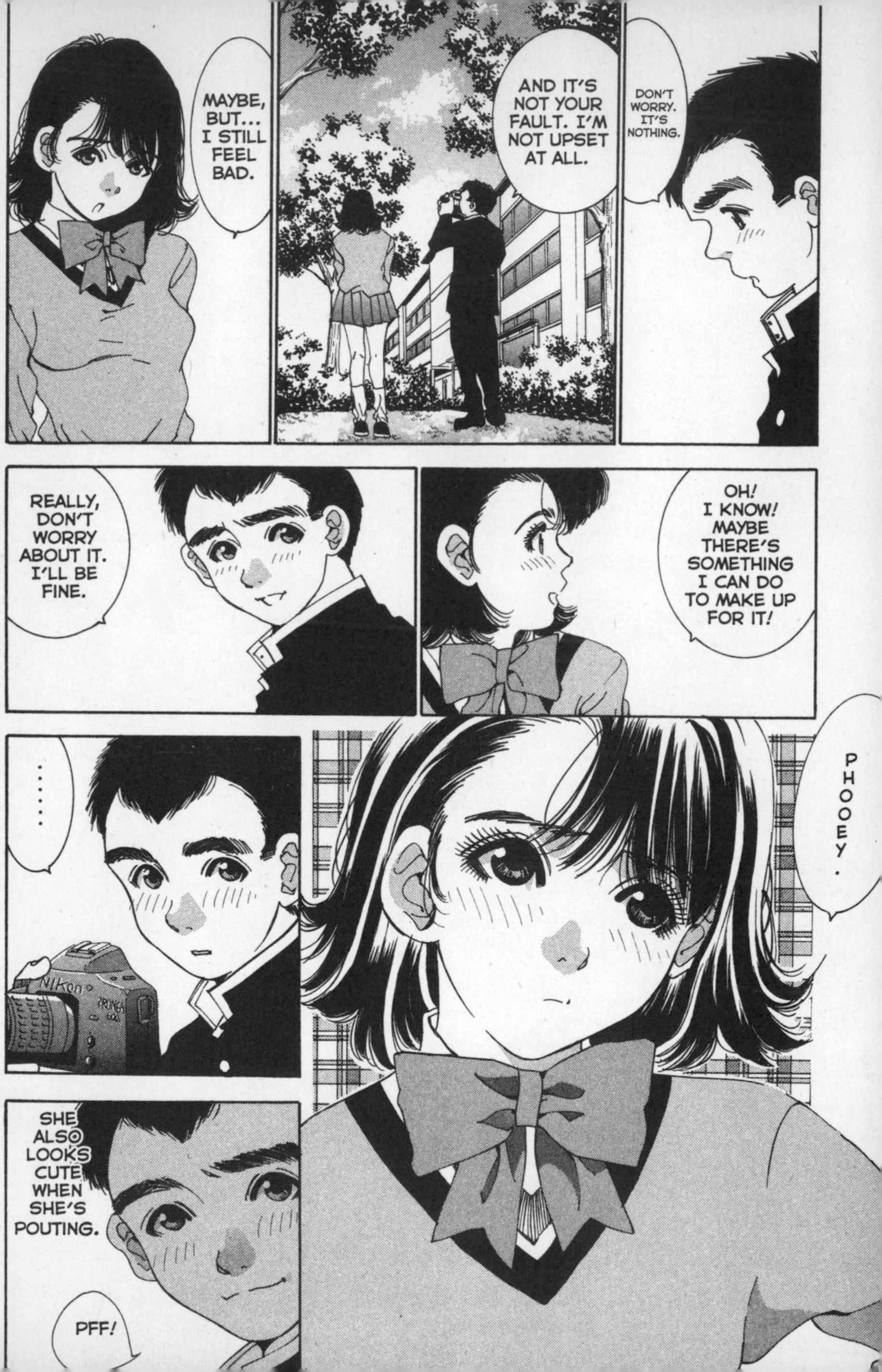
DON'T WORRY. IT'S NOTHING.
AND IT'S NOT YOUR FAULT. I'M NOT UPSET AT ALL.
MAYBE, BUT... I STILL FEEL BAD.
OH! I KNOW! MAYBE THERE'S SOMETHING I CAN DO TO MAKE UP FOR IT!
REALLY, DON'T WORRY ABOUT IT. I'LL BE FINE.
PHOOEY.
......
SHE ALSO LOOKS CUTE WHEN SHE'S POUTING.
PFF!

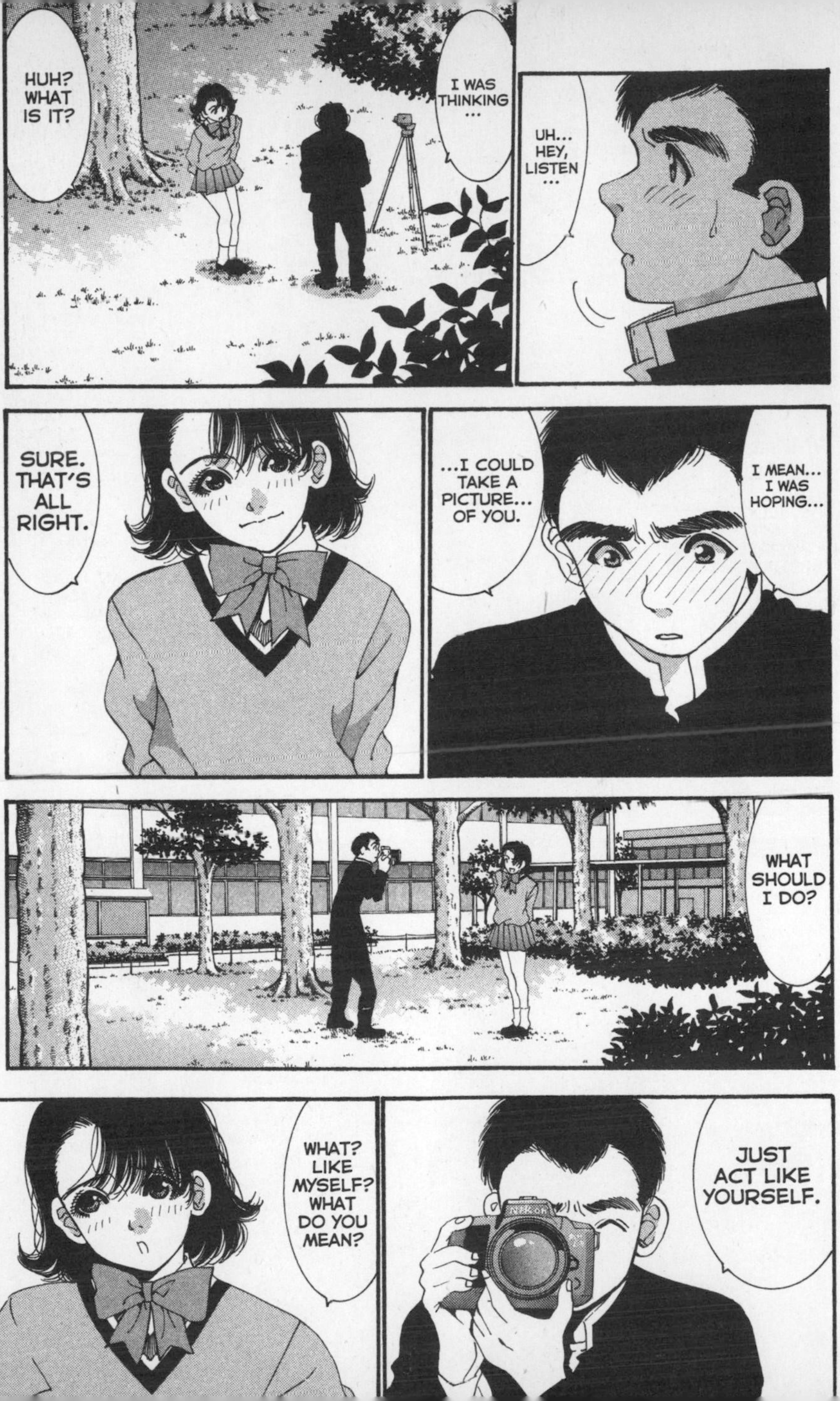
UH... HEY, LISTEN ...
I WAS THINKING ...
HUH? WHAT IS IT?
I MEAN... I WAS HOPING...
...I COULD TAKE A PICTURE... OF YOU.
SURE. THAT'S ALL RIGHT.
WHAT SHOULD I DO?
JUST ACT LIKE YOURSELF.
WHAT? LIKE MYSELF? WHAT DO YOU MEAN?

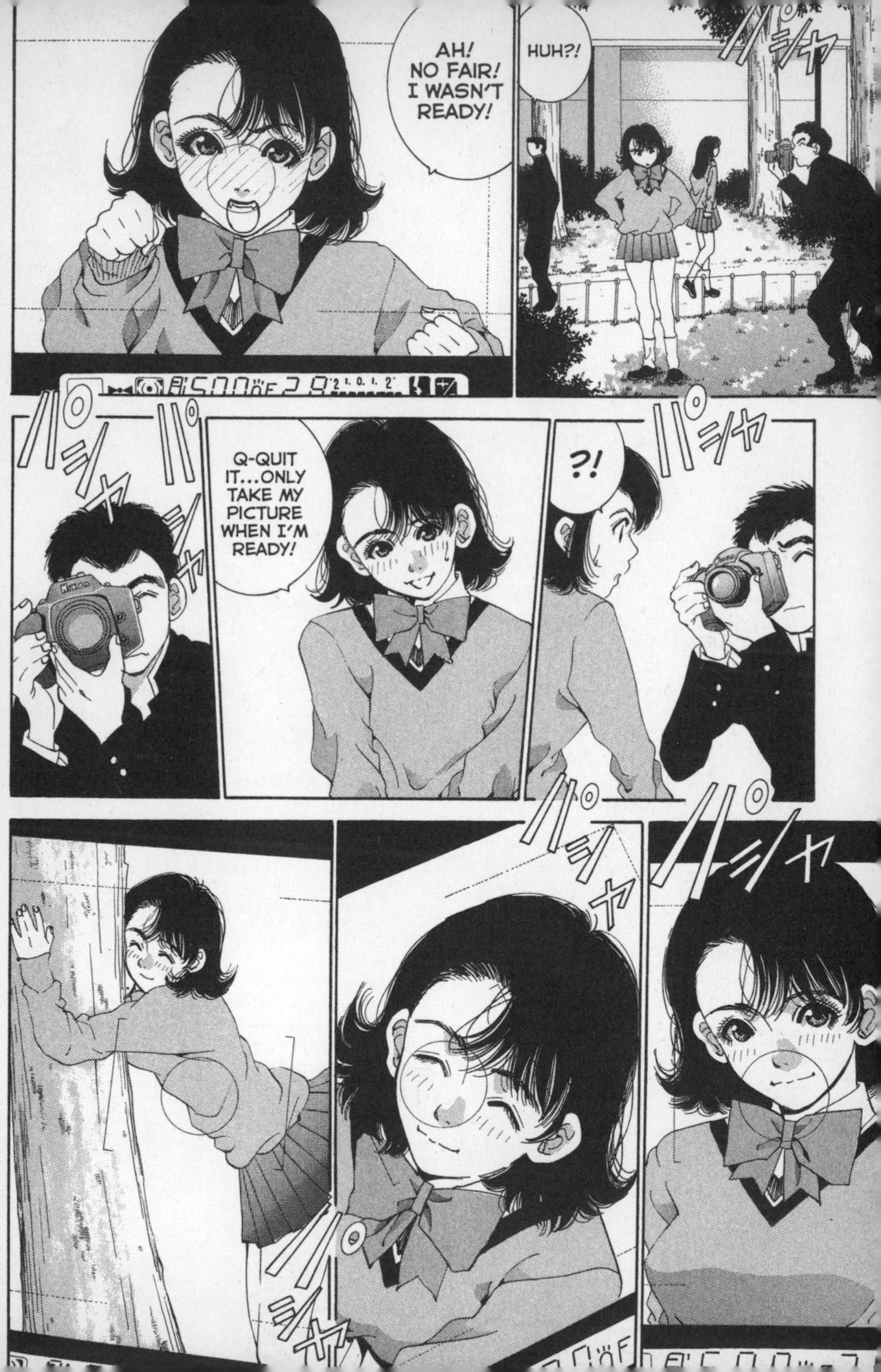
パシャ
HUH?!
AH! NO FAIR! I WASN'T READY!
パシャ
?!
Q-QUIT IT...ONLY TAKE MY PICTURE WHEN I'M READY!
パシャ
パシャ
パシャ
パシャ
パシャ

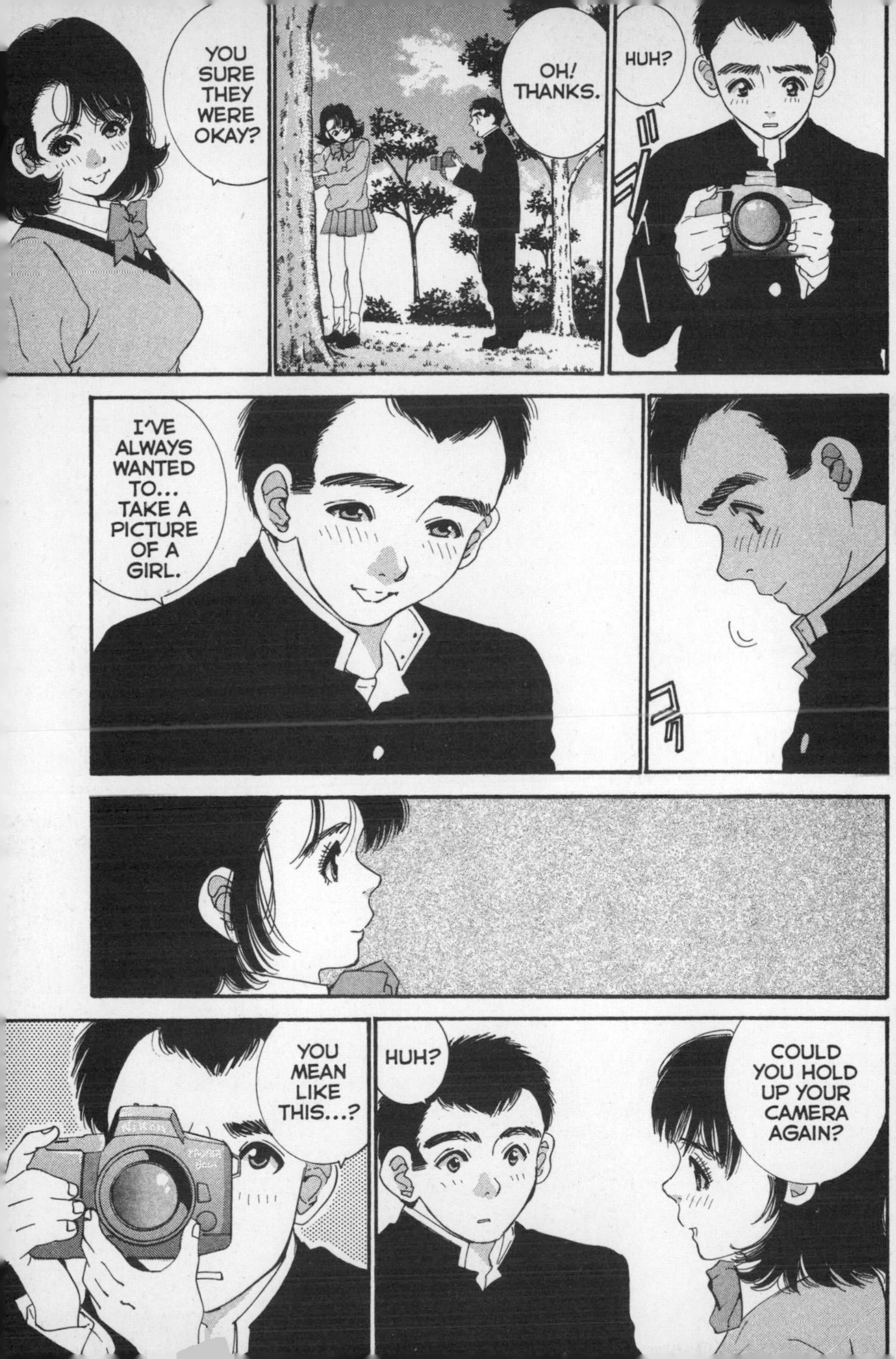
HUH?
OH! THANKS.
YOU SURE THEY WERE OKAY?
I'VE ALWAYS WANTED TO... TAKE A PICTURE OF A GIRL.
COULD YOU HOLD UP YOUR CAMERA AGAIN?
HUH?
YOU MEAN LIKE THIS...?

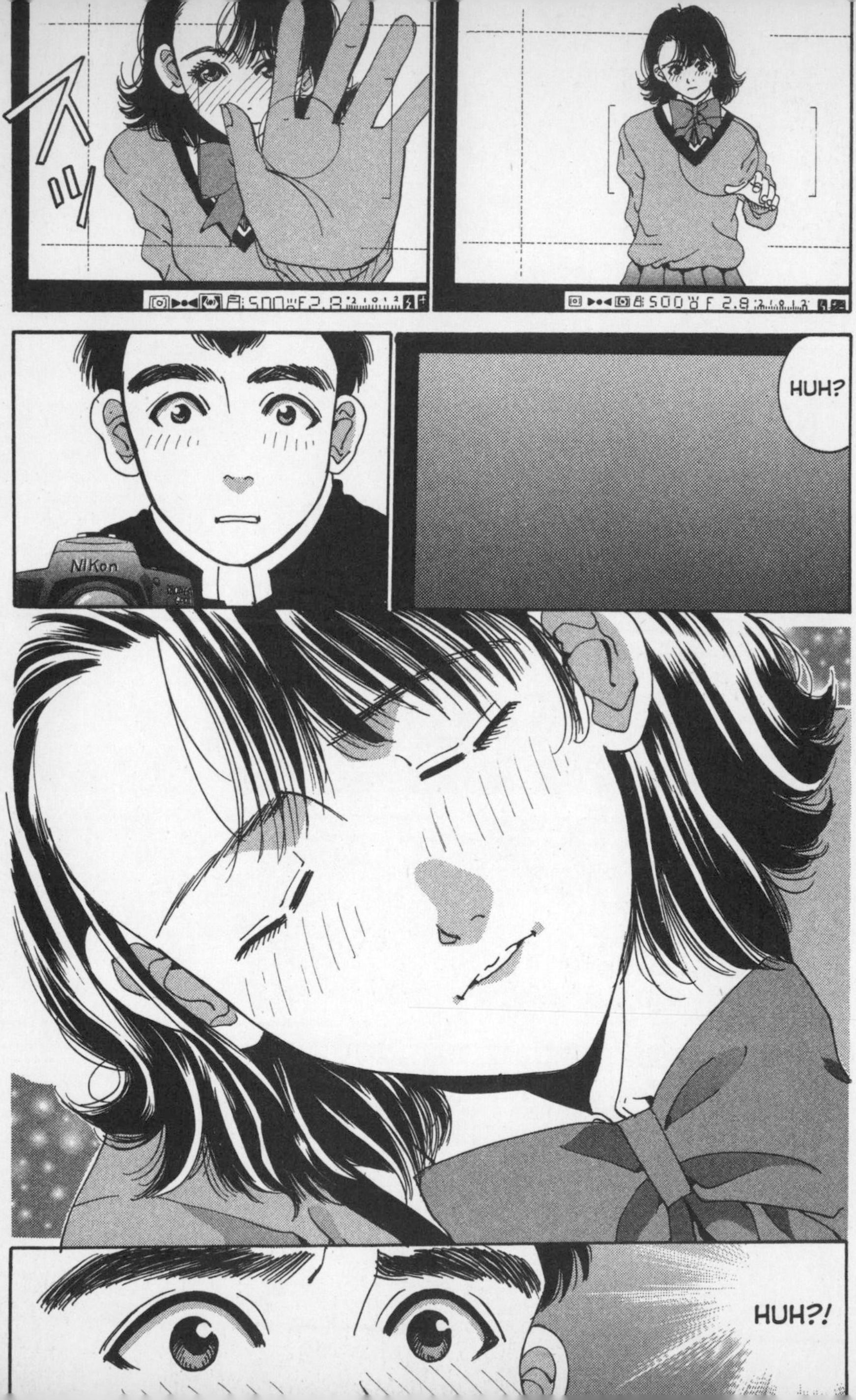
HUH?
NIKON
HUH?!

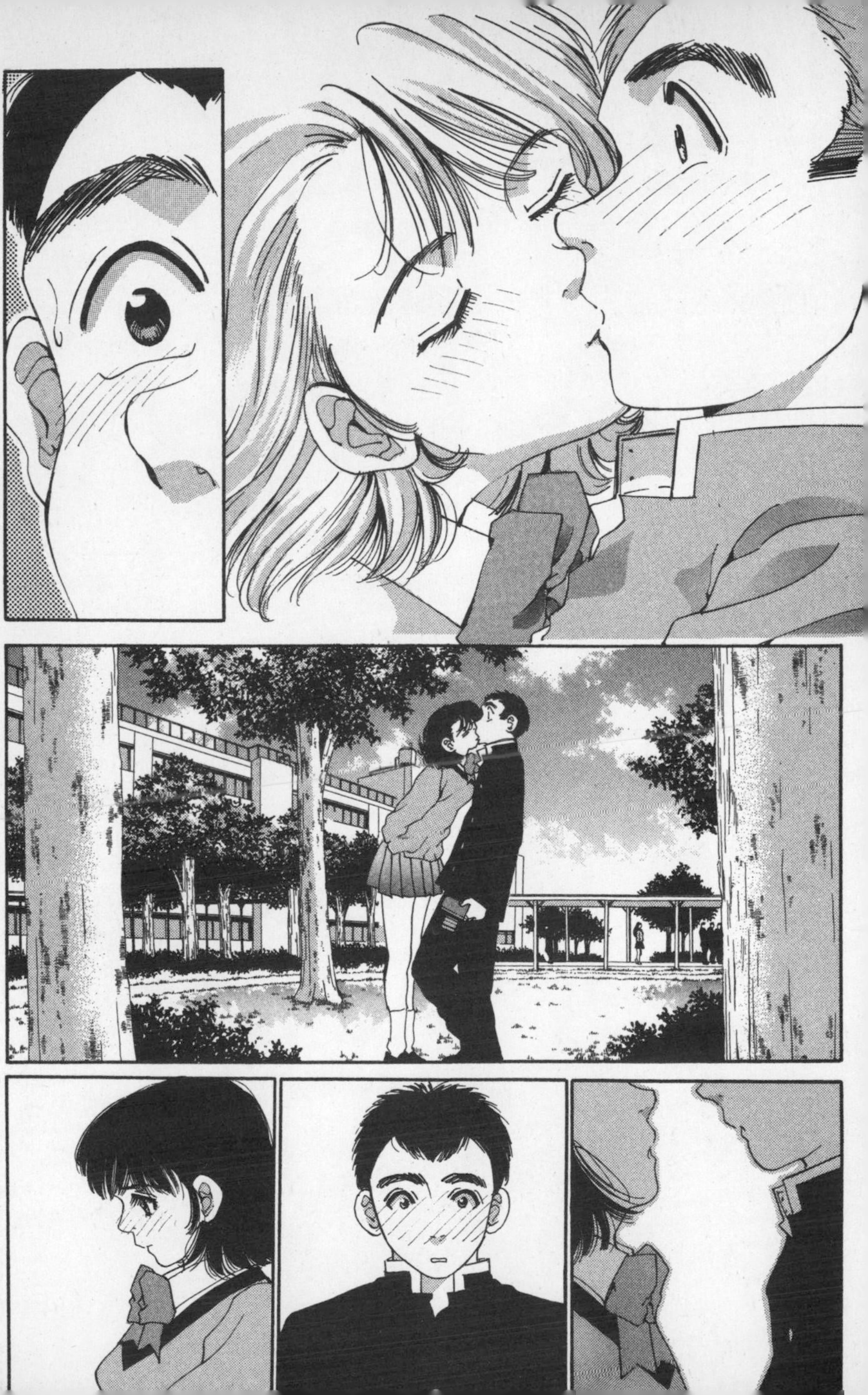

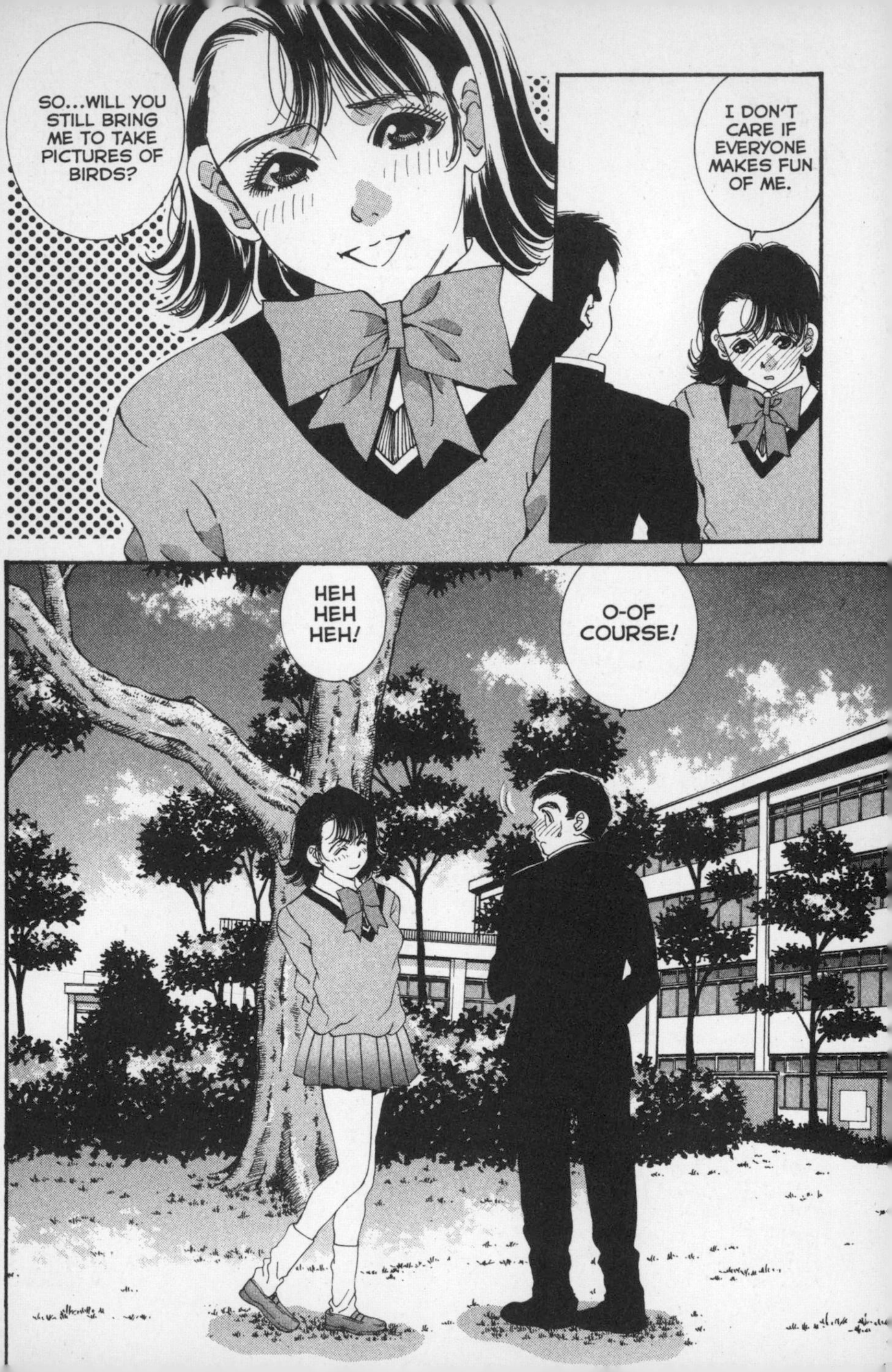
I DON'T CARE IF EVERYONE MAKES FUN OF ME.
SO...WILL YOU STILL BRING ME TO TAKE PICTURES OF BIRDS?
O-OF COURSE!
HEH HEH HEH!

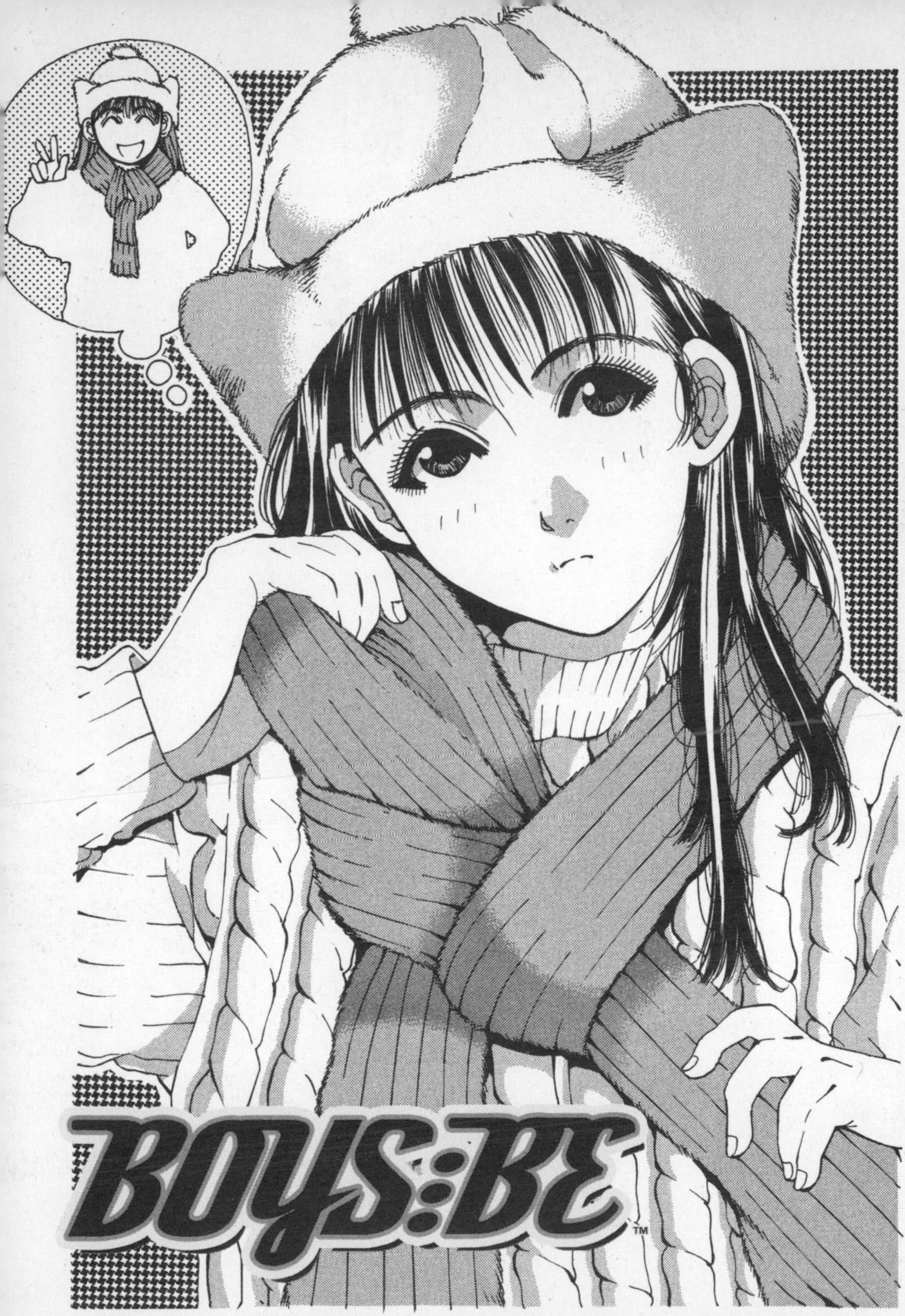
BOYS:BE™

Report 10 - My Secret Communication With You!

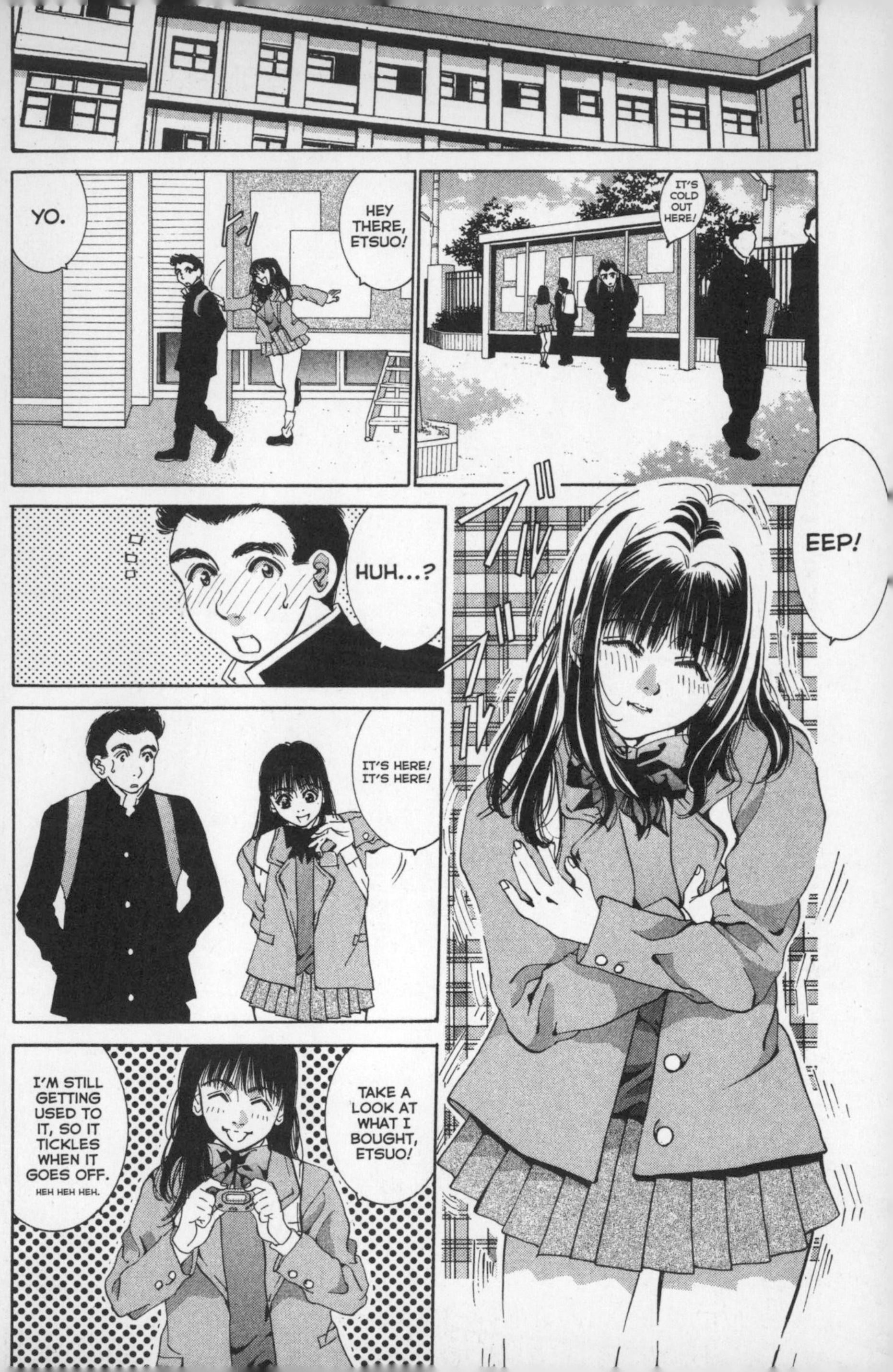
IT'S COLD OUT HERE!
HEY THERE, ETSUO!
YO.
EEP!
HUH...?
IT'S HERE! IT'S HERE!
TAKE A LOOK AT WHAT I BOUGHT, ETSUO!
I'M STILL GETTING USED TO IT, SO IT TICKLES WHEN IT GOES OFF.
HEH HEH HEH.

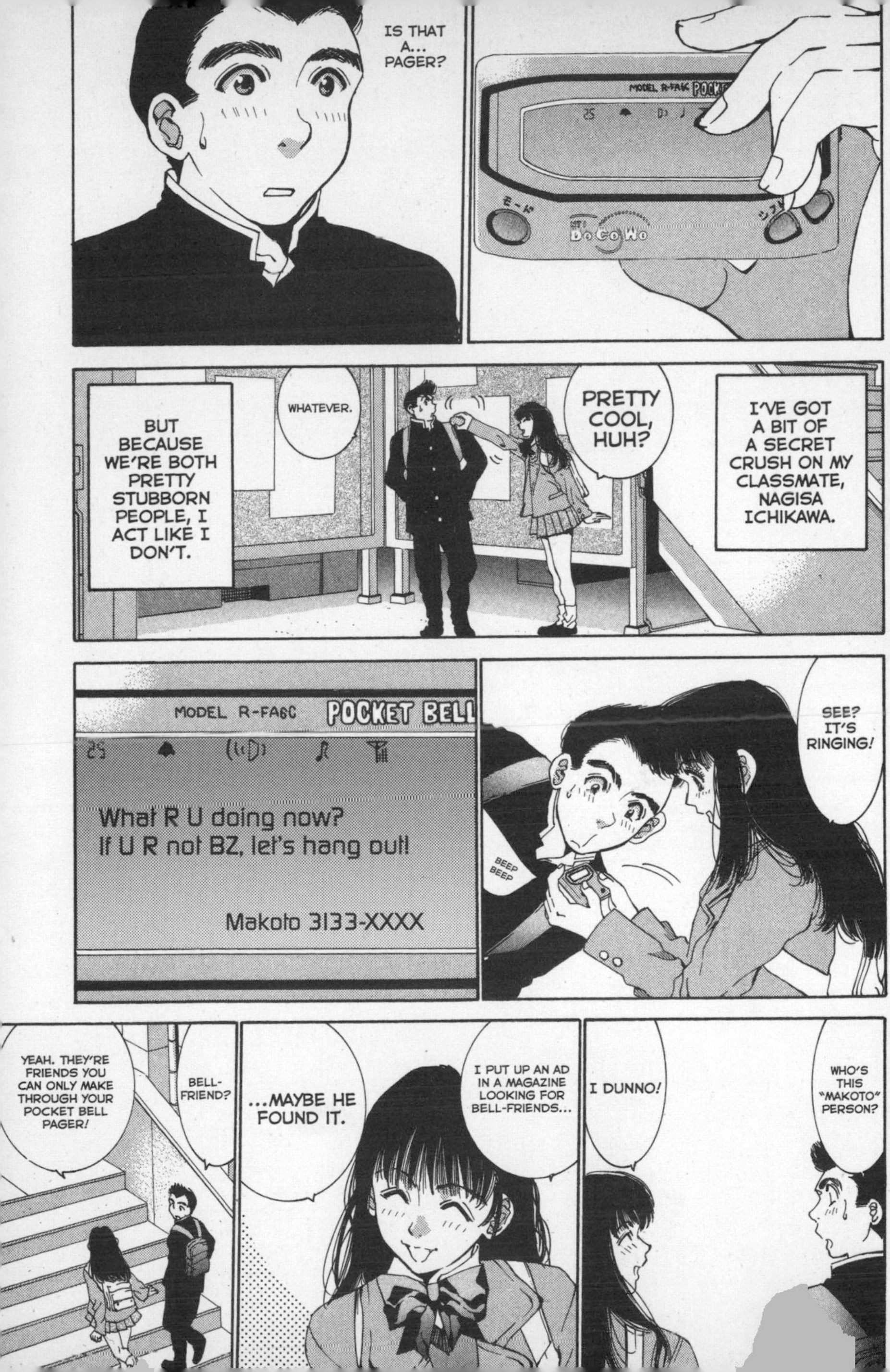
IS THAT A... PAGER?
I'VE GOT A BIT OF A SECRET CRUSH ON MY CLASSMATE, NAGISA ICHIKAWA.
PRETTY COOL, HUH?
WHATEVER.
BUT BECAUSE WE'RE BOTH PRETTY STUBBORN PEOPLE, I ACT LIKE I DON'T.
SEE? IT'S RINGING!
BEEP BEEP
MODEL R-FA6C POCKET BELL
What R U doing now?
If U R not BZ, let's hang out!
Makoto 3133-XXXX
WHO'S THIS "MAKOTO" PERSON?
I DUNNO!
I PUT UP AN AD IN A MAGAZINE LOOKING FOR BELL-FRIENDS...
...MAYBE HE FOUND IT.
BELL-FRIEND?
YEAH. THEY'RE FRIENDS YOU CAN ONLY MAKE THROUGH YOUR POCKET BELL PAGER!

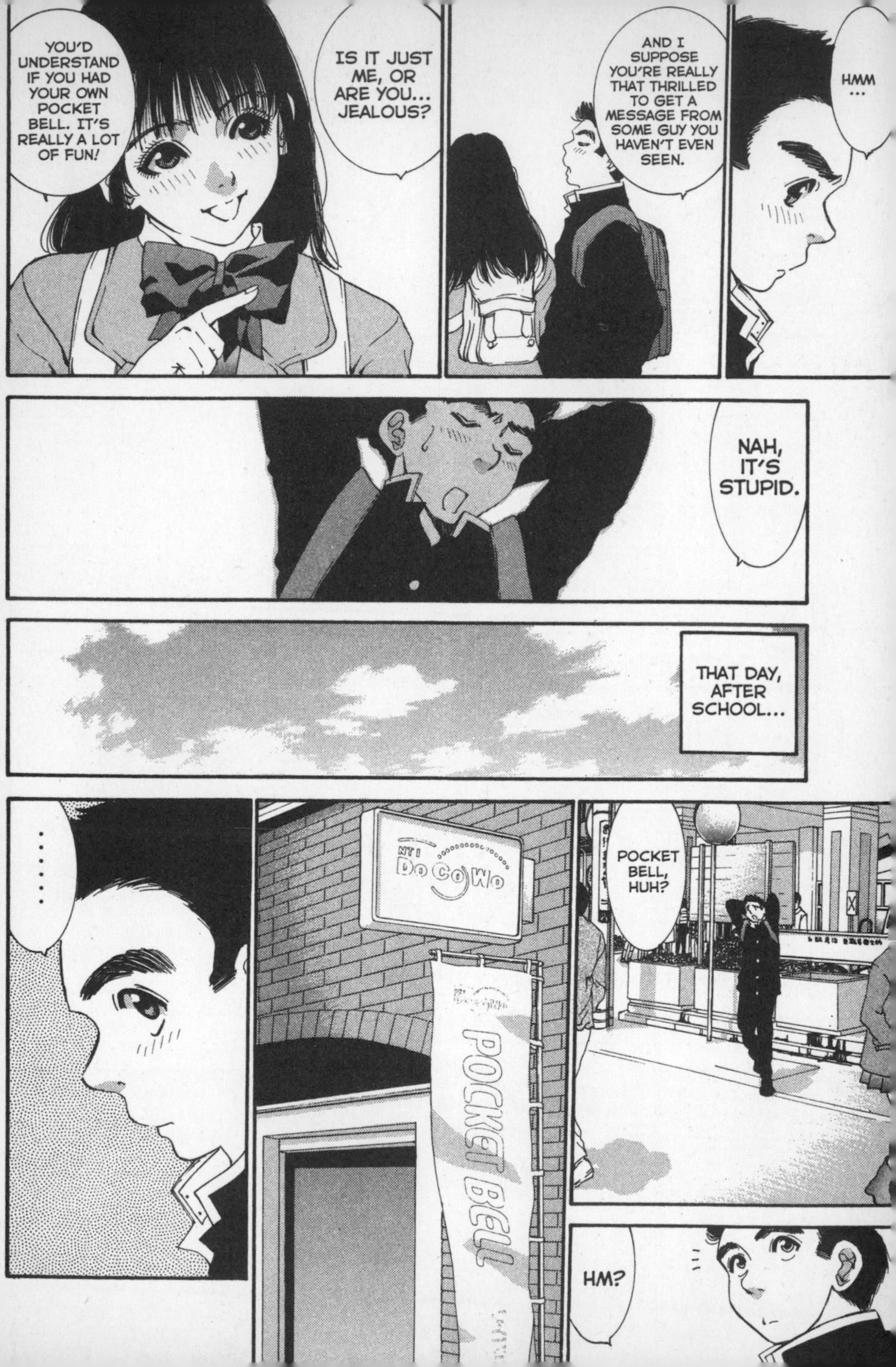
HMM...
AND I SUPPOSE YOU'RE REALLY THAT THRILLED TO GET A MESSAGE FROM SOME GUY YOU HAVEN'T EVEN SEEN.
IS IT JUST ME, OR ARE YOU... JEALOUS?
YOU'D UNDERSTAND IF YOU HAD YOUR OWN POCKET BELL. IT'S REALLY A LOT OF FUN!
NAH, IT'S STUPID.
THAT DAY, AFTER SCHOOL...
POCKET BELL, HUH?
HM?
POCKET BELL
......

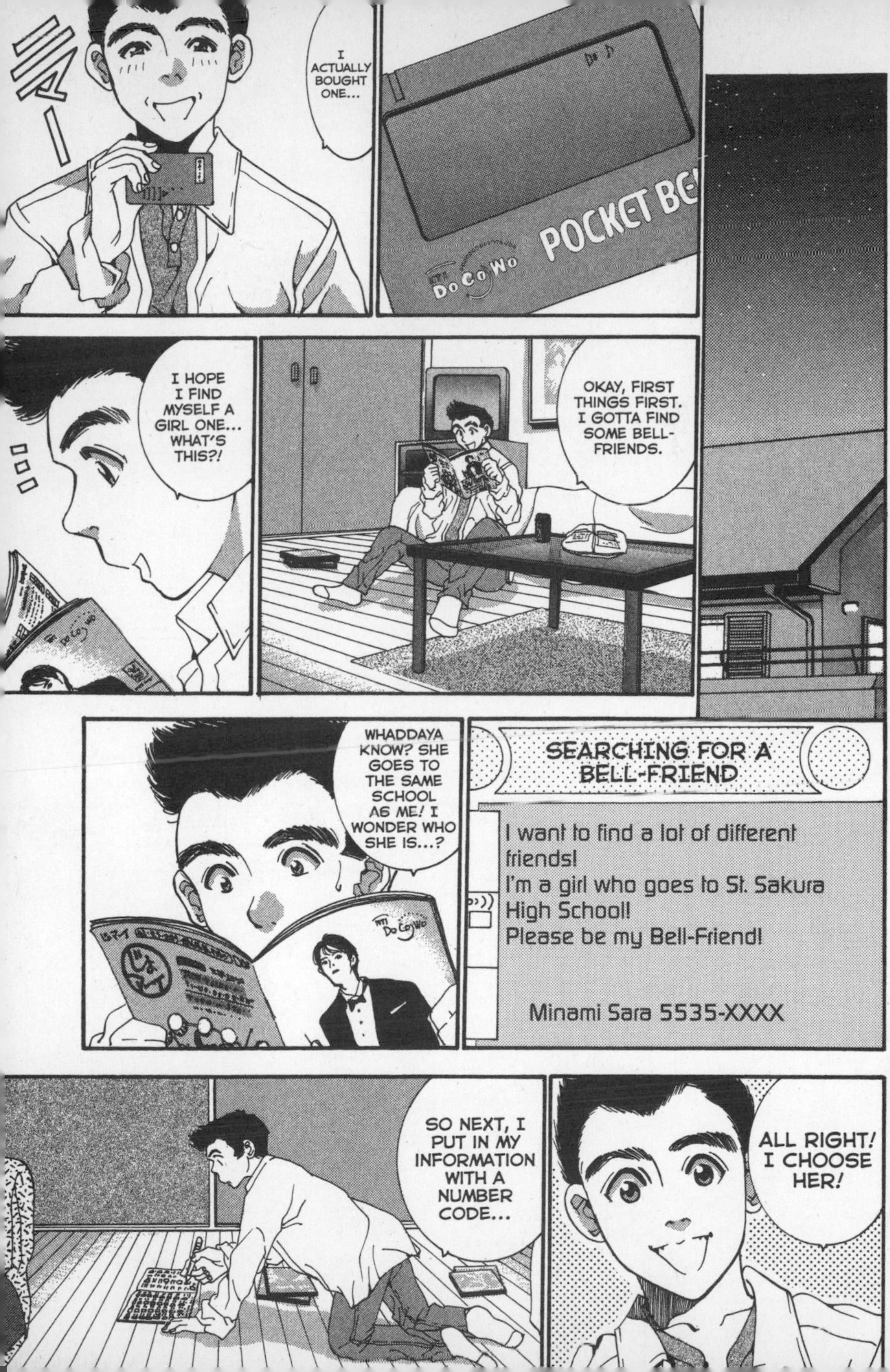
DoCoWo
POCKET BE
I ACTUALLY BOUGHT ONE...
OKAY, FIRST THINGS FIRST. I GOTTA FIND SOME BELL-FRIENDS.
I HOPE I FIND MYSELF A GIRL ONE... WHAT'S THIS?!
SEARCHING FOR A BELL-FRIEND
I want to find a lot of different friends!
I'm a girl who goes to St. Sakura High School!
Please be my Bell-Friend!
Minami Sara 5535-XXXX
WHADDAYA KNOW? SHE GOES TO THE SAME SCHOOL AS ME! I WONDER WHO SHE IS...?
ALL RIGHT! I CHOOSE HER!
SO NEXT, I PUT IN MY INFORMATION WITH A NUMBER CODE...

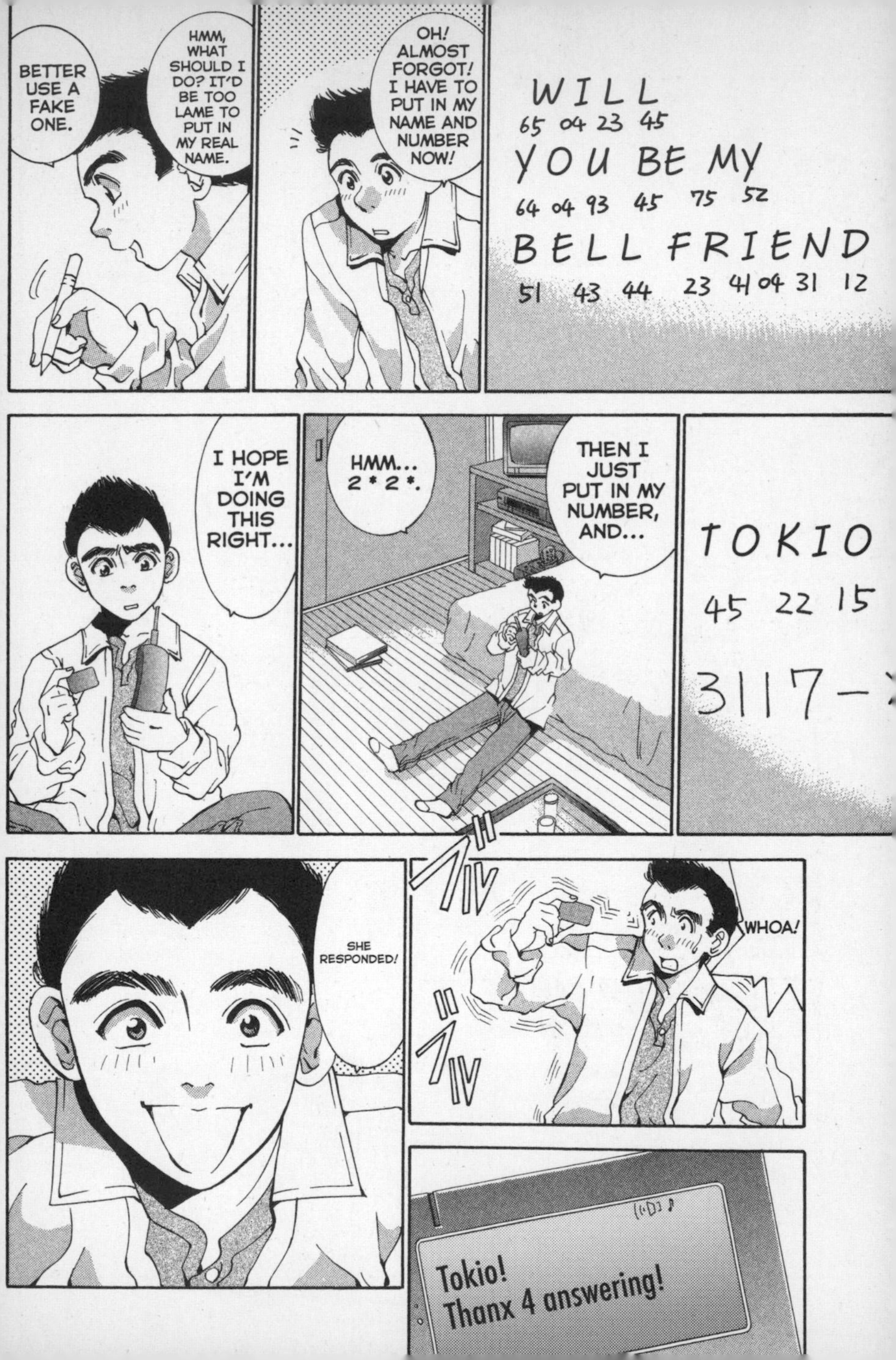
WILL
65 04 23 45
YOU BE MY
64 04 93 45 75 52
BELL FRIEND
51 43 44 23 41 04 31 12
OH! ALMOST FORGOT! I HAVE TO PUT IN MY NAME AND NUMBER NOW!
HMM, WHAT SHOULD I DO? IT'D BE TOO LAME TO PUT IN MY REAL NAME.
BETTER USE A FAKE ONE.
TOKIO
45 22 15
3117-
THEN I JUST PUT IN MY NUMBER, AND...
HMM... 2 * 2 *.
I HOPE I'M DOING THIS RIGHT...
WHOA!
Tokio! Thanx 4 answering!
SHE RESPONDED!

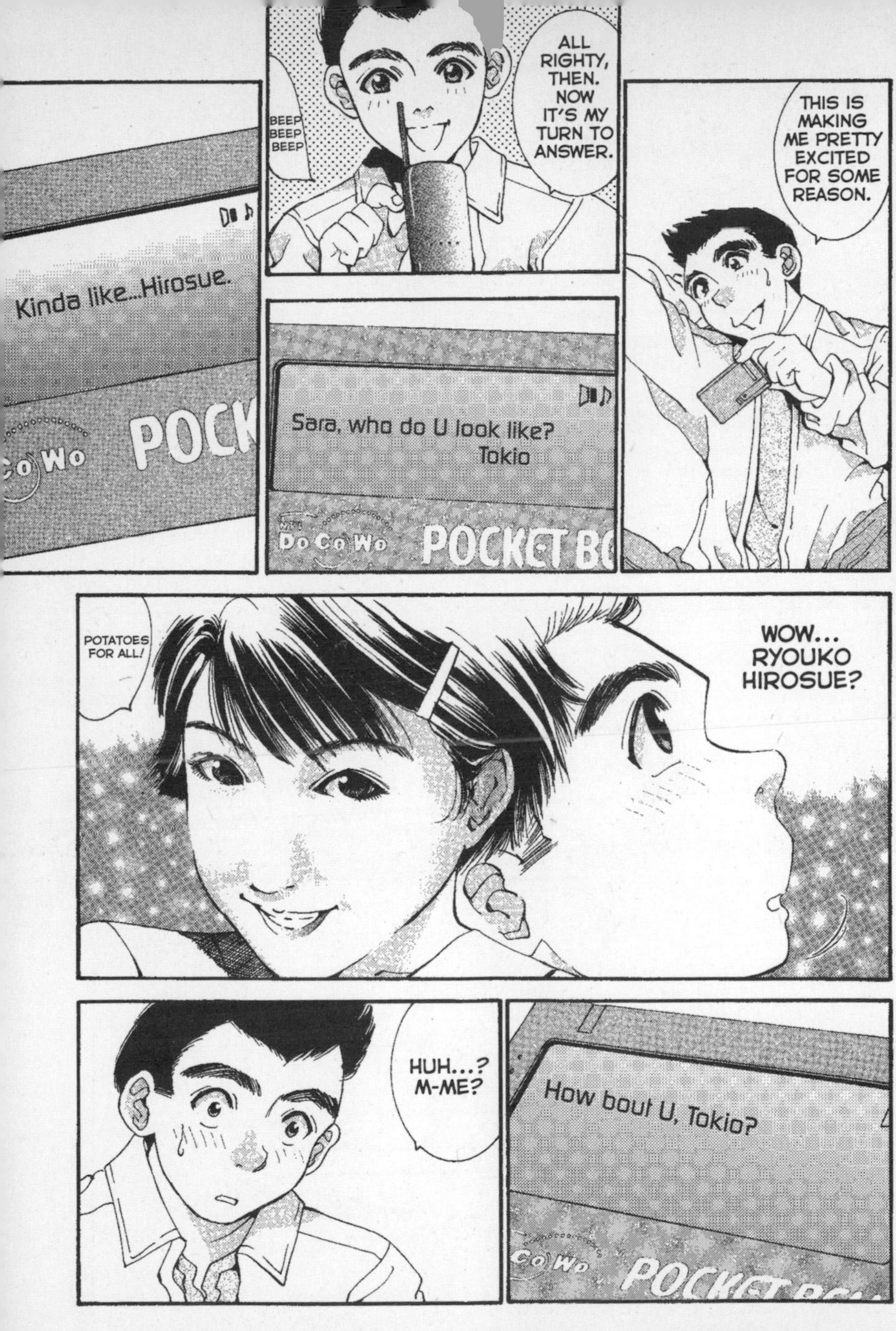

THIS IS MAKING ME PRETTY EXCITED FOR SOME REASON.
ALL RIGHTY, THEN. NOW IT'S MY TURN TO ANSWER.
BEEP BEEP BEEP
Sara, who do U look like? Tokio
DoCoWo
Kinda like...Hirosue.
WOW... RYOUKO HIROSUE?
POTATOES FOR ALL!
How bout U, Tokio?
HUH...? M-ME?

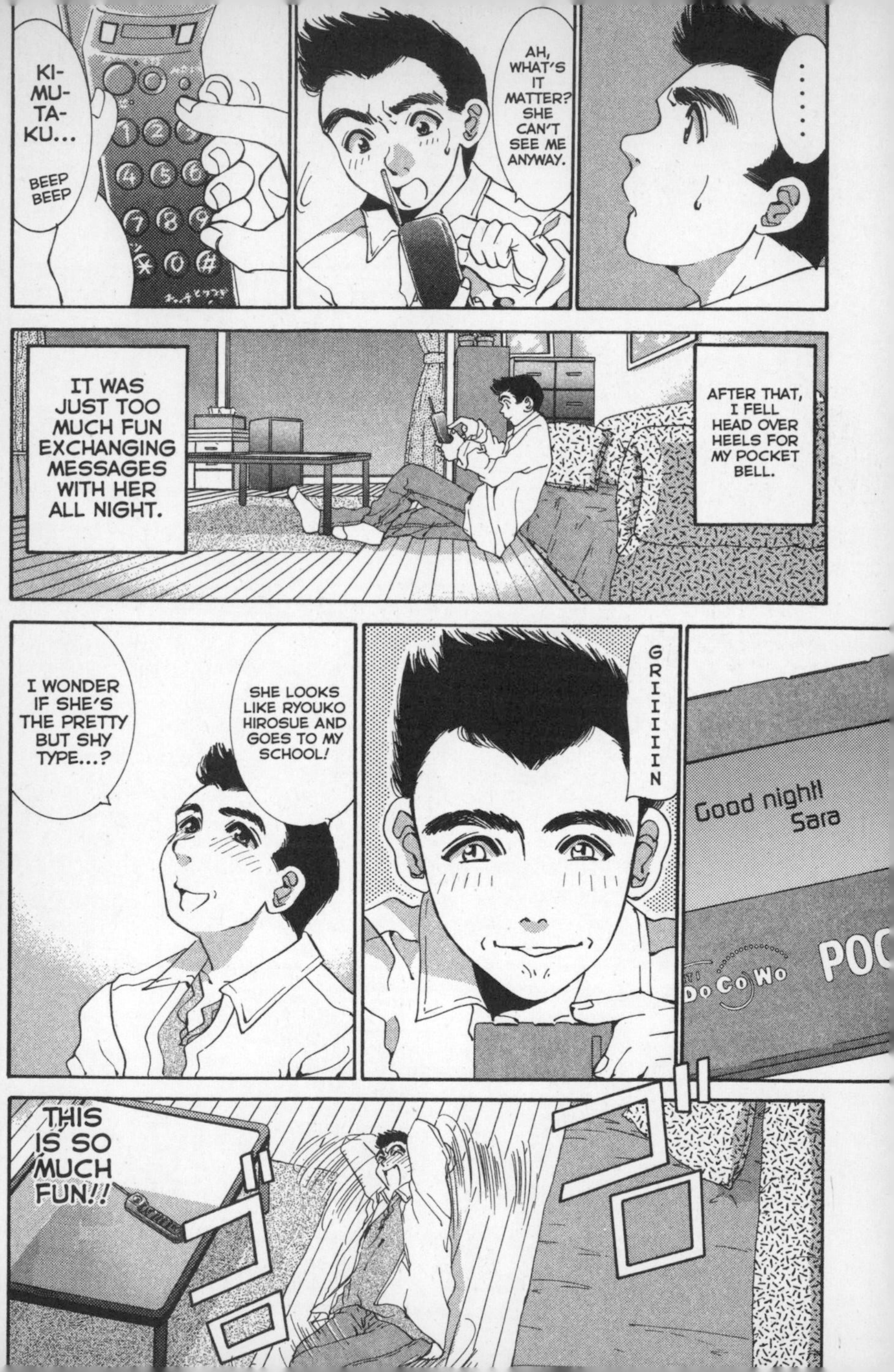
......
AH, WHAT'S IT MATTER? SHE CAN'T SEE ME ANYWAY.
KI-MU-TA-KU...
BEEP BEEP
AFTER THAT, I FELL HEAD OVER HEELS FOR MY POCKET BELL.
IT WAS JUST TOO MUCH FUN EXCHANGING MESSAGES WITH HER ALL NIGHT.
Good night! Sara
GRIIIIIN
SHE LOOKS LIKE RYOUKO HIROSUE AND GOES TO MY SCHOOL!
I WONDER IF SHE'S THE PRETTY BUT SHY TYPE...?
THIS IS SO MUCH FUN!!

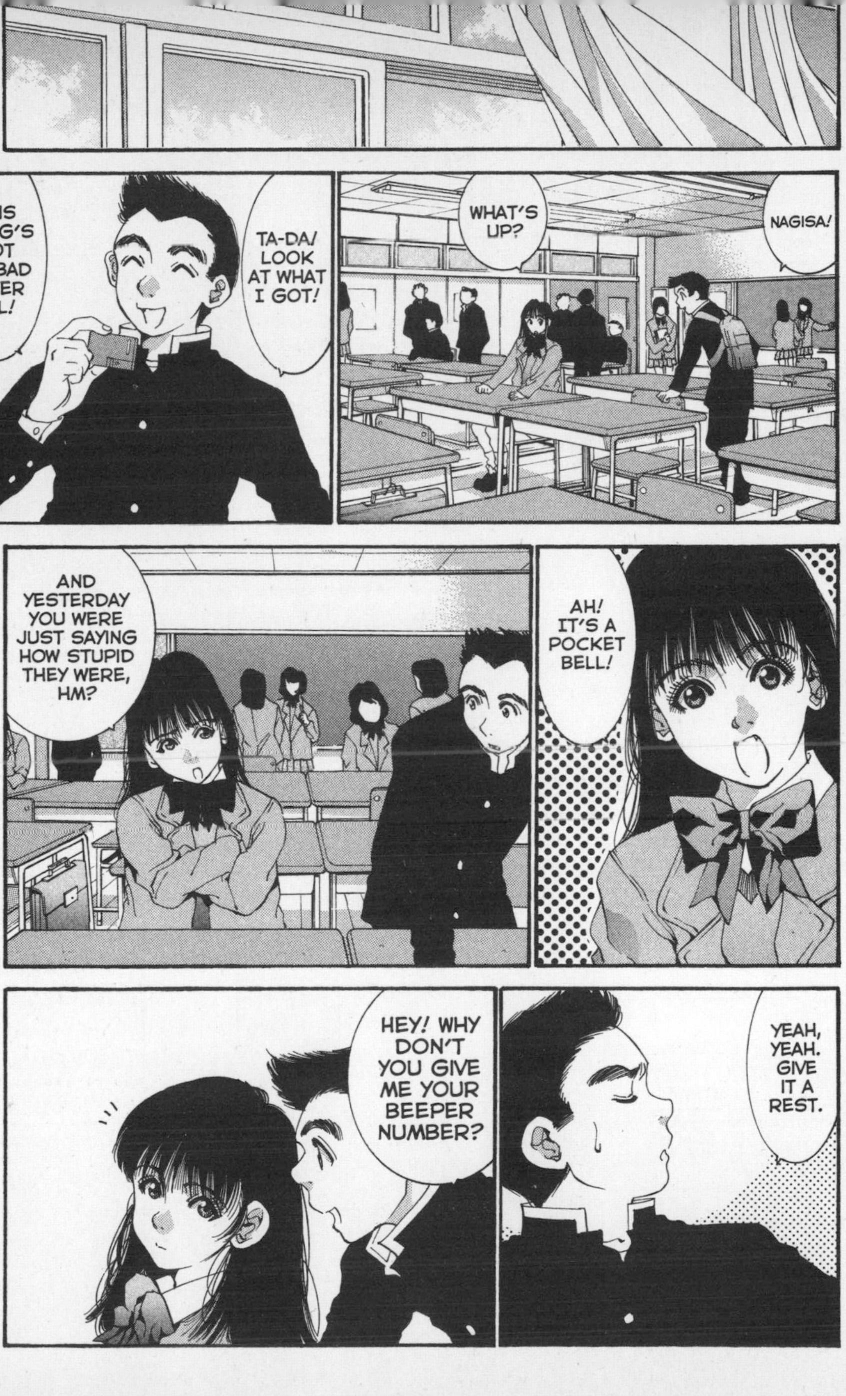
NAGISA!
WHAT'S UP?
TA-DA! LOOK AT WHAT I GOT!
THIS THING'S NOT SO BAD AFTER ALL!
AH! IT'S A POCKET BELL!
AND YESTERDAY YOU WERE JUST SAYING HOW STUPID THEY WERE, HM?
YEAH, YEAH. GIVE IT A REST.
HEY! WHY DON'T YOU GIVE ME YOUR BEEPER NUMBER?

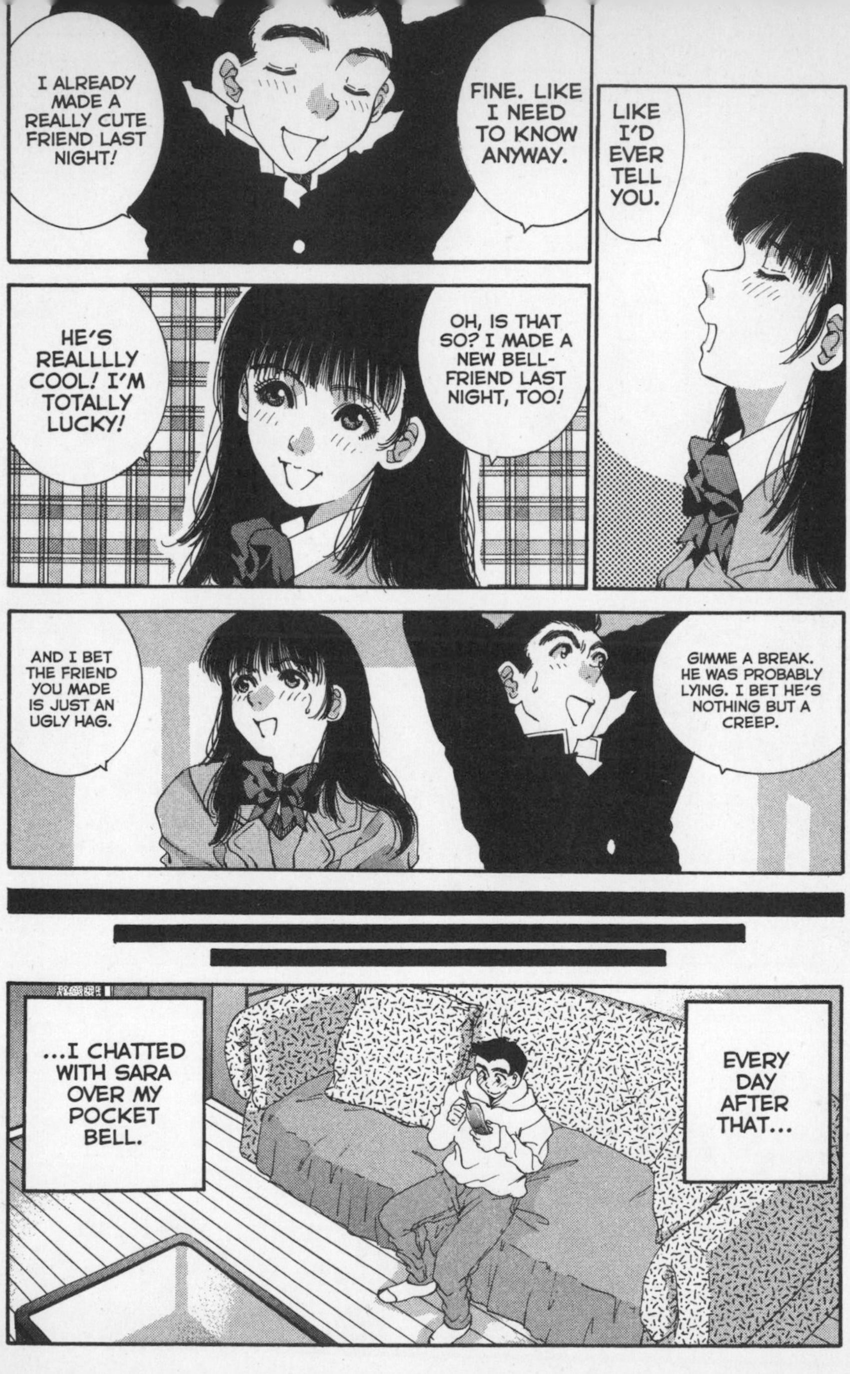
LIKE I'D EVER TELL YOU.
FINE. LIKE I NEED TO KNOW ANYWAY.
I ALREADY MADE A REALLY CUTE FRIEND LAST NIGHT!
OH, IS THAT SO? I MADE A NEW BELL-FRIEND LAST NIGHT, TOO!
HE'S REALLLLY COOL! I'M TOTALLY LUCKY!
GIMME A BREAK. HE WAS PROBABLY LYING. I BET HE'S NOTHING BUT A CREEP.
AND I BET THE FRIEND YOU MADE IS JUST AN UGLY HAG.
EVERY DAY AFTER THAT...
...I CHATTED WITH SARA OVER MY POCKET BELL.

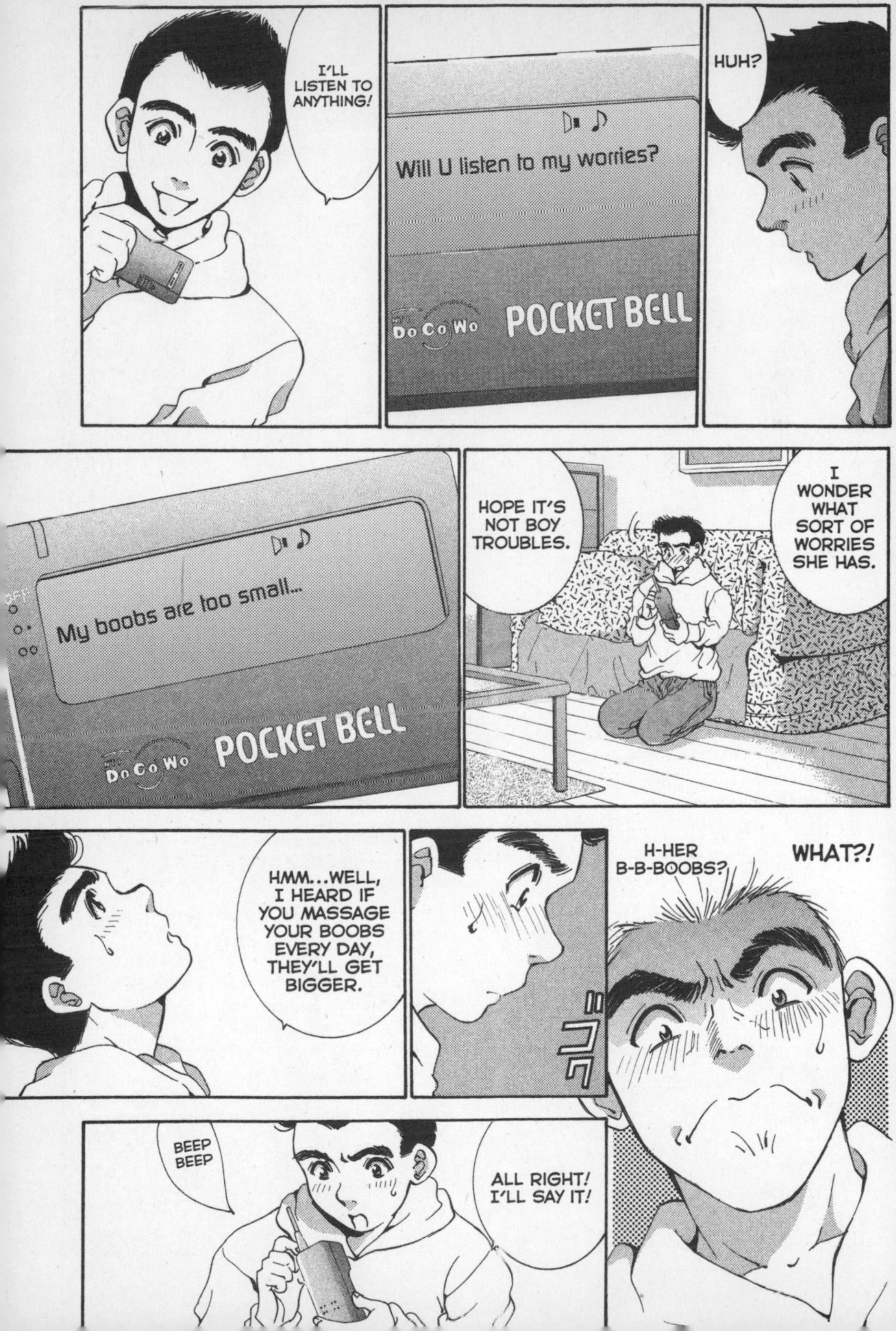
HUH?
Will U listen to my worries?
DoCoWo
POCKET BELL
I'LL LISTEN TO ANYTHING!
I WONDER WHAT SORT OF WORRIES SHE HAS.
HOPE IT'S NOT BOY TROUBLES.
My boobs are too small...
DoCoWo
POCKET BELL
WHAT?!
H-HER B-B-BOOBS?
HMM...WELL, I HEARD IF YOU MASSAGE YOUR BOOBS EVERY DAY, THEY'LL GET BIGGER.
ALL RIGHT! I'LL SAY IT!
BEEP BEEP

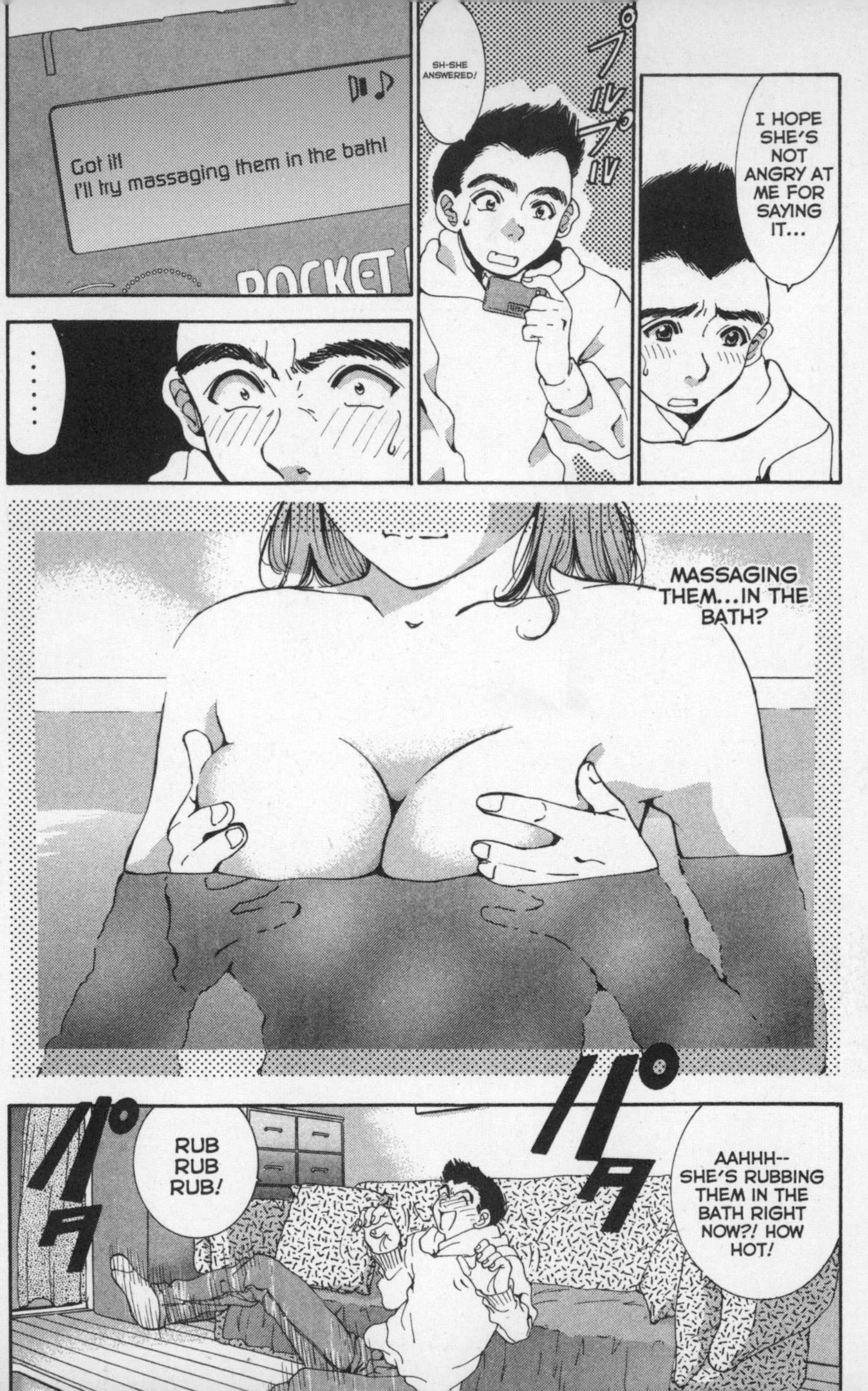

I HOPE SHE'S NOT ANGRY AT ME FOR SAYING IT...
SH-SHE ANSWERED!
Got it!
I'll try massaging them in the bath!
POCKET
......
MASSAGING THEM...IN THE BATH?
パタ
AAHHH-- SHE'S RUBBING THEM IN THE BATH RIGHT NOW?! HOW HOT!
RUB RUB RUB!
パタ

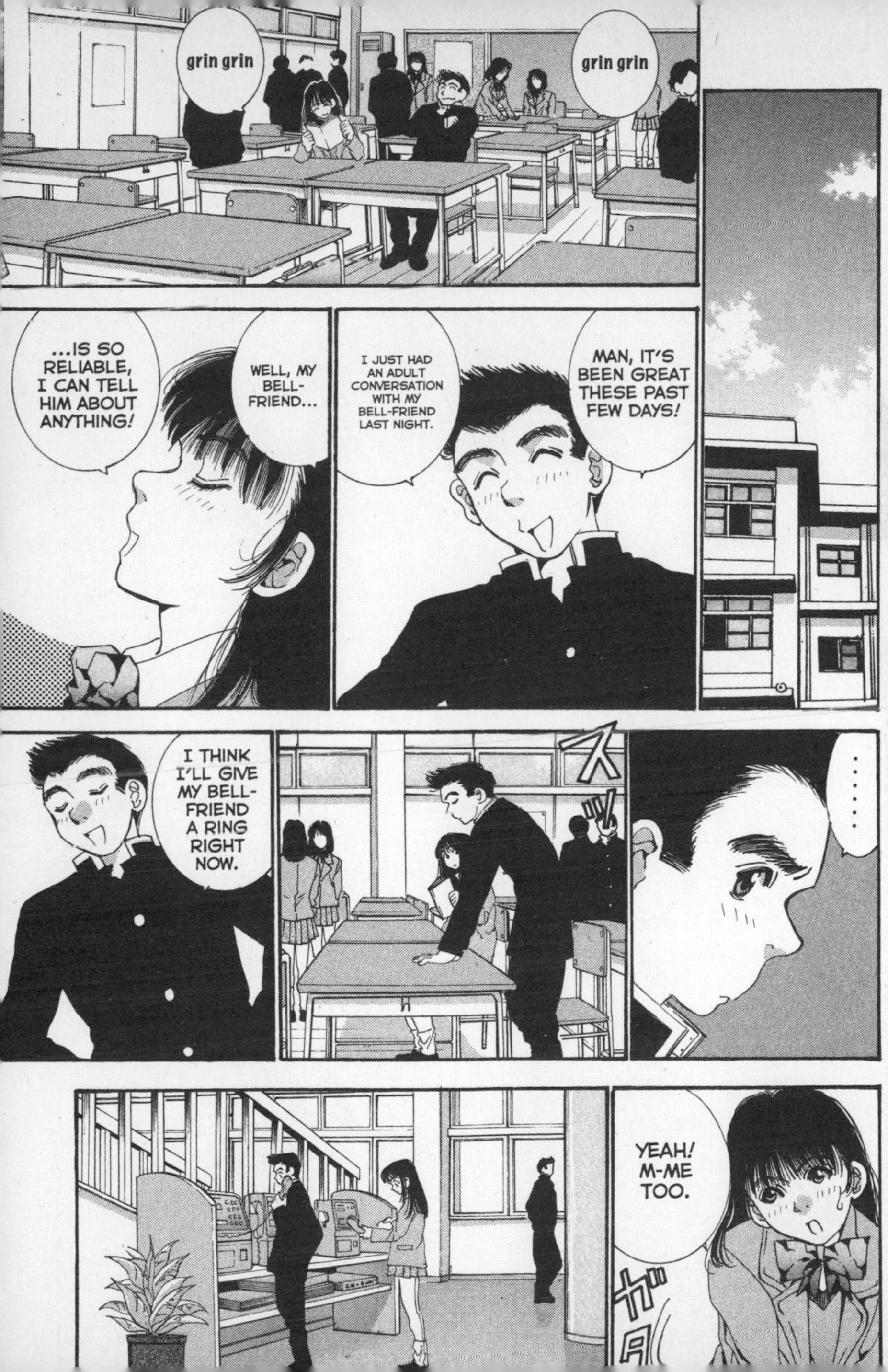
grin grin
grin grin
MAN, IT'S BEEN GREAT THESE PAST FEW DAYS!
I JUST HAD AN ADULT CONVERSATION WITH MY BELL-FRIEND LAST NIGHT.
WELL, MY BELL-FRIEND...
...IS SO RELIABLE, I CAN TELL HIM ABOUT ANYTHING!
......
I THINK I'LL GIVE MY BELL-FRIEND A RING RIGHT NOW.
YEAH! M-ME TOO.

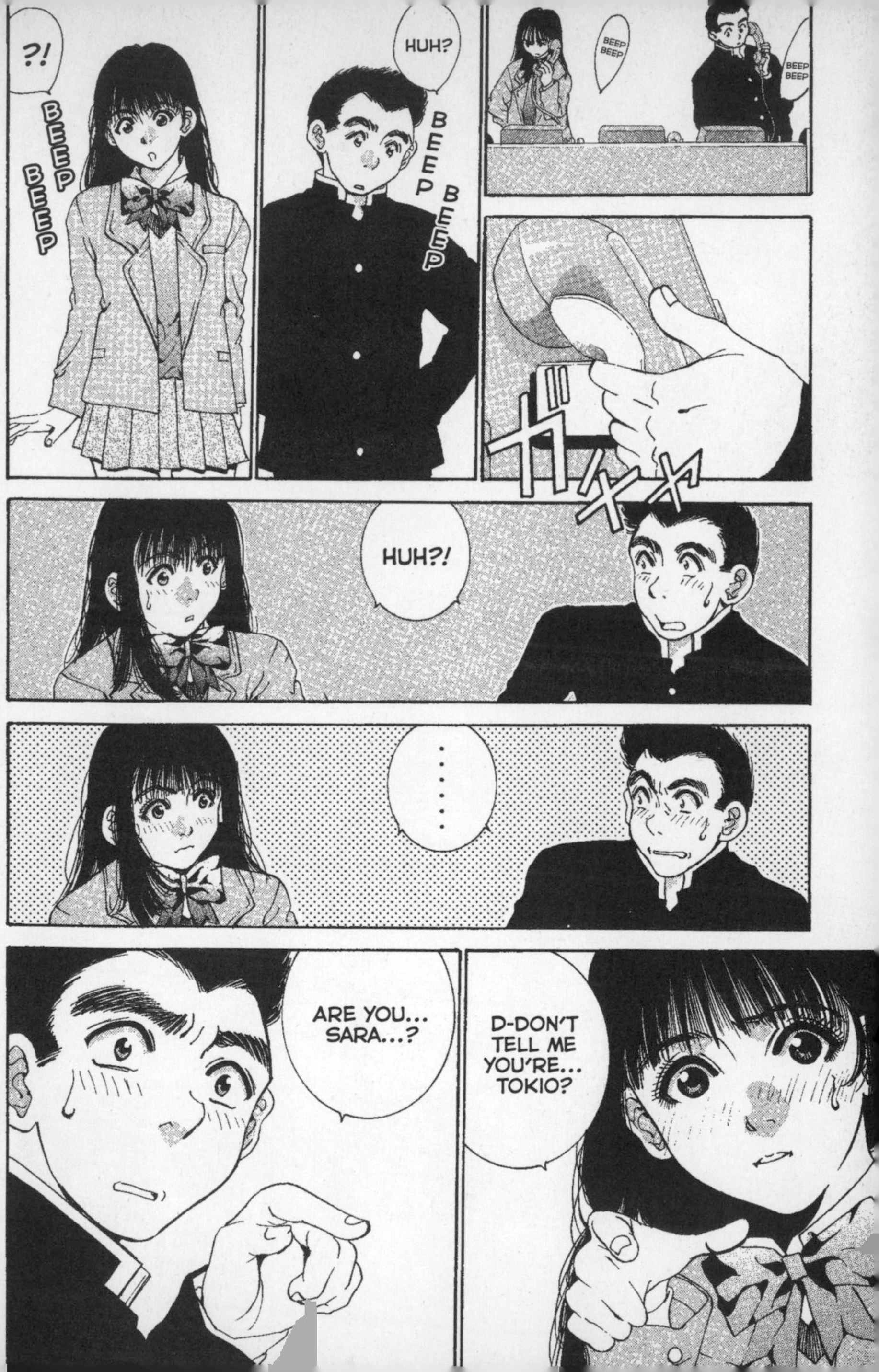
BEEP BEEP
BEEP BEEP
HUH?
BEEP BEEEP
?!
BEEEP BEEEP
HUH?!
.....
D-DON'T TELL ME YOU'RE... TOKIO?
ARE YOU... SARA...?

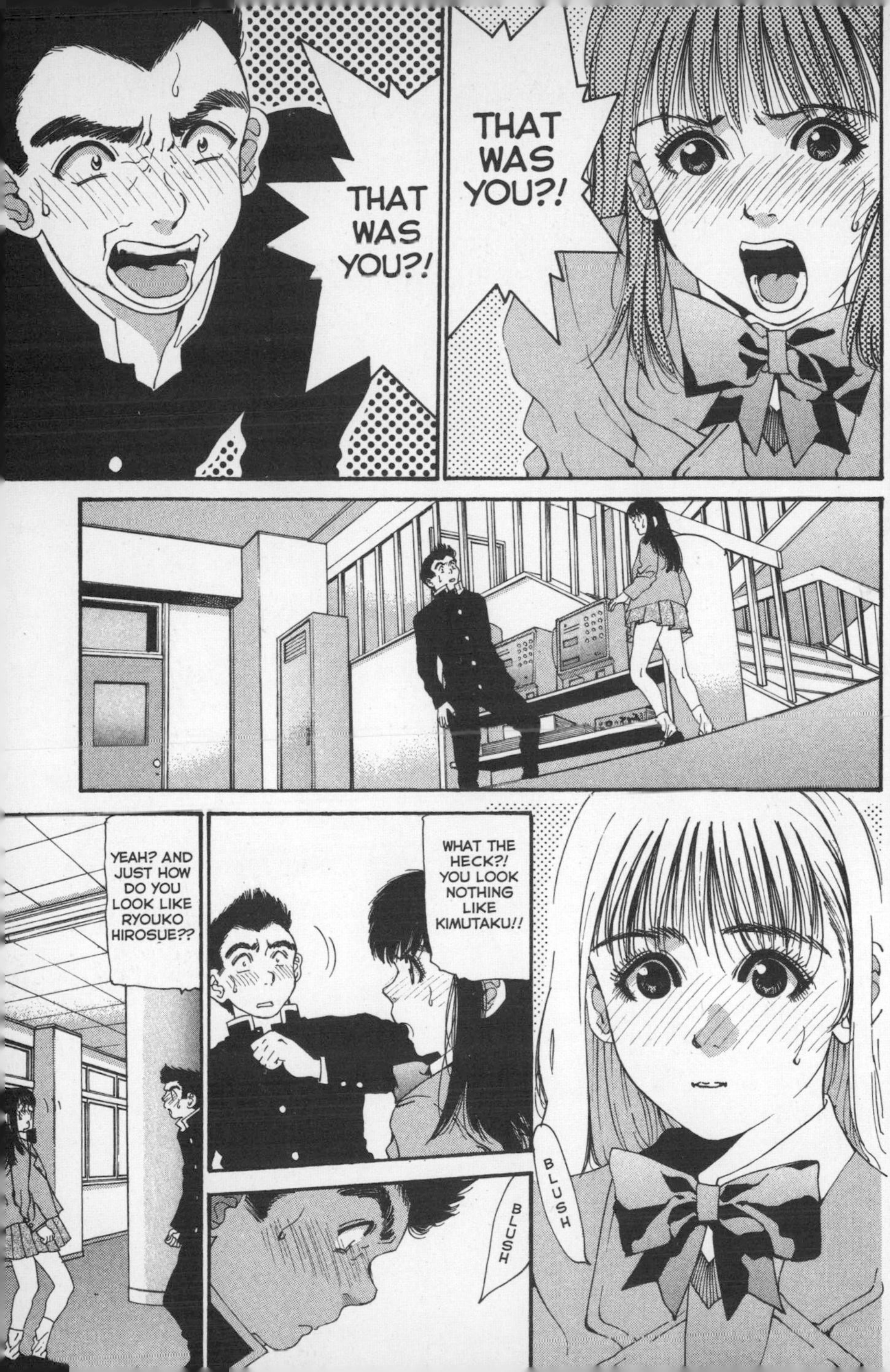
THAT WAS YOU?!
THAT WAS YOU?!
BLUSH
WHAT THE HECK?! YOU LOOK NOTHING LIKE KIMUTAKU!!
BLUSH
YEAH? AND JUST HOW DO YOU LOOK LIKE RYOUKO HIROSUE??

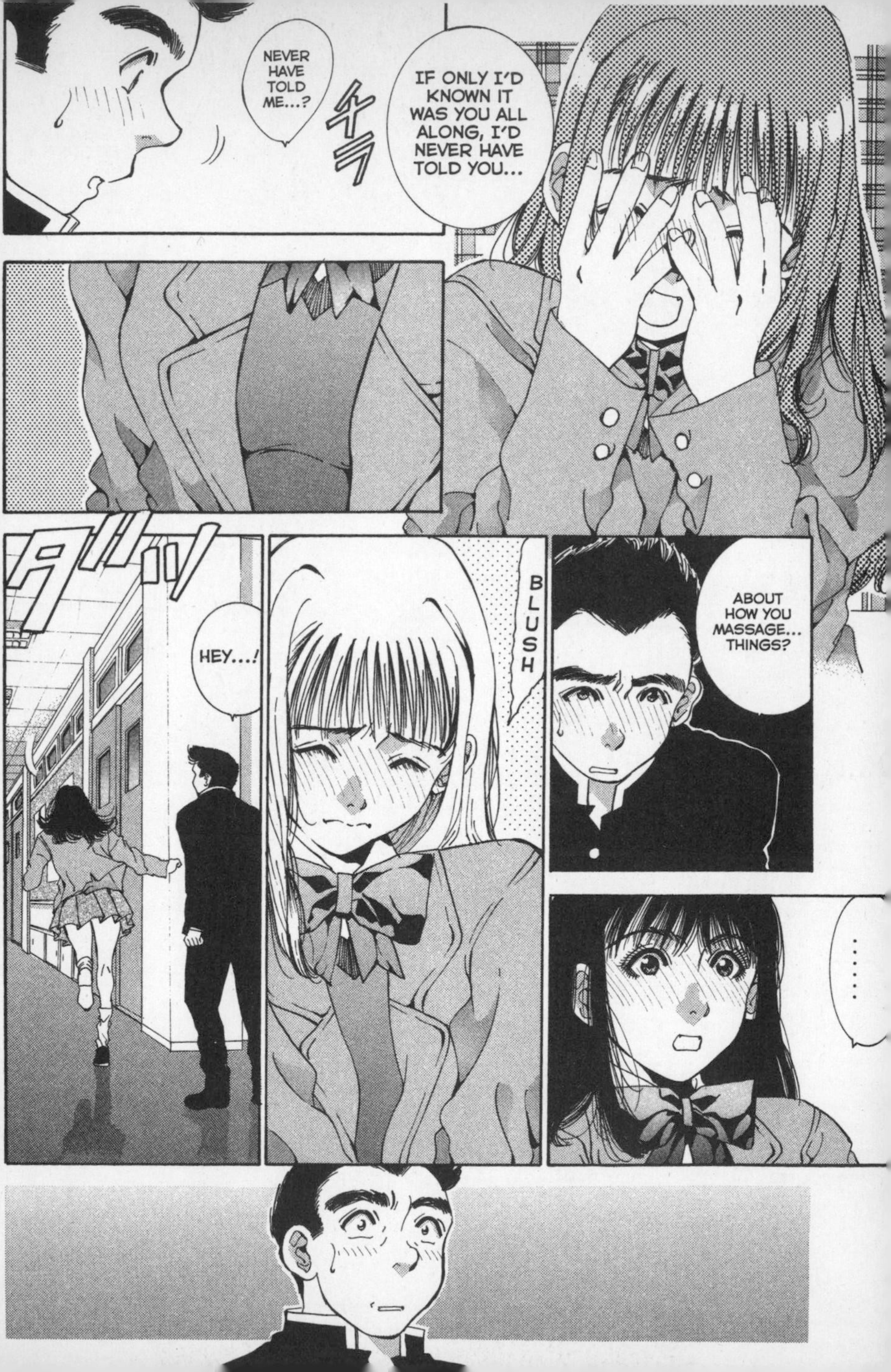
IF ONLY I'D KNOWN IT WAS YOU ALL ALONG, I'D NEVER HAVE TOLD YOU...
チラ
NEVER HAVE TOLD ME...?
ABOUT HOW YOU MASSAGE... THINGS?
......
BLUSH
ダッ
HEY...!

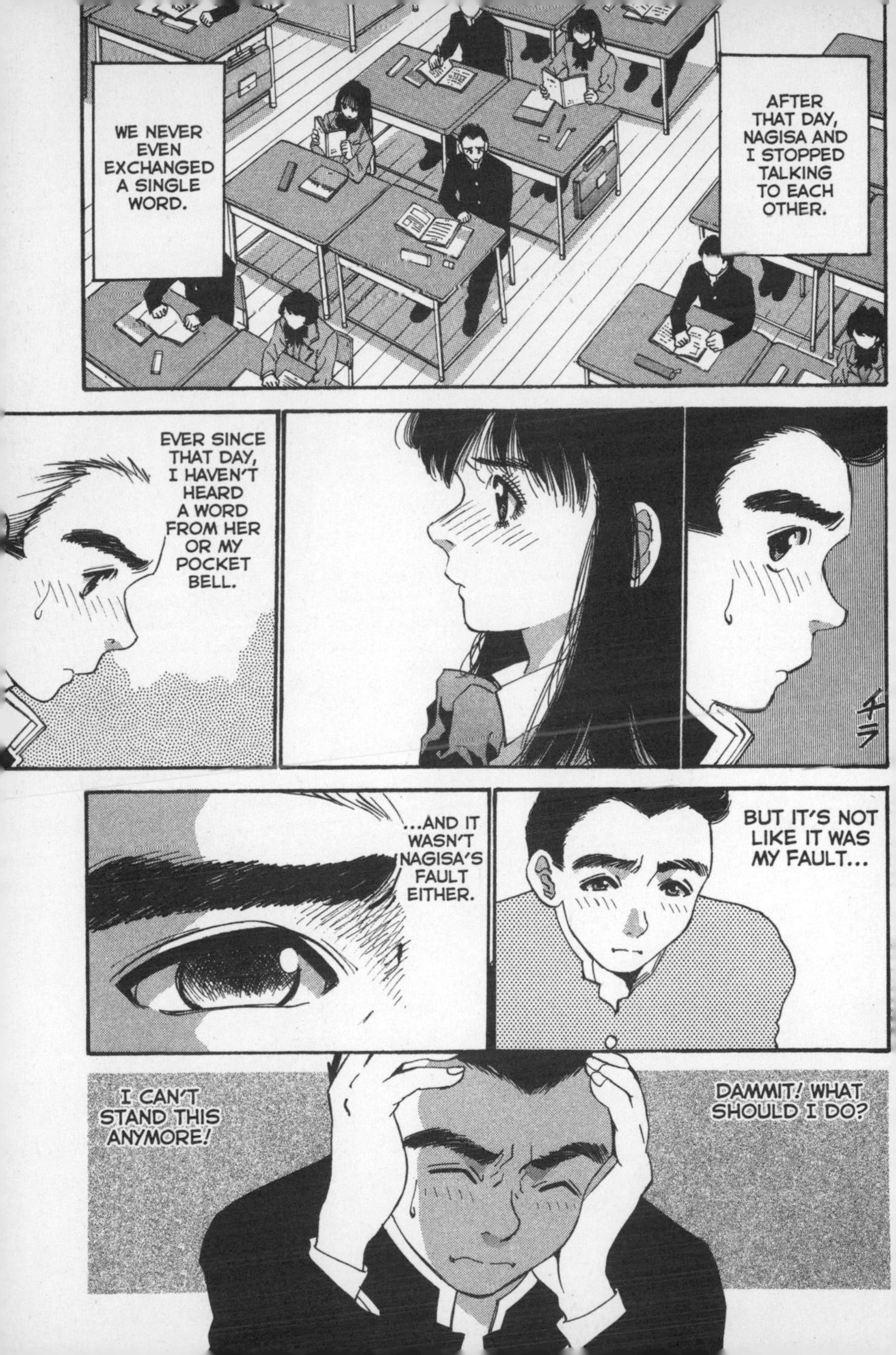
AFTER THAT DAY, NAGISA AND I STOPPED TALKING TO EACH OTHER.
WE NEVER EVEN EXCHANGED A SINGLE WORD.
チラ
EVER SINCE THAT DAY, I HAVEN'T HEARD A WORD FROM HER OR MY POCKET BELL.
BUT IT'S NOT LIKE IT WAS MY FAULT...
...AND IT WASN'T NAGISA'S FAULT EITHER.
DAMMIT! WHAT SHOULD I DO?
I CAN'T STAND THIS ANYMORE!

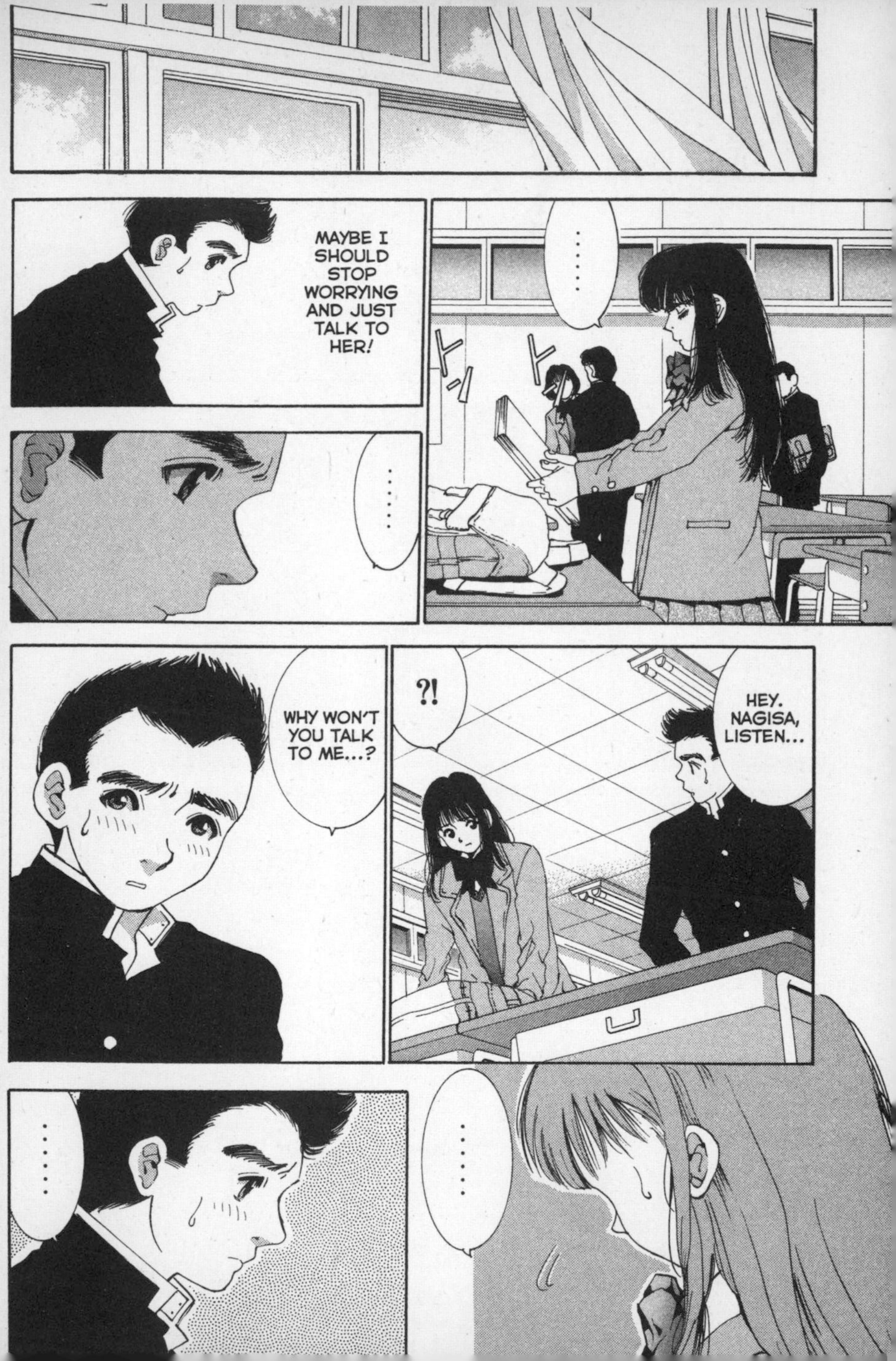
......
MAYBE I SHOULD STOP WORRYING AND JUST TALK TO HER!
......
HEY. NAGISA, LISTEN...
?!
WHY WON'T YOU TALK TO ME...?
......
......

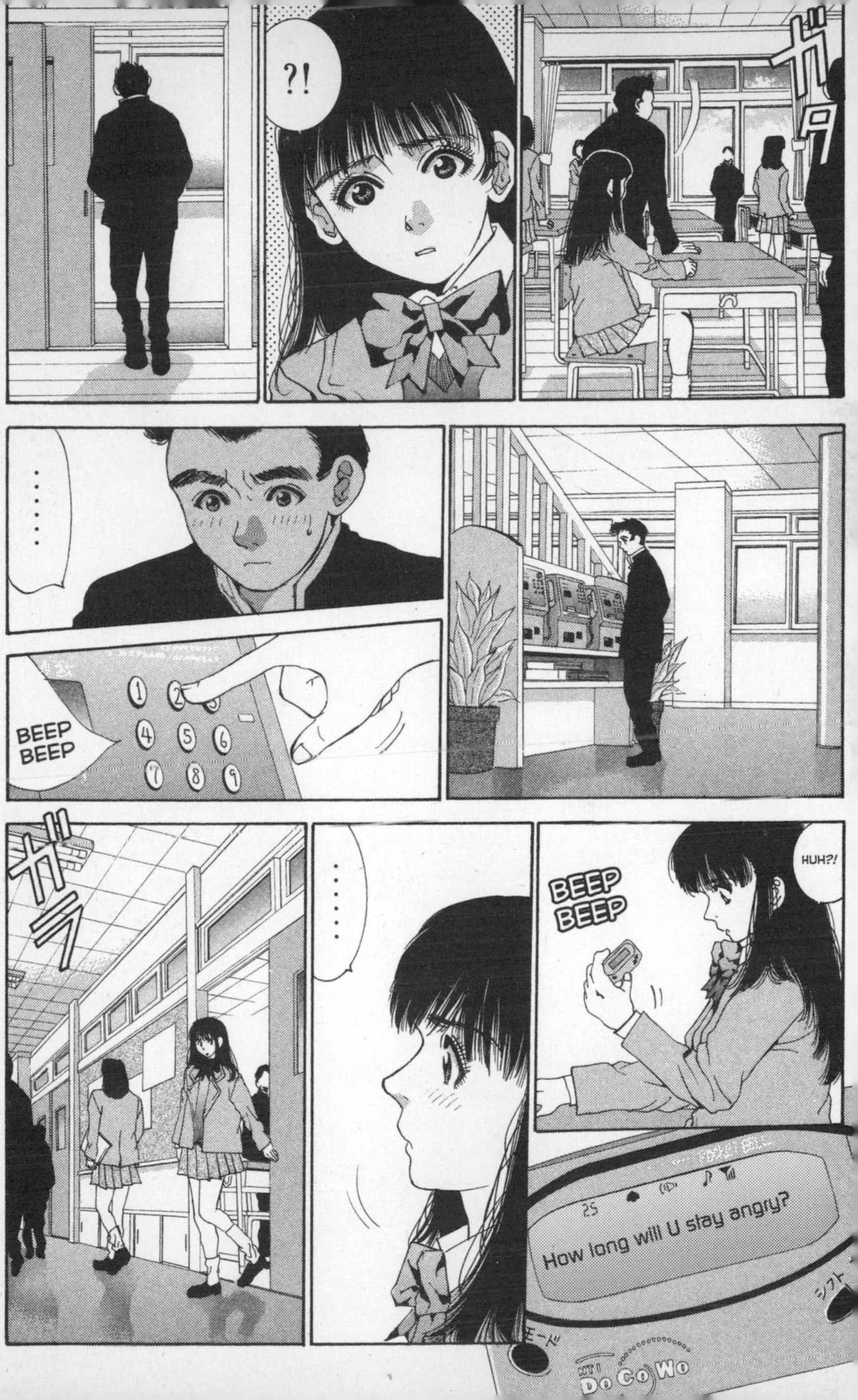
ガタ
?!
......
BEEP BEEP
HUH?!
BEEP BEEP
How long will U stay angry?
シフト
モード
DoCoMo
......
ガラ

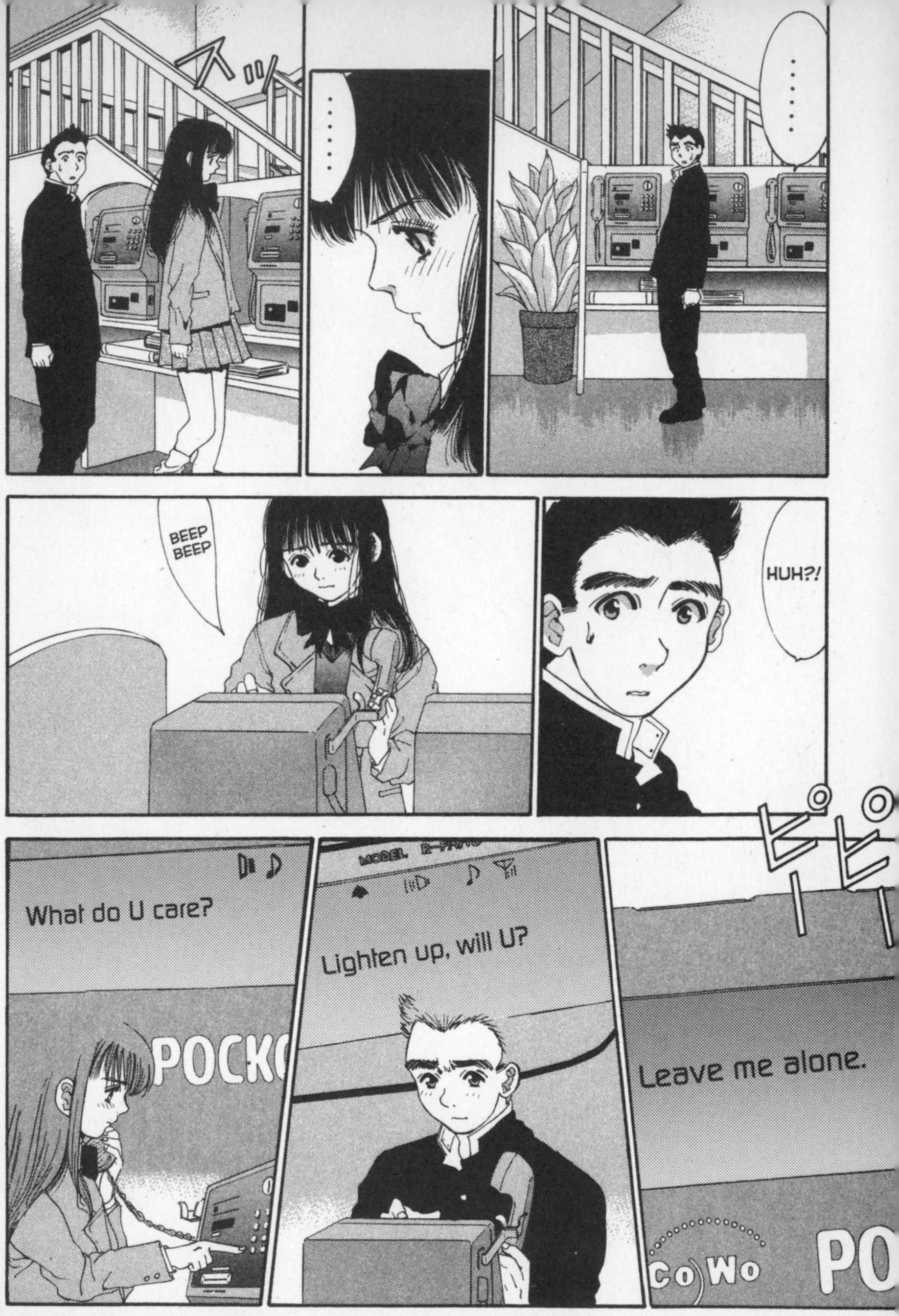
......
......
HUH?!
BEEP BEEP
ピーピー
Leave me alone.
PO
Lighten up, will U?
What do U care?
POCKO

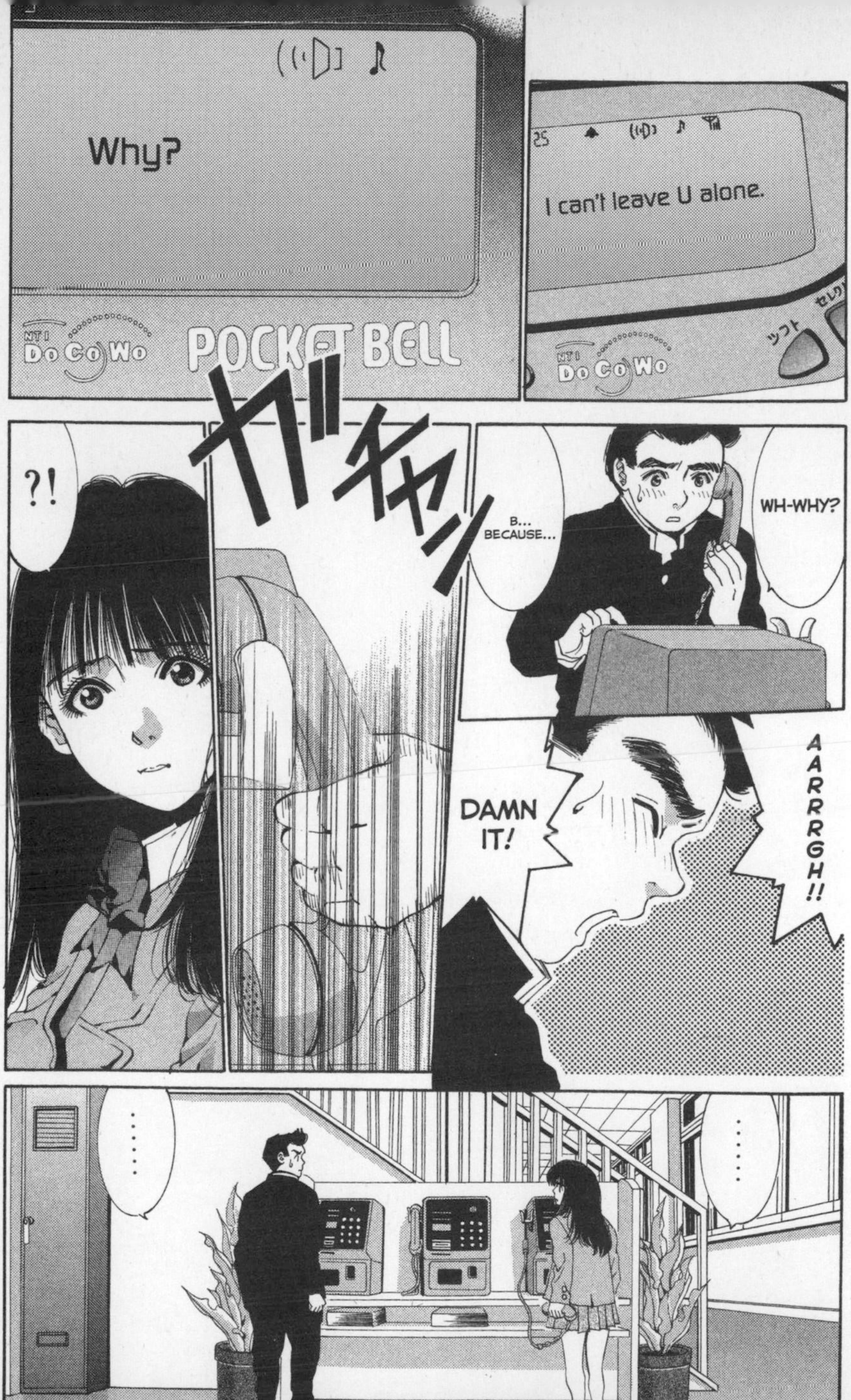
25
I can't leave U alone.
DoCoWo
Why?
DoCoWo
POCKET BELL
WH-WHY?
B... BECAUSE...
AARRRGH!!
DAMN IT!
ガチャン
?!
......
......

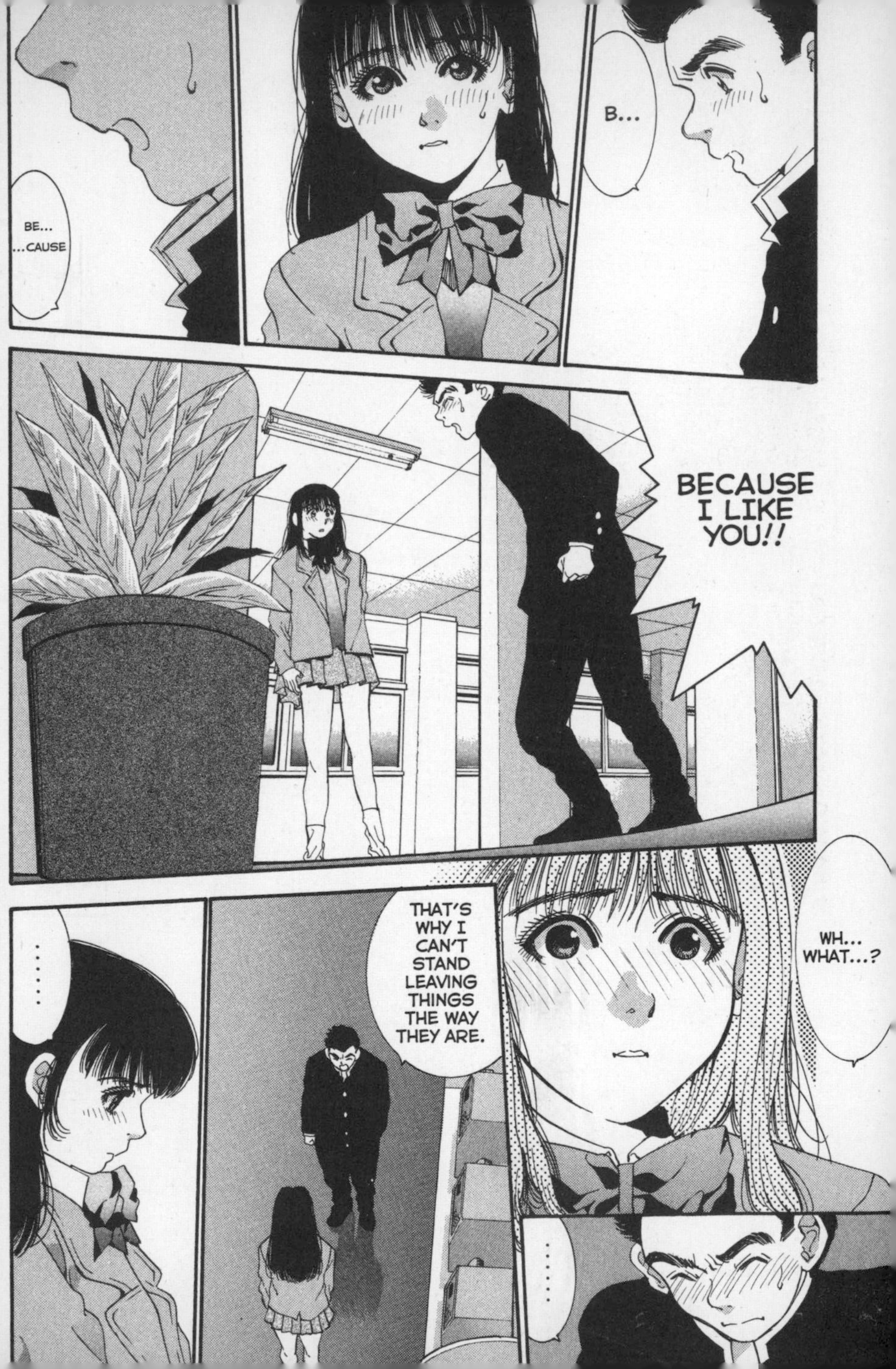
B...
BE... ...CAUSE
BECAUSE I LIKE YOU!!
WH... WHAT...?
......
THAT'S WHY I CAN'T STAND LEAVING THINGS THE WAY THEY ARE.
......

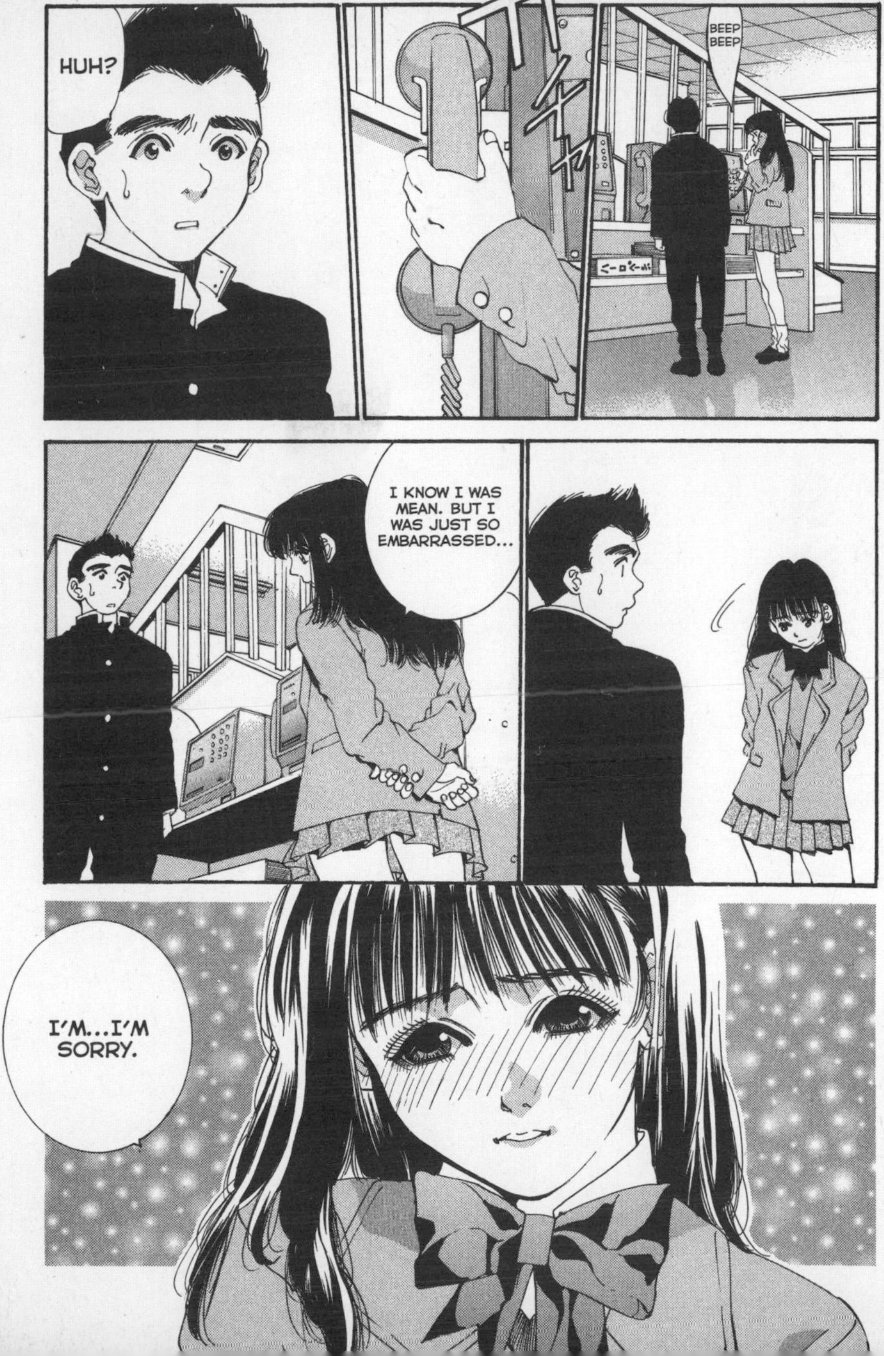
BEEP BEEP
HUH?
I KNOW I WAS MEAN. BUT I WAS JUST SO EMBARRASSED...
I'M...I'M SORRY.

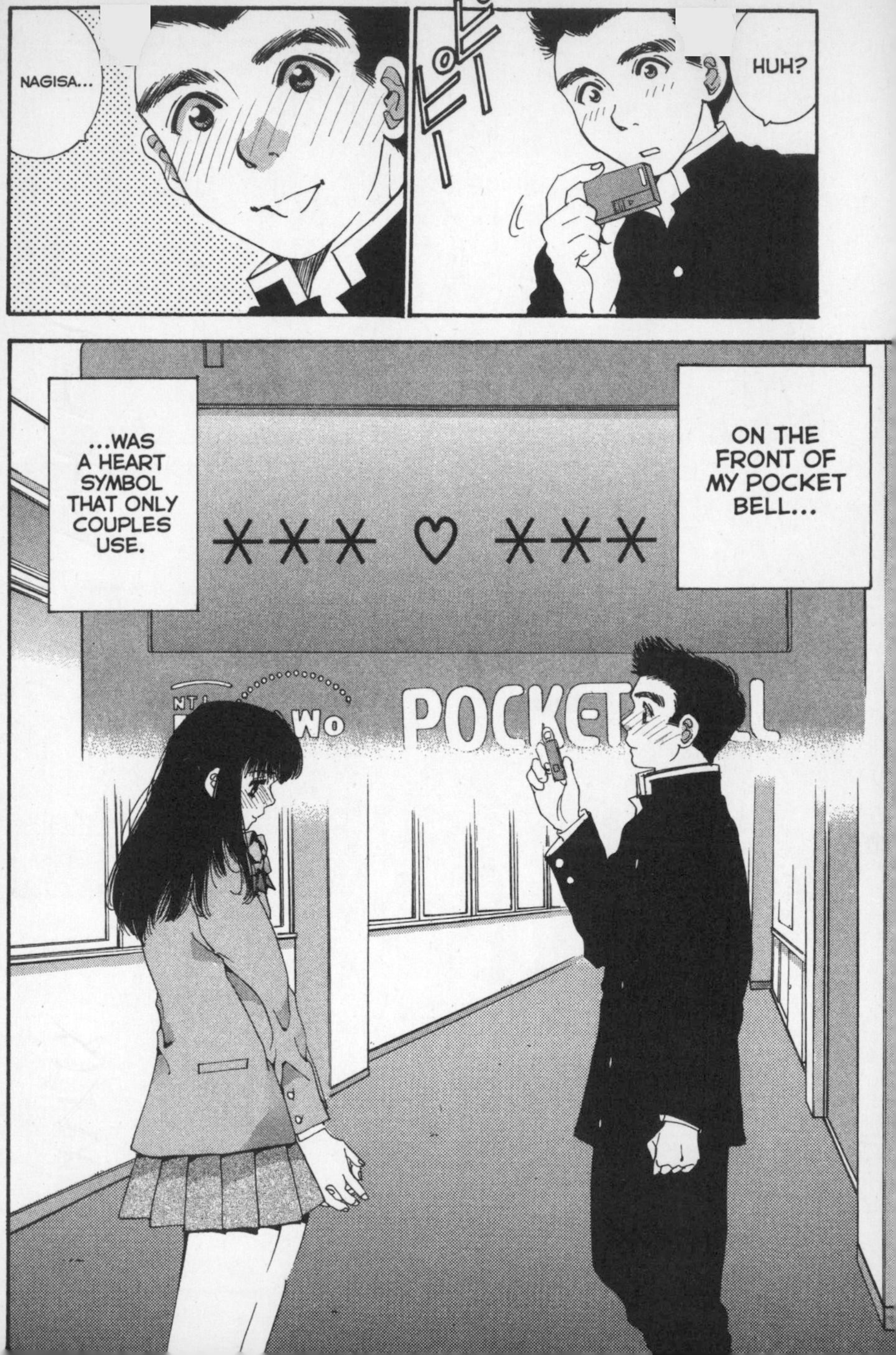
HUH?
NAGISA...
ON THE FRONT OF MY POCKET BELL...
*** ♡ ***
...WAS A HEART SYMBOL THAT ONLY COUPLES USE.

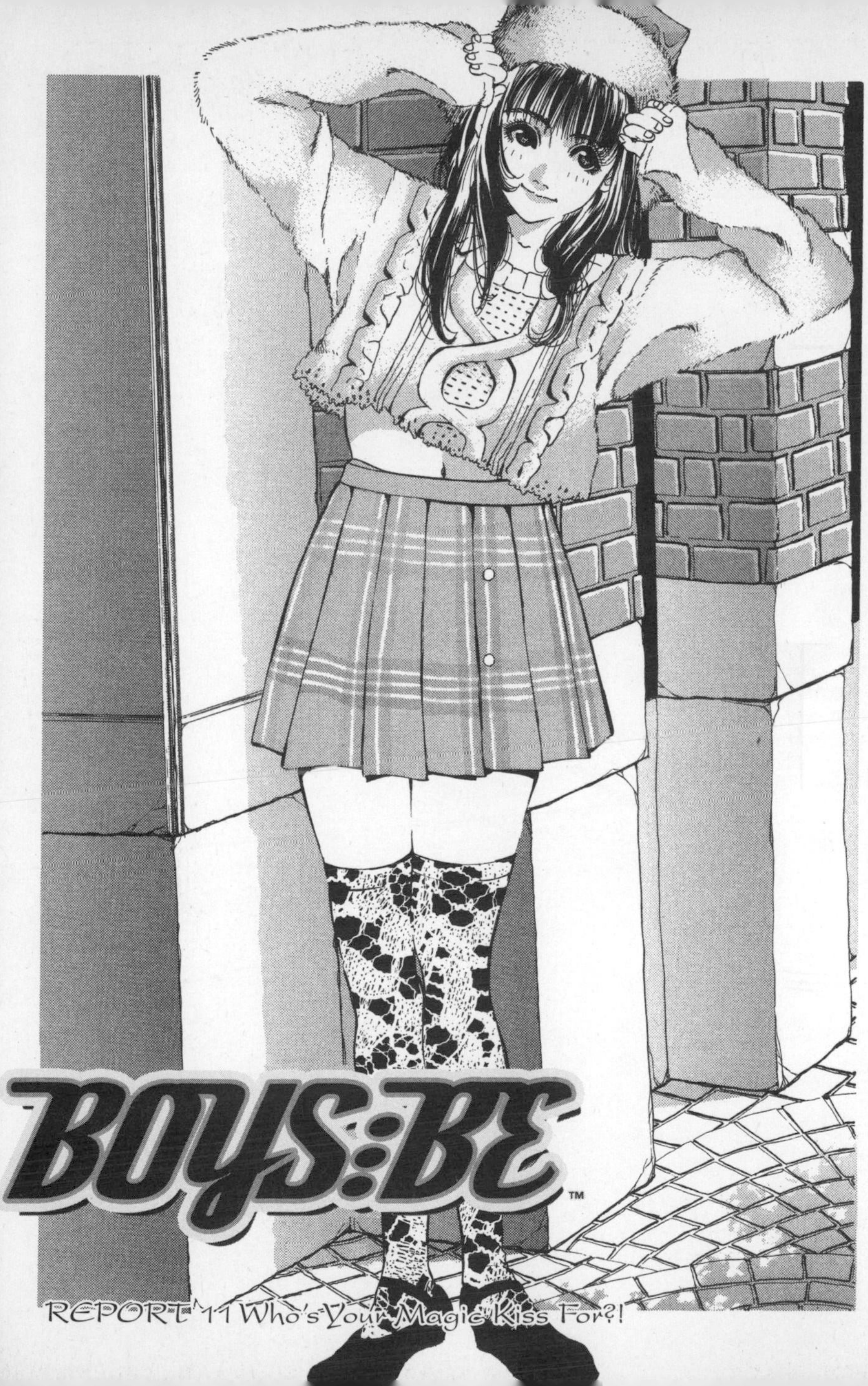
BOYS BE™
REPORT 11 Who's Your Magic Kiss For?!

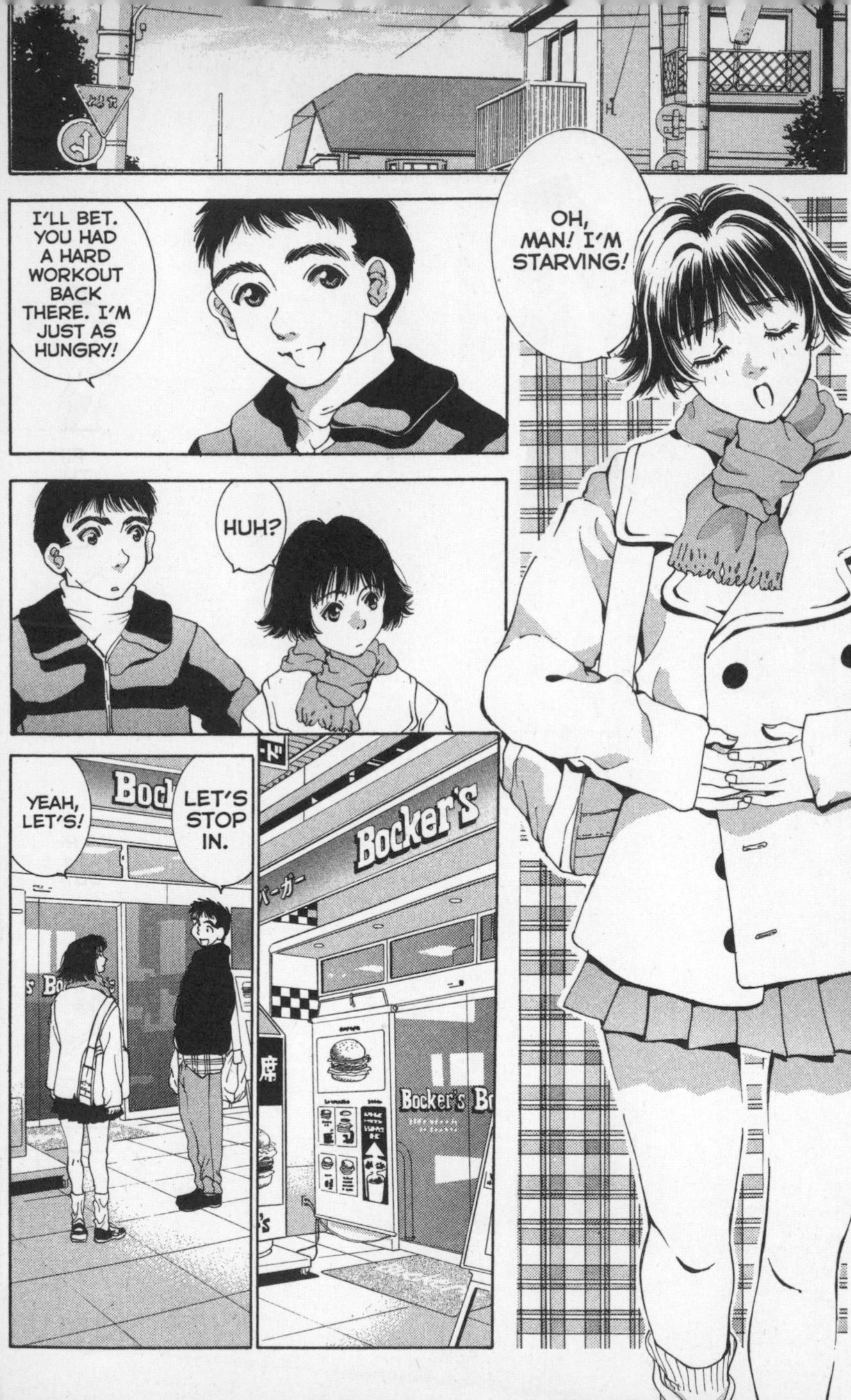
OH, MAN! I'M STARVING!
I'LL BET. YOU HAD A HARD WORKOUT BACK THERE. I'M JUST AS HUNGRY!
HUH?
Bocker's
LET'S STOP IN.
YEAH, LET'S!

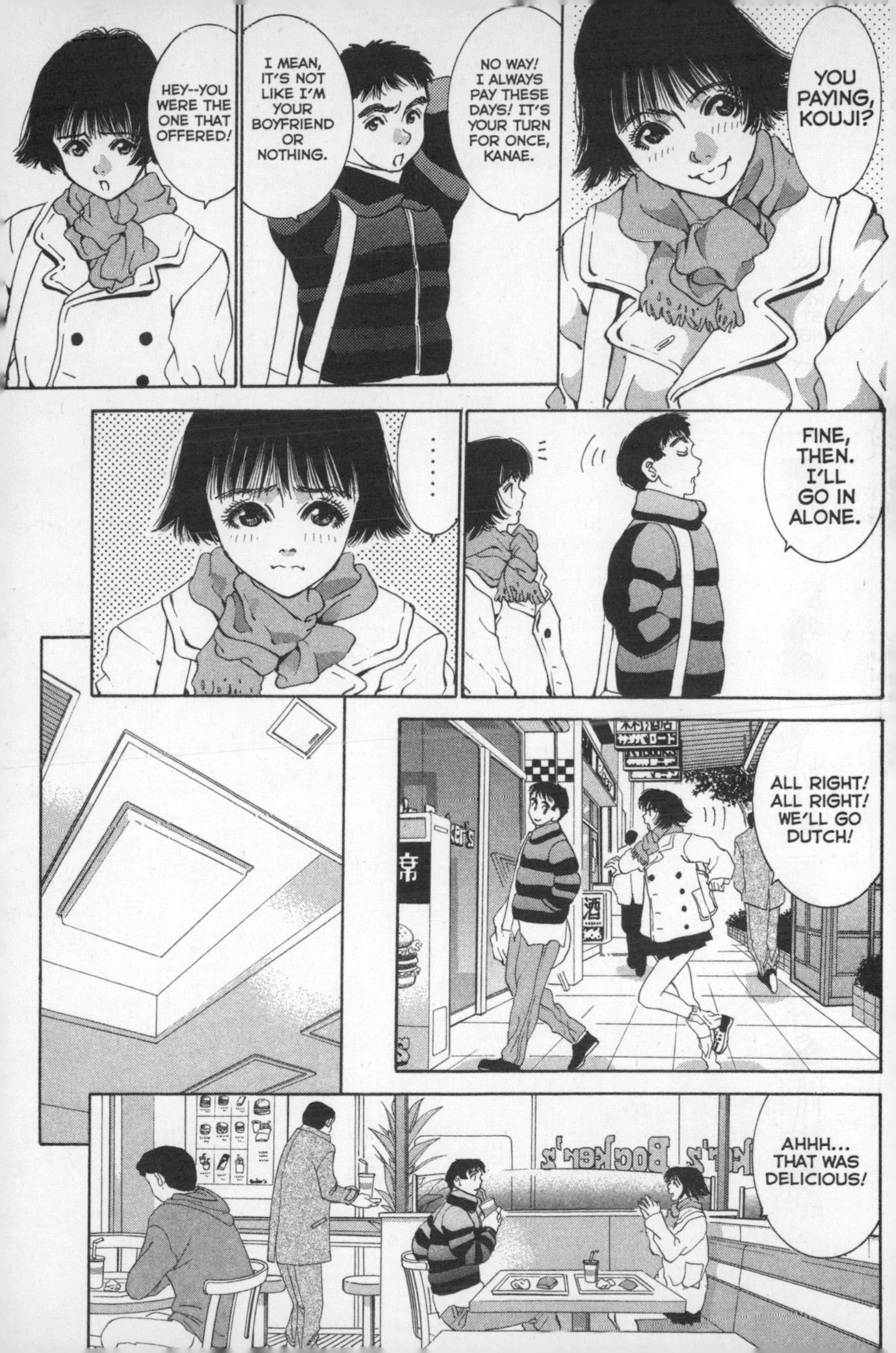
YOU PAYING, KOUJI?
NO WAY! I ALWAYS PAY THESE DAYS! IT'S YOUR TURN FOR ONCE, KANAE.
I MEAN, IT'S NOT LIKE I'M YOUR BOYFRIEND OR NOTHING.
HEY--YOU WERE THE ONE THAT OFFERED!
FINE, THEN. I'LL GO IN ALONE.
......
ALL RIGHT! ALL RIGHT! WE'LL GO DUTCH!
AHHH... THAT WAS DELICIOUS!

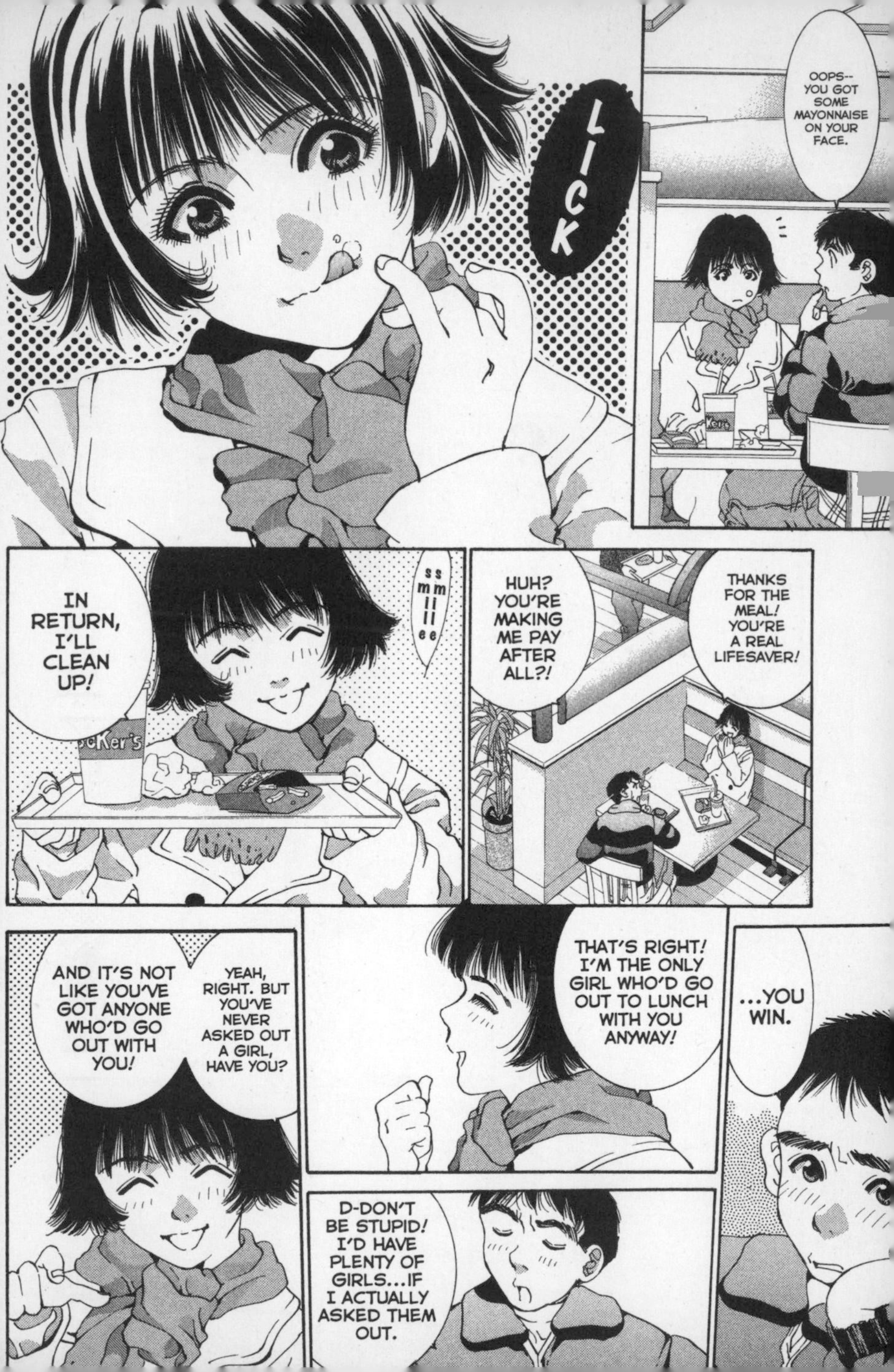
OOPS-- YOU GOT SOME MAYONNAISE ON YOUR FACE.
LICK
THANKS FOR THE MEAL! YOU'RE A REAL LIFESAVER!
HUH? YOU'RE MAKING ME PAY AFTER ALL?!
ssmmiillee
IN RETURN, I'LL CLEAN UP!
...YOU WIN.
THAT'S RIGHT! I'M THE ONLY GIRL WHO'D GO OUT TO LUNCH WITH YOU ANYWAY!
D-DON'T BE STUPID! I'D HAVE PLENTY OF GIRLS...IF I ACTUALLY ASKED THEM OUT.
YEAH, RIGHT. BUT YOU'VE NEVER ASKED OUT A GIRL, HAVE YOU?
AND IT'S NOT LIKE YOU'VE GOT ANYONE WHO'D GO OUT WITH YOU!

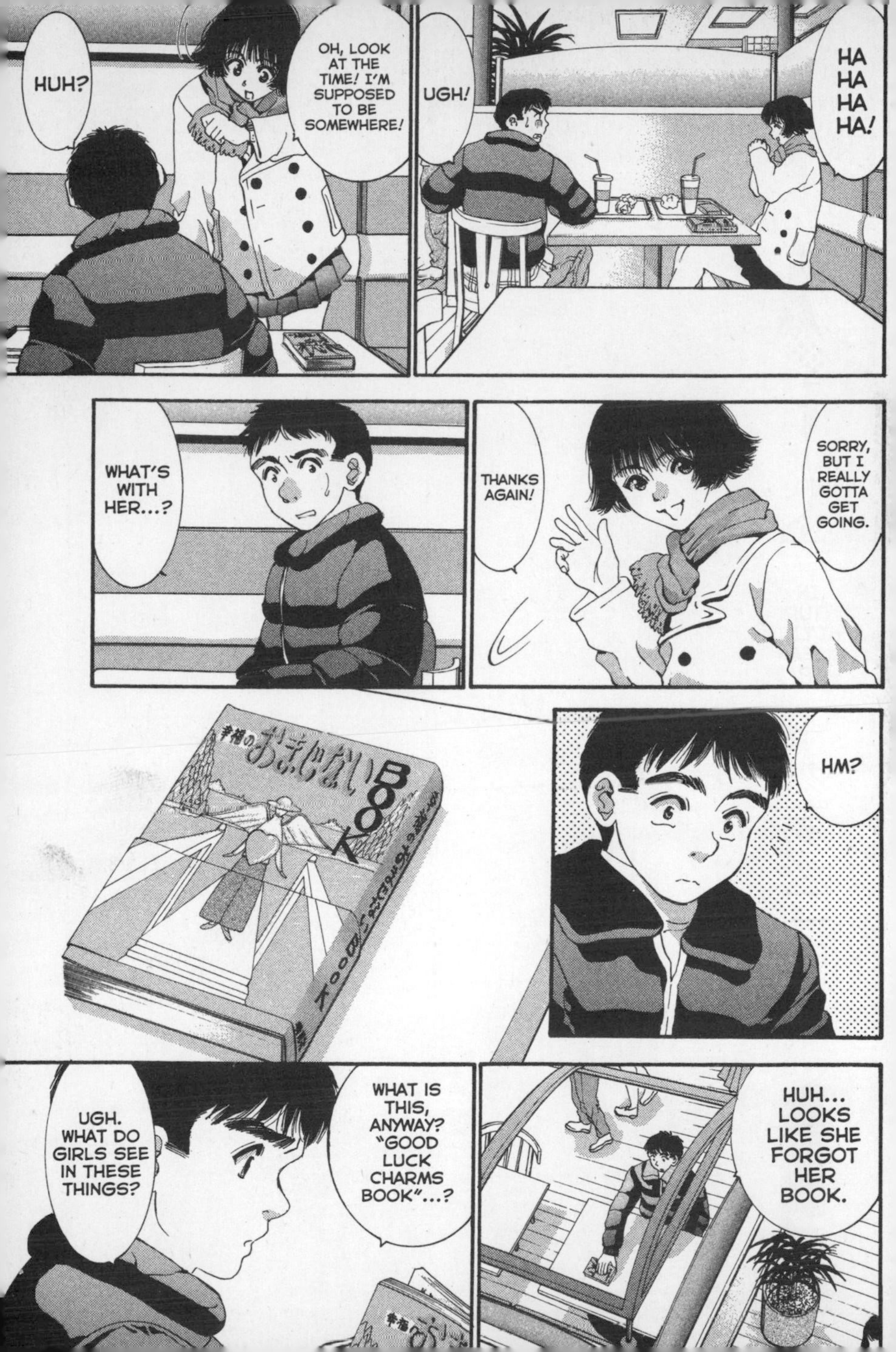
HA HA HA HA!
UGH!
OH, LOOK AT THE TIME! I'M SUPPOSED TO BE SOMEWHERE!
HUH?
SORRY, BUT I REALLY GOTTA GET GOING.
THANKS AGAIN!
WHAT'S WITH HER...?
HM?
幸福のおまじないBOOK
HUH... LOOKS LIKE SHE FORGOT HER BOOK.
WHAT IS THIS, ANYWAY? "GOOD LUCK CHARMS BOOK"...?
UGH. WHAT DO GIRLS SEE IN THESE THINGS?

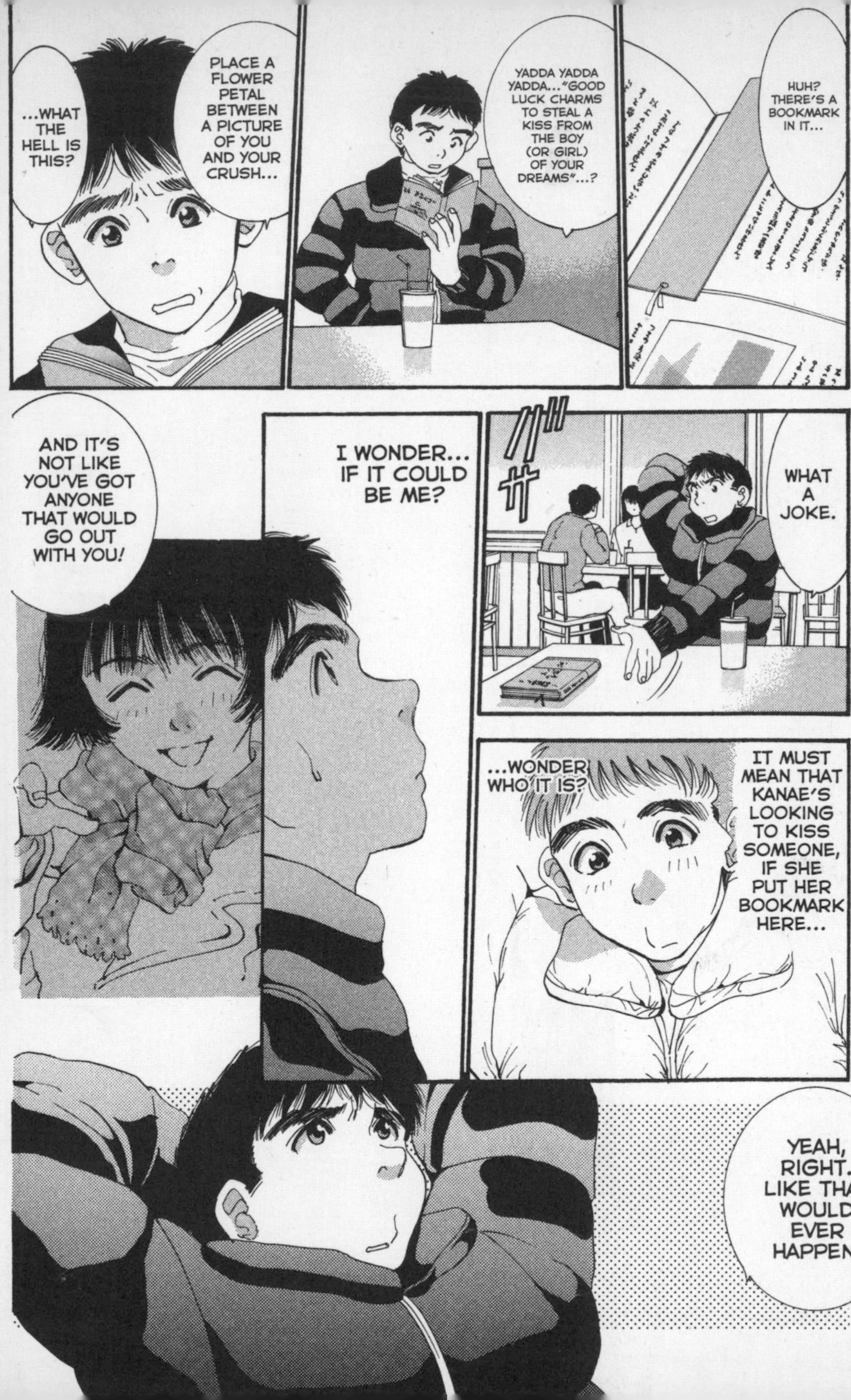
HUH? THERE'S A BOOKMARK IN IT...
YADDA YADDA YADDA... "GOOD LUCK CHARMS TO STEAL A KISS FROM THE BOY (OR GIRL) OF YOUR DREAMS"...?
PLACE A FLOWER PETAL BETWEEN A PICTURE OF YOU AND YOUR CRUSH...
...WHAT THE HELL IS THIS?
WHAT A JOKE.
IT MUST MEAN THAT KANAE'S LOOKING TO KISS SOMEONE, IF SHE PUT HER BOOKMARK HERE...
...WONDER WHO IT IS?
I WONDER... IF IT COULD BE ME?
AND IT'S NOT LIKE YOU'VE GOT ANYONE THAT WOULD GO OUT WITH YOU!
YEAH, RIGHT. LIKE THAT WOULD EVER HAPPEN.

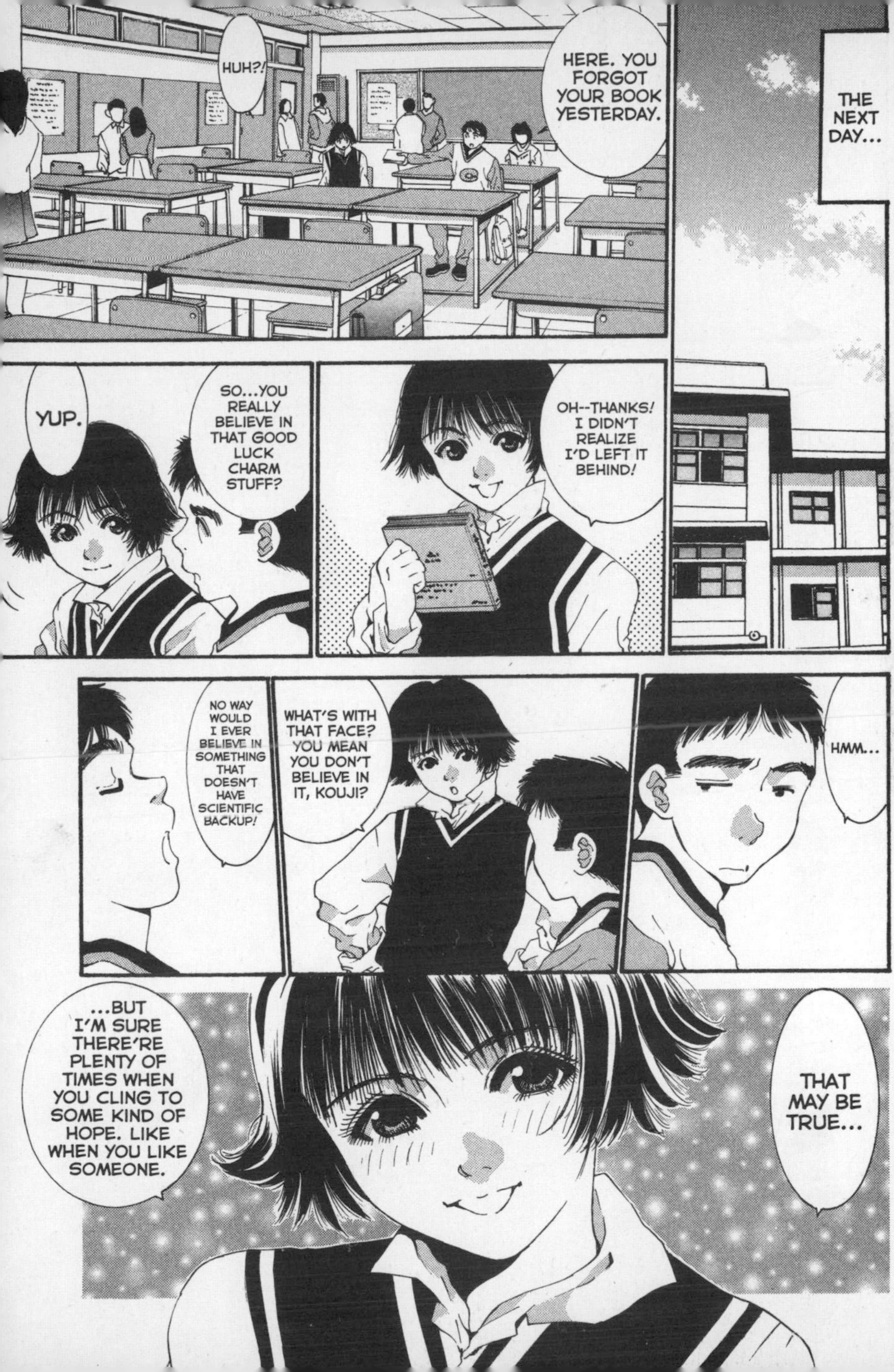
THE NEXT DAY...
HERE. YOU FORGOT YOUR BOOK YESTERDAY.
HUH?!
OH--THANKS! I DIDN'T REALIZE I'D LEFT IT BEHIND!
SO...YOU REALLY BELIEVE IN THAT GOOD LUCK CHARM STUFF?
YUP.
HMM...
WHAT'S WITH THAT FACE? YOU MEAN YOU DON'T BELIEVE IN IT, KOUJI?
NO WAY WOULD I EVER BELIEVE IN SOMETHING THAT DOESN'T HAVE SCIENTIFIC BACKUP!
THAT MAY BE TRUE...
...BUT I'M SURE THERE'RE PLENTY OF TIMES WHEN YOU CLING TO SOME KIND OF HOPE. LIKE WHEN YOU LIKE SOMEONE.

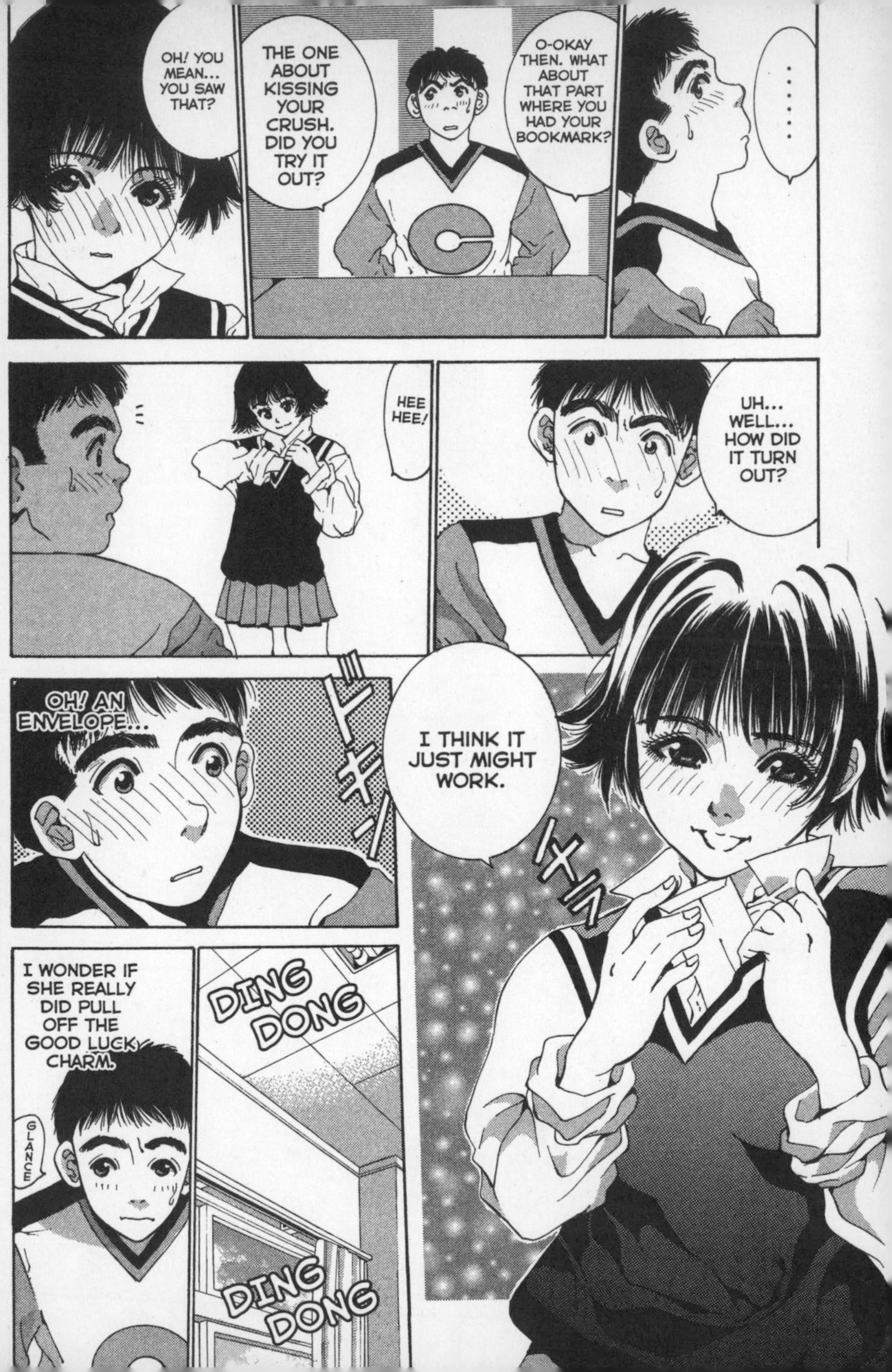
......
O-OKAY THEN. WHAT ABOUT THAT PART WHERE YOU HAD YOUR BOOKMARK?
THE ONE ABOUT KISSING YOUR CRUSH. DID YOU TRY IT OUT?
OH! YOU MEAN... YOU SAW THAT?
UH... WELL... HOW DID IT TURN OUT?
HEE HEE!
I THINK IT JUST MIGHT WORK.
OH! AN ENVELOPE...
DING DONG
DING DONG
I WONDER IF SHE REALLY DID PULL OFF THE GOOD LUCK CHARM.
GLANCE

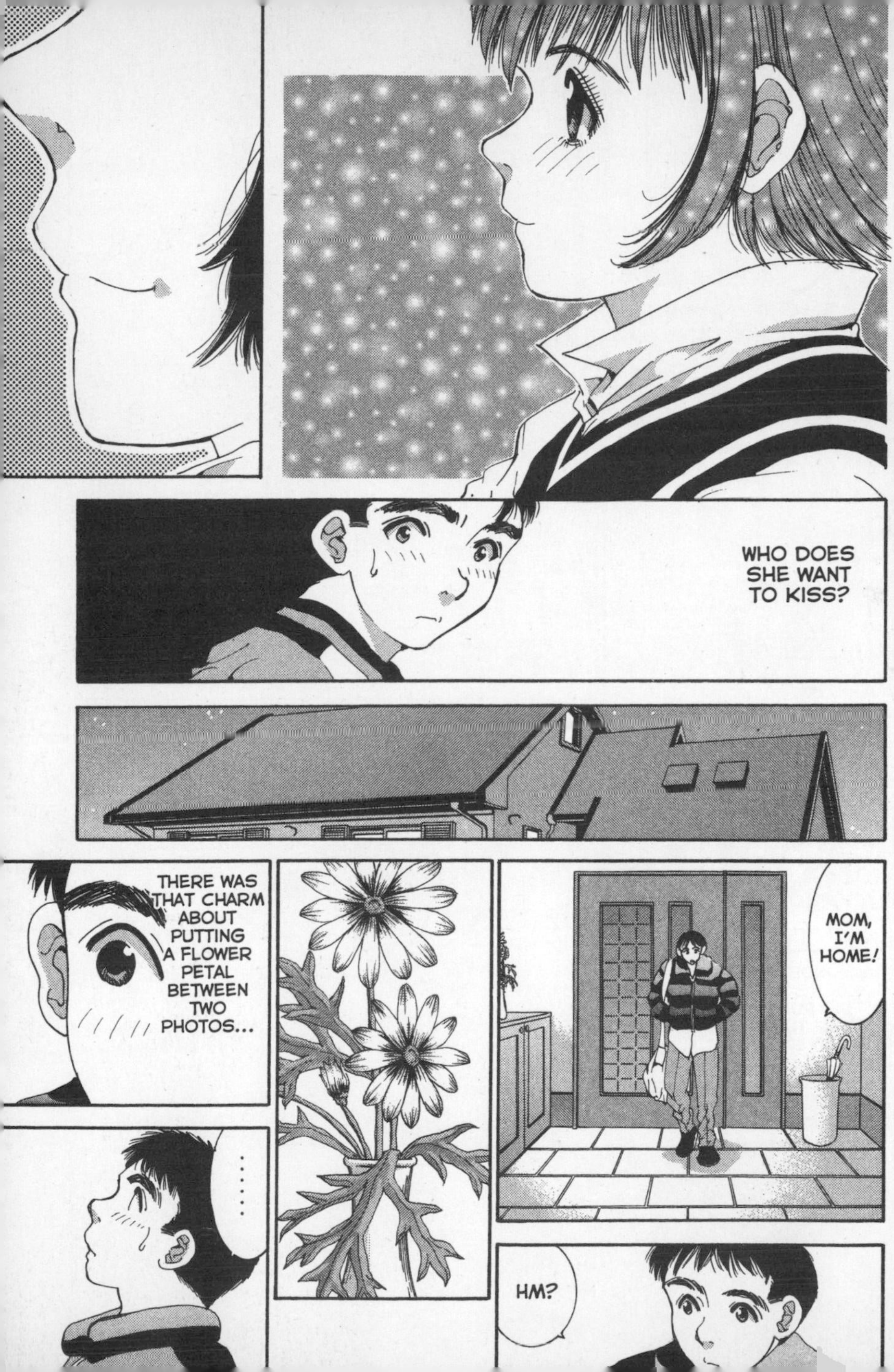
WHO DOES SHE WANT TO KISS?
MOM, I'M HOME!
HM?
THERE WAS THAT CHARM ABOUT PUTTING A FLOWER PETAL BETWEEN TWO PHOTOS...
......

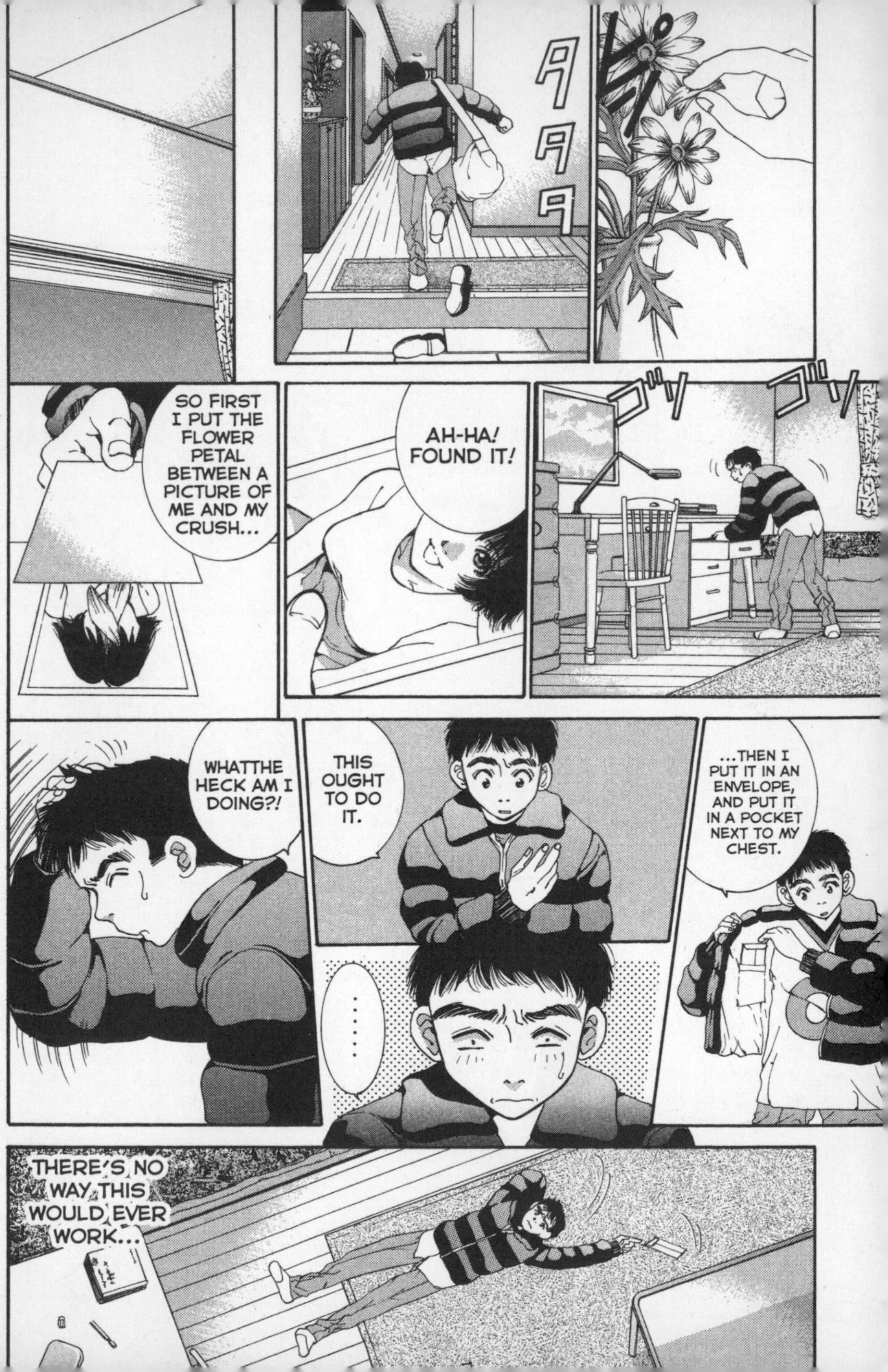
タタタ
AH-HA! FOUND IT!
SO FIRST I PUT THE FLOWER PETAL BETWEEN A PICTURE OF ME AND MY CRUSH...
...THEN I PUT IT IN AN ENVELOPE, AND PUT IT IN A POCKET NEXT TO MY CHEST.
THIS OUGHT TO DO IT.
......
WHATTHE HECK AM I DOING?!
THERE'S NO WAY THIS WOULD EVER WORK...

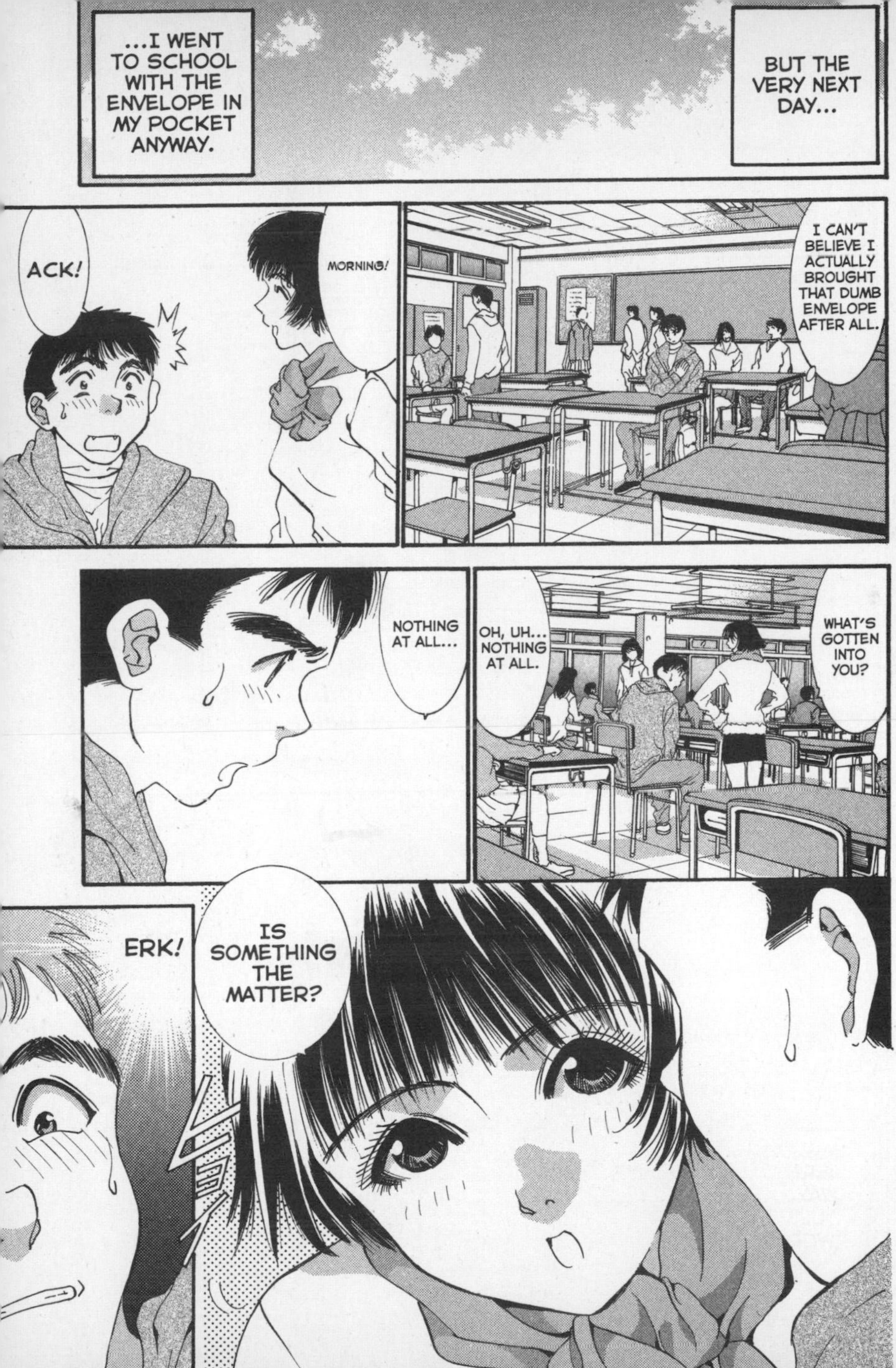
BUT THE VERY NEXT DAY...
...I WENT TO SCHOOL WITH THE ENVELOPE IN MY POCKET ANYWAY.
I CAN'T BELIEVE I ACTUALLY BROUGHT THAT DUMB ENVELOPE AFTER ALL.
MORNING!
ACK!
WHAT'S GOTTEN INTO YOU?
OH, UH... NOTHING AT ALL.
NOTHING AT ALL...
IS SOMETHING THE MATTER?
ERK!

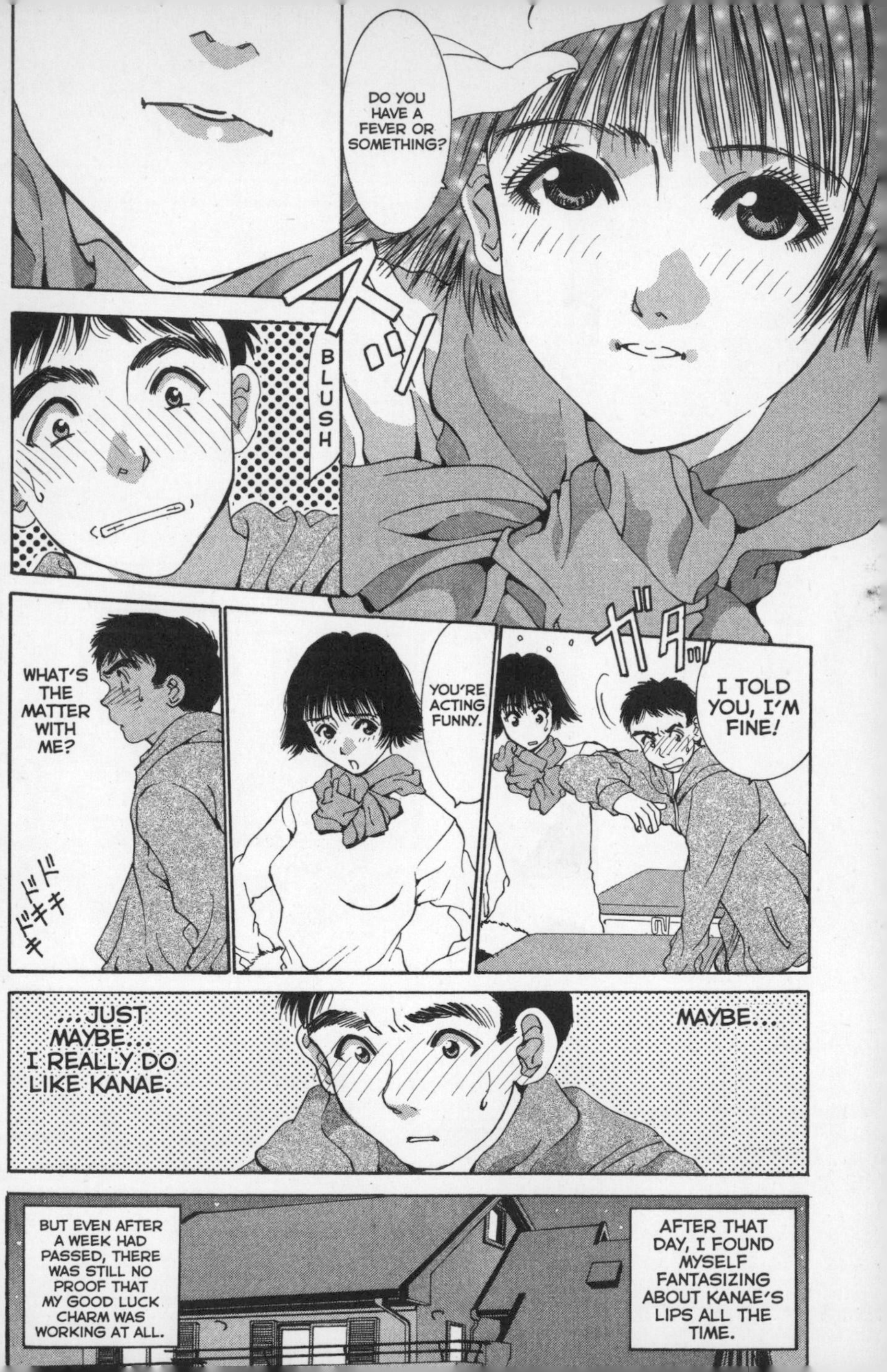
DO YOU HAVE A FEVER OR SOMETHING?
BLUSH
ガタッ
I TOLD YOU, I'M FINE!
YOU'RE ACTING FUNNY.
WHAT'S THE MATTER WITH ME?
ドキドキ
MAYBE...
...JUST MAYBE... I REALLY DO LIKE KANAE.
AFTER THAT DAY, I FOUND MYSELF FANTASIZING ABOUT KANAE'S LIPS ALL THE TIME.
BUT EVEN AFTER A WEEK HAD PASSED, THERE WAS STILL NO PROOF THAT MY GOOD LUCK CHARM WAS WORKING AT ALL.

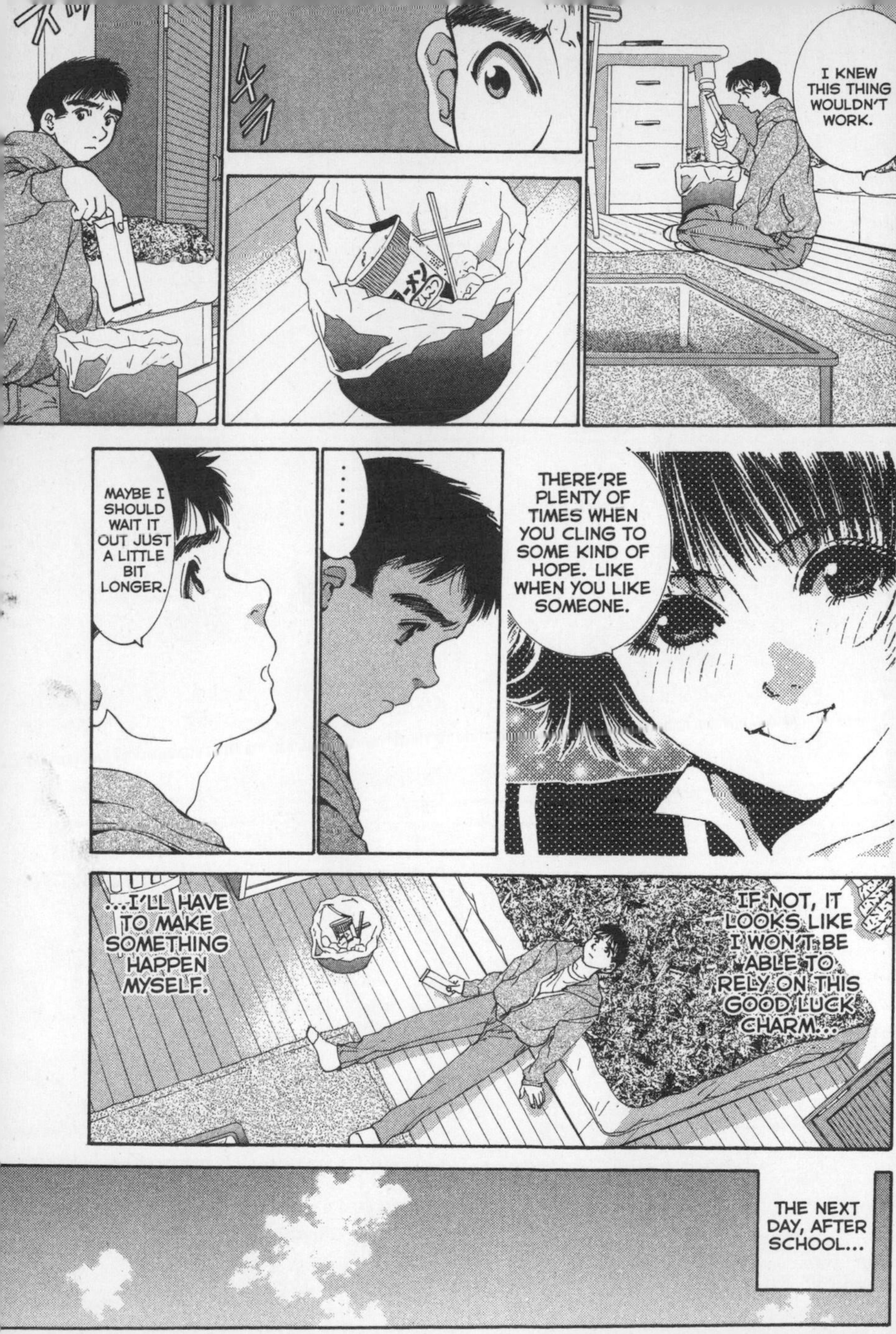
I KNEW THIS THING WOULDN'T WORK.
THERE'RE PLENTY OF TIMES WHEN YOU CLING TO SOME KIND OF HOPE. LIKE WHEN YOU LIKE SOMEONE.
......
MAYBE I SHOULD WAIT IT OUT JUST A LITTLE BIT LONGER.
IF NOT, IT LOOKS LIKE I WON'T BE ABLE TO RELY ON THIS GOOD LUCK CHARM...
...I'LL HAVE TO MAKE SOMETHING HAPPEN MYSELF.
THE NEXT DAY, AFTER SCHOOL...

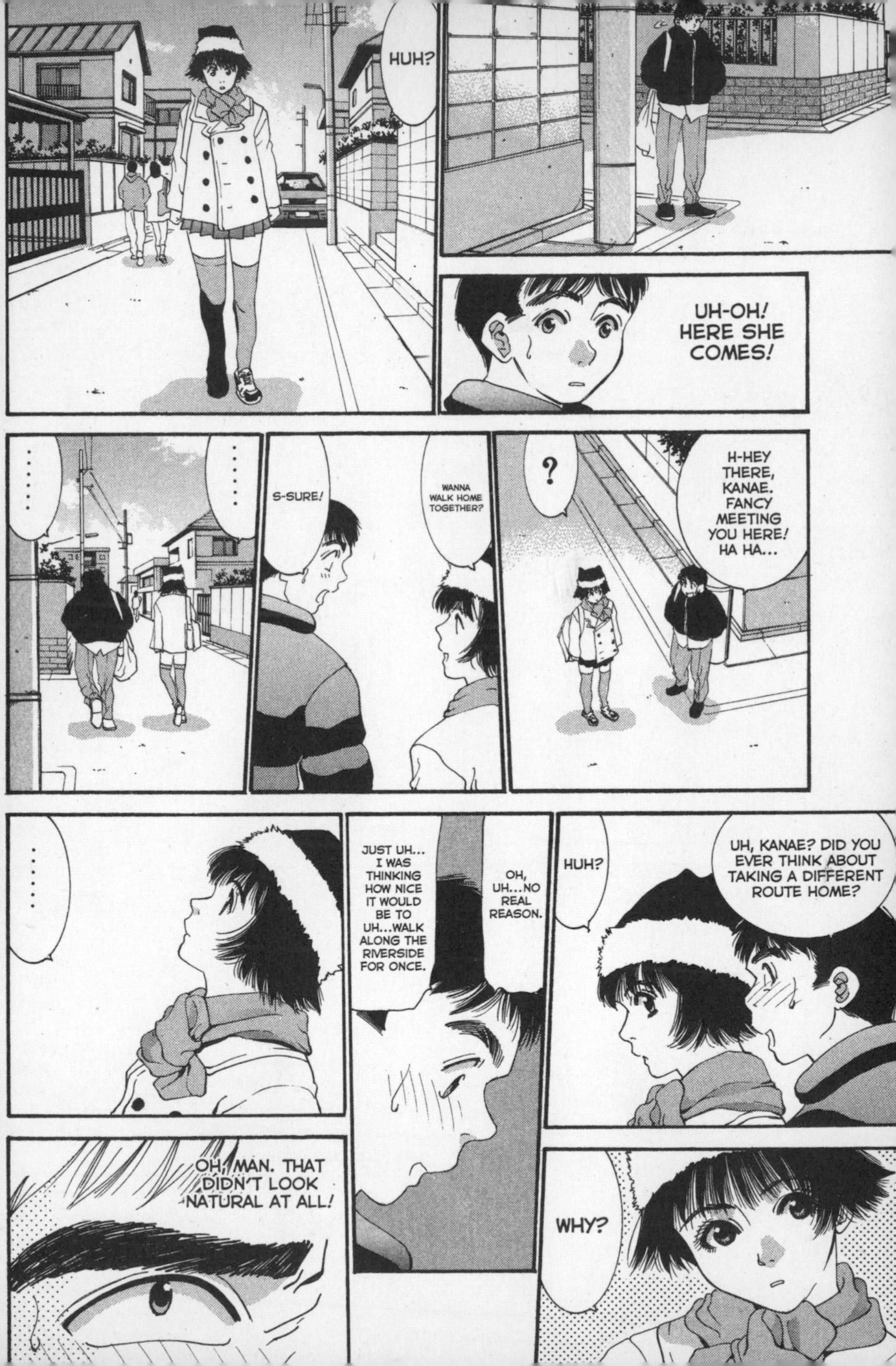
UH-OH! HERE SHE COMES!
HUH?
H-HEY THERE, KANAE. FANCY MEETING YOU HERE! HA HA...
?
WANNA WALK HOME TOGETHER?
S-SURE!
......
......
UH, KANAE? DID YOU EVER THINK ABOUT TAKING A DIFFERENT ROUTE HOME?
HUH?
WHY?
OH, UH...NO REAL REASON.
JUST UH... I WAS THINKING HOW NICE IT WOULD BE TO UH...WALK ALONG THE RIVERSIDE FOR ONCE.
......
OH, MAN. THAT DIDN'T LOOK NATURAL AT ALL!

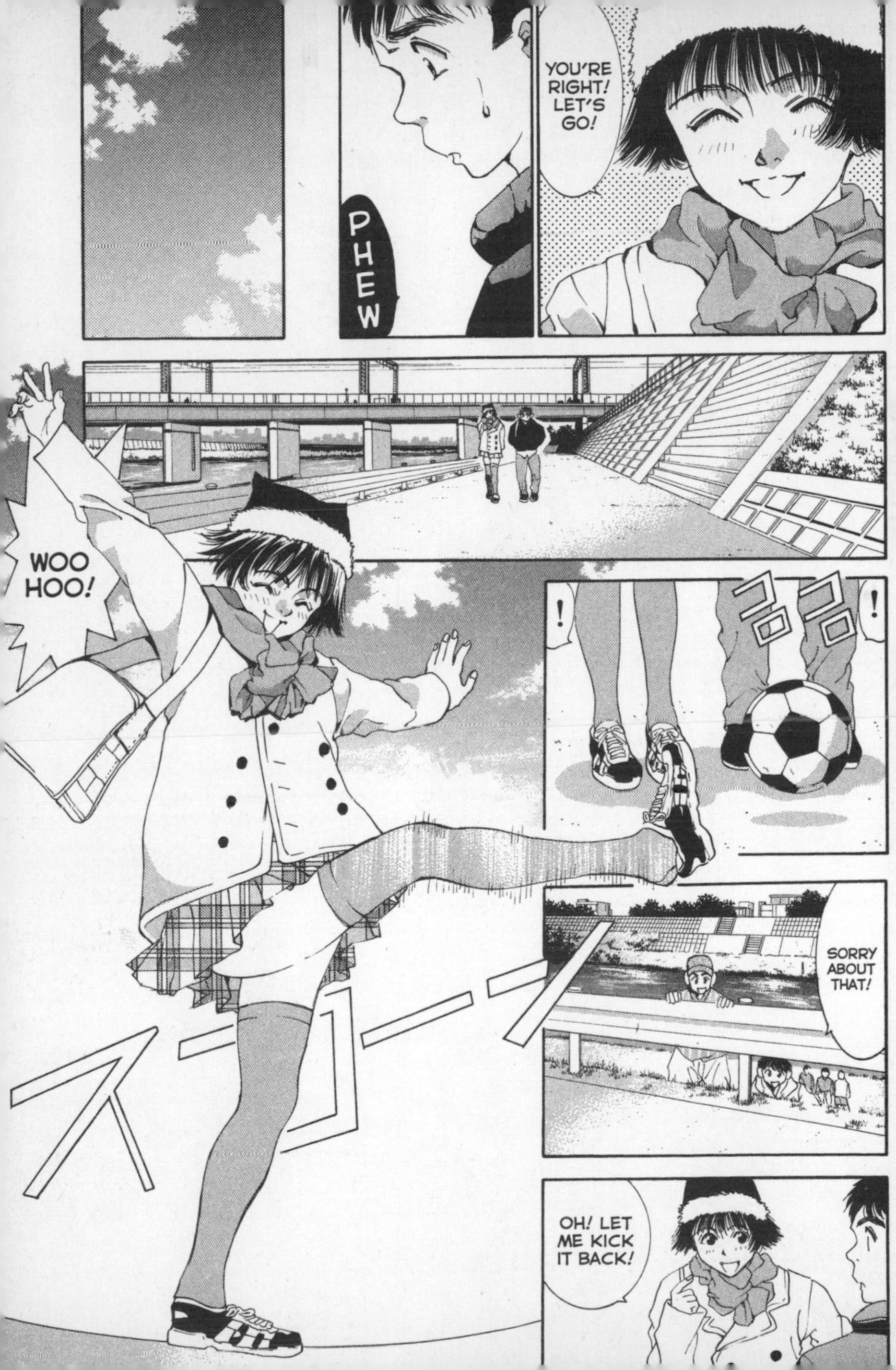
YOU'RE RIGHT! LET'S GO!
PHEW
!
!
SORRY ABOUT THAT!
OH! LET ME KICK IT BACK!
WOO HOO!

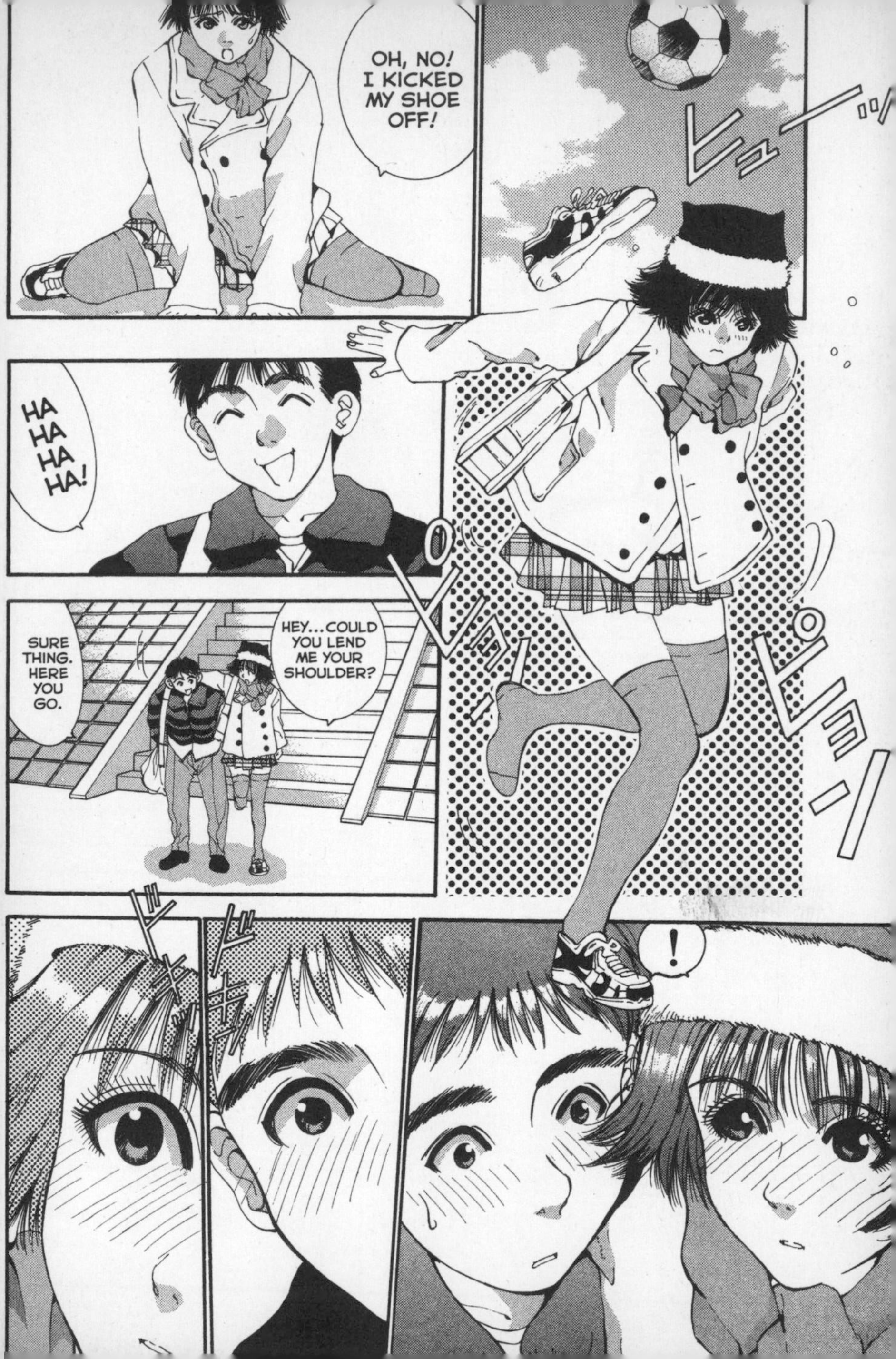

OH, NO! I KICKED MY SHOE OFF!
HA HA HA HA!
HEY...COULD YOU LEND ME YOUR SHOULDER?
SURE THING. HERE YOU GO.
!

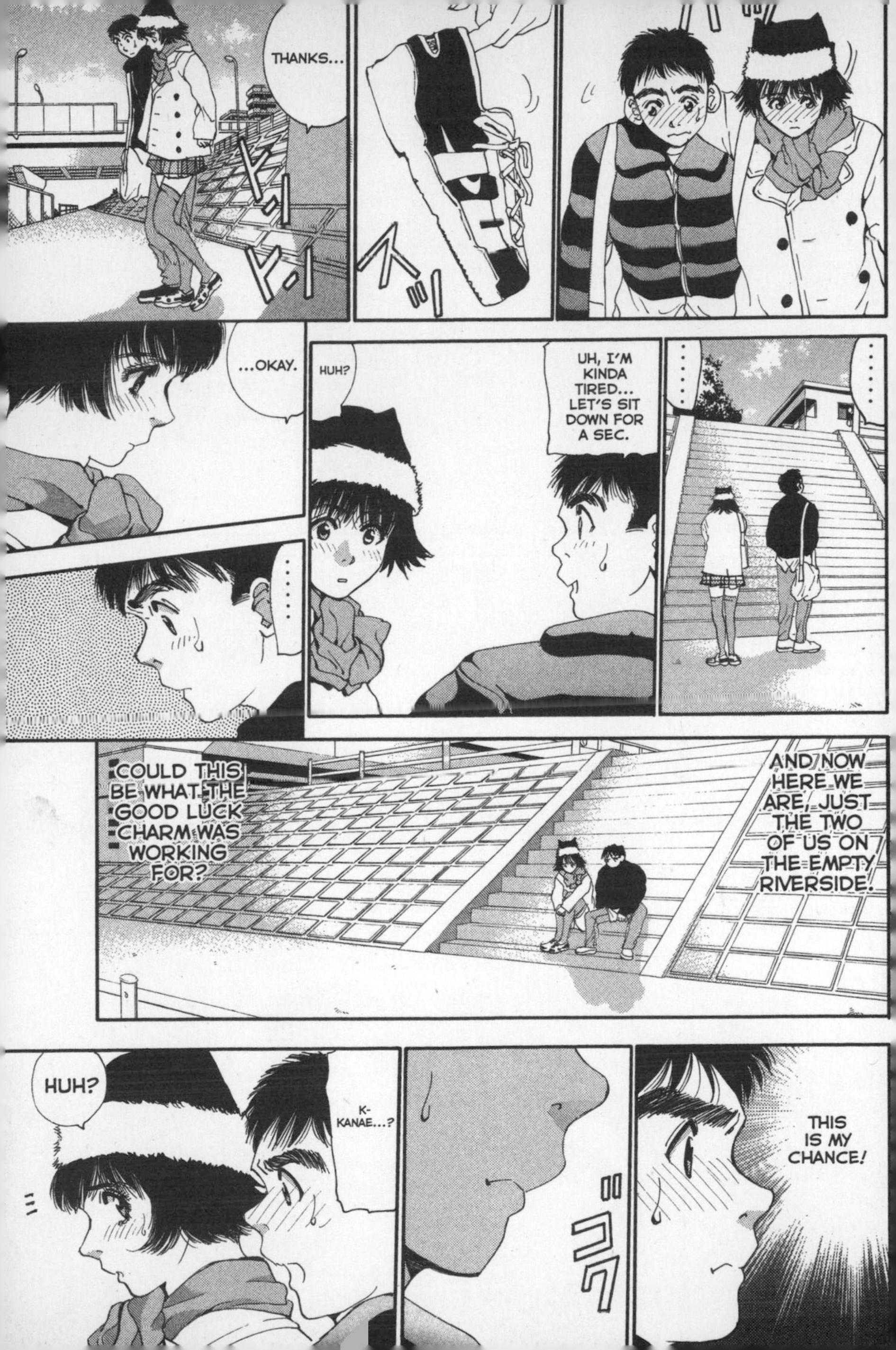
THANKS...
......
UH, I'M KINDA TIRED... LET'S SIT DOWN FOR A SEC.
HUH?
...OKAY.
......
AND NOW HERE WE ARE, JUST THE TWO OF US ON THE EMPTY RIVERSIDE.
COULD THIS BE WHAT THE GOOD LUCK CHARM WAS WORKING FOR?
THIS IS MY CHANCE!
K-KANAE...?
HUH?

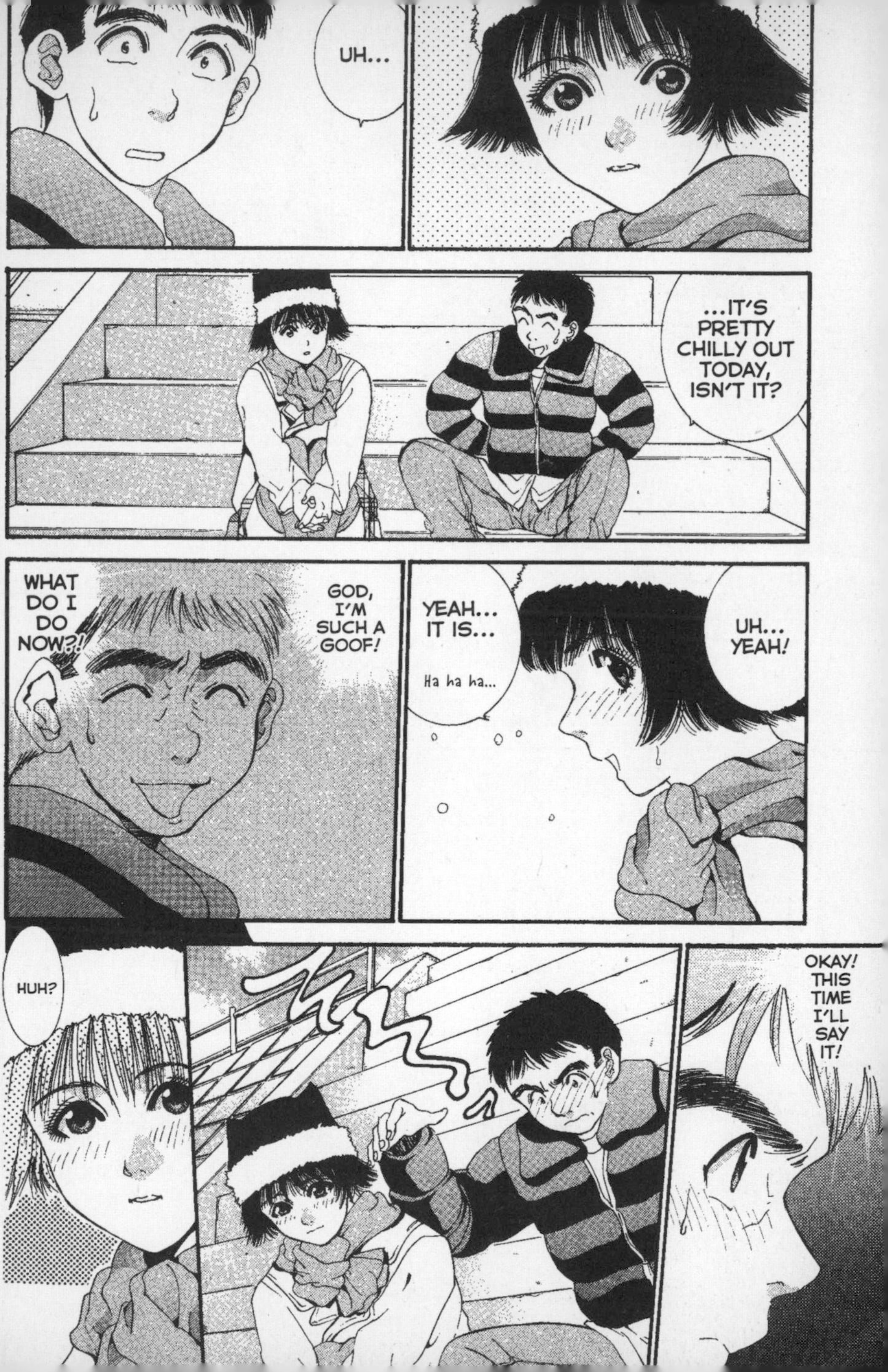
UH...
...IT'S PRETTY CHILLY OUT TODAY, ISN'T IT?
UH... YEAH!
YEAH... IT IS...
Ha ha ha...
GOD, I'M SUCH A GOOF!
WHAT DO I DO NOW?!
OKAY! THIS TIME I'LL SAY IT!
HUH?

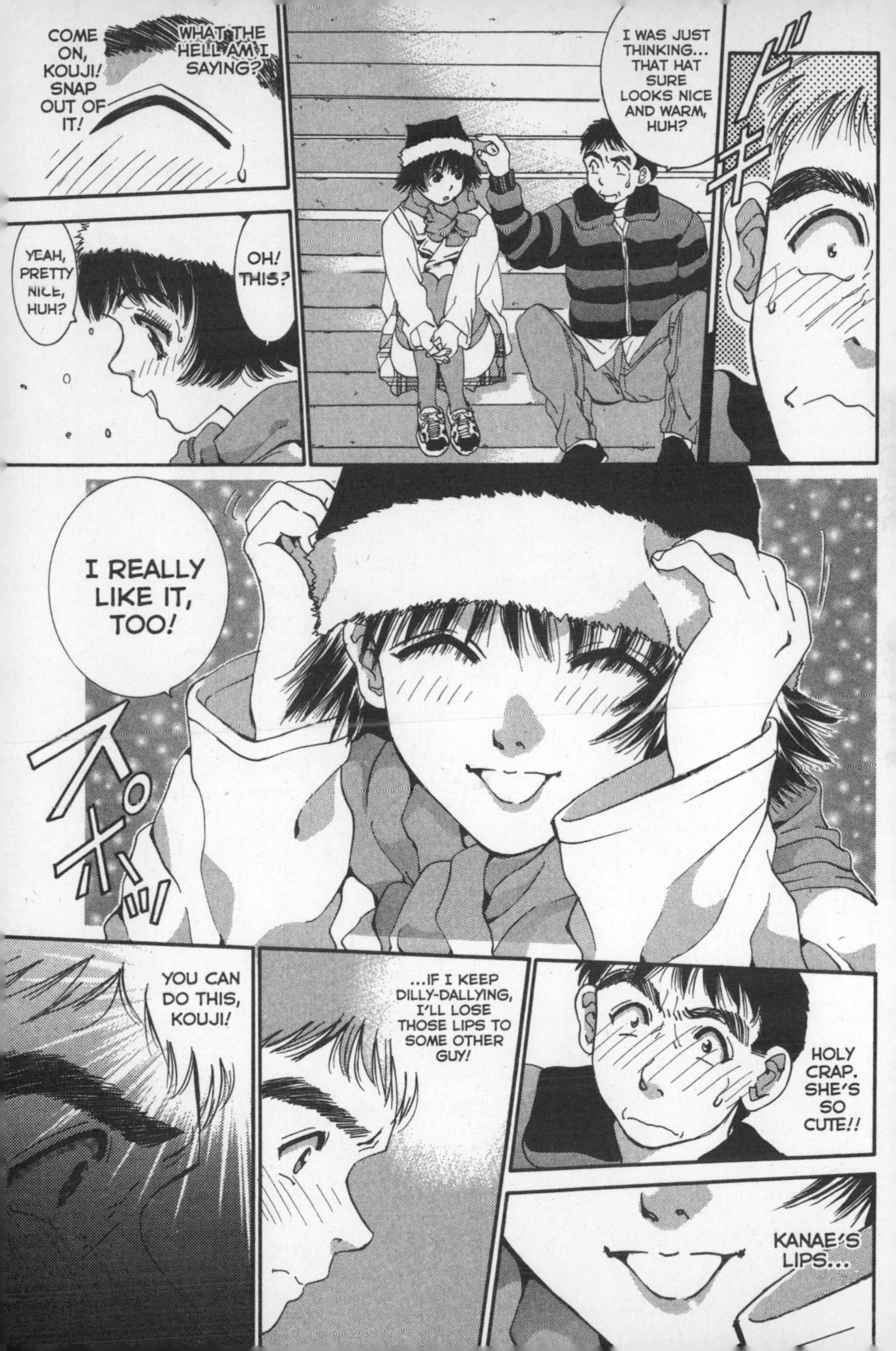
I WAS JUST THINKING... THAT HAT SURE LOOKS NICE AND WARM, HUH?
WHAT THE HELL AM I SAYING?
COME ON, KOUJI! SNAP OUT OF IT!
OH! THIS?
YEAH, PRETTY NICE, HUH?
I REALLY LIKE IT, TOO!
HOLY CRAP. SHE'S SO CUTE!!
KANAE'S LIPS...
...IF I KEEP DILLY-DALLYING, I'LL LOSE THOSE LIPS TO SOME OTHER GUY!
YOU CAN DO THIS, KOUJI!

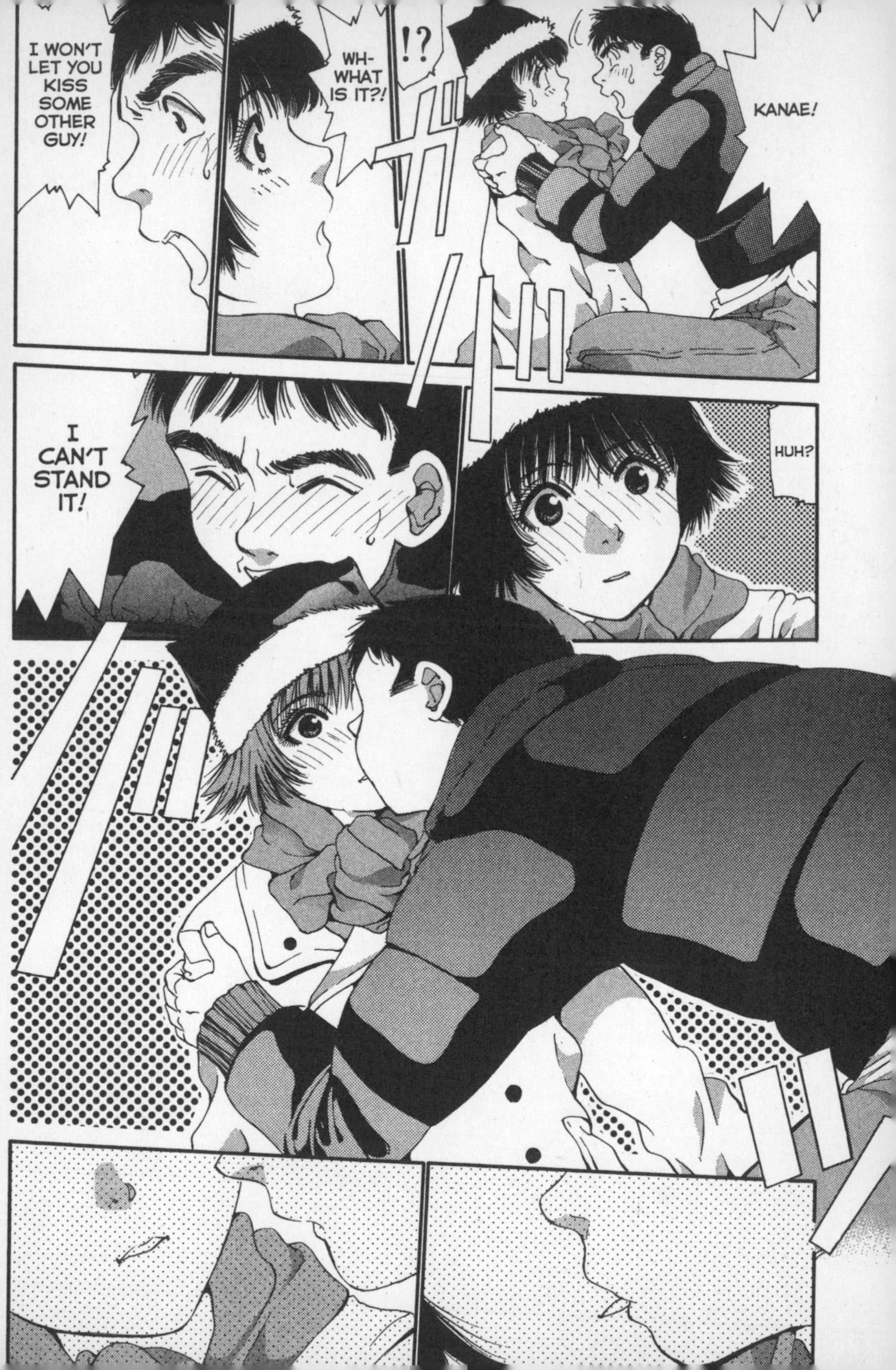
KANAE!
!?
ガ
WH- WHAT IS IT?!
I WON'T LET YOU KISS SOME OTHER GUY!
HUH?
I CAN'T STAND IT!

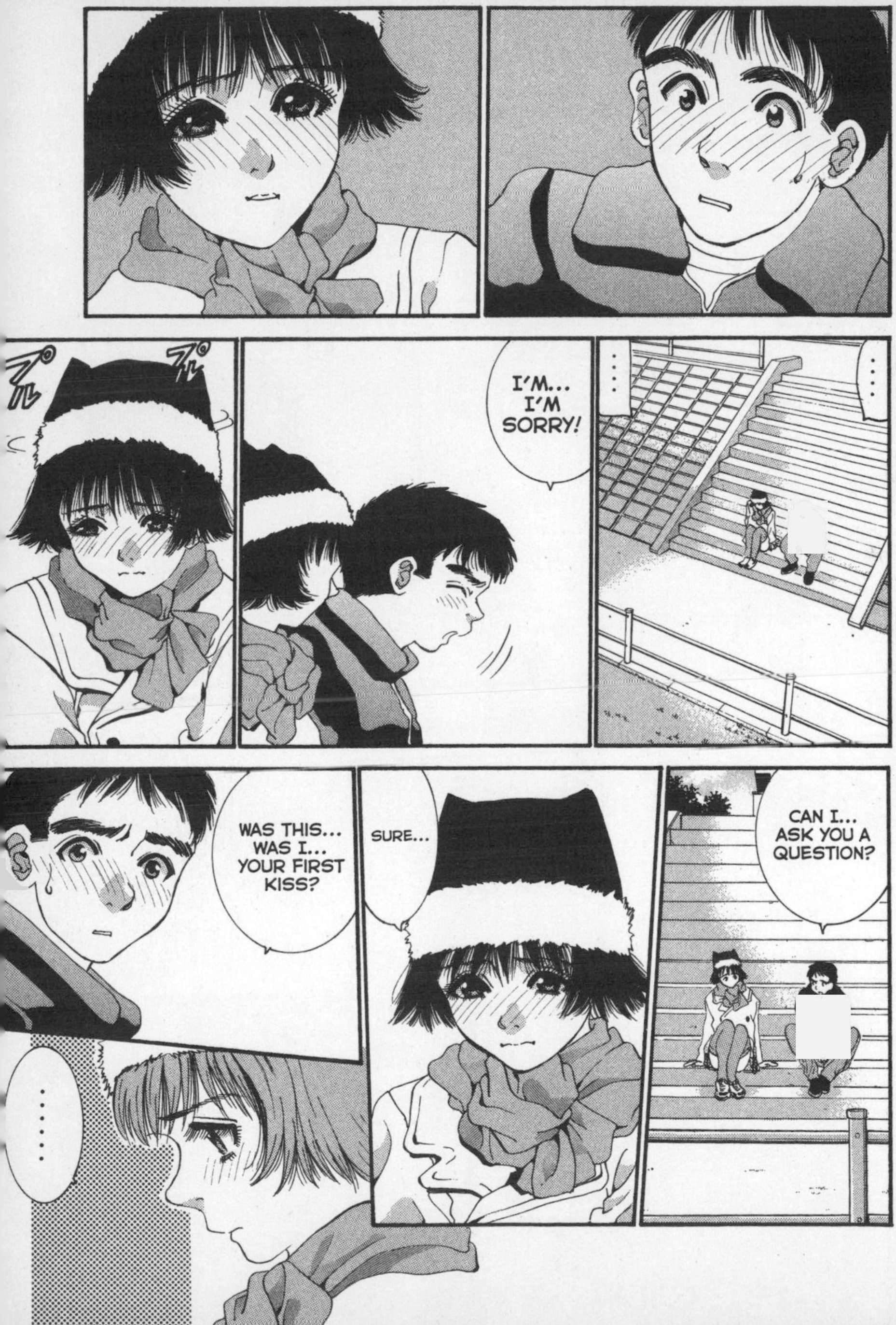
.....
.....
I'M... I'M SORRY!
CAN I... ASK YOU A QUESTION?
SURE...
WAS THIS... WAS I... YOUR FIRST KISS?
......

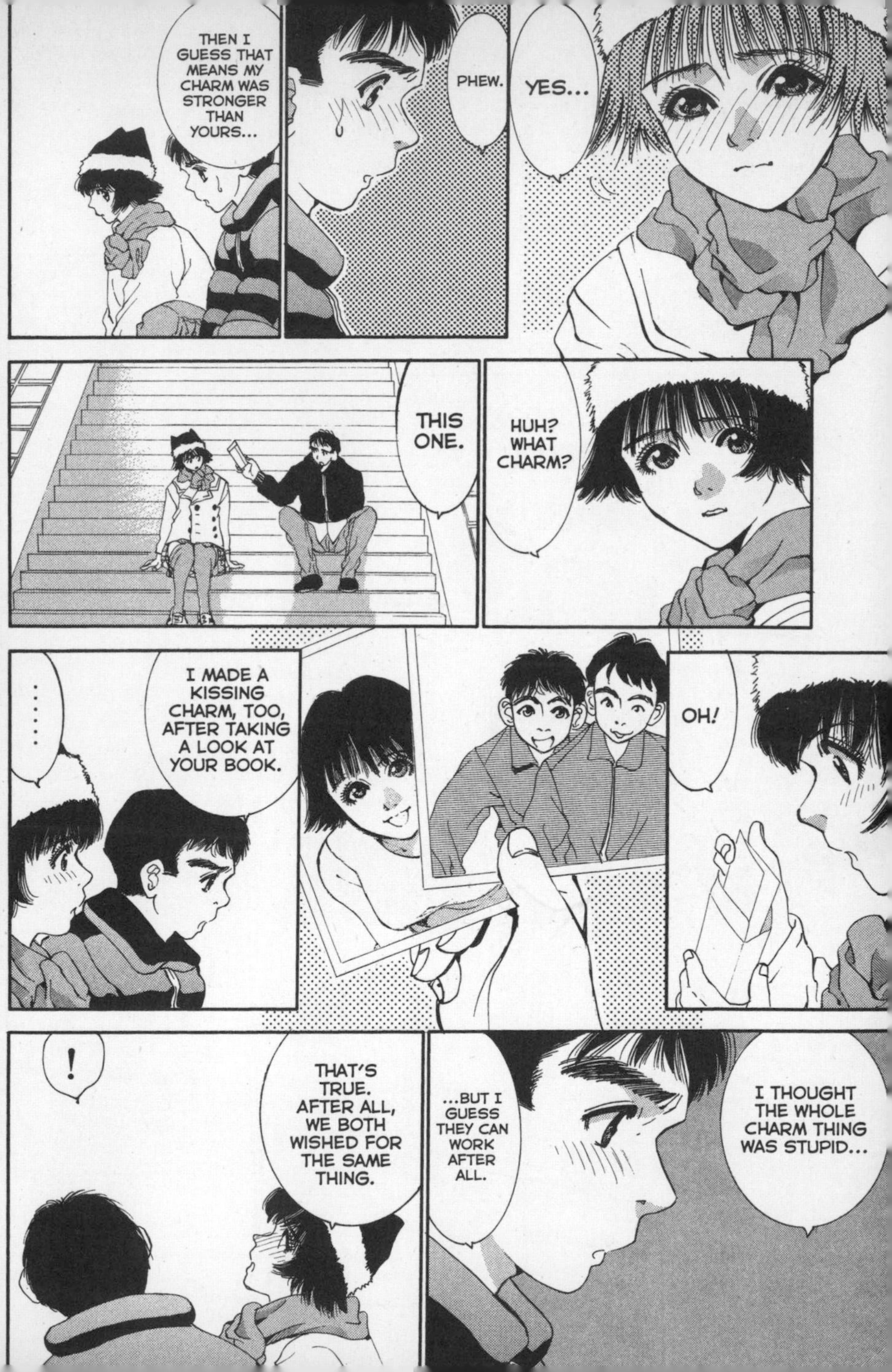
YES...
PHEW.
THEN I GUESS THAT MEANS MY CHARM WAS STRONGER THAN YOURS...
HUH? WHAT CHARM?
THIS ONE.
OH!
I MADE A KISSING CHARM, TOO, AFTER TAKING A LOOK AT YOUR BOOK.
......
I THOUGHT THE WHOLE CHARM THING WAS STUPID...
...BUT I GUESS THEY CAN WORK AFTER ALL.
THAT'S TRUE. AFTER ALL, WE BOTH WISHED FOR THE SAME THING.
!

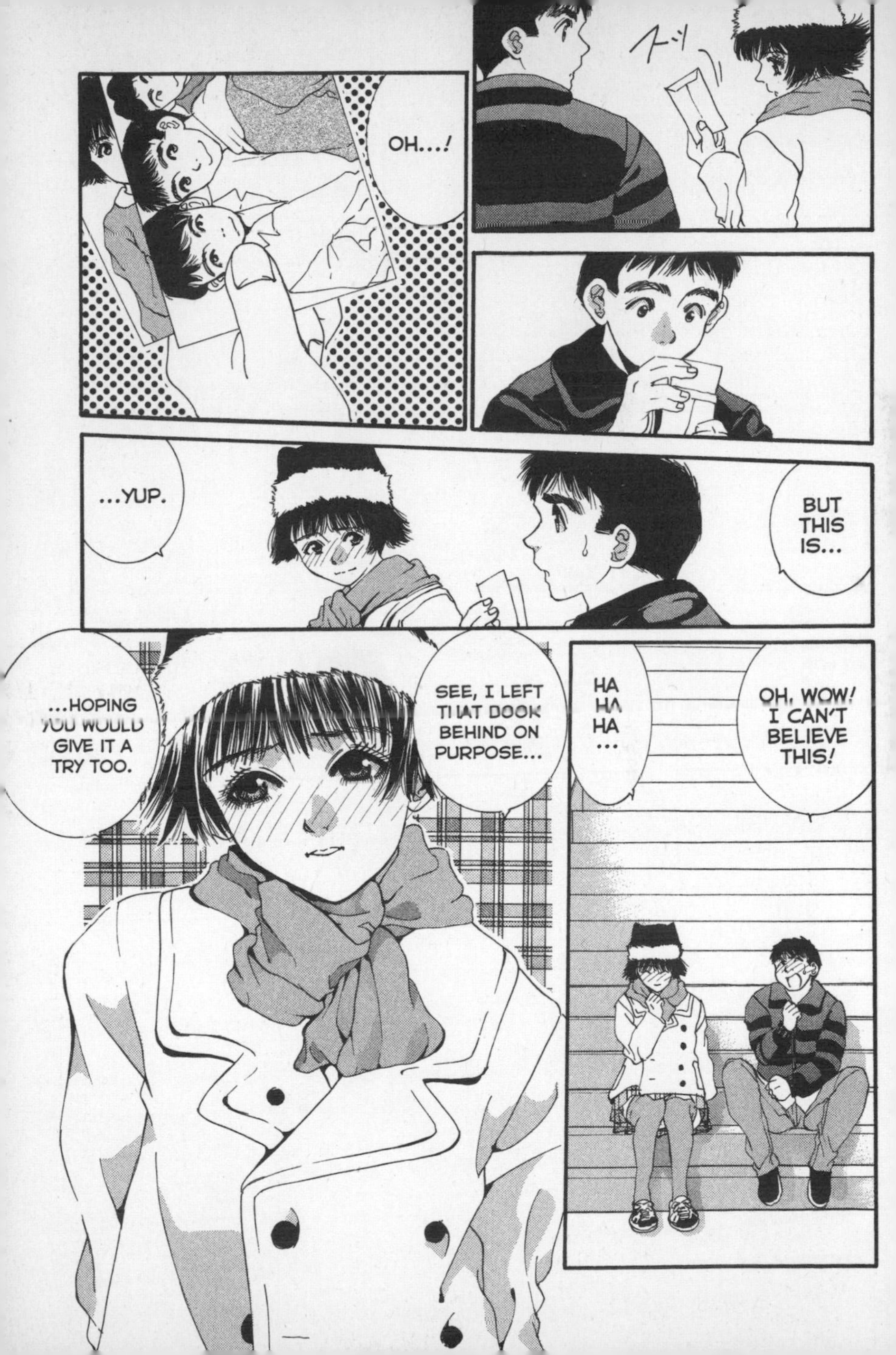
スッ
OH...!
BUT THIS IS...
...YUP.
OH, WOW! I CAN'T BELIEVE THIS!
HA HA HA ...
SEE, I LEFT THAT BOOK BEHIND ON PURPOSE...
...HOPING YOU WOULD GIVE IT A TRY TOO.

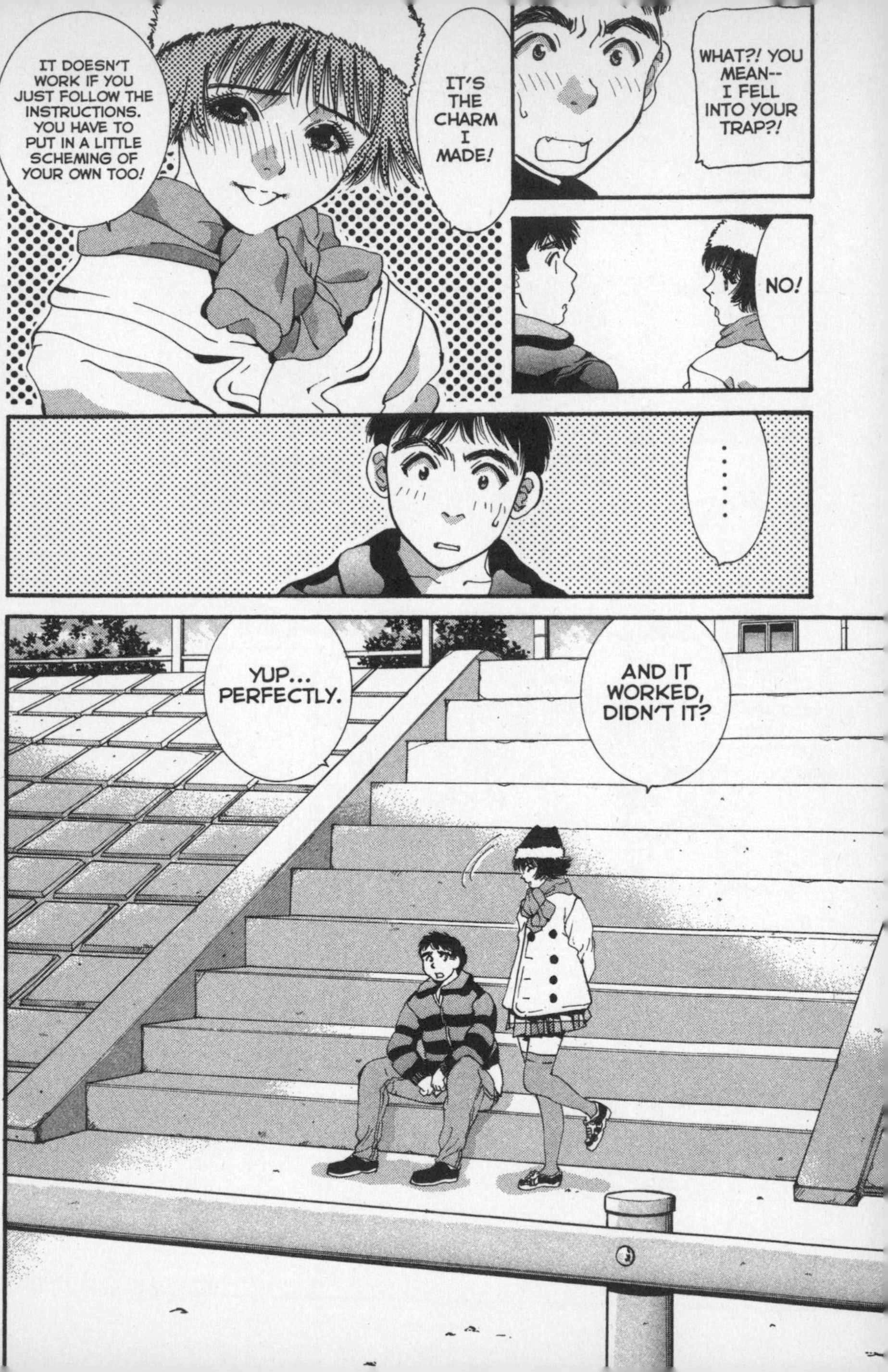
WHAT?! YOU MEAN-- I FELL INTO YOUR TRAP?!
NO!
IT'S THE CHARM I MADE!
IT DOESN'T WORK IF YOU JUST FOLLOW THE INSTRUCTIONS. YOU HAVE TO PUT IN A LITTLE SCHEMING OF YOUR OWN TOO!
......
AND IT WORKED, DIDN'T IT?
YUP... PERFECTLY.

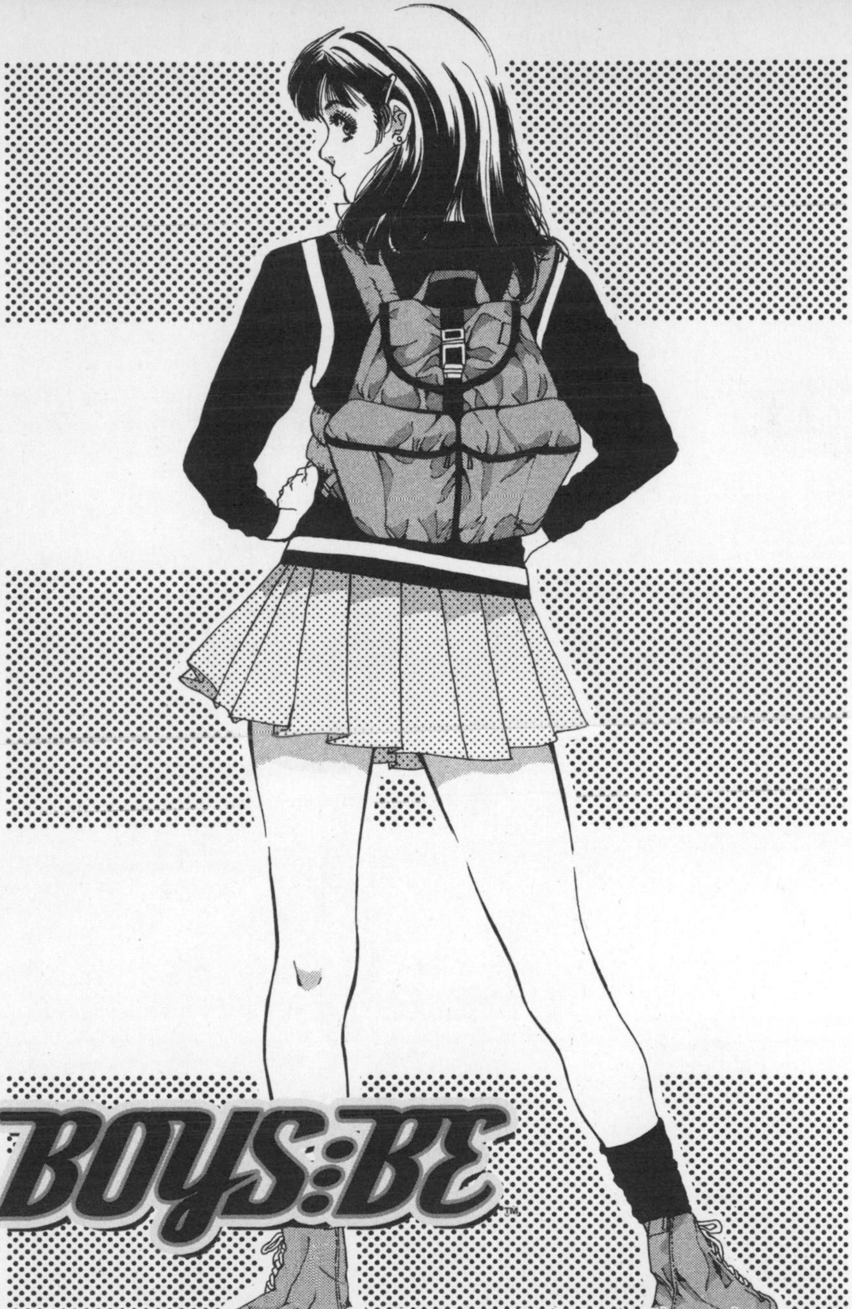
BOYS BE™
Report 12 Longing for Dream-Colored Chocolate

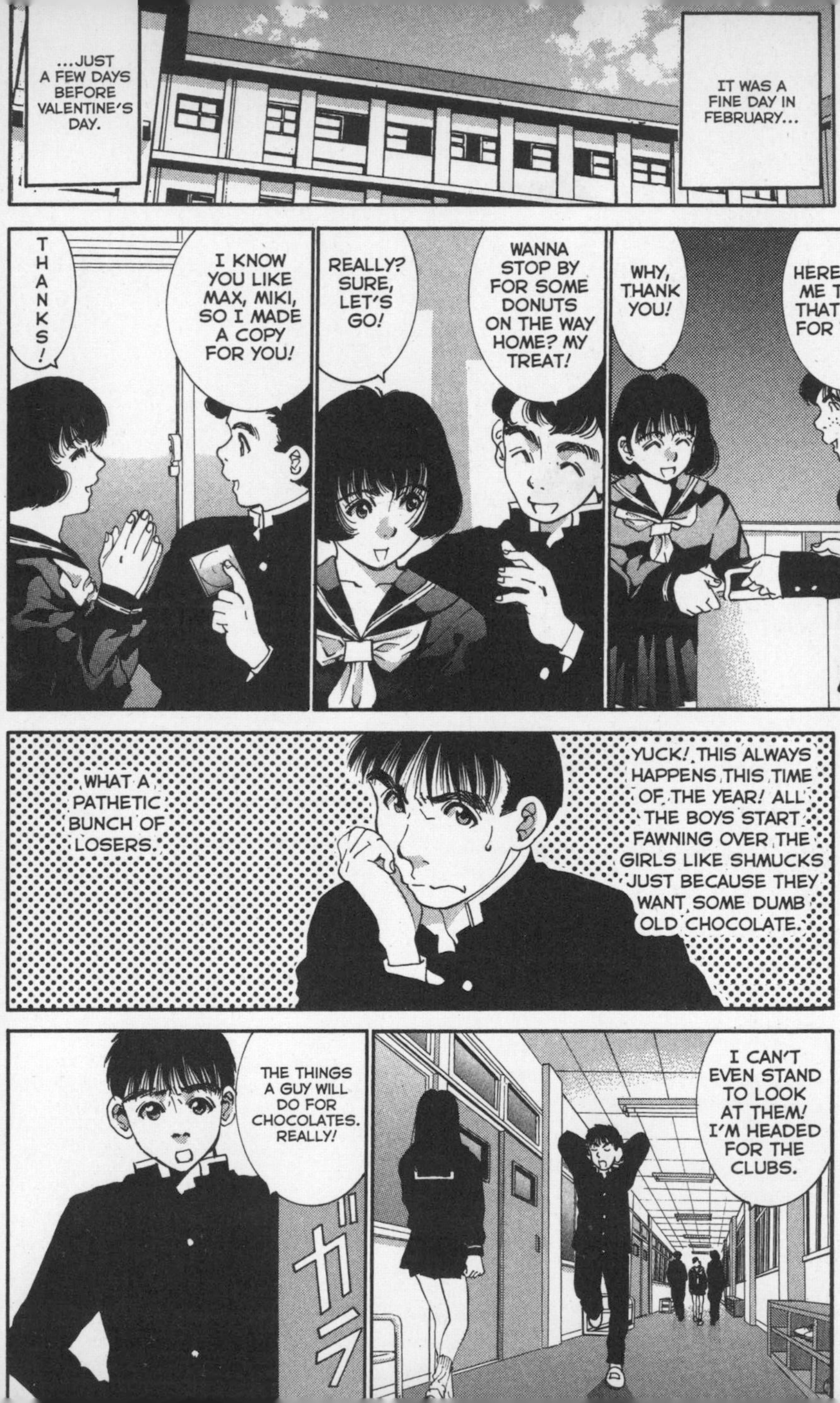

IT WAS A FINE DAY IN FEBRUARY...
...JUST A FEW DAYS BEFORE VALENTINE'S DAY.
HERE, LET ME TAKE THAT OUT FOR YOU.
WHY, THANK YOU!
WANNA STOP BY FOR SOME DONUTS ON THE WAY HOME? MY TREAT!
REALLY? SURE, LET'S GO!
I KNOW YOU LIKE MAX, MIKI, SO I MADE A COPY FOR YOU!
THANKS!
YUCK! THIS ALWAYS HAPPENS THIS TIME OF THE YEAR! ALL THE BOYS START FAWNING OVER THE GIRLS LIKE SHMUCKS JUST BECAUSE THEY WANT SOME DUMB OLD CHOCOLATE.
WHAT A PATHETIC BUNCH OF LOSERS.
I CAN'T EVEN STAND TO LOOK AT THEM! I'M HEADED FOR THE CLUBS.
ガラ
THE THINGS A GUY WILL DO FOR CHOCOLATES. REALLY!

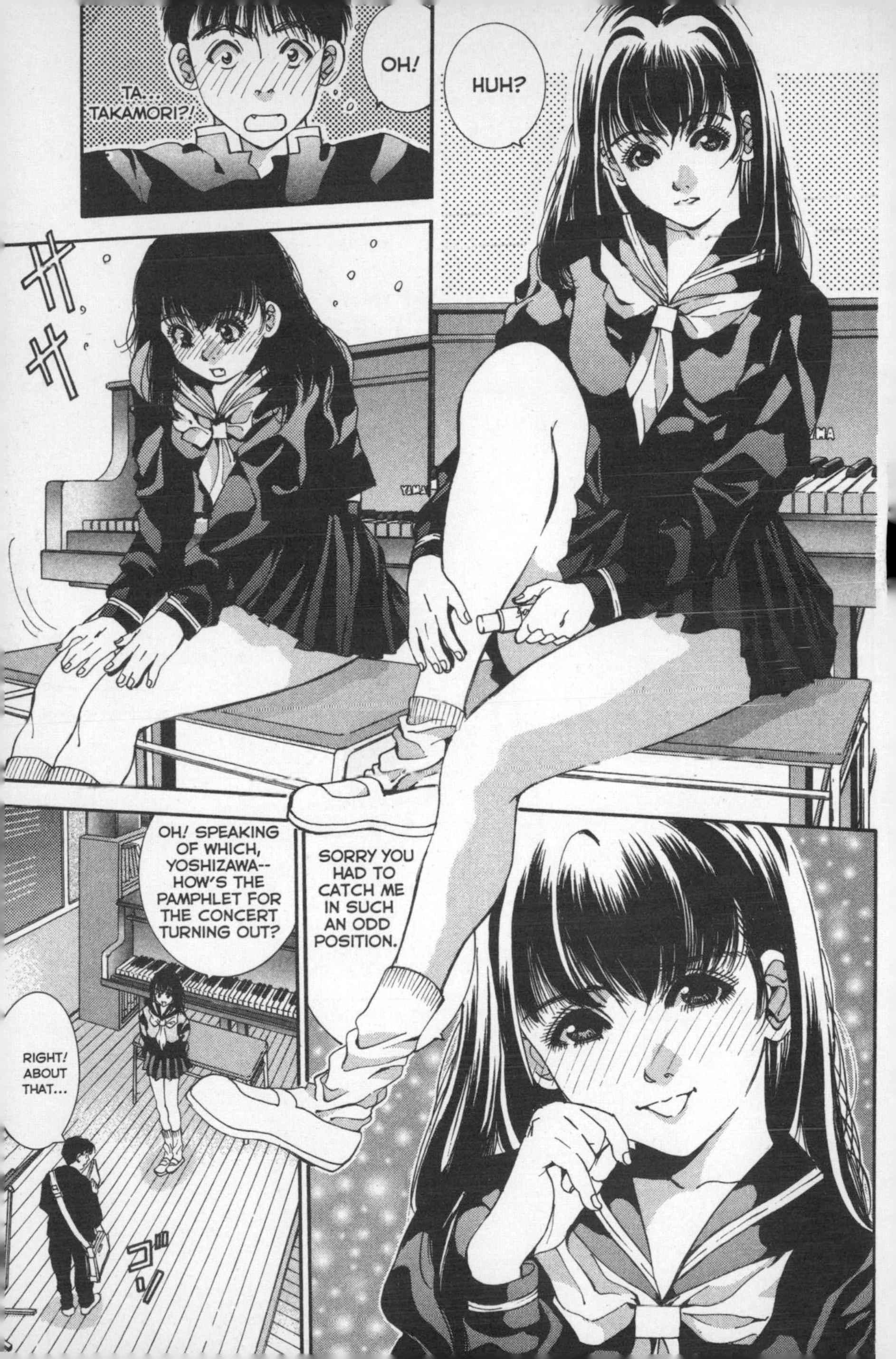
HUH?
OH!
TA... TAKAMORI?!
SORRY YOU HAD TO CATCH ME IN SUCH AN ODD POSITION.
OH! SPEAKING OF WHICH, YOSHIZAWA-- HOW'S THE PAMPHLET FOR THE CONCERT TURNING OUT?
RIGHT! ABOUT THAT...

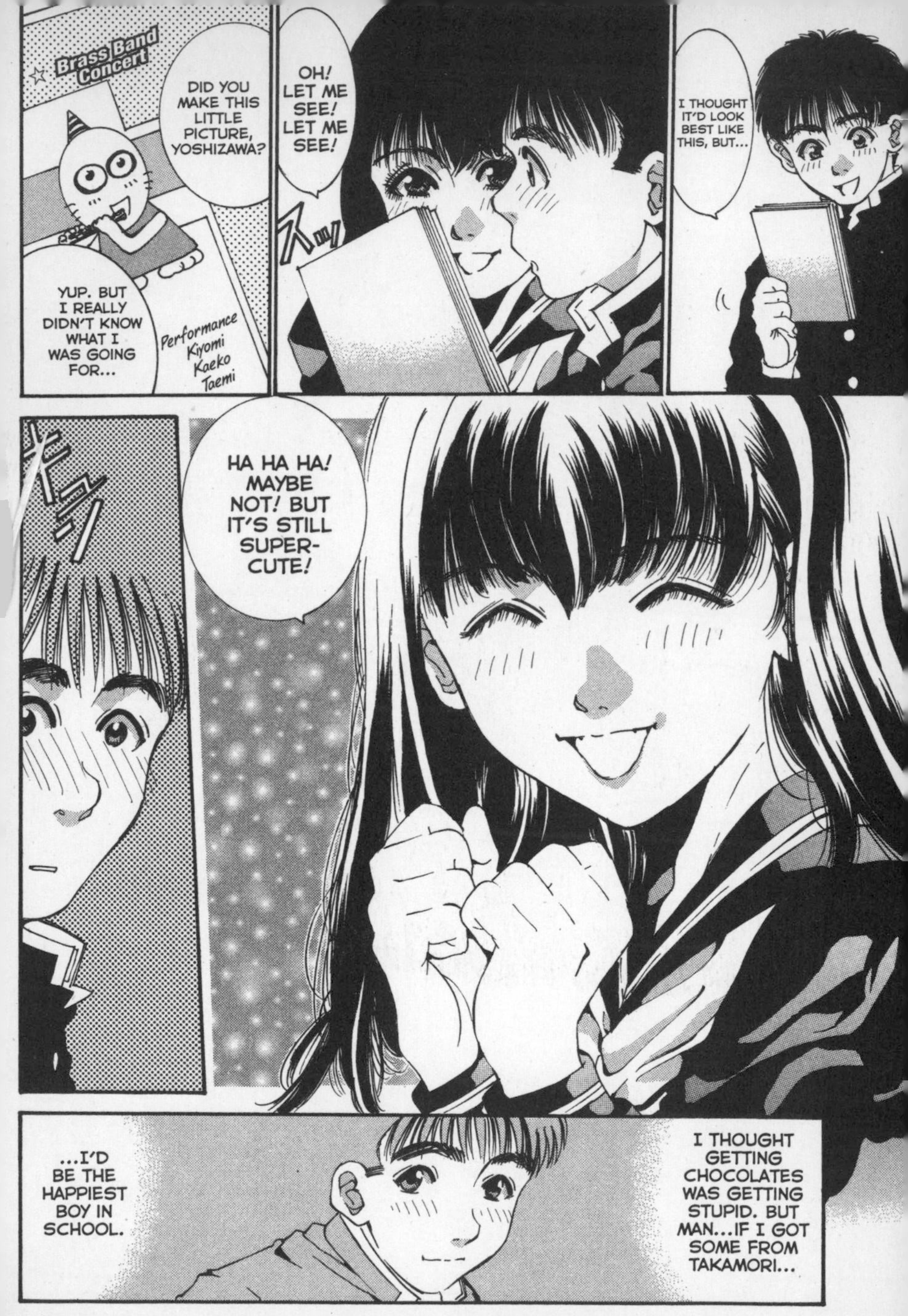
I THOUGHT IT'D LOOK BEST LIKE THIS, BUT...
OH! LET ME SEE! LET ME SEE!
DID YOU MAKE THIS LITTLE PICTURE, YOSHIZAWA?
Brass Band Concert
YUP. BUT I REALLY DIDN'T KNOW WHAT I WAS GOING FOR...
Performance Kiyomi Kaeko Taemi
HA HA HA! MAYBE NOT! BUT IT'S STILL SUPER-CUTE!
I THOUGHT GETTING CHOCOLATES WAS GETTING STUPID. BUT MAN...IF I GOT SOME FROM TAKAMORI...
...I'D BE THE HAPPIEST BOY IN SCHOOL.

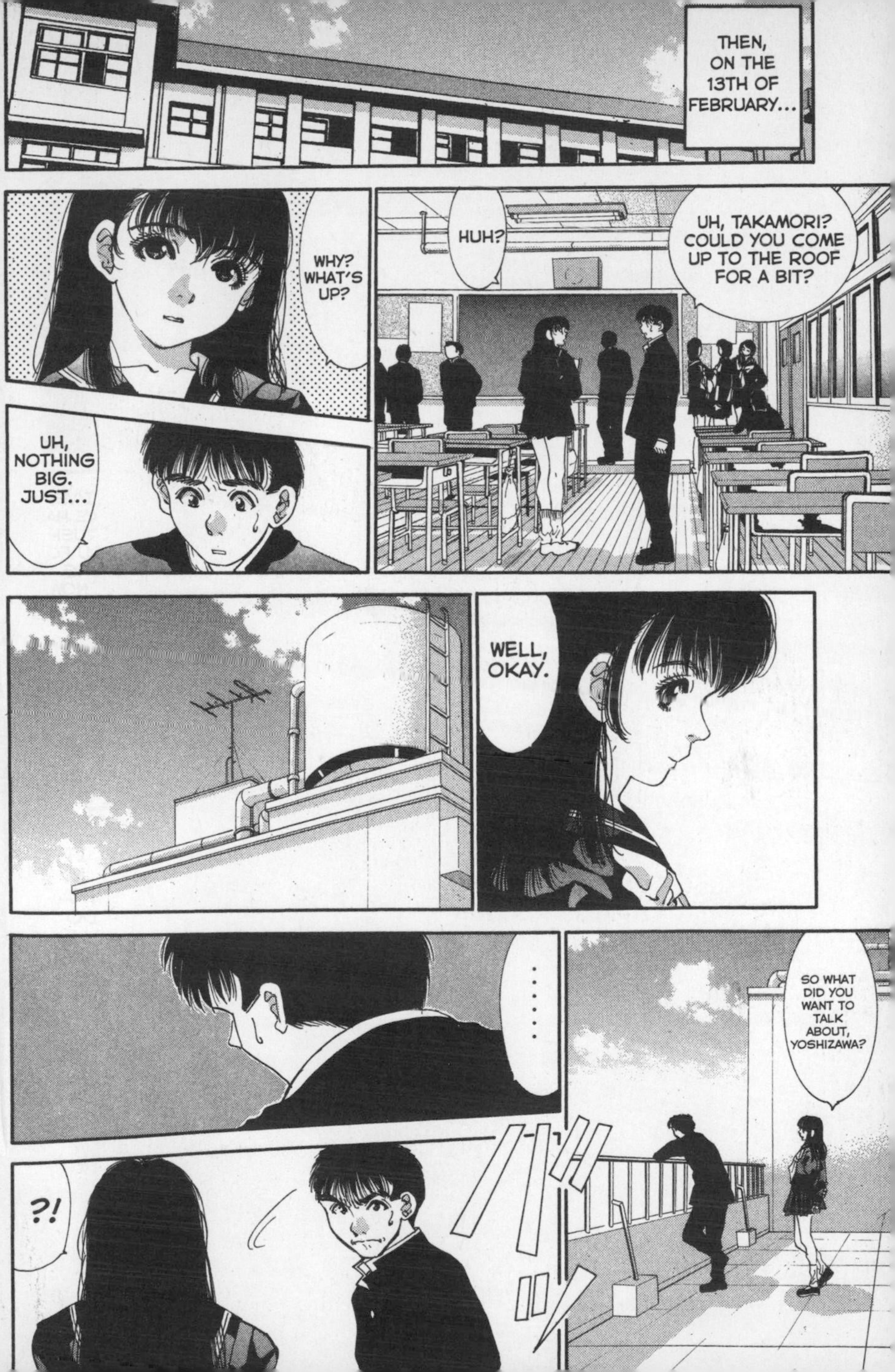
THEN, ON THE 13TH OF FEBRUARY...
UH, TAKAMORI? COULD YOU COME UP TO THE ROOF FOR A BIT?
HUH?
WHY? WHAT'S UP?
UH, NOTHING BIG. JUST...
WELL, OKAY.
SO WHAT DID YOU WANT TO TALK ABOUT, YOSHIZAWA?
......
?!

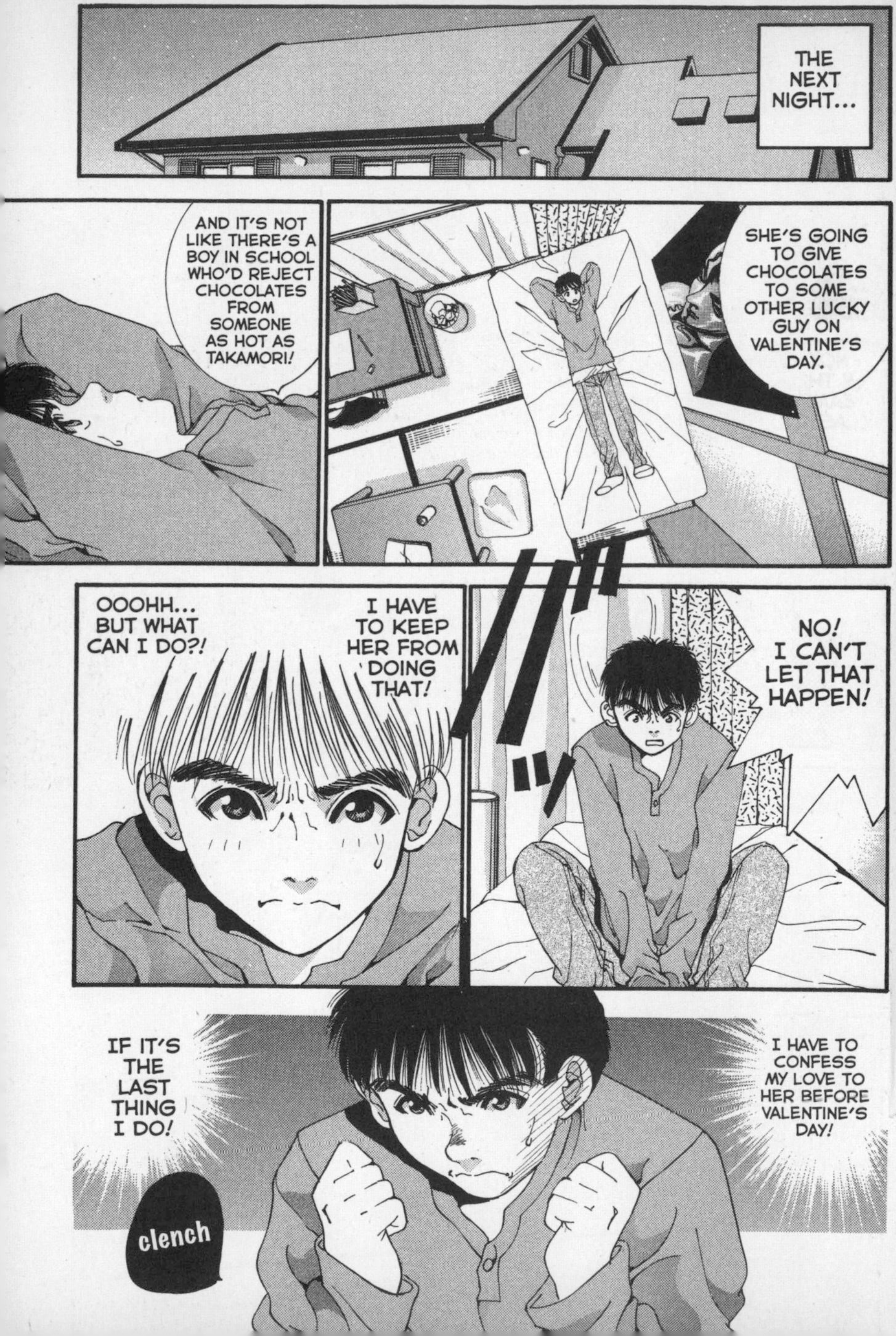
THE NEXT NIGHT...
SHE'S GOING TO GIVE CHOCOLATES TO SOME OTHER LUCKY GUY ON VALENTINE'S DAY.
AND IT'S NOT LIKE THERE'S A BOY IN SCHOOL WHO'D REJECT CHOCOLATES FROM SOMEONE AS HOT AS TAKAMORI!
NO! I CAN'T LET THAT HAPPEN!
I HAVE TO KEEP HER FROM DOING THAT!
OOOHH... BUT WHAT CAN I DO?!
I HAVE TO CONFESS MY LOVE TO HER BEFORE VALENTINE'S DAY!
IF IT'S THE LAST THING I DO!
clench

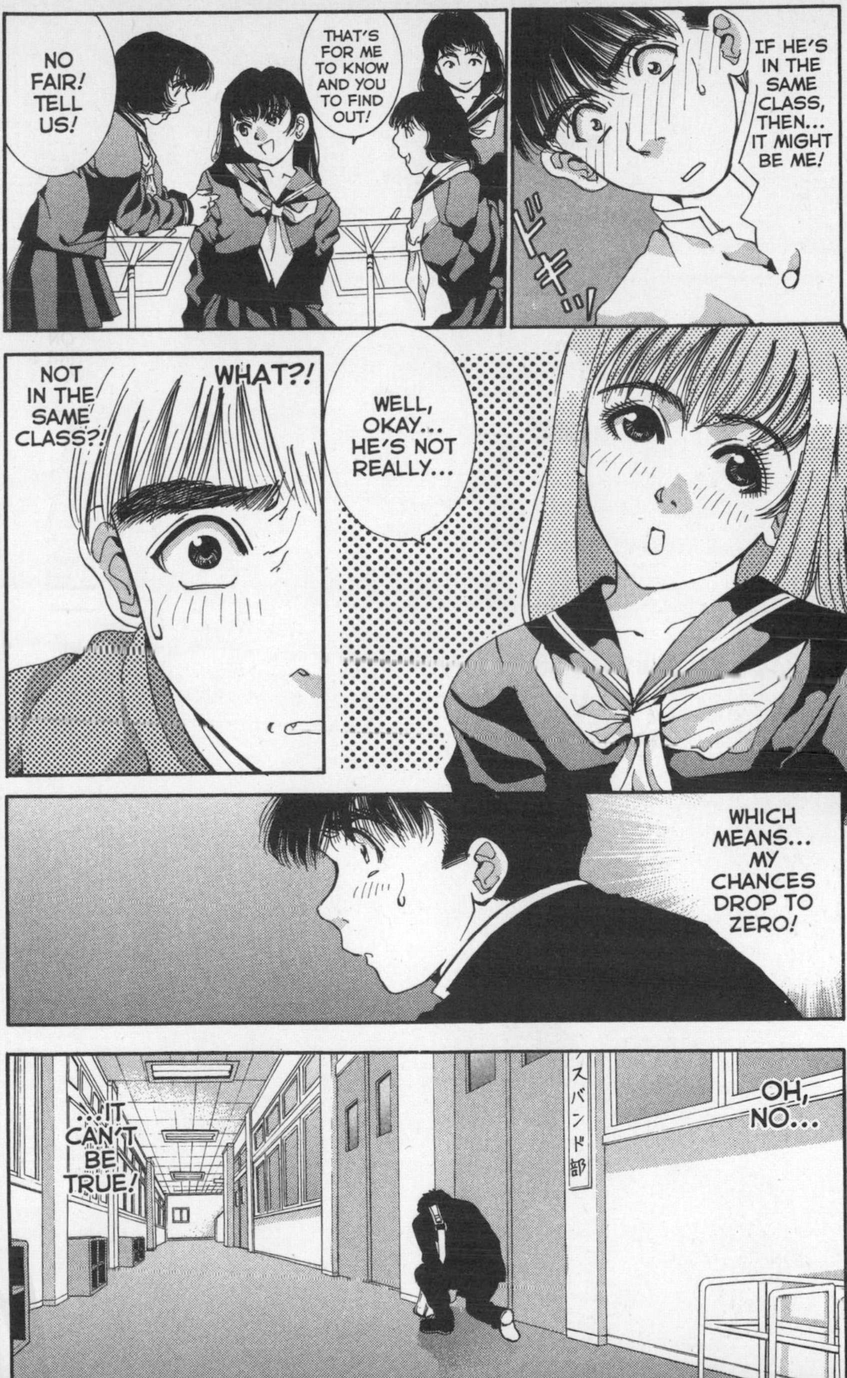
IF HE'S IN THE SAME CLASS, THEN... IT MIGHT BE ME!
ドキッ!
THAT'S FOR ME TO KNOW AND YOU TO FIND OUT!
NO FAIR! TELL US!
WELL, OKAY... HE'S NOT REALLY...
WHAT?!
NOT IN THE SAME CLASS?!
WHICH MEANS... MY CHANCES DROP TO ZERO!
OH, NO...
スバンド部
...IT CAN'T BE TRUE!

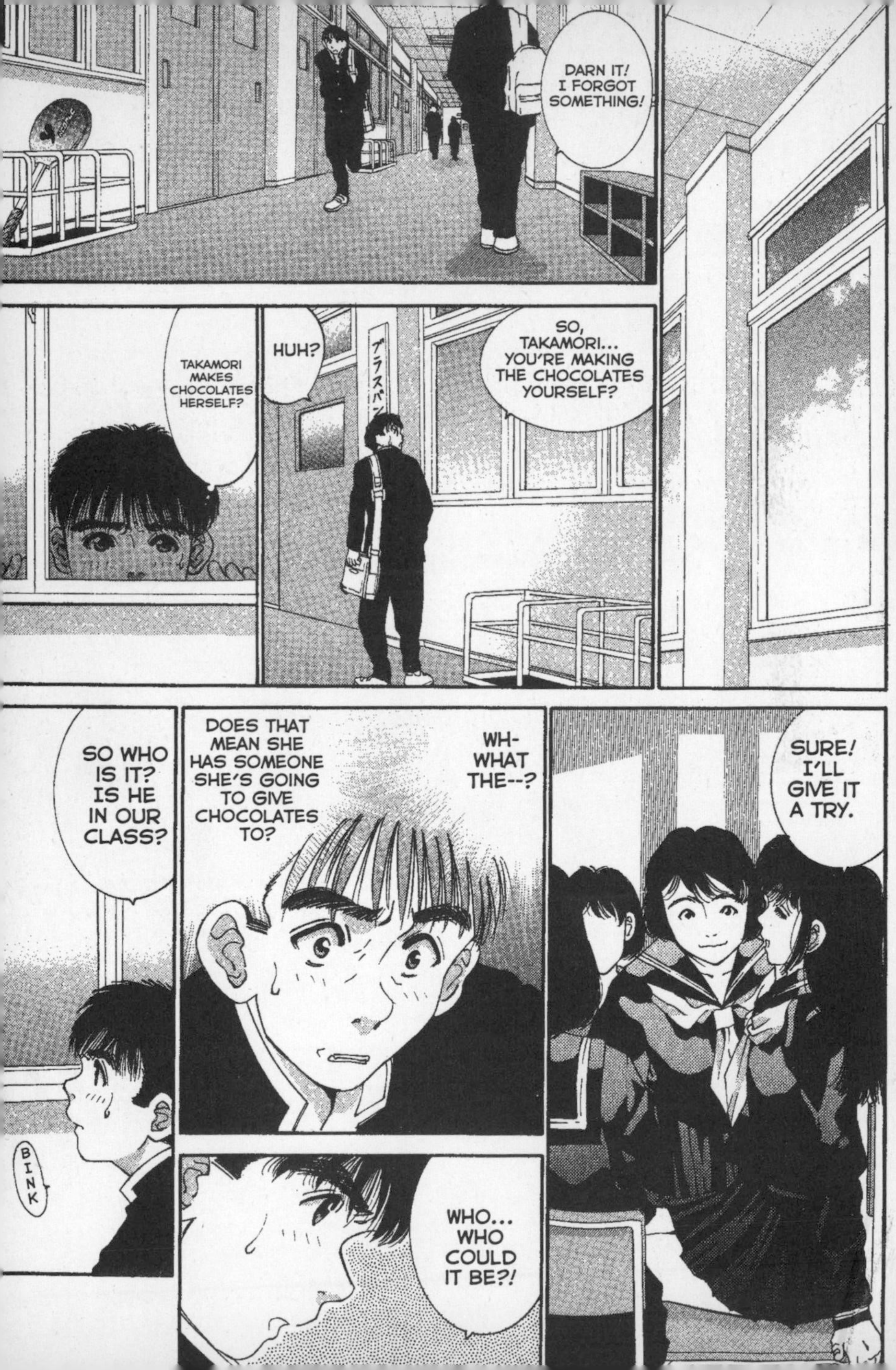
DARN IT! I FORGOT SOMETHING!
SO, TAKAMORI... YOU'RE MAKING THE CHOCOLATES YOURSELF?
ブラスバン
HUH?
TAKAMORI MAKES CHOCOLATES HERSELF?
SURE! I'LL GIVE IT A TRY.
WH- WHAT THE--?
DOES THAT MEAN SHE HAS SOMEONE SHE'S GOING TO GIVE CHOCOLATES TO?
WHO... WHO COULD IT BE?!
SO WHO IS IT? IS HE IN OUR CLASS?
BINK

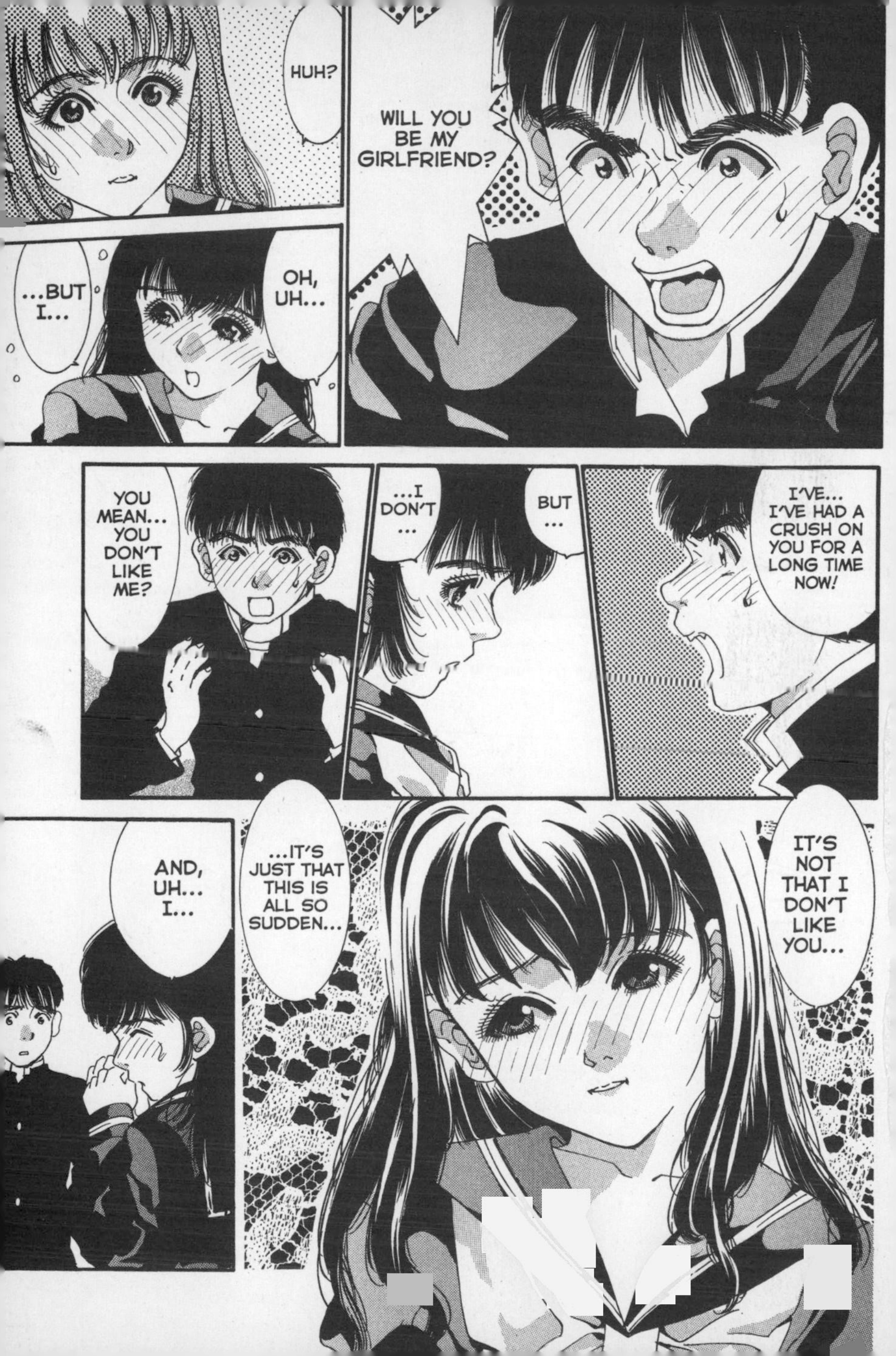
WILL YOU BE MY GIRLFRIEND?
HUH?
OH, UH...
...BUT I...
I'VE... I'VE HAD A CRUSH ON YOU FOR A LONG TIME NOW!
BUT ...
...I DON'T ...
YOU MEAN... YOU DON'T LIKE ME?
IT'S NOT THAT I DON'T LIKE YOU...
...IT'S JUST THAT THIS IS ALL SO SUDDEN...
AND, UH... I...

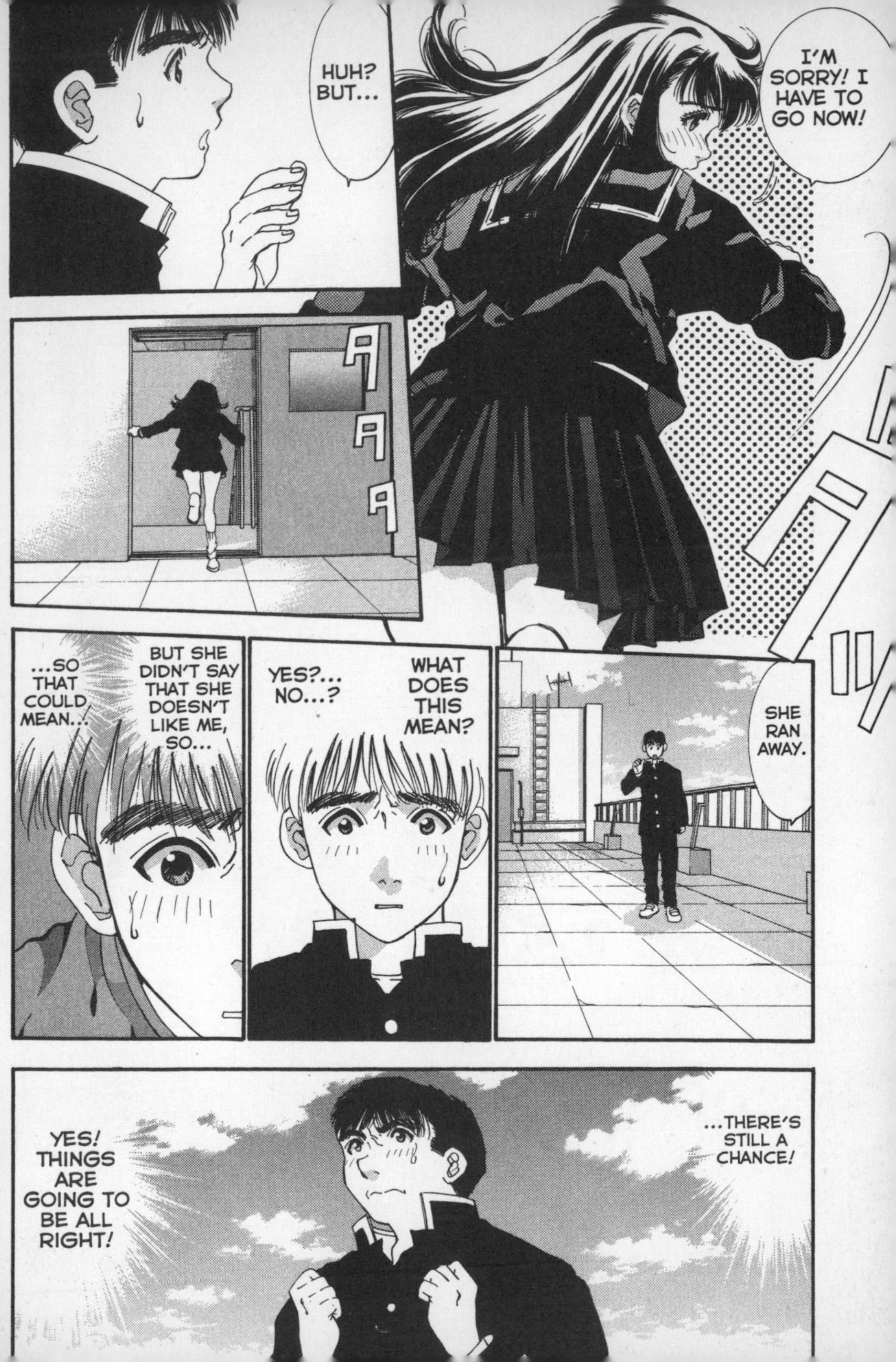
I'M SORRY! I HAVE TO GO NOW!
HUH? BUT...
SHE RAN AWAY.
WHAT DOES THIS MEAN?
YES?... NO...?
BUT SHE DIDN'T SAY THAT SHE DOESN'T LIKE ME, SO...
...SO THAT COULD MEAN...
...THERE'S STILL A CHANCE!
YES! THINGS ARE GOING TO BE ALL RIGHT!

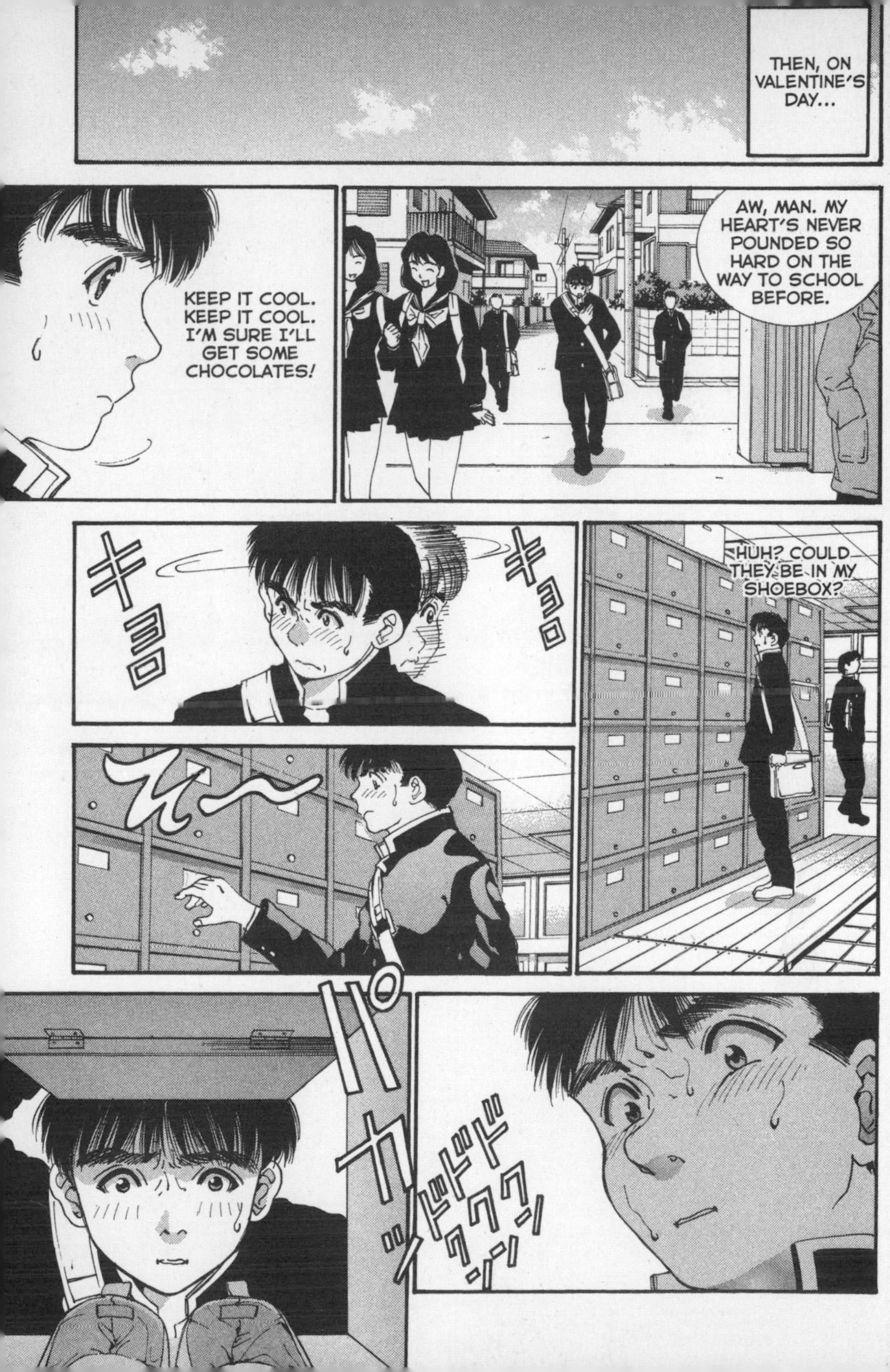
THEN, ON VALENTINE'S DAY...
AW, MAN. MY HEART'S NEVER POUNDED SO HARD ON THE WAY TO SCHOOL BEFORE.
KEEP IT COOL. KEEP IT COOL. I'M SURE I'LL GET SOME CHOCOLATES!
HUH? COULD THEY BE IN MY SHOEBOX?
キョロ
キョロ
ん〜
パカ

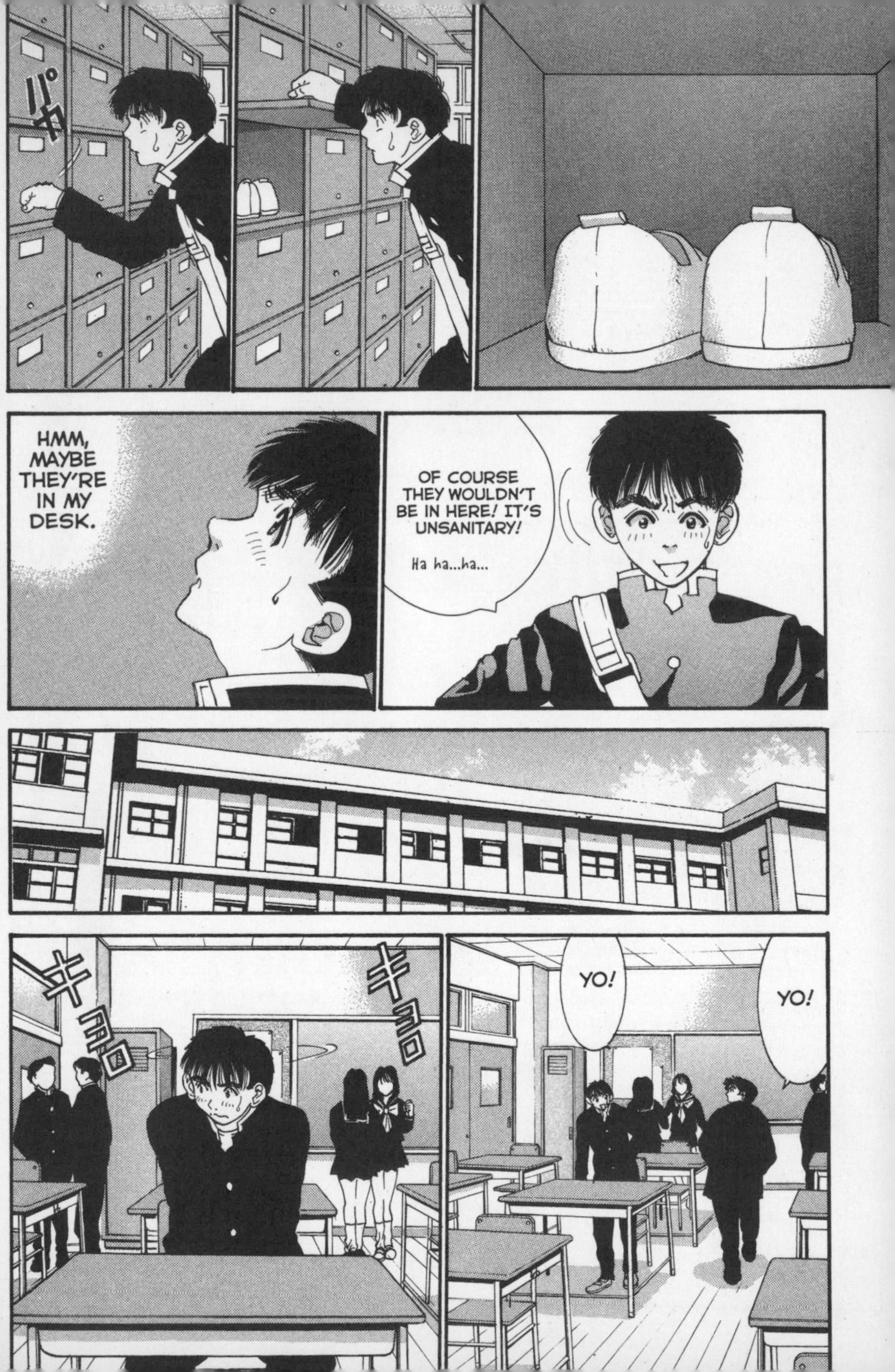
パカ
OF COURSE THEY WOULDN'T BE IN HERE! IT'S UNSANITARY!
Ha ha...ha...
HMM, MAYBE THEY'RE IN MY DESK.
YO!
YO!
キョロ
キョロ

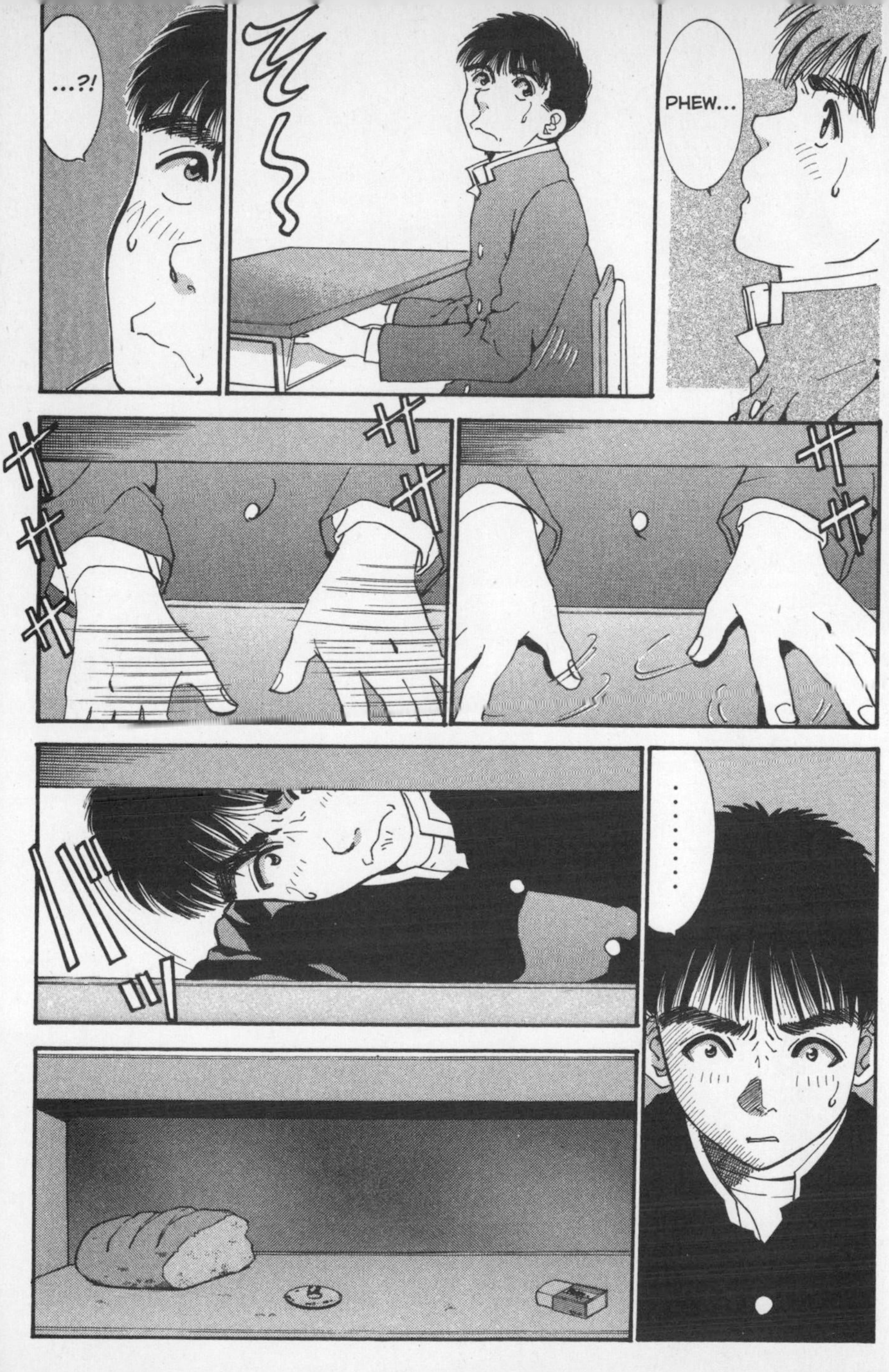
PHEW...
...?!
......

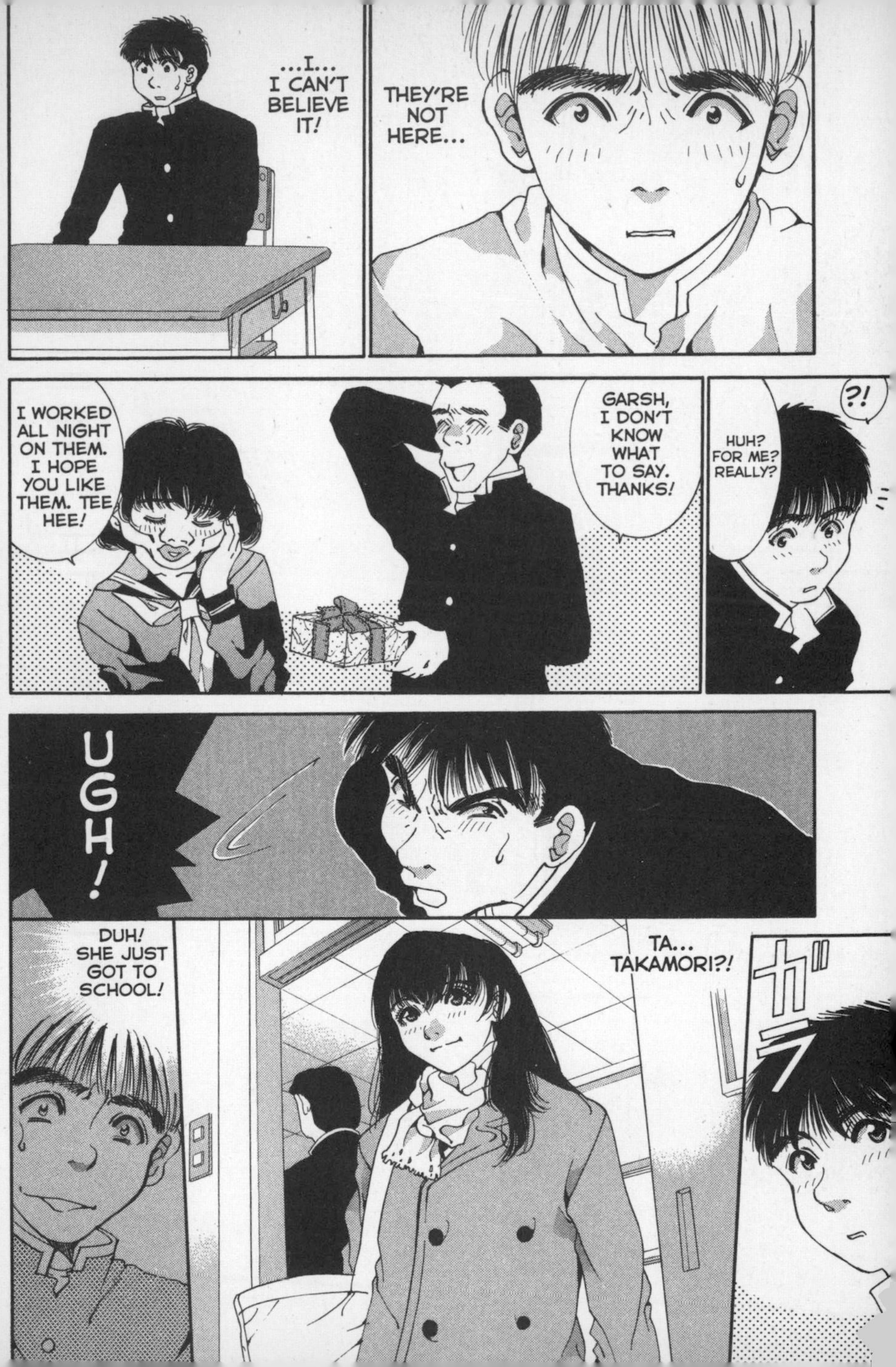
THEY'RE NOT HERE...
...I... I CAN'T BELIEVE IT!
?!
HUH? FOR ME? REALLY?
GARSH, I DON'T KNOW WHAT TO SAY. THANKS!
I WORKED ALL NIGHT ON THEM. I HOPE YOU LIKE THEM. TEE HEE!
UGH!
ガラ
TA... TAKAMORI?!
DUH! SHE JUST GOT TO SCHOOL!

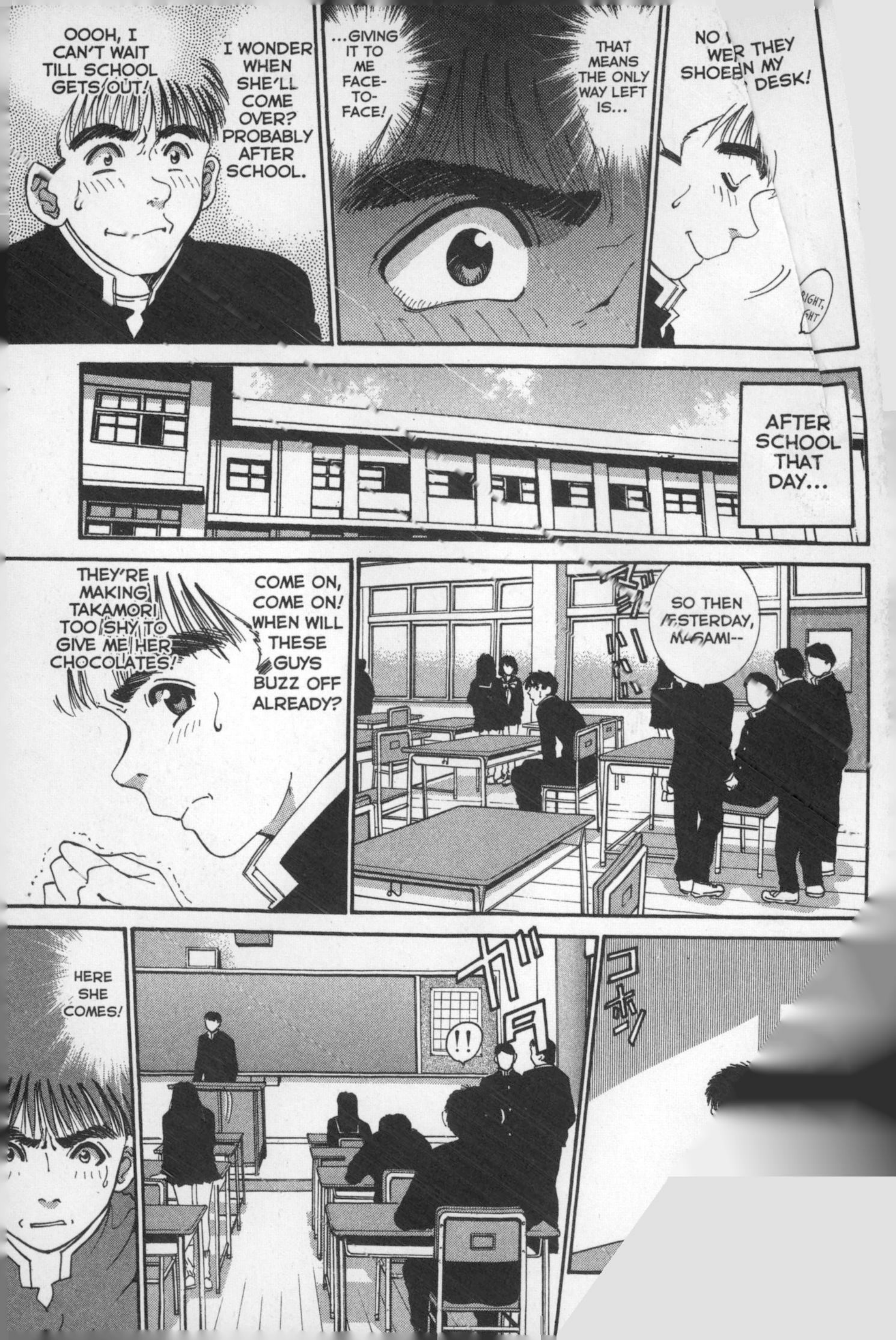
THAT MEANS THE ONLY WAY LEFT IS...
...GIVING IT TO ME FACE-TO-FACE!
I WONDER WHEN SHE'LL COME OVER? PROBABLY AFTER SCHOOL.
OOOH, I CAN'T WAIT TILL SCHOOL GETS OUT!
AFTER SCHOOL THAT DAY...
SO THEN
COME ON, COME ON! WHEN WILL THESE GUYS BUZZ OFF ALREADY?
THEY'RE MAKING TAKAMORI TOO SHY TO GIVE ME HER CHOCOLATES!
!!
HERE SHE COMES!

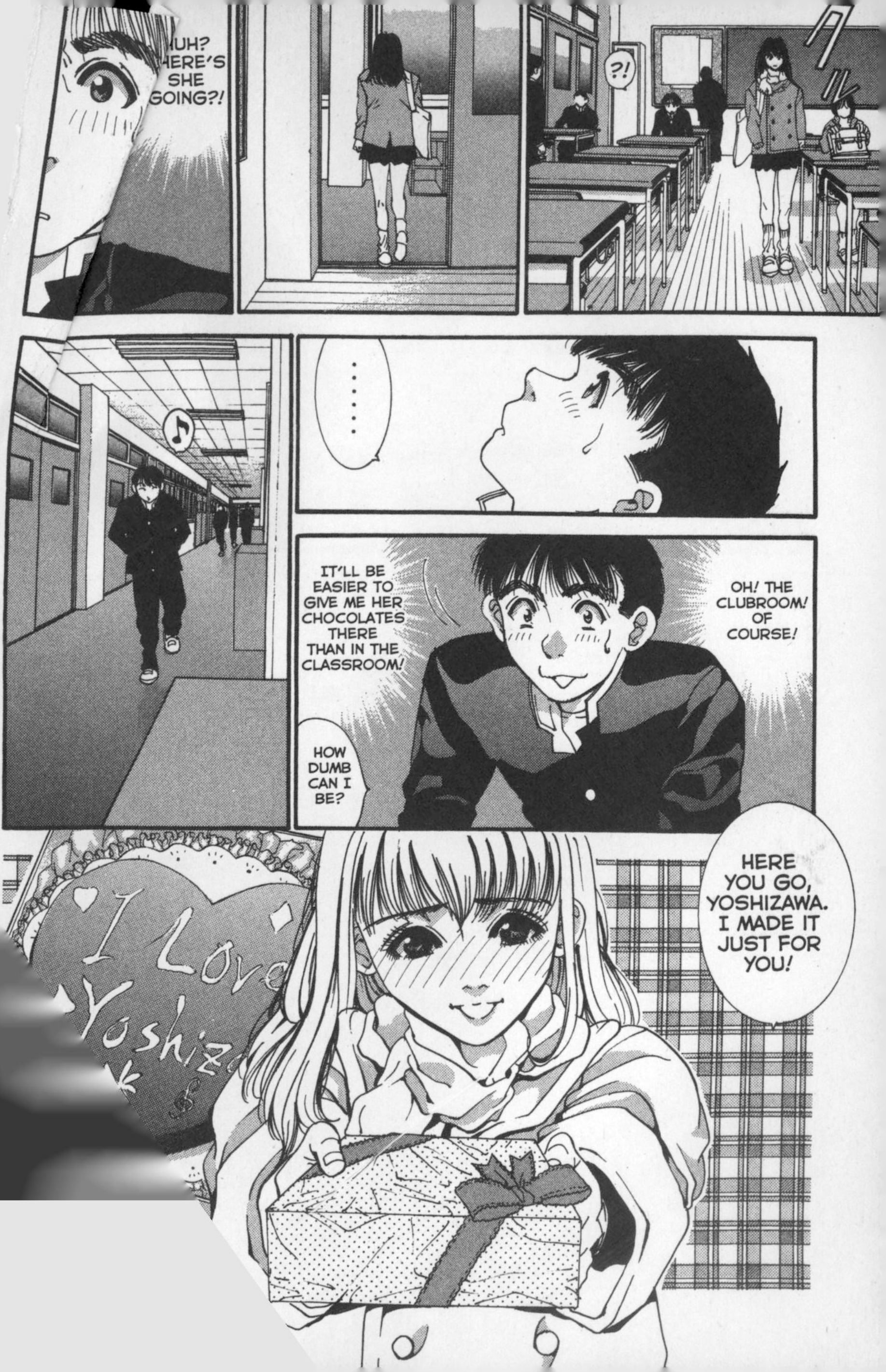
?!
HUH? HERE'S SHE GOING?!
......
OH! THE CLUBROOM! OF COURSE!
IT'LL BE EASIER TO GIVE ME HER CHOCOLATES THERE THAN IN THE CLASSROOM!
HOW DUMB CAN I BE?
HERE YOU GO, YOSHIZAWA. I MADE IT JUST FOR YOU!
I Love

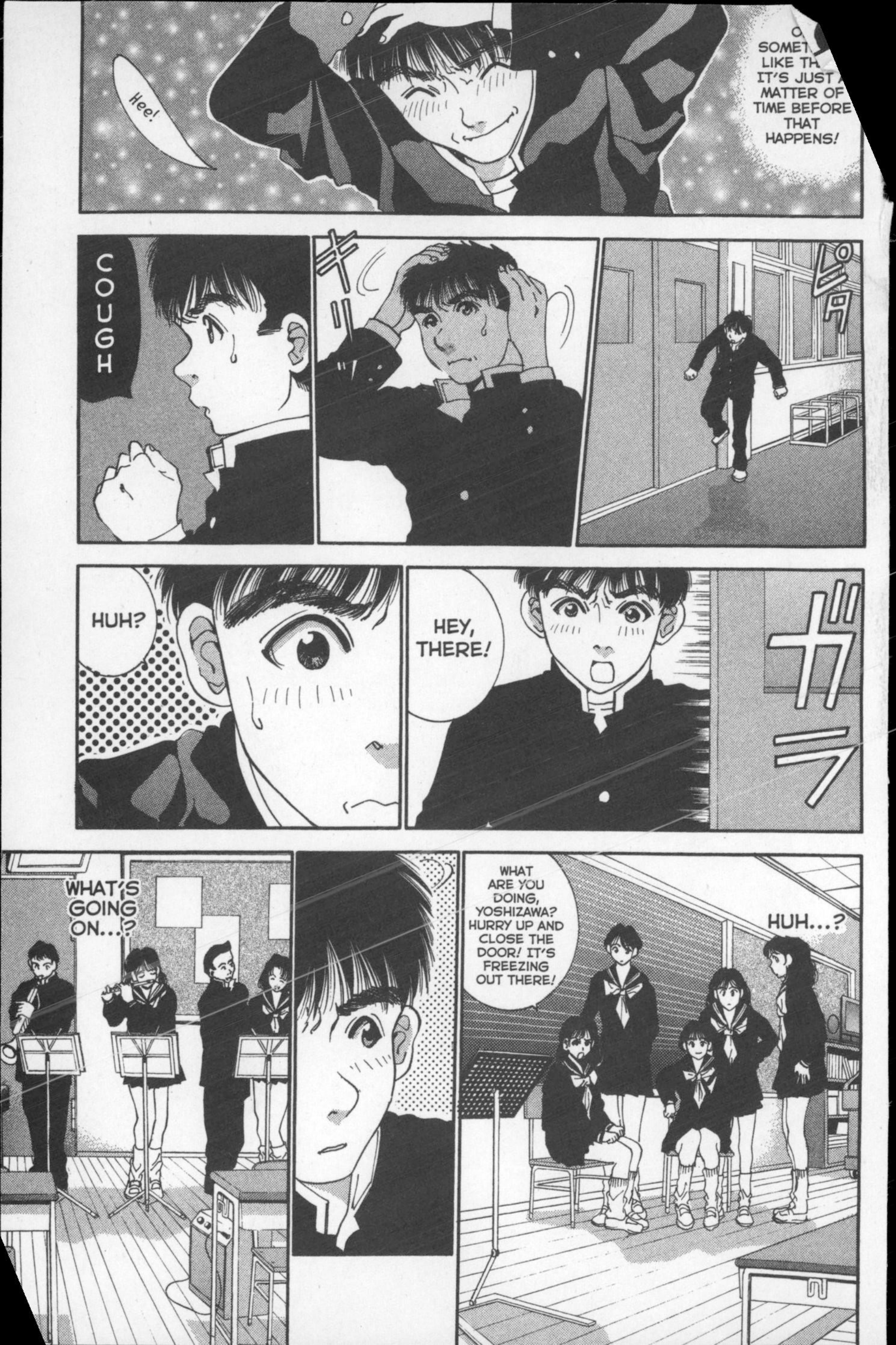
IT'S JUST A MATTER OF TIME BEFORE THAT HAPPENS!
Hee!
ピタ
COUGH
ガラ
HEY, THERE!
HUH?
WHAT ARE YOU DOING, YOSHIZAWA? HURRY UP AND CLOSE THE DOOR! IT'S FREEZING OUT THERE!
HUH...?
WHAT'S GOING ON...?

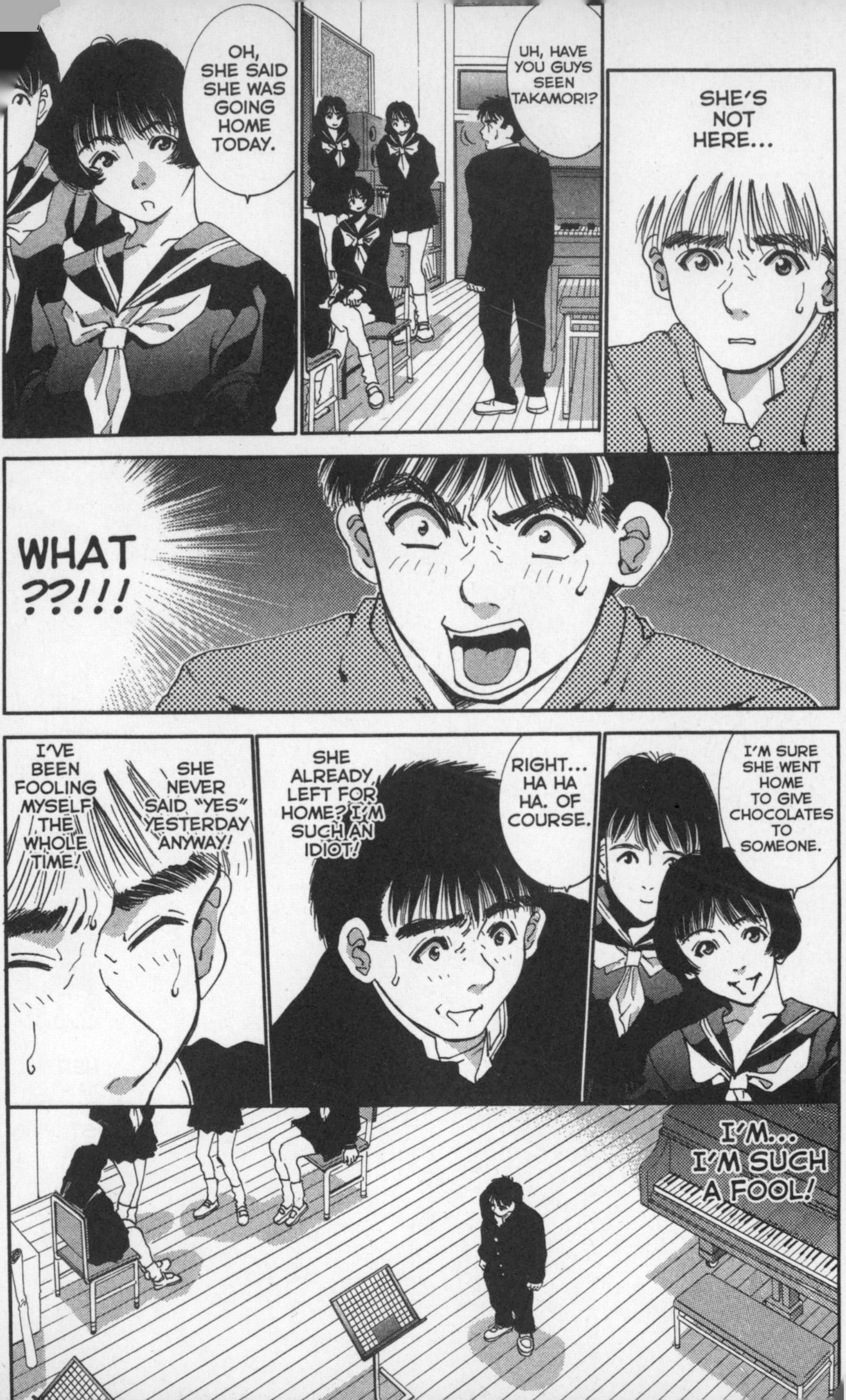
SHE'S NOT HERE...
UH, HAVE YOU GUYS SEEN TAKAMORI?
OH, SHE SAID SHE WAS GOING HOME TODAY.
WHAT ??!!!
I'M SURE SHE WENT HOME TO GIVE CHOCOLATES TO SOMEONE.
RIGHT... HA HA HA. OF COURSE.
SHE ALREADY LEFT FOR HOME? I'M SUCH AN IDIOT!
SHE NEVER SAID "YES" YESTERDAY ANYWAY!
I'VE BEEN FOOLING MYSELF THE WHOLE TIME!
I'M... I'M SUCH A FOOL!

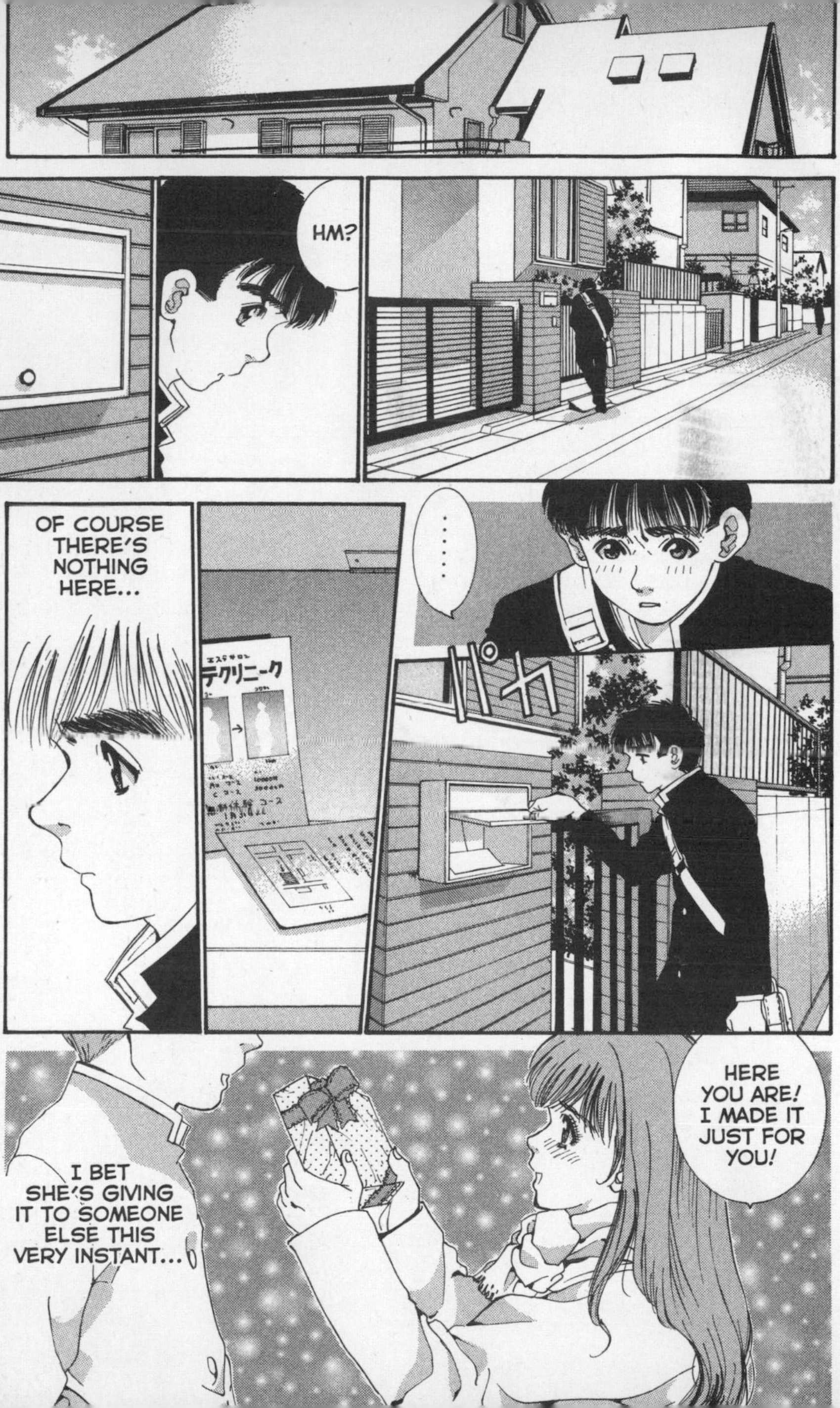
HM?
......
パカ
テクリニーク
OF COURSE THERE'S NOTHING HERE...
HERE YOU ARE! I MADE IT JUST FOR YOU!
I BET SHE'S GIVING IT TO SOMEONE ELSE THIS VERY INSTANT...

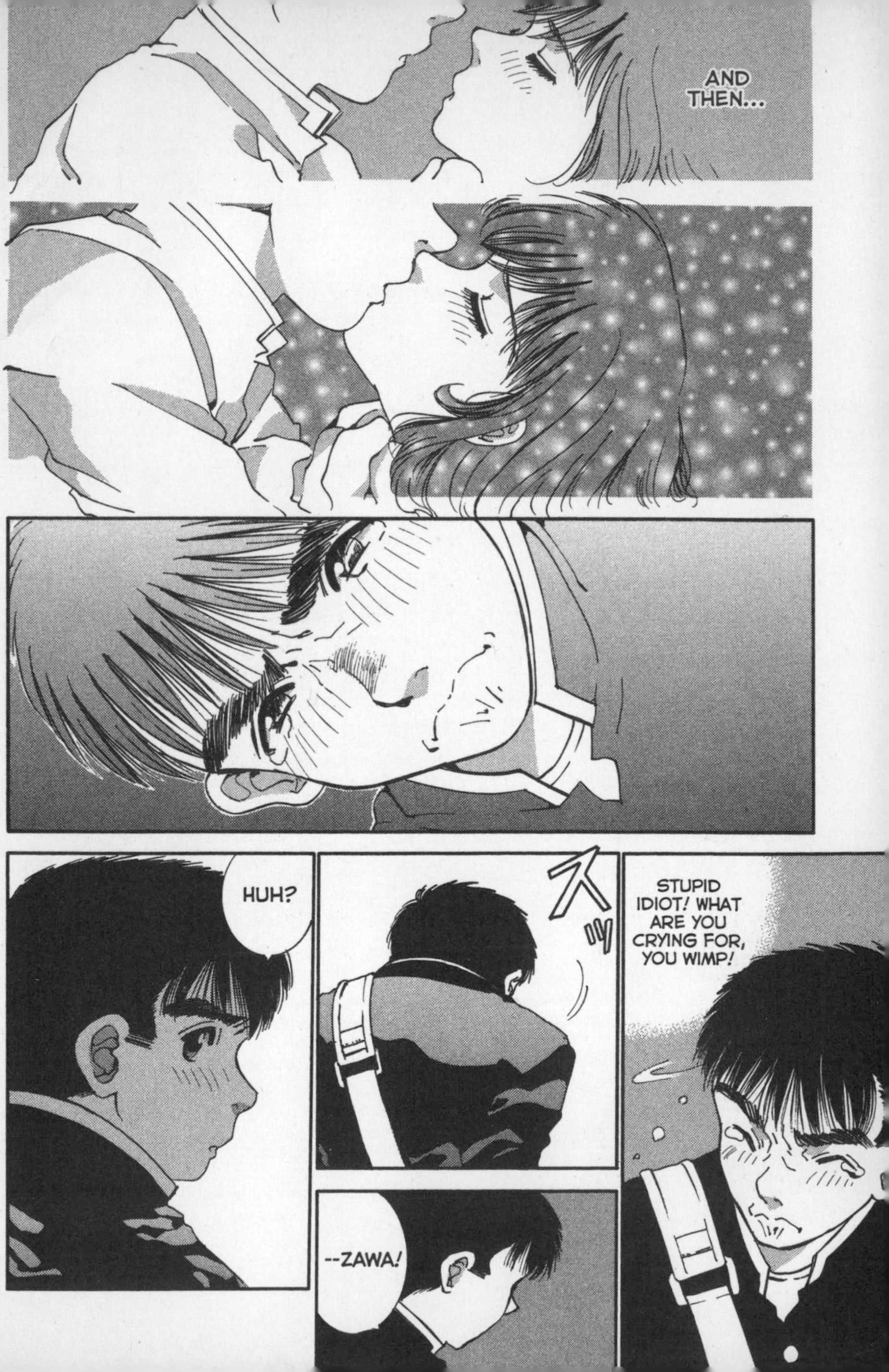
AND THEN...
STUPID IDIOT! WHAT ARE YOU CRYING FOR, YOU WIMP!
スッ
--ZAWA!
HUH?

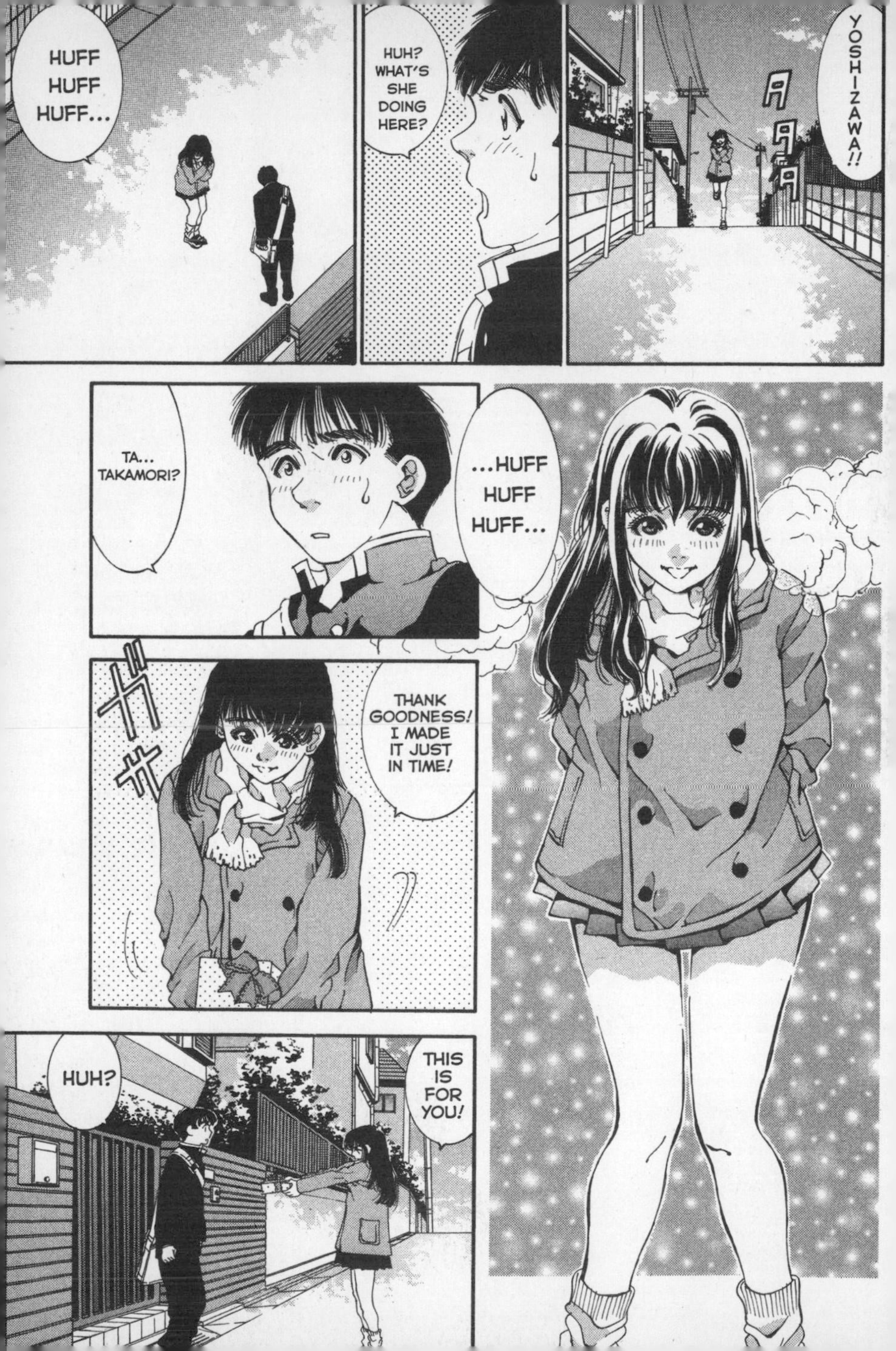
YOSHIZAWA!!
タタタ
HUH? WHAT'S SHE DOING HERE?
HUFF HUFF HUFF...
...HUFF HUFF HUFF...
TA... TAKAMORI?
THANK GOODNESS! I MADE IT JUST IN TIME!
THIS IS FOR YOU!
HUH?

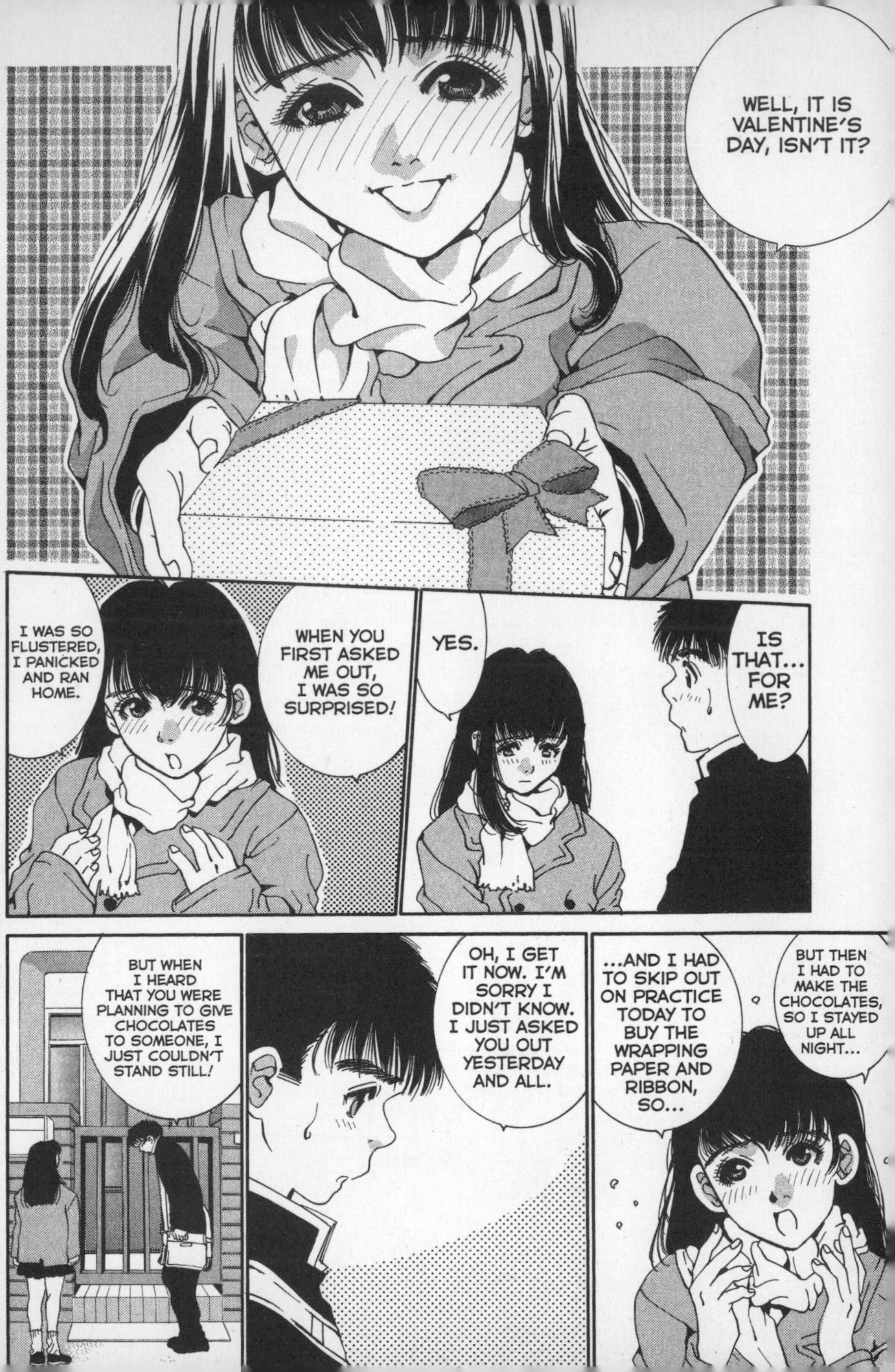
WELL, IT IS VALENTINE'S DAY, ISN'T IT?
IS THAT... FOR ME?
YES.
WHEN YOU FIRST ASKED ME OUT, I WAS SO SURPRISED!
I WAS SO FLUSTERED, I PANICKED AND RAN HOME.
BUT THEN I HAD TO MAKE THE CHOCOLATES, SO I STAYED UP ALL NIGHT...
...AND I HAD TO SKIP OUT ON PRACTICE TODAY TO BUY THE WRAPPING PAPER AND RIBBON, SO...
OH, I GET IT NOW. I'M SORRY I DIDN'T KNOW. I JUST ASKED YOU OUT YESTERDAY AND ALL.
BUT WHEN I HEARD THAT YOU WERE PLANNING TO GIVE CHOCOLATES TO SOMEONE, I JUST COULDN'T STAND STILL!

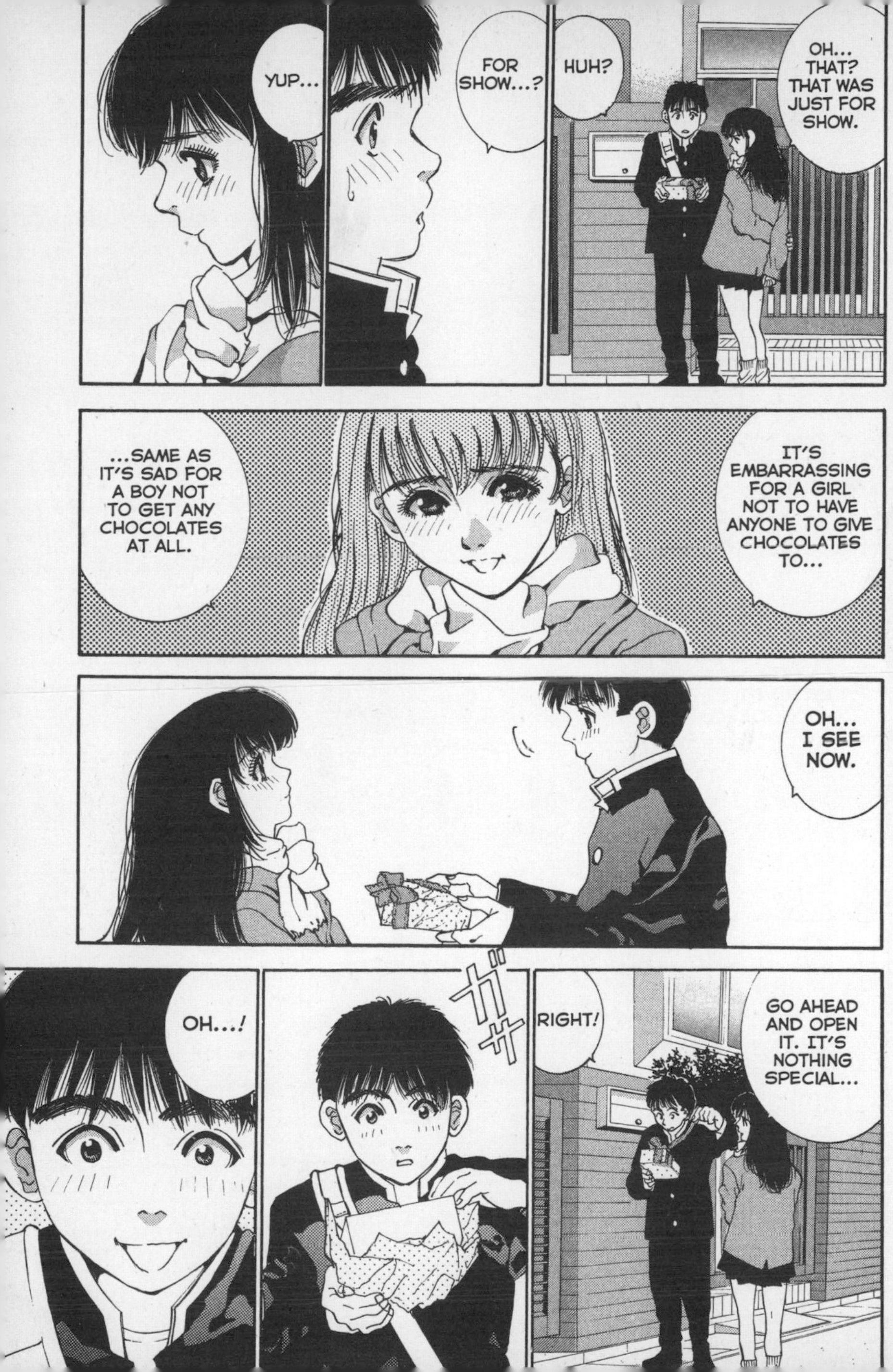
OH... THAT? THAT WAS JUST FOR SHOW.
HUH?
FOR SHOW...?
YUP...
IT'S EMBARRASSING FOR A GIRL NOT TO HAVE ANYONE TO GIVE CHOCOLATES TO...
...SAME AS IT'S SAD FOR A BOY NOT TO GET ANY CHOCOLATES AT ALL.
OH... I SEE NOW.
GO AHEAD AND OPEN IT. IT'S NOTHING SPECIAL...
RIGHT!
ガサ
OH...!

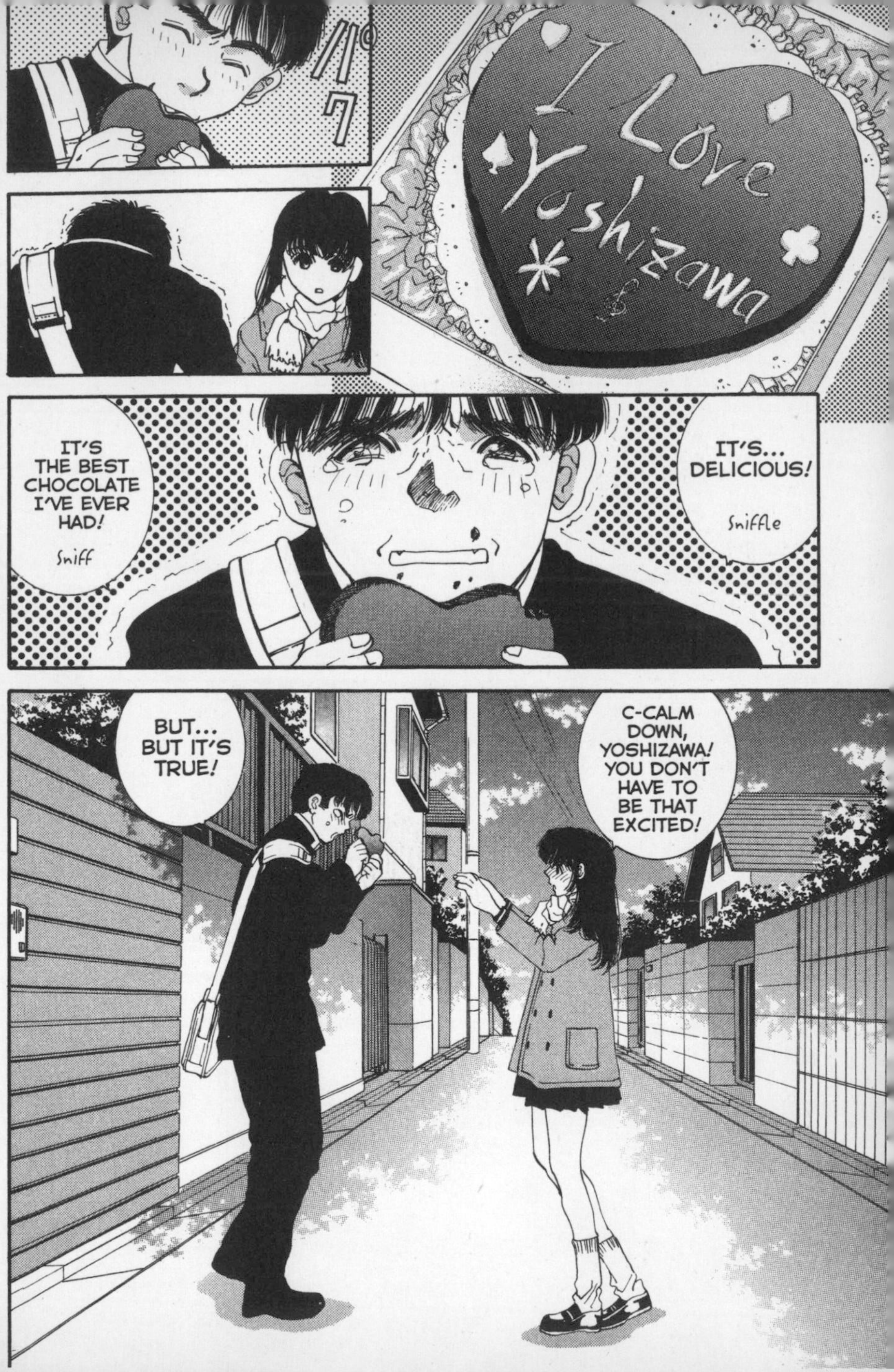
I Love Yoshizawa
パク
IT'S... DELICIOUS!
Sniffle
IT'S THE BEST CHOCOLATE I'VE EVER HAD!
Sniff
C-CALM DOWN, YOSHIZAWA! YOU DON'T HAVE TO BE THAT EXCITED!
BUT... BUT IT'S TRUE!

BOYS BE

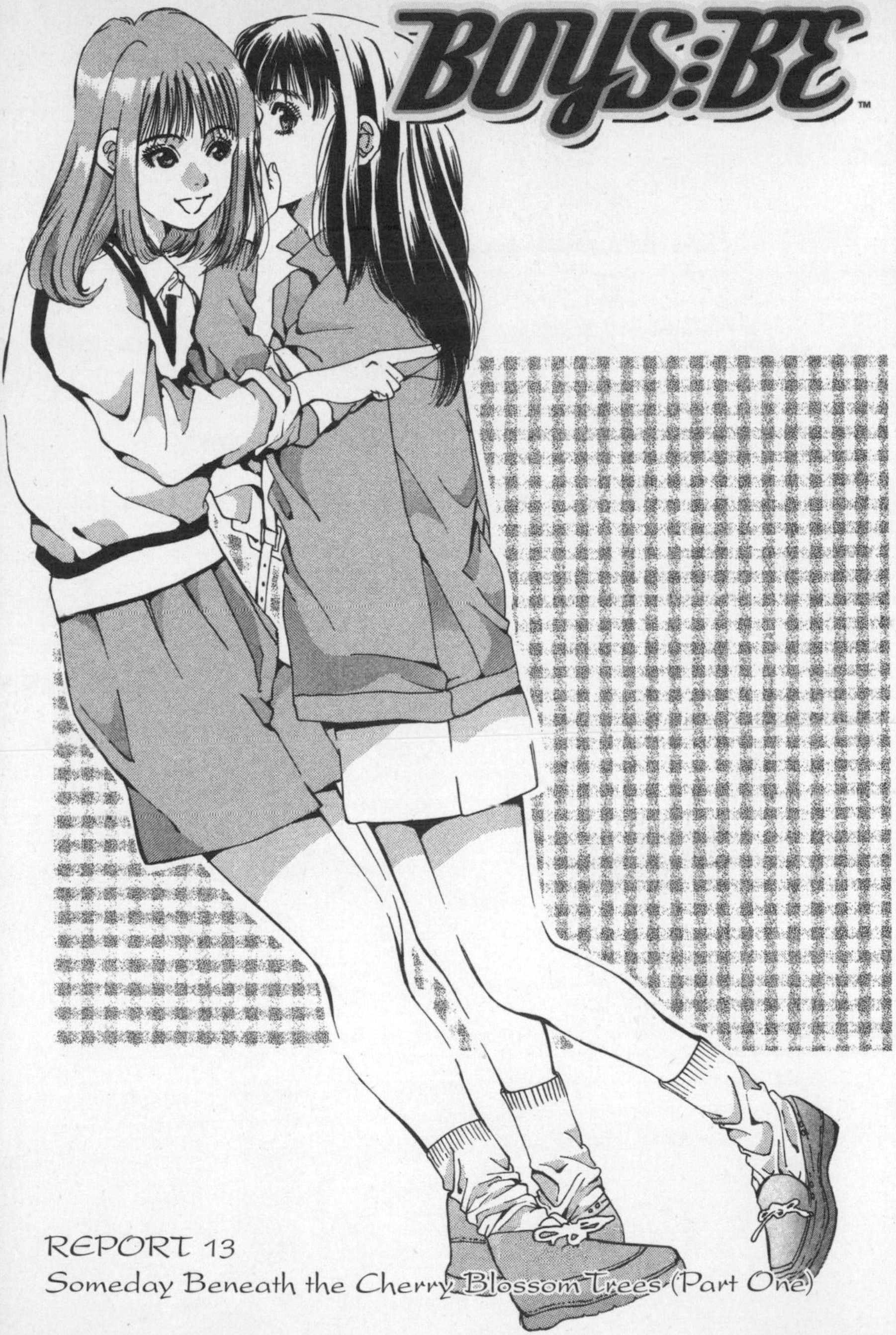

REPORT 13

Someday Beneath the Cherry Blossom Trees (Part One)

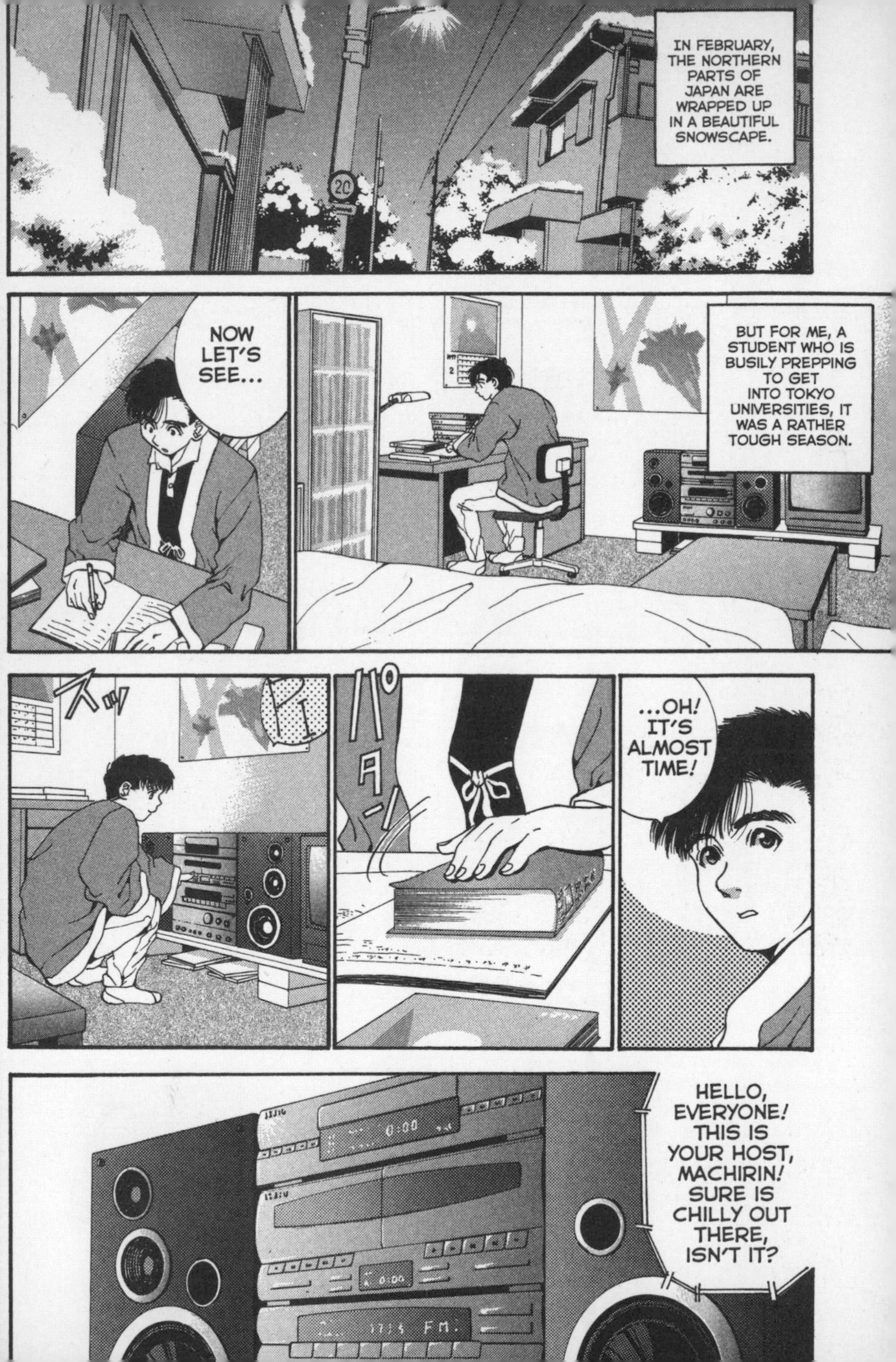
IN FEBRUARY, THE NORTHERN PARTS OF JAPAN ARE WRAPPED UP IN A BEAUTIFUL SNOWSCAPE.
BUT FOR ME, A STUDENT WHO IS BUSILY PREPPING TO GET INTO TOKYO UNIVERSITIES, IT WAS A RATHER TOUGH SEASON.
NOW LET'S SEE...
...OH! IT'S ALMOST TIME!
HELLO, EVERYONE! THIS IS YOUR HOST, MACHIRIN! SURE IS CHILLY OUT THERE, ISN'T IT?

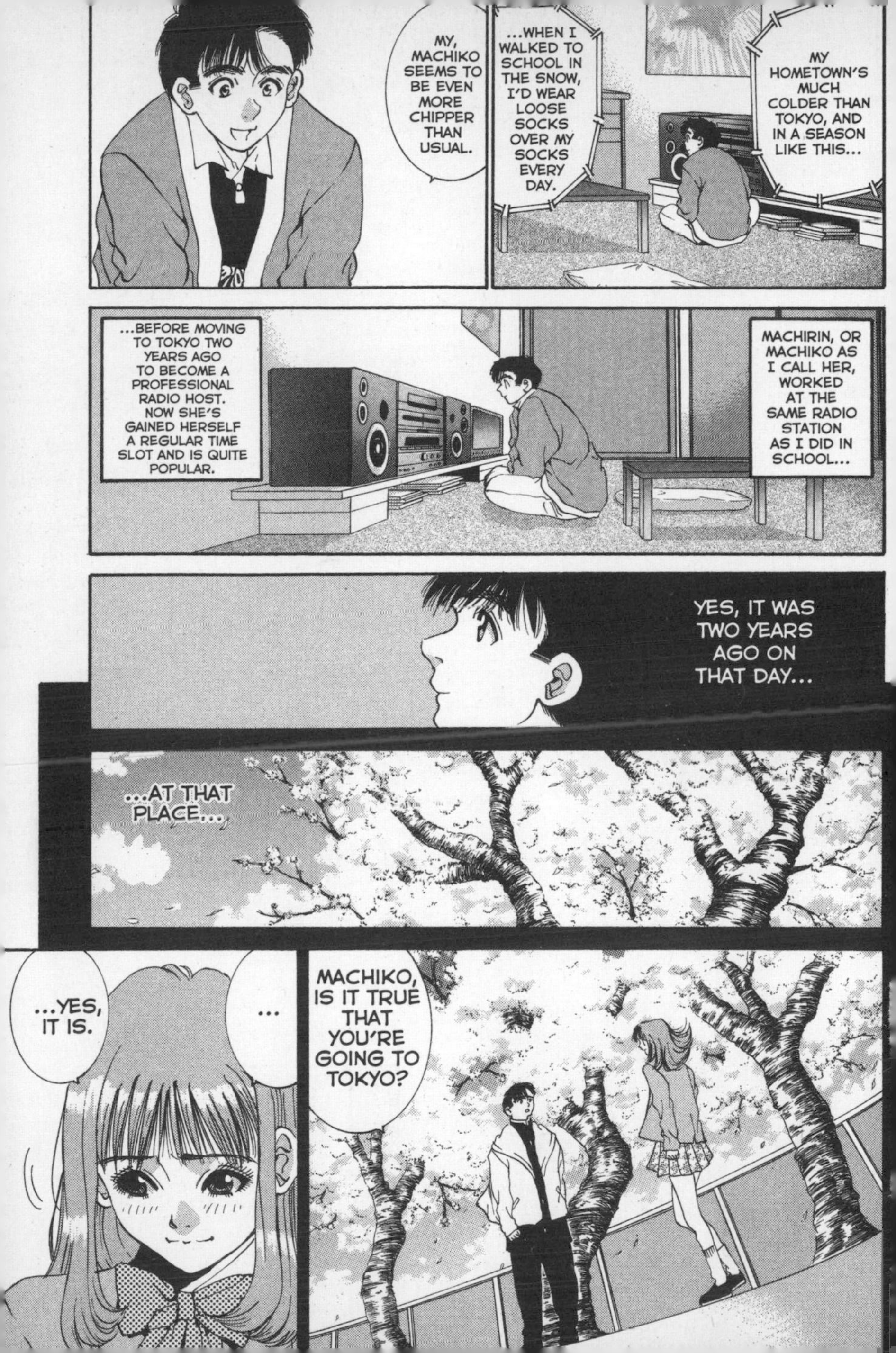
MY HOMETOWN'S MUCH COLDER THAN TOKYO, AND IN A SEASON LIKE THIS...
...WHEN I WALKED TO SCHOOL IN THE SNOW, I'D WEAR LOOSE SOCKS OVER MY SOCKS EVERY DAY.
MY, MACHIKO SEEMS TO BE EVEN MORE CHIPPER THAN USUAL.
MACHIRIN, OR MACHIKO AS I CALL HER, WORKED AT THE SAME RADIO STATION AS I DID IN SCHOOL...
...BEFORE MOVING TO TOKYO TWO YEARS AGO TO BECOME A PROFESSIONAL RADIO HOST. NOW SHE'S GAINED HERSELF A REGULAR TIME SLOT AND IS QUITE POPULAR.
YES, IT WAS TWO YEARS AGO ON THAT DAY...
...AT THAT PLACE...
MACHIKO, IS IT TRUE THAT YOU'RE GOING TO TOKYO?
...
...YES, IT IS.

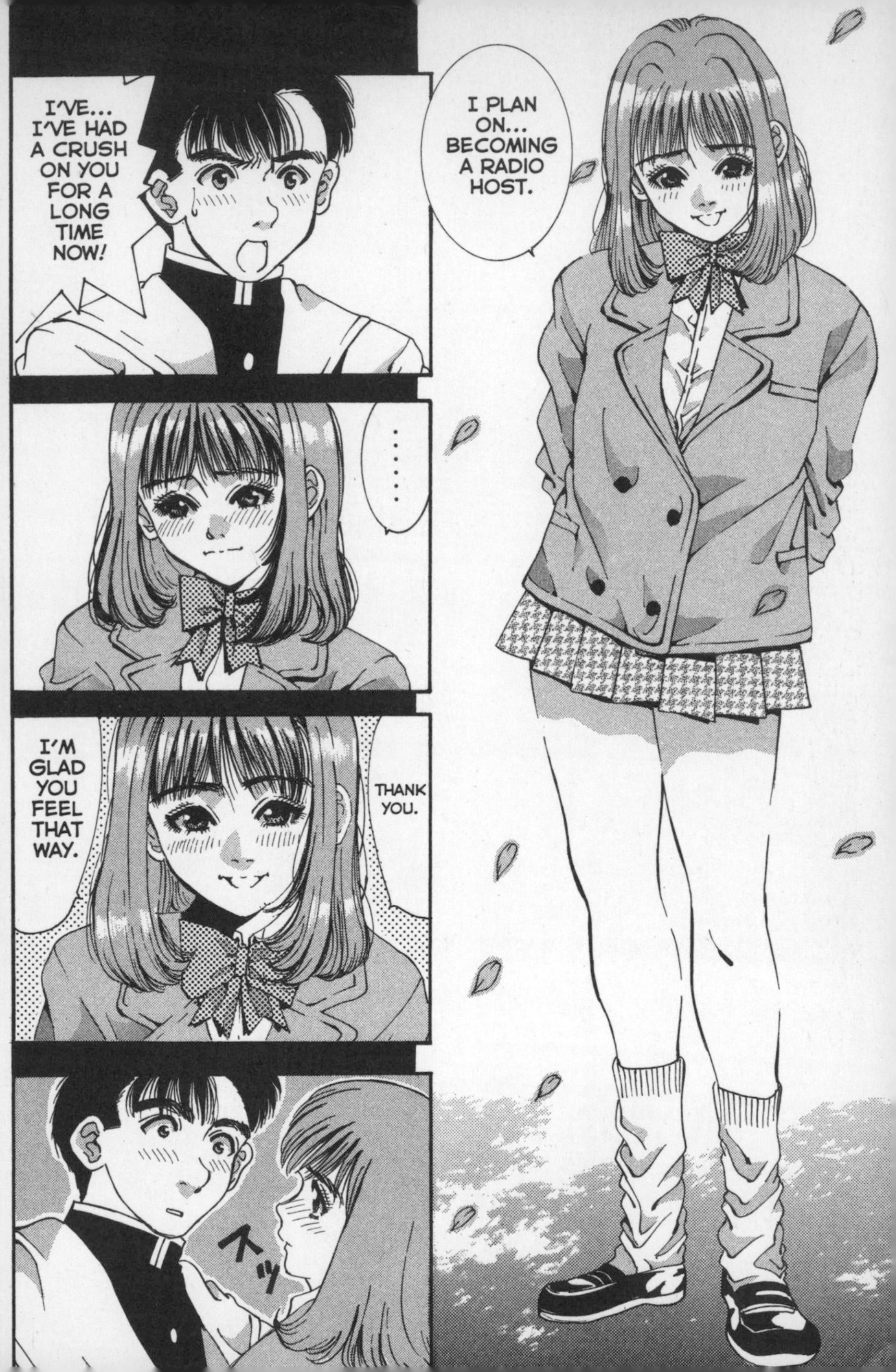
I PLAN ON... BECOMING A RADIO HOST.
I'VE... I'VE HAD A CRUSH ON YOU FOR A LONG TIME NOW!
......
THANK YOU.
I'M GLAD YOU FEEL THAT WAY.

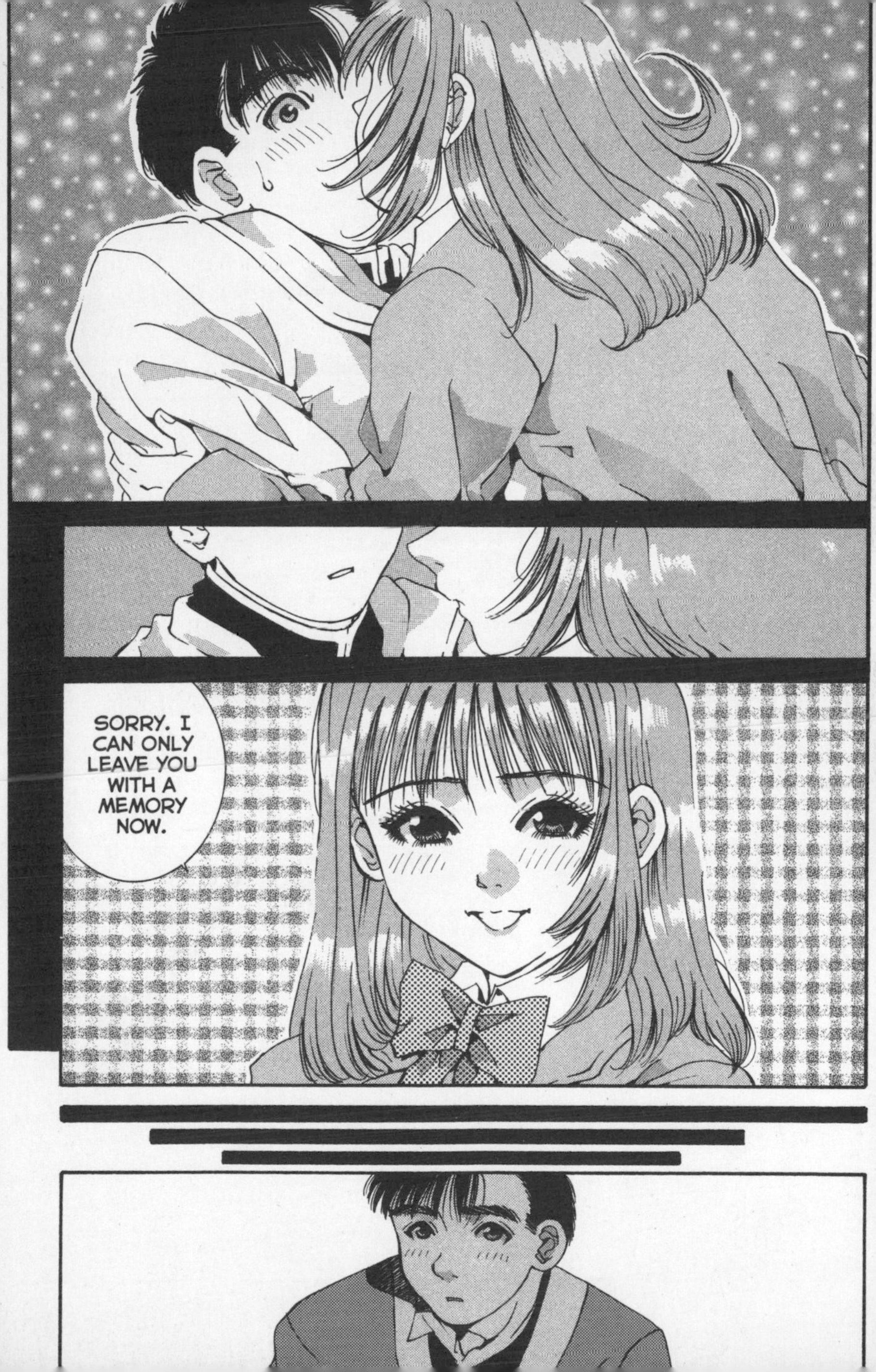
SORRY. I CAN ONLY LEAVE YOU WITH A MEMORY NOW.

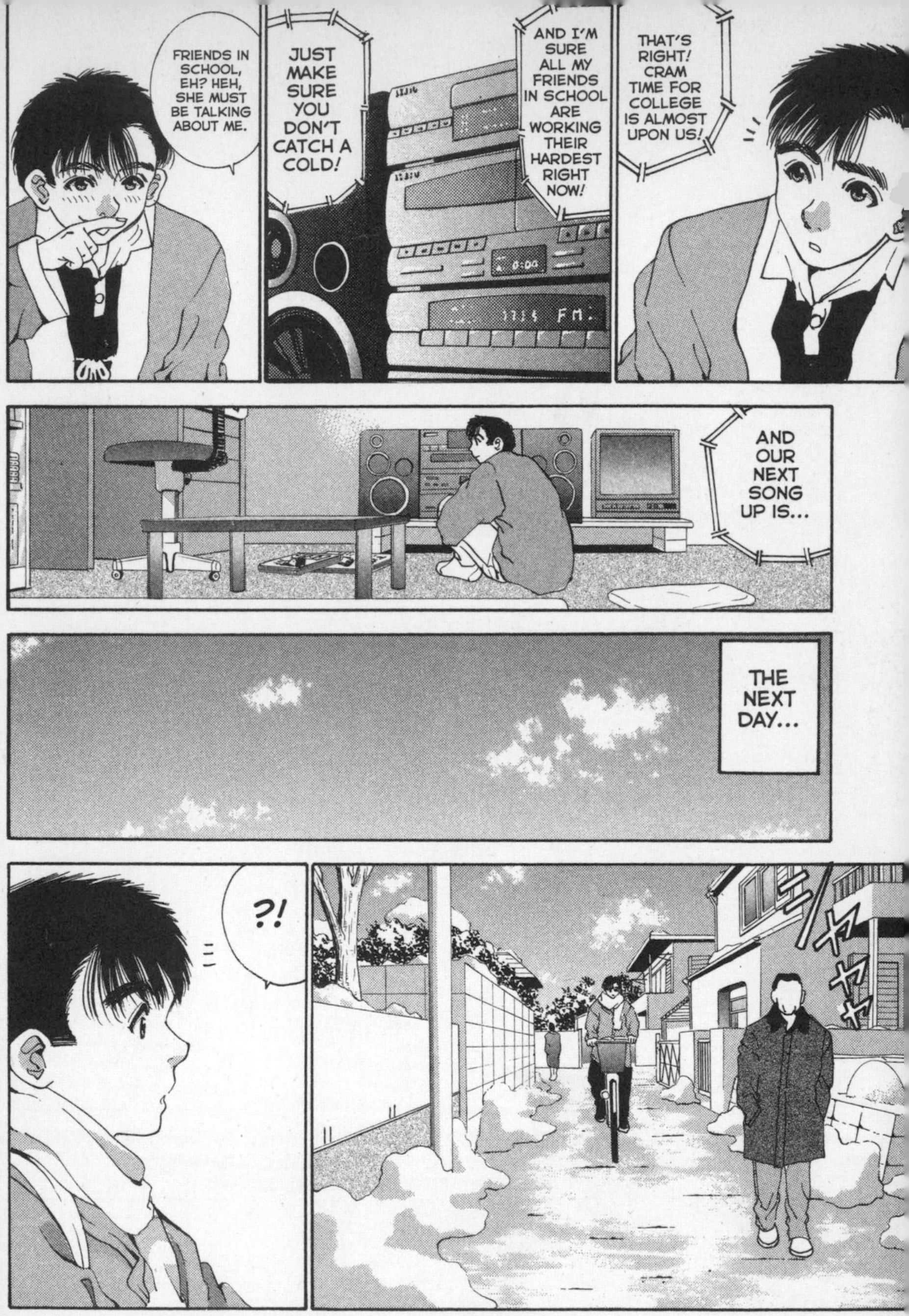
THAT'S RIGHT! CRAM TIME FOR COLLEGE IS ALMOST UPON US!
AND I'M SURE ALL MY FRIENDS IN SCHOOL ARE WORKING THEIR HARDEST RIGHT NOW!
JUST MAKE SURE YOU DON'T CATCH A COLD!
FRIENDS IN SCHOOL, EH? HEH, SHE MUST BE TALKING ABOUT ME.
AND OUR NEXT SONG UP IS...
THE NEXT DAY...
?!

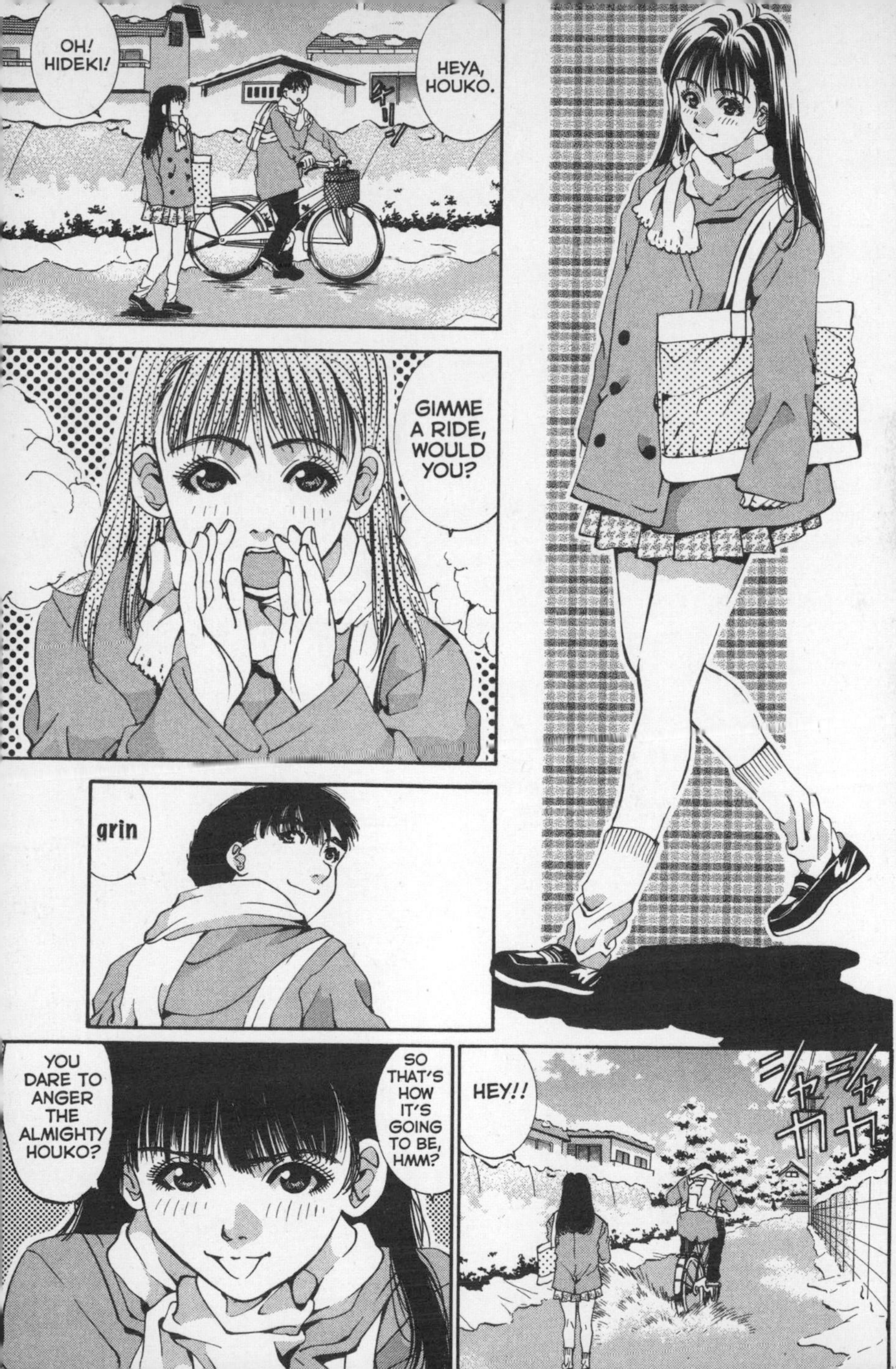
HEYA, HOUKO.
OH! HIDEKI!
GIMME A RIDE, WOULD YOU?
grin
HEY!!
SO THAT'S HOW IT'S GOING TO BE, HMM?
YOU DARE TO ANGER THE ALMIGHTY HOUKO?

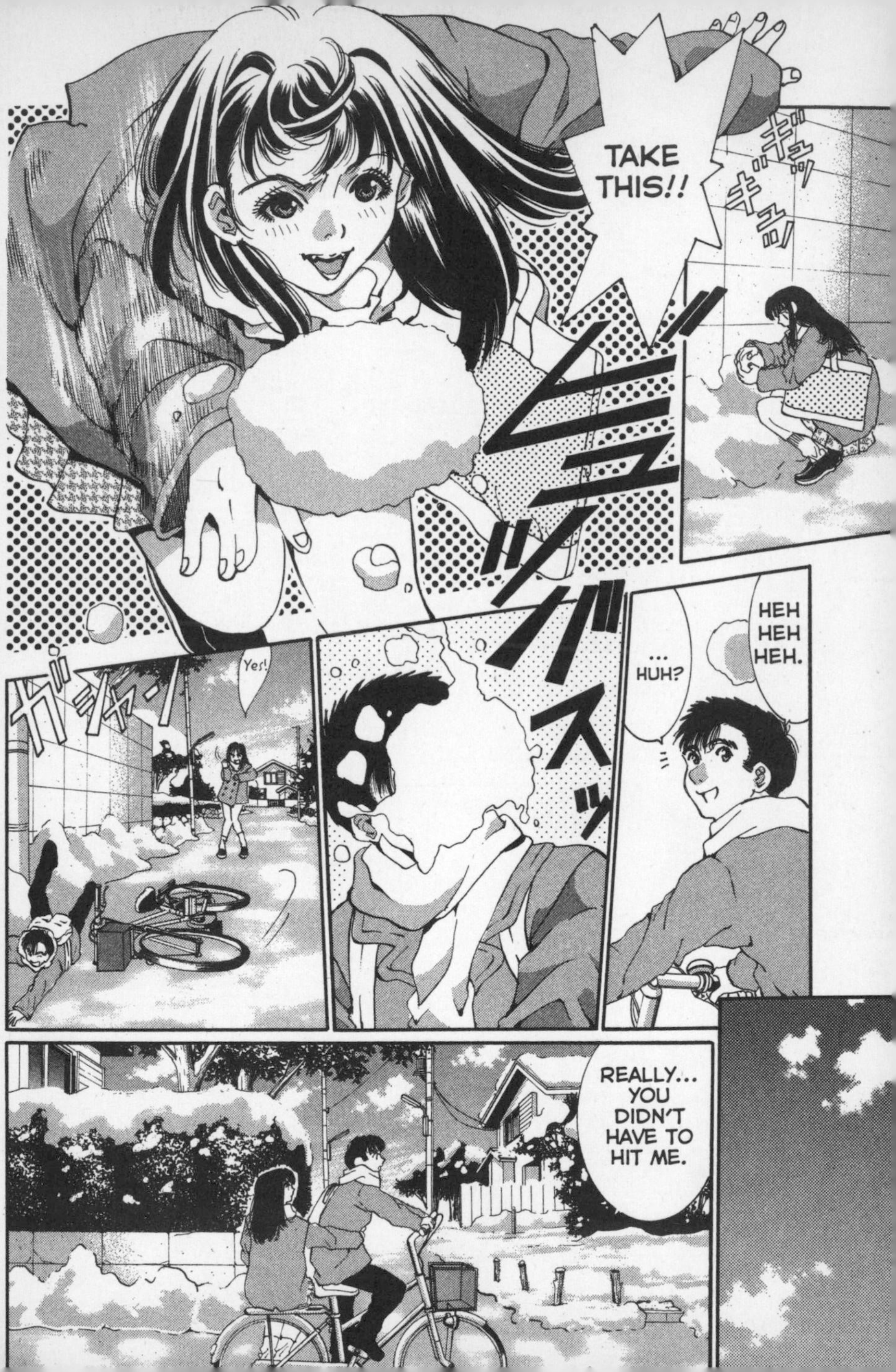
ギュッ ギュッ
TAKE THIS!!
ビュッ
HEH HEH HEH.
... HUH?
バスッ
Yes!
ガシャーン
REALLY... YOU DIDN'T HAVE TO HIT ME.

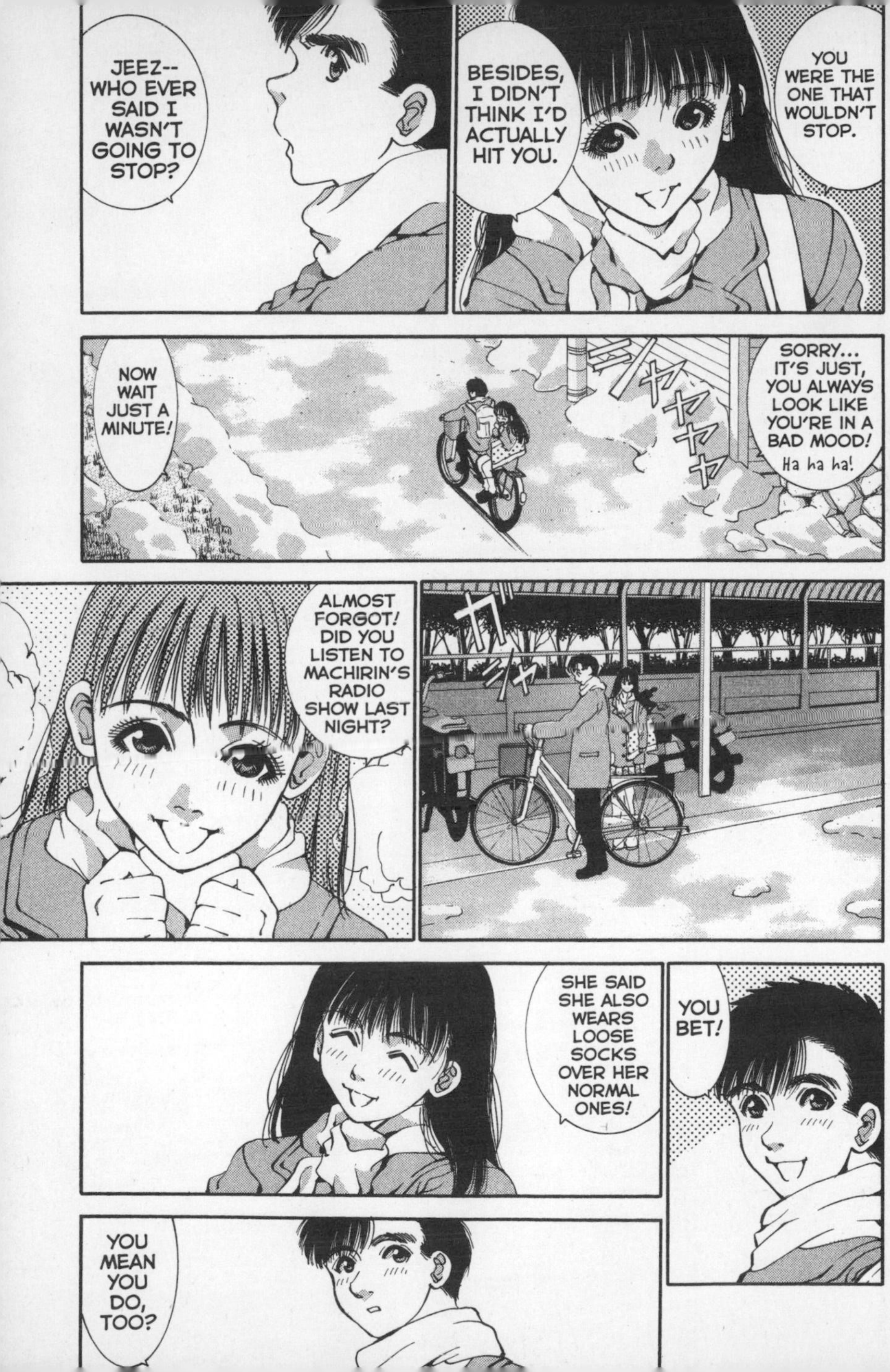
YOU WERE THE ONE THAT WOULDN'T STOP.
BESIDES, I DIDN'T THINK I'D ACTUALLY HIT YOU.
JEEZ-- WHO EVER SAID I WASN'T GOING TO STOP?
SORRY... IT'S JUST, YOU ALWAYS LOOK LIKE YOU'RE IN A BAD MOOD!
Ha ha ha!
NOW WAIT JUST A MINUTE!
ALMOST FORGOT! DID YOU LISTEN TO MACHIRIN'S RADIO SHOW LAST NIGHT?
YOU BET!
SHE SAID SHE ALSO WEARS LOOSE SOCKS OVER HER NORMAL ONES!
YOU MEAN YOU DO, TOO?

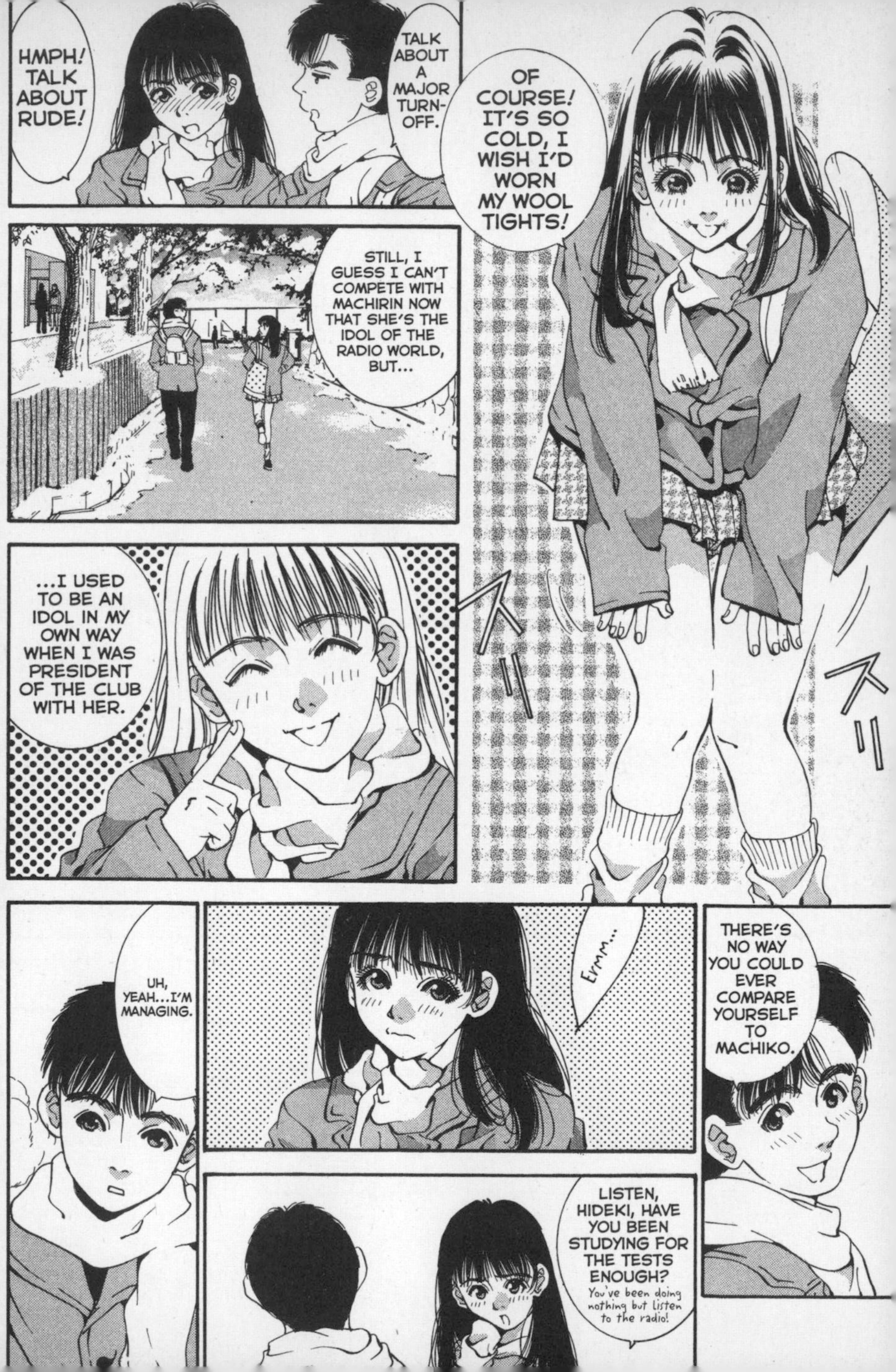
OF COURSE! IT'S SO COLD, I WISH I'D WORN MY WOOL TIGHTS!
スリ
スリ
TALK ABOUT A MAJOR TURN-OFF.
HMPH! TALK ABOUT RUDE!
STILL, I GUESS I CAN'T COMPETE WITH MACHIRIN NOW THAT SHE'S THE IDOL OF THE RADIO WORLD, BUT...
...I USED TO BE AN IDOL IN MY OWN WAY WHEN I WAS PRESIDENT OF THE CLUB WITH HER.
THERE'S NO WAY YOU COULD EVER COMPARE YOURSELF TO MACHIKO.
Ermm...
LISTEN, HIDEKI, HAVE YOU BEEN STUDYING FOR THE TESTS ENOUGH?
You've been doing nothing but listen to the radio!
UH, YEAH...I'M MANAGING.

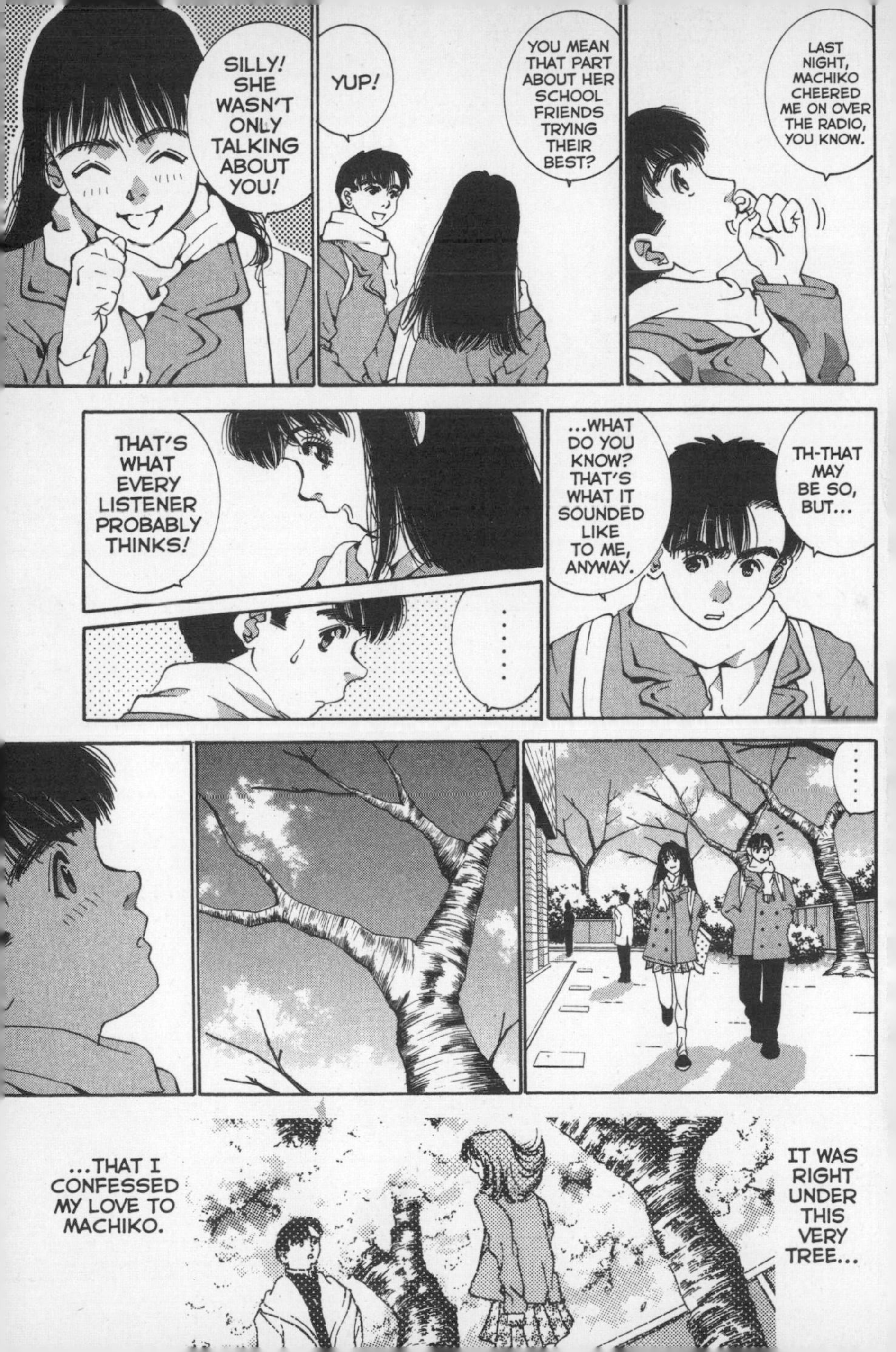
LAST NIGHT, MACHIKO CHEERED ME ON OVER THE RADIO, YOU KNOW.
YOU MEAN THAT PART ABOUT HER SCHOOL FRIENDS TRYING THEIR BEST?
YUP!
SILLY! SHE WASN'T ONLY TALKING ABOUT YOU!
TH-THAT MAY BE SO, BUT...
...WHAT DO YOU KNOW? THAT'S WHAT IT SOUNDED LIKE TO ME, ANYWAY.
THAT'S WHAT EVERY LISTENER PROBABLY THINKS!
......
......
...
IT WAS RIGHT UNDER THIS VERY TREE...
...THAT I CONFESSED MY LOVE TO MACHIKO.

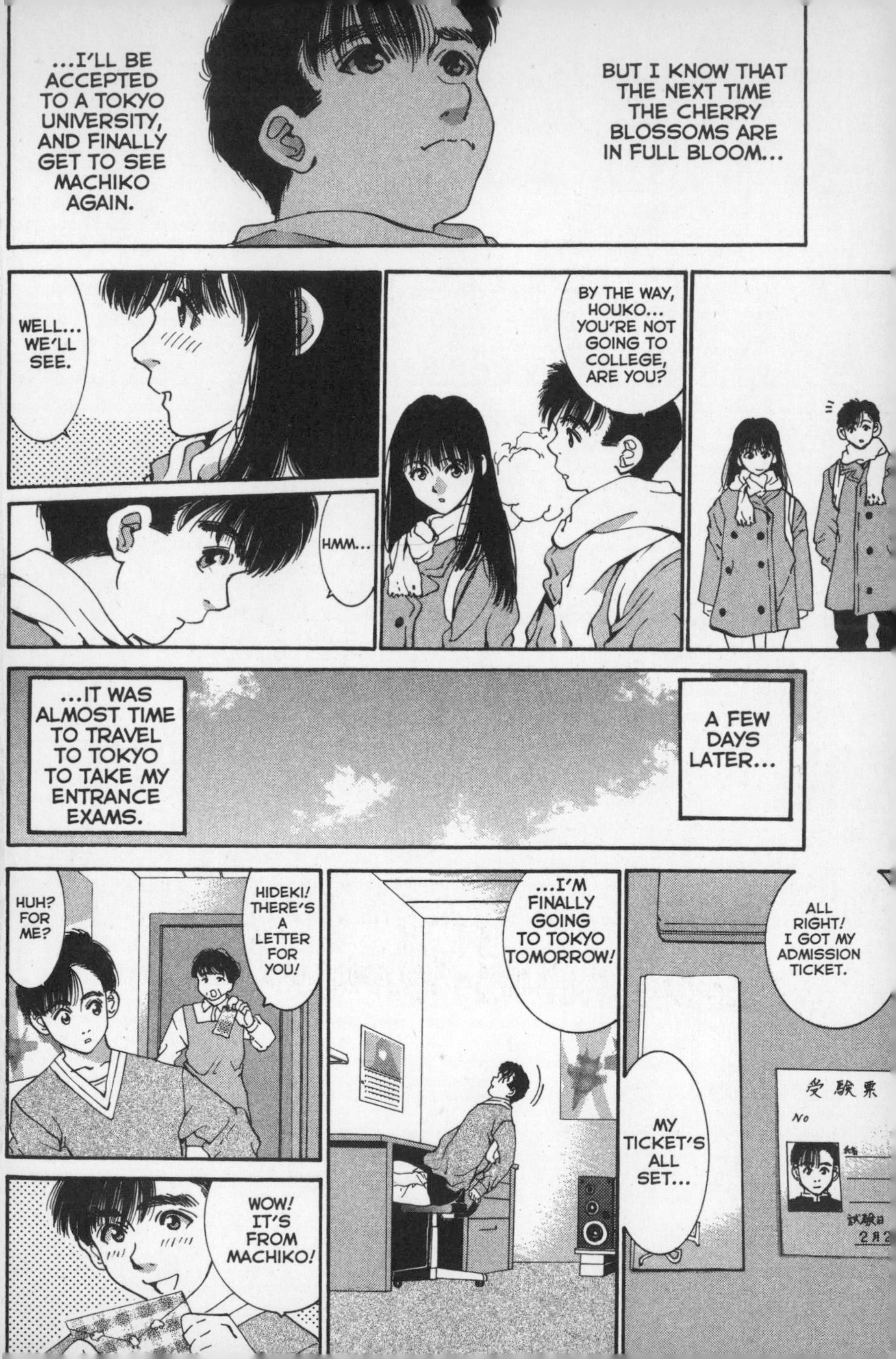
BUT I KNOW THAT THE NEXT TIME THE CHERRY BLOSSOMS ARE IN FULL BLOOM...
...I'LL BE ACCEPTED TO A TOKYO UNIVERSITY, AND FINALLY GET TO SEE MACHIKO AGAIN.
BY THE WAY, HOUKO... YOU'RE NOT GOING TO COLLEGE, ARE YOU?
WELL... WE'LL SEE.
HMM...
A FEW DAYS LATER...
...IT WAS ALMOST TIME TO TRAVEL TO TOKYO TO TAKE MY ENTRANCE EXAMS.
ALL RIGHT! I GOT MY ADMISSION TICKET.
受験票
MY TICKET'S ALL SET...
...I'M FINALLY GOING TO TOKYO TOMORROW!
HIDEKI! THERE'S A LETTER FOR YOU!
HUH? FOR ME?
WOW! IT'S FROM MACHIKO!

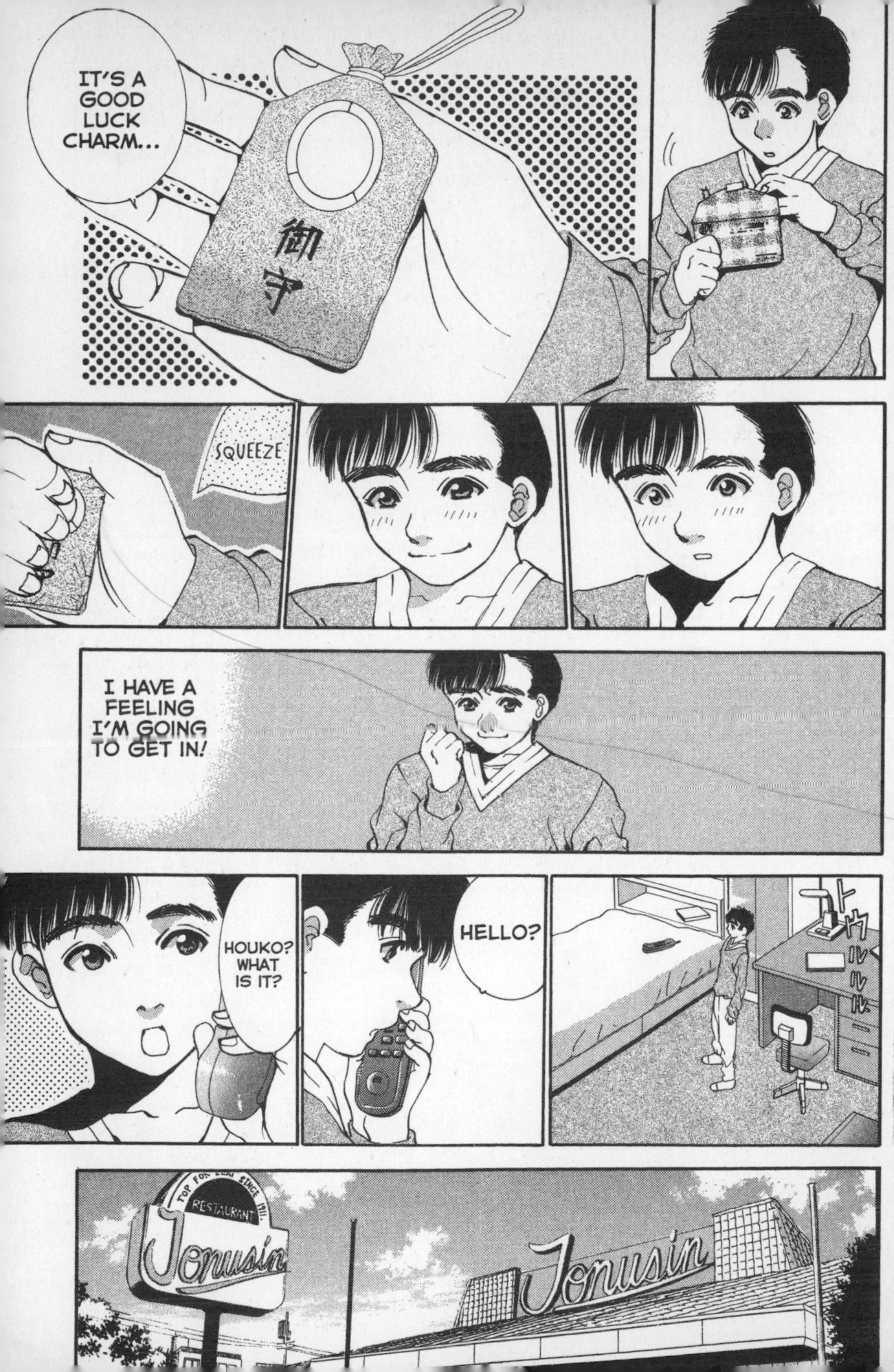
IT'S A GOOD LUCK CHARM...
御守
SQUEEZE
I HAVE A FEELING I'M GOING TO GET IN!
トゥルルル
HELLO?
HOUKO? WHAT IS IT?
RESTAURANT
Jonusin
Jonusin

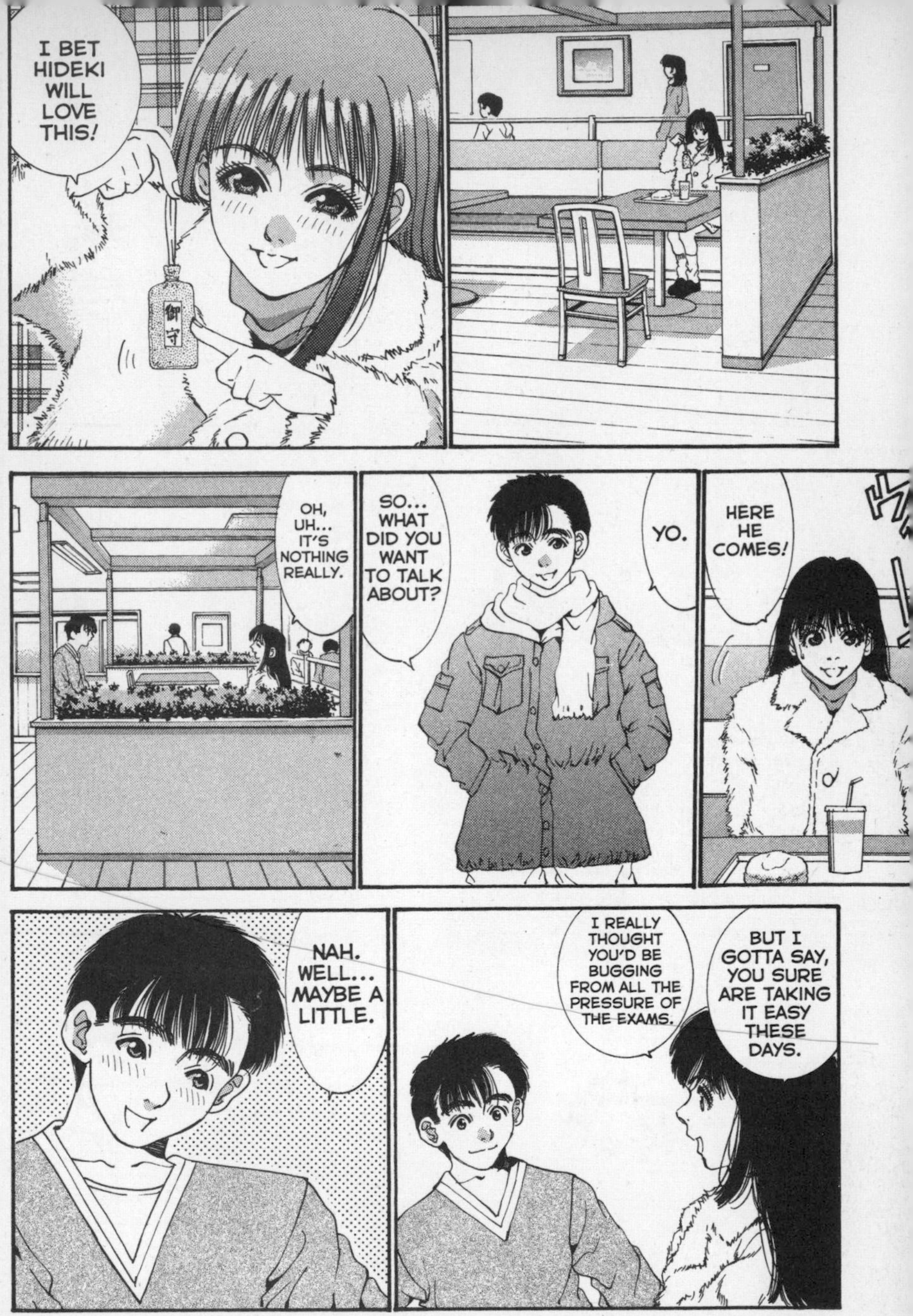
I BET HIDEKI WILL LOVE THIS!
御守
HERE HE COMES!
YO.
SO... WHAT DID YOU WANT TO TALK ABOUT?
OH, UH... IT'S NOTHING REALLY.
BUT I GOTTA SAY, YOU SURE ARE TAKING IT EASY THESE DAYS.
I REALLY THOUGHT YOU'D BE BUGGING FROM ALL THE PRESSURE OF THE EXAMS.
NAH. WELL... MAYBE A LITTLE.

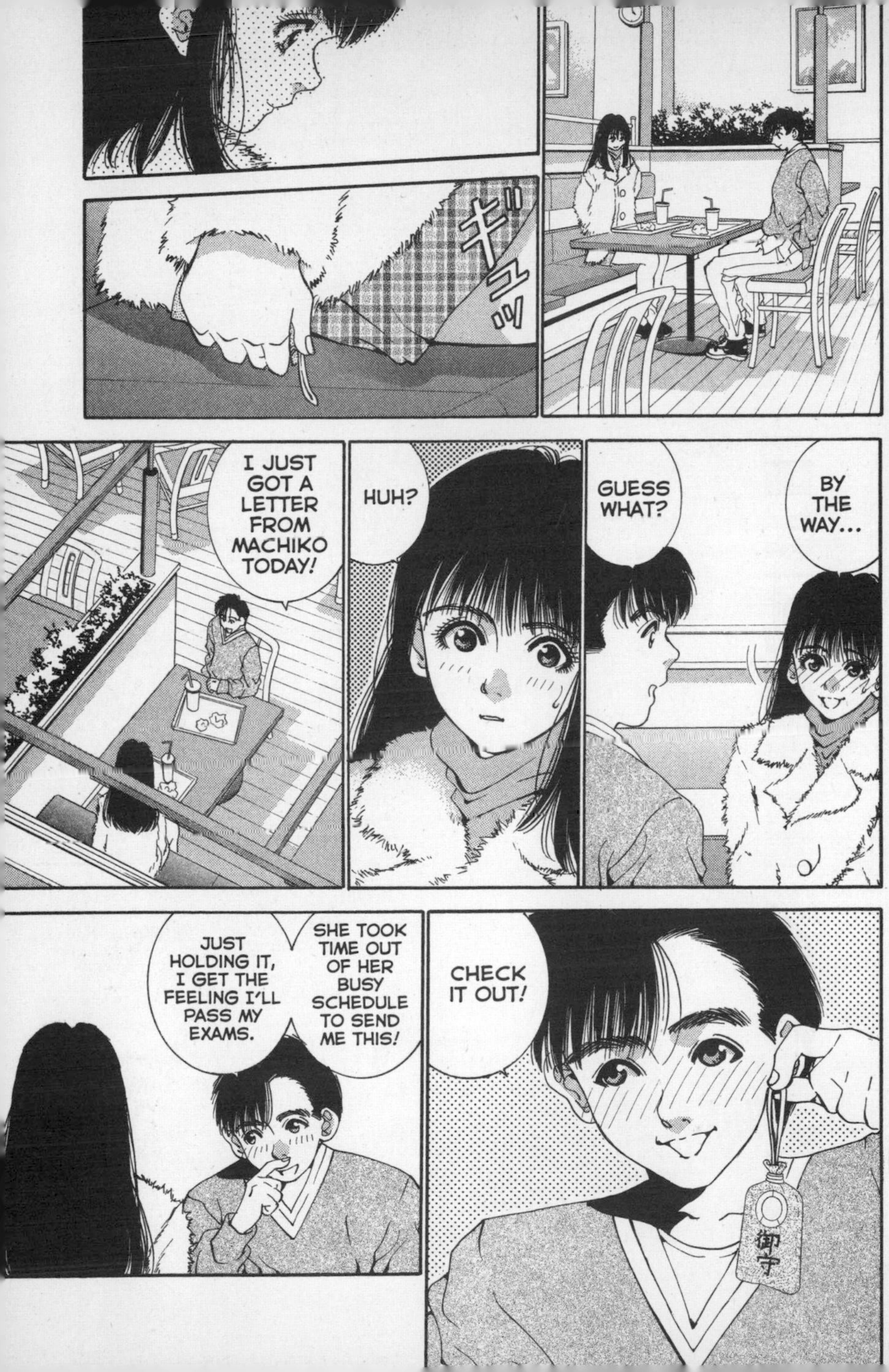
ギュッ
BY THE WAY...
GUESS WHAT?
HUH?
I JUST GOT A LETTER FROM MACHIKO TODAY!
CHECK IT OUT!
御守
SHE TOOK TIME OUT OF HER BUSY SCHEDULE TO SEND ME THIS!
JUST HOLDING IT, I GET THE FEELING I'LL PASS MY EXAMS.

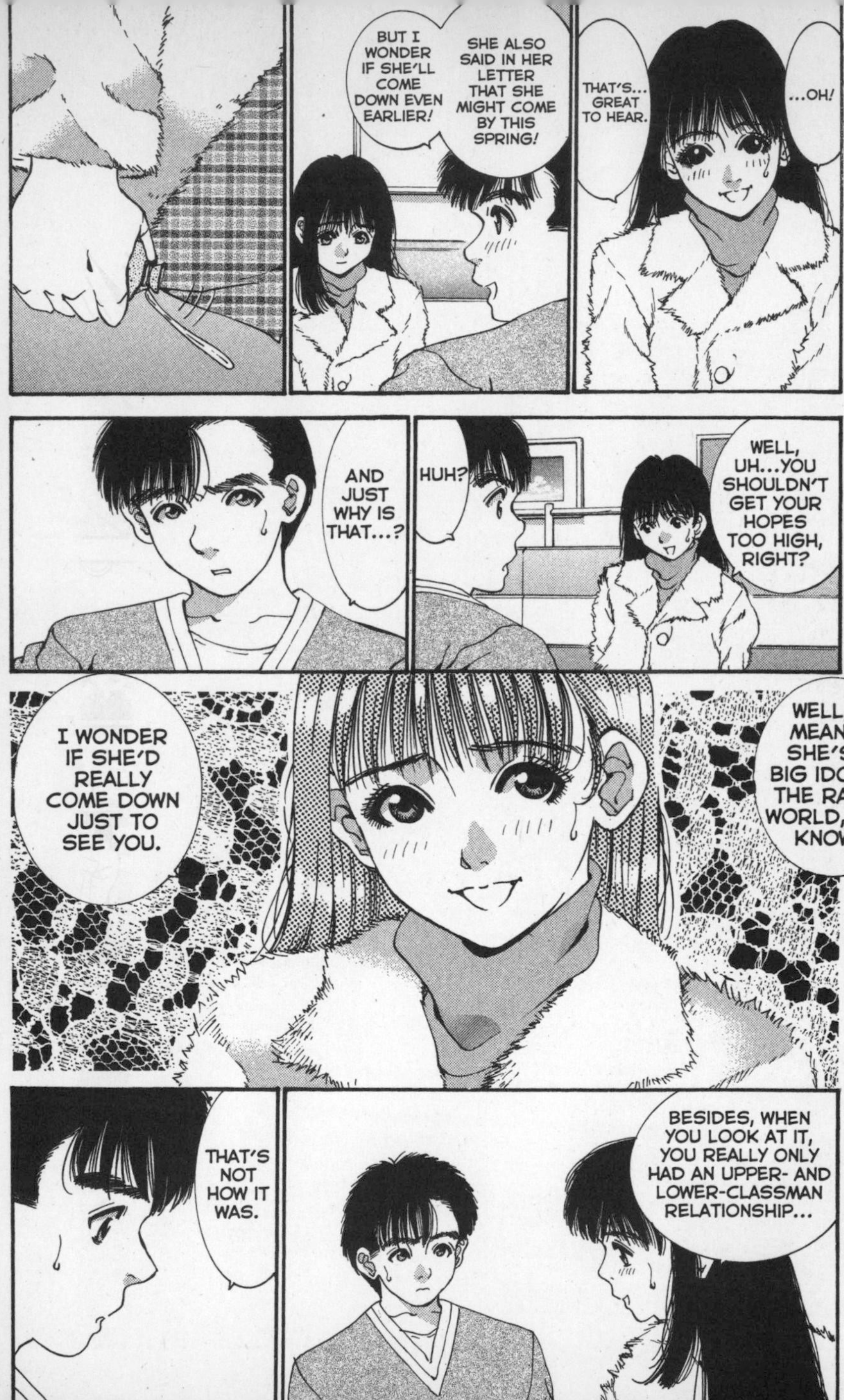
...OH!
THAT'S... GREAT TO HEAR.
SHE ALSO SAID IN HER LETTER THAT SHE MIGHT COME BY THIS SPRING!
BUT I WONDER IF SHE'LL COME DOWN EVEN EARLIER!
WELL, UH...YOU SHOULDN'T GET YOUR HOPES TOO HIGH, RIGHT?
HUH?
AND JUST WHY IS THAT...?
WELL, I MEAN... SHE'S A BIG IDOL IN THE RADIO WORLD, YOU KNOW?
I WONDER IF SHE'D REALLY COME DOWN JUST TO SEE YOU.
BESIDES, WHEN YOU LOOK AT IT, YOU REALLY ONLY HAD AN UPPER- AND LOWER-CLASSMAN RELATIONSHIP...
THAT'S NOT HOW IT WAS.

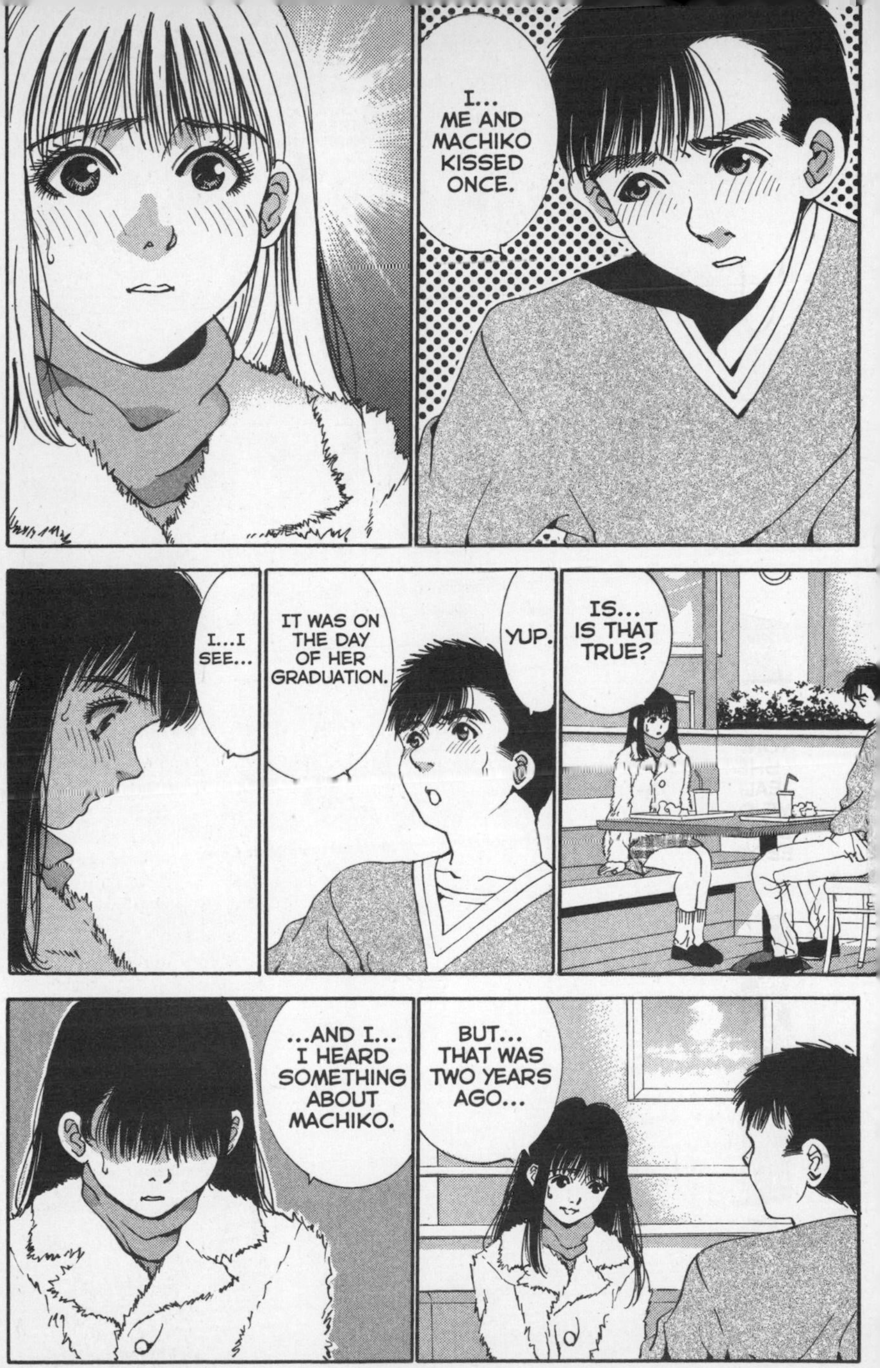
I... ME AND MACHIKO KISSED ONCE.
IS... IS THAT TRUE?
YUP.
IT WAS ON THE DAY OF HER GRADUATION.
I...I SEE...
BUT... THAT WAS TWO YEARS AGO...
...AND I... I HEARD SOMETHING ABOUT MACHIKO.

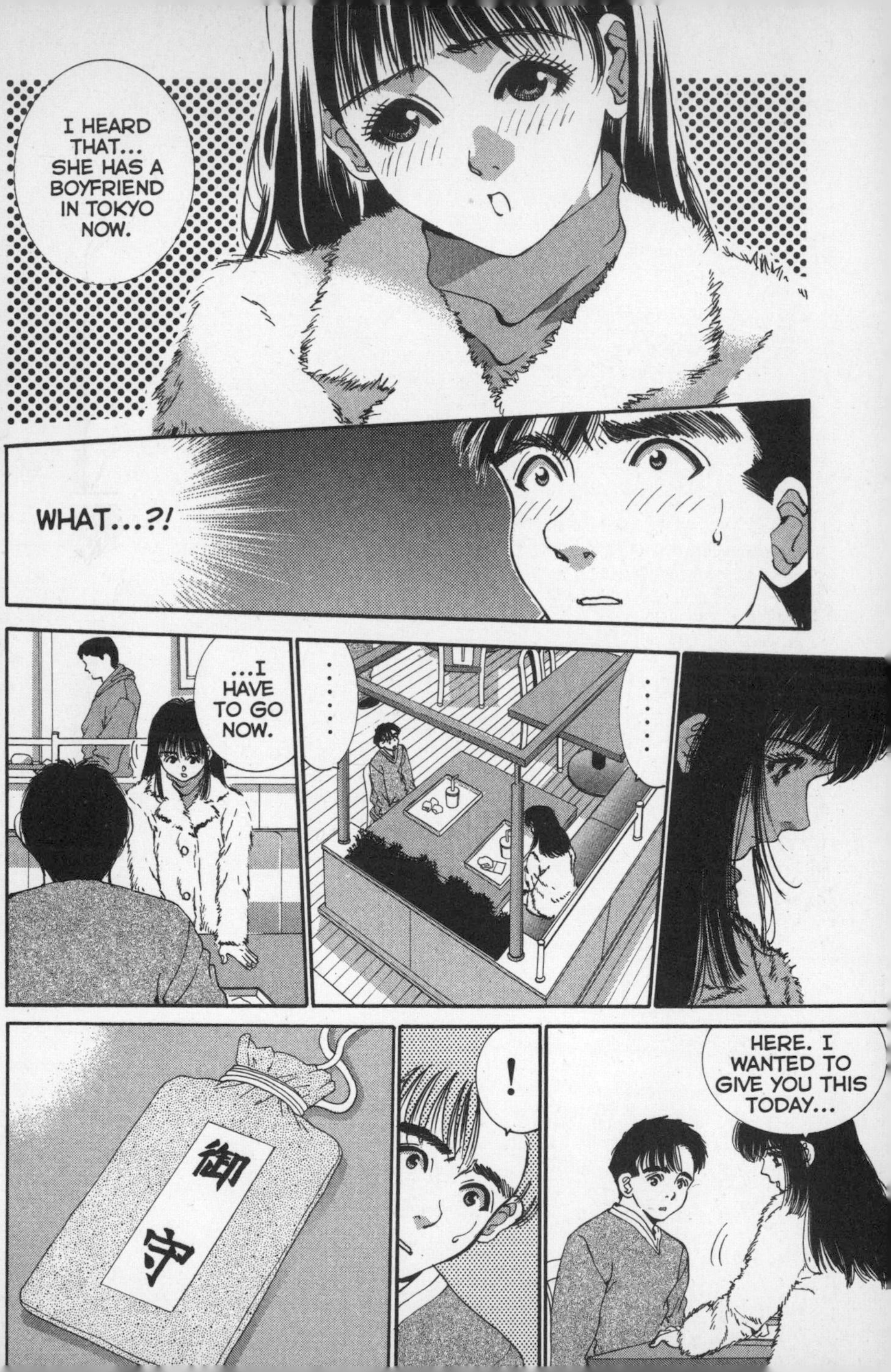
I HEARD THAT... SHE HAS A BOYFRIEND IN TOKYO NOW.
WHAT...?!
......
......
...I HAVE TO GO NOW.
HERE. I WANTED TO GIVE YOU THIS TODAY...
!
御守

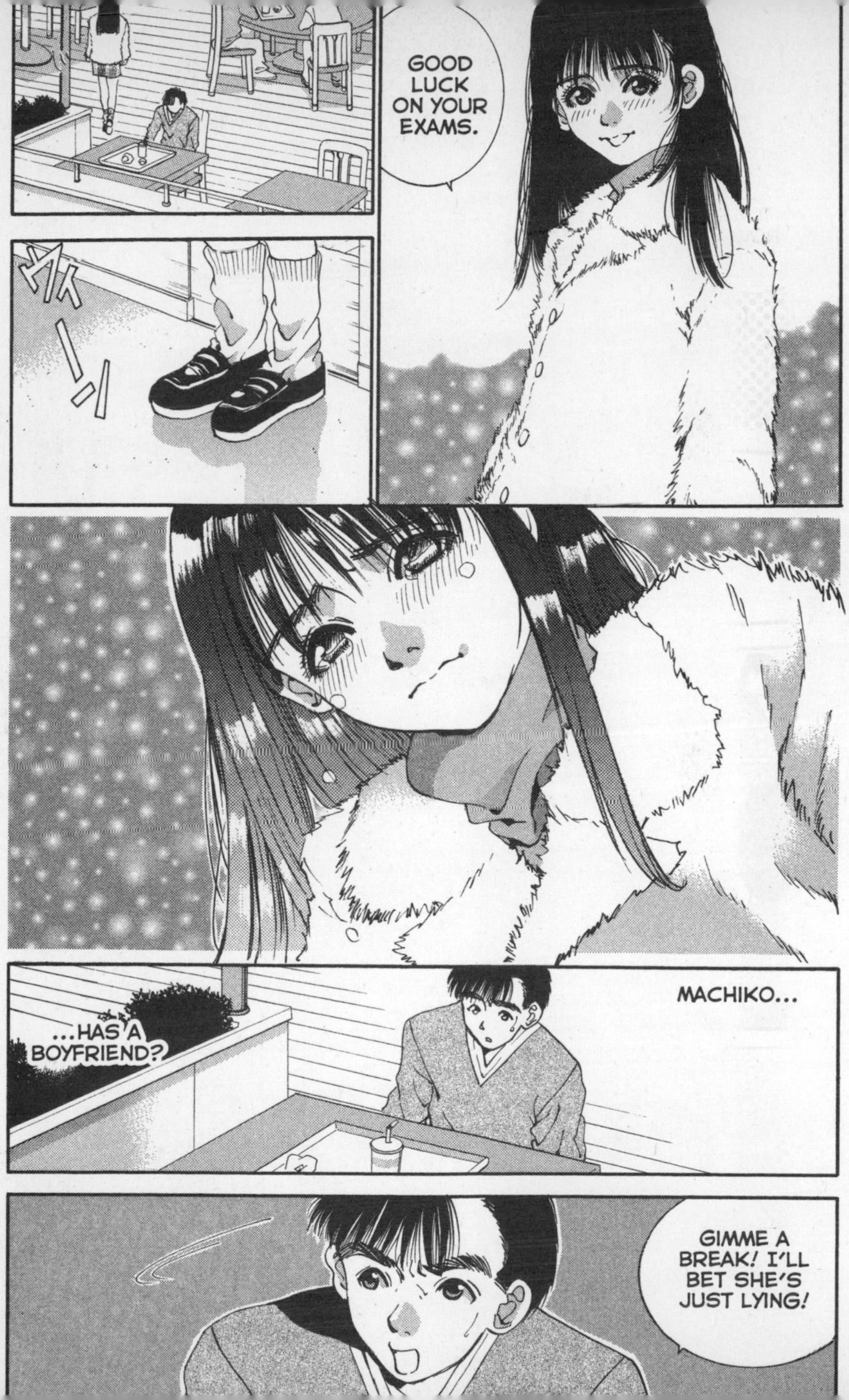
GOOD LUCK ON YOUR EXAMS.
MACHIKO...
...HAS A BOYFRIEND?
GIMME A BREAK! I'LL BET SHE'S JUST LYING!

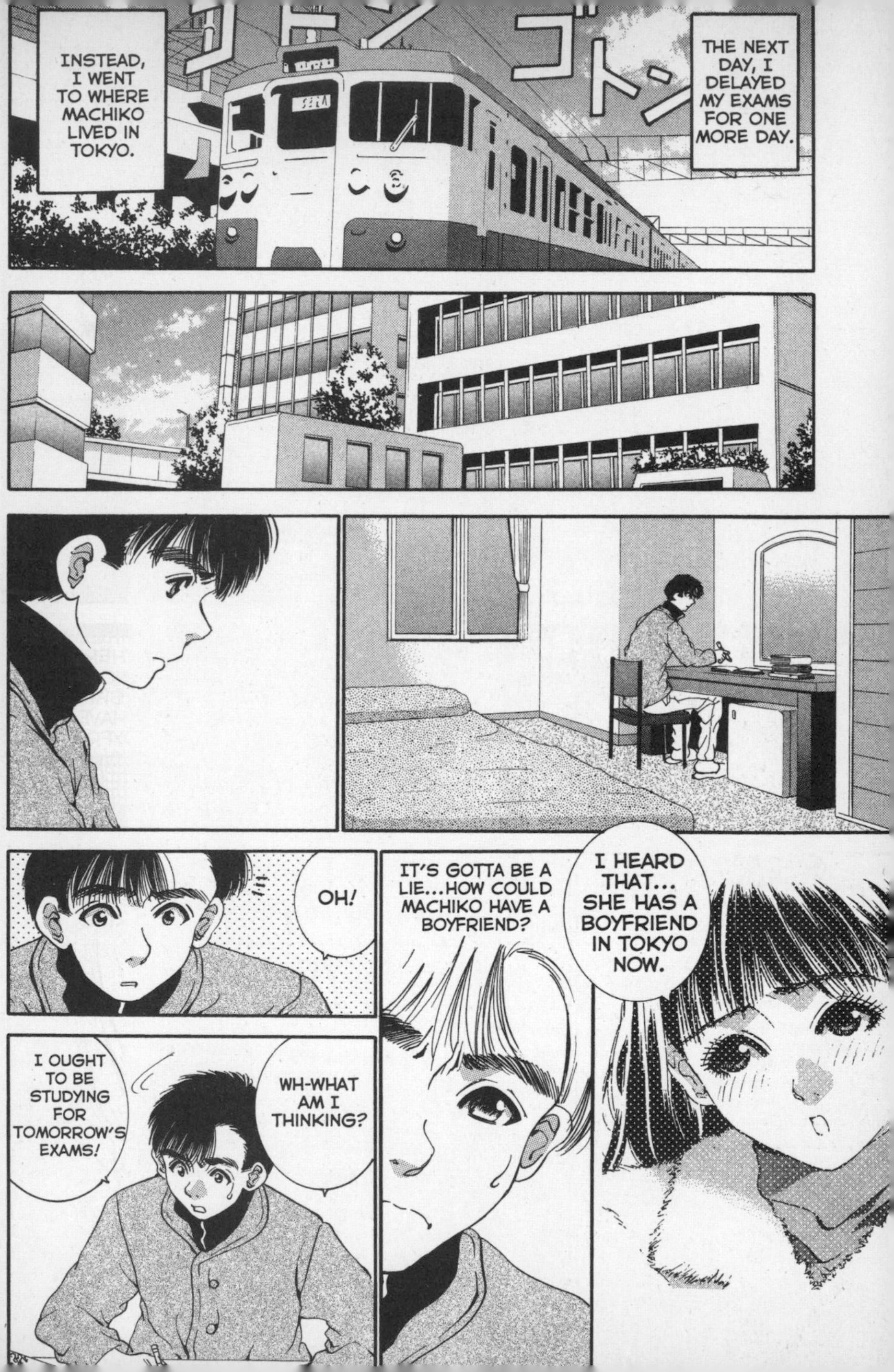
THE NEXT DAY, I DELAYED MY EXAMS FOR ONE MORE DAY.
INSTEAD, I WENT TO WHERE MACHIKO LIVED IN TOKYO.
I HEARD THAT... SHE HAS A BOYFRIEND IN TOKYO NOW.
IT'S GOTTA BE A LIE...HOW COULD MACHIKO HAVE A BOYFRIEND?
OH!
WH-WHAT AM I THINKING?
I OUGHT TO BE STUDYING FOR TOMORROW'S EXAMS!

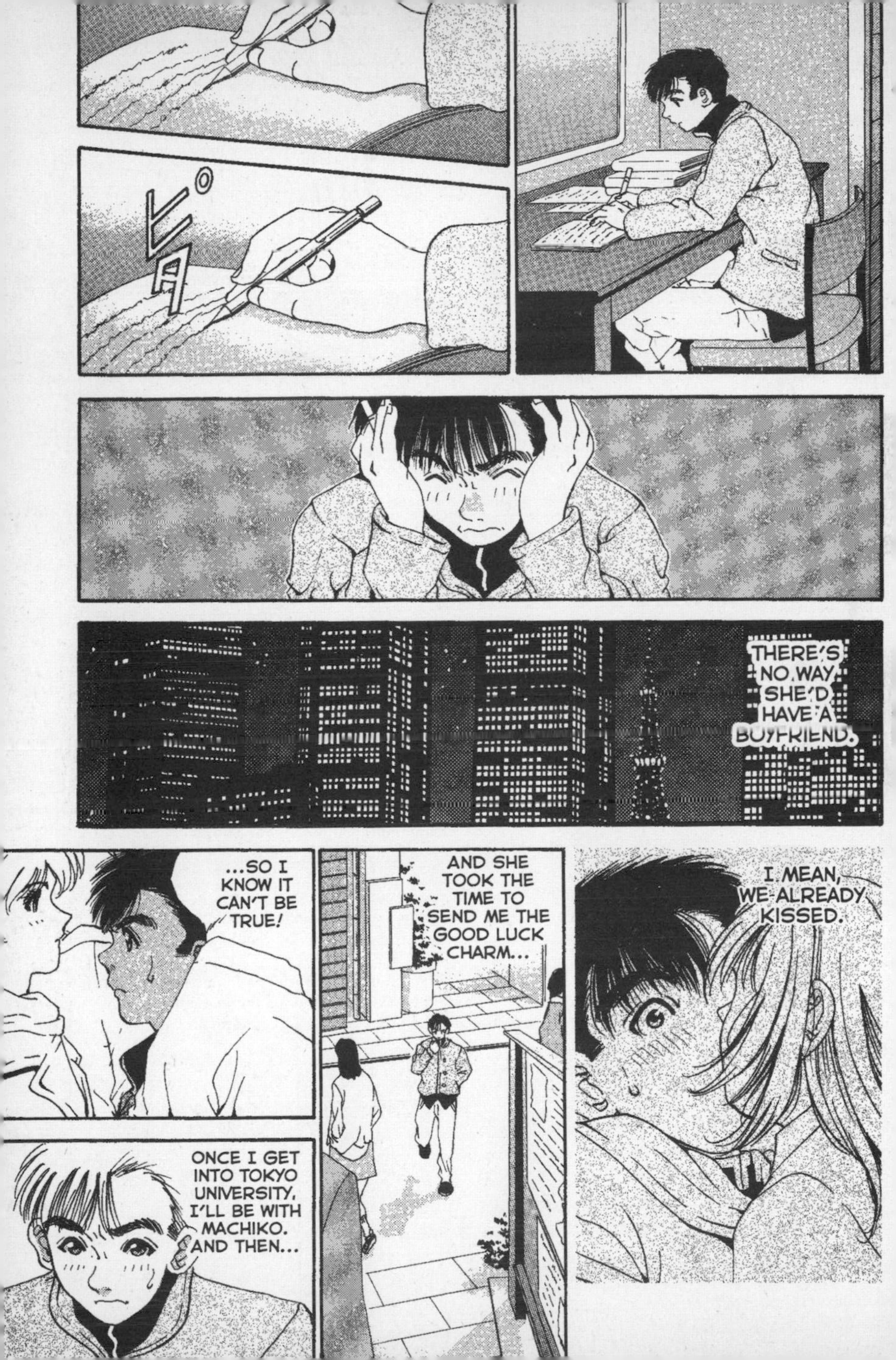
ピタ
THERE'S NO WAY SHE'D HAVE A BOYFRIEND.
I MEAN, WE ALREADY KISSED.
AND SHE TOOK THE TIME TO SEND ME THE GOOD LUCK CHARM...
...SO I KNOW IT CAN'T BE TRUE!
ONCE I GET INTO TOKYO UNIVERSITY, I'LL BE WITH MACHIKO. AND THEN...

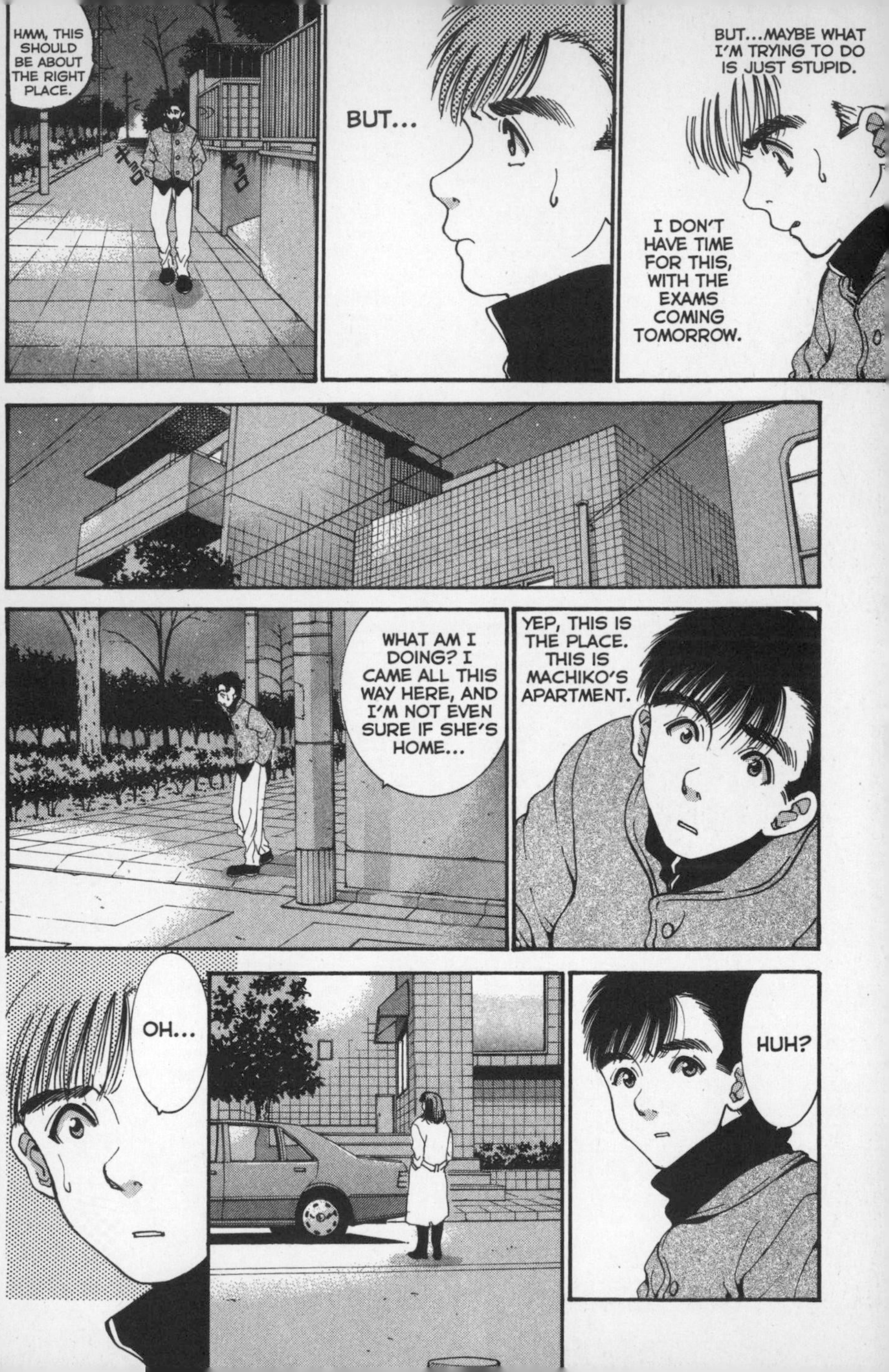
BUT...MAYBE WHAT I'M TRYING TO DO IS JUST STUPID.
I DON'T HAVE TIME FOR THIS, WITH THE EXAMS COMING TOMORROW.
BUT...
HMM, THIS SHOULD BE ABOUT THE RIGHT PLACE.
YEP, THIS IS THE PLACE. THIS IS MACHIKO'S APARTMENT.
WHAT AM I DOING? I CAME ALL THIS WAY HERE, AND I'M NOT EVEN SURE IF SHE'S HOME...
HUH?
OH...

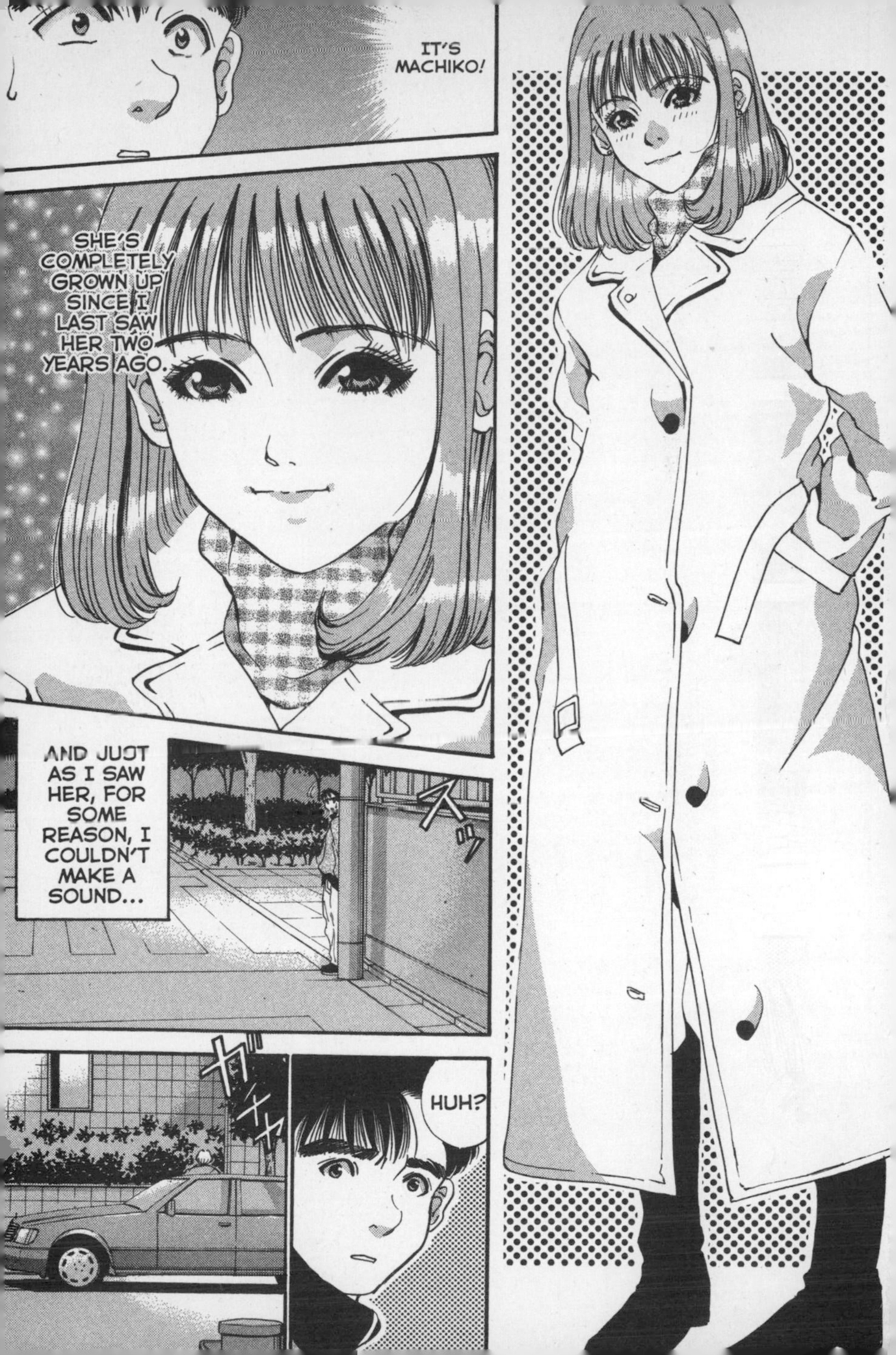
IT'S MACHIKO!
SHE'S COMPLETELY GROWN UP SINCE I LAST SAW HER TWO YEARS AGO.
AND JUST AS I SAW HER, FOR SOME REASON, I COULDN'T MAKE A SOUND...
HUH?

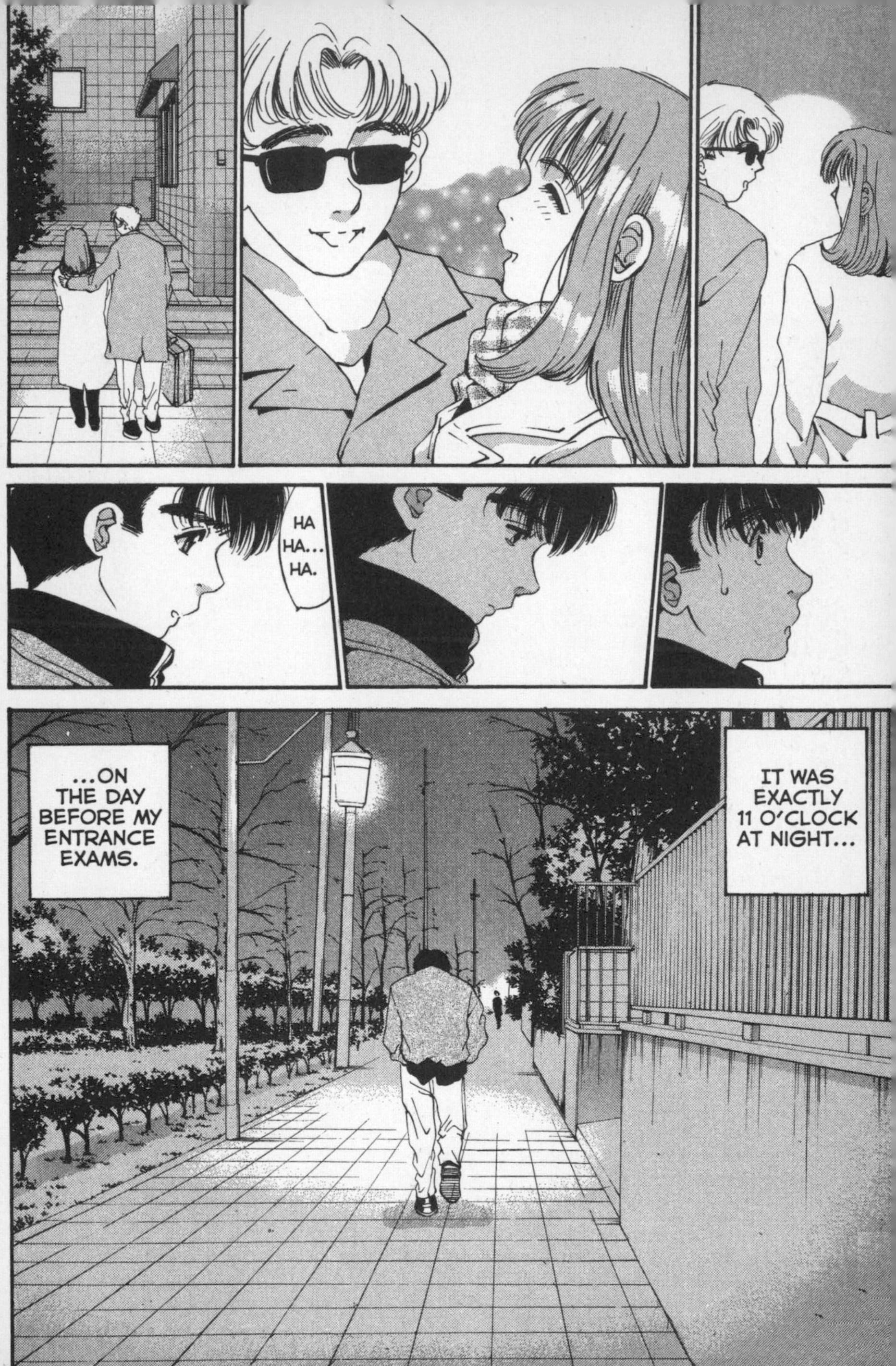
HA HA... HA.
IT WAS EXACTLY 11 O'CLOCK AT NIGHT...
...ON THE DAY BEFORE MY ENTRANCE EXAMS.

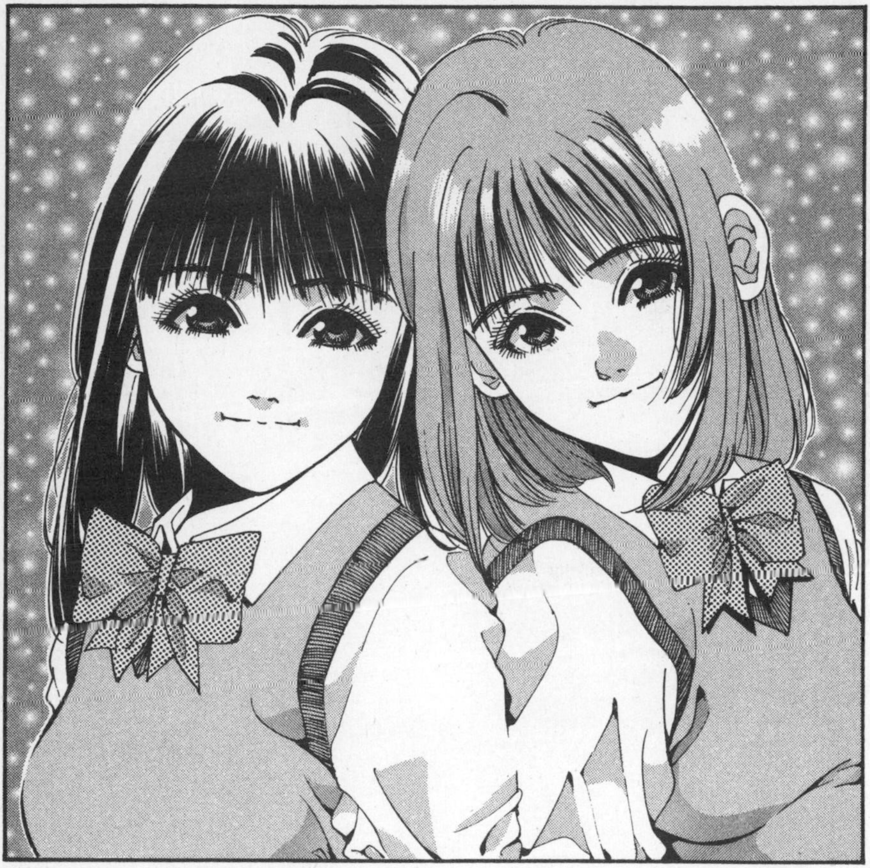

BOYS:BE™

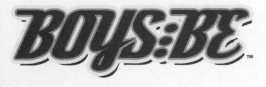

REPORT 14
Someday Beneath the Cherry Blossom Trees (Part Two)

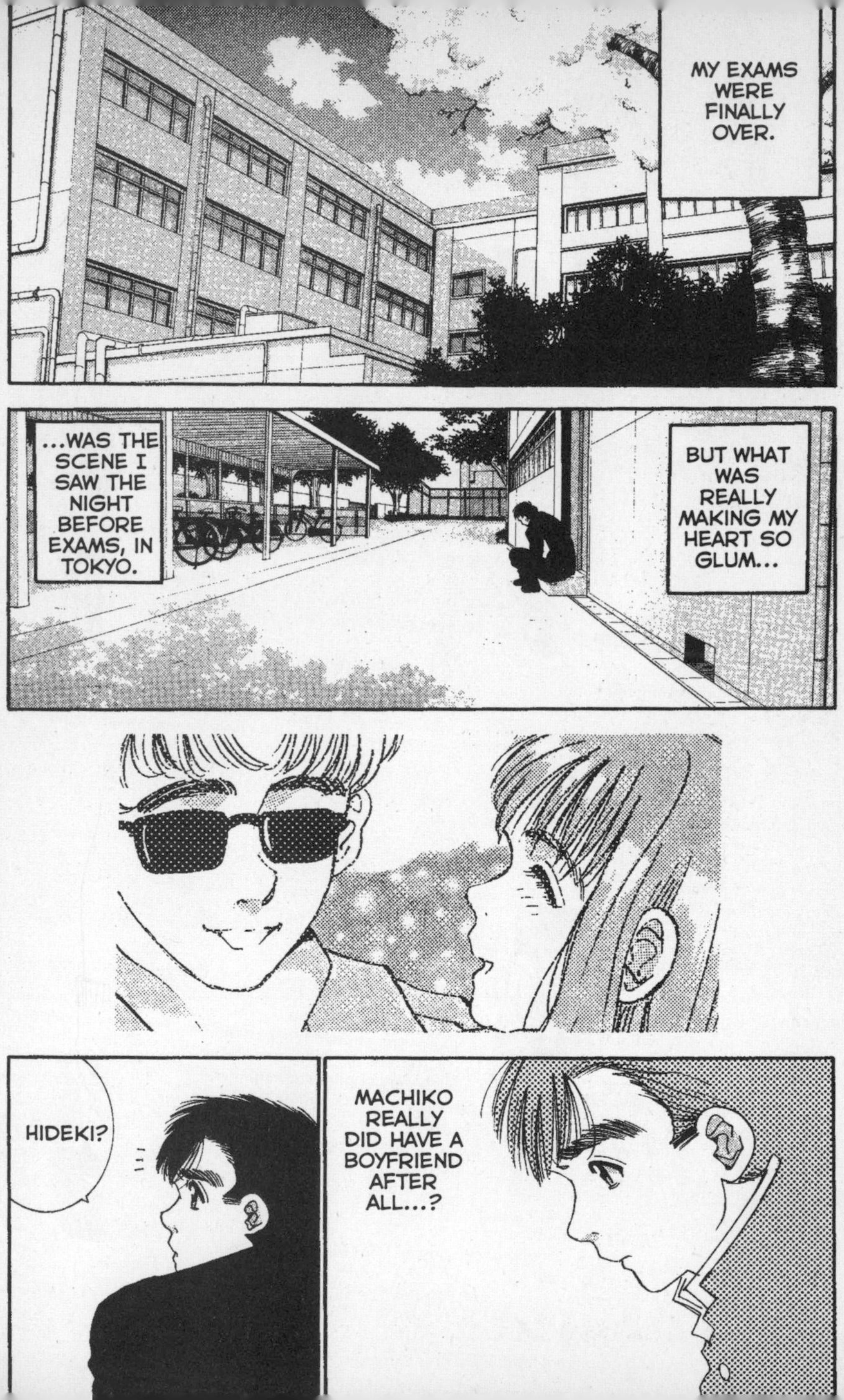
MY EXAMS WERE FINALLY OVER.
BUT WHAT WAS REALLY MAKING MY HEART SO GLUM...
...WAS THE SCENE I SAW THE NIGHT BEFORE EXAMS, IN TOKYO.
MACHIKO REALLY DID HAVE A BOYFRIEND AFTER ALL...?
HIDEKI?

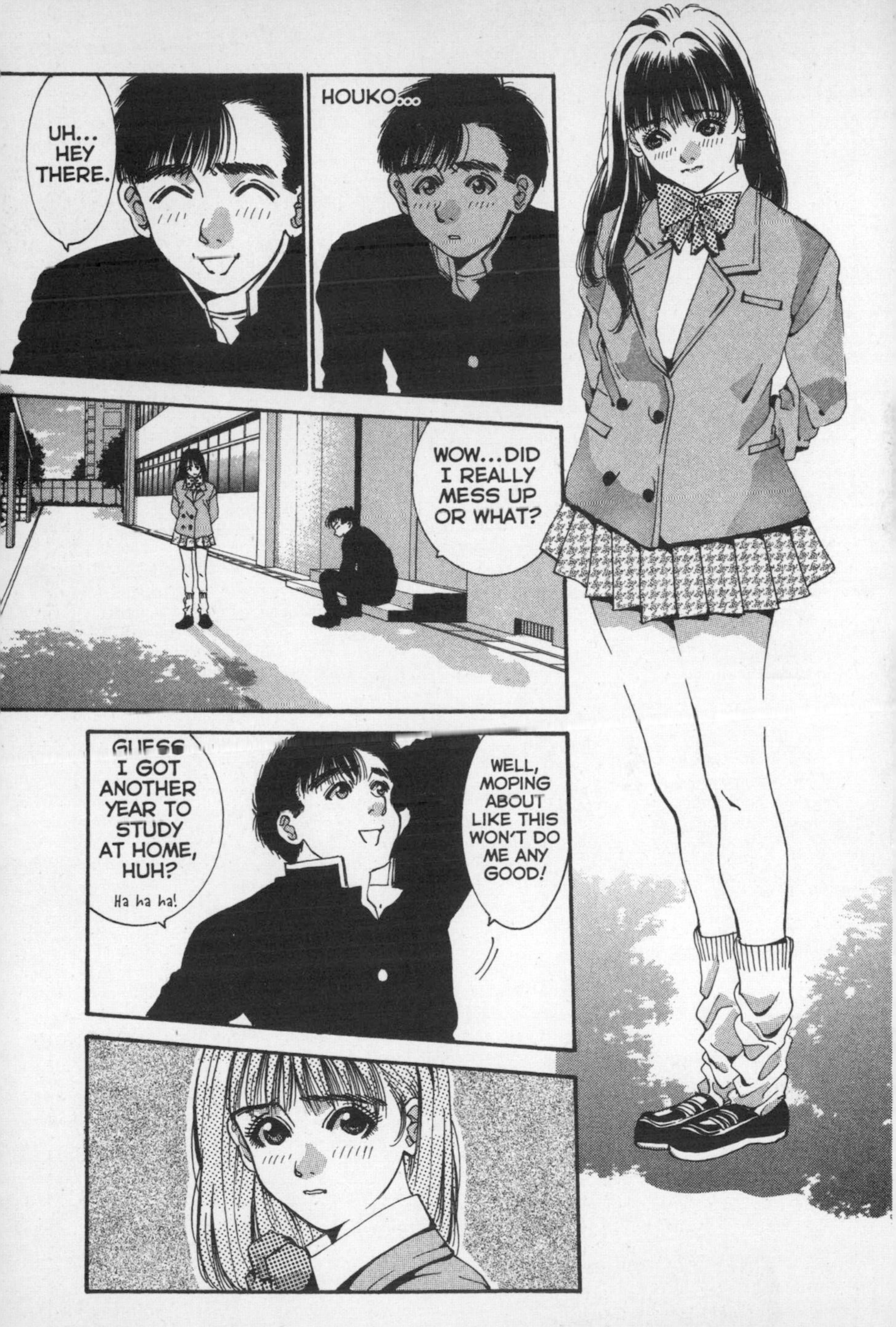
HOUKO...
UH... HEY THERE.
WOW...DID I REALLY MESS UP OR WHAT?
WELL, MOPING ABOUT LIKE THIS WON'T DO ME ANY GOOD!
GUESS I GOT ANOTHER YEAR TO STUDY AT HOME, HUH?
Ha ha ha!

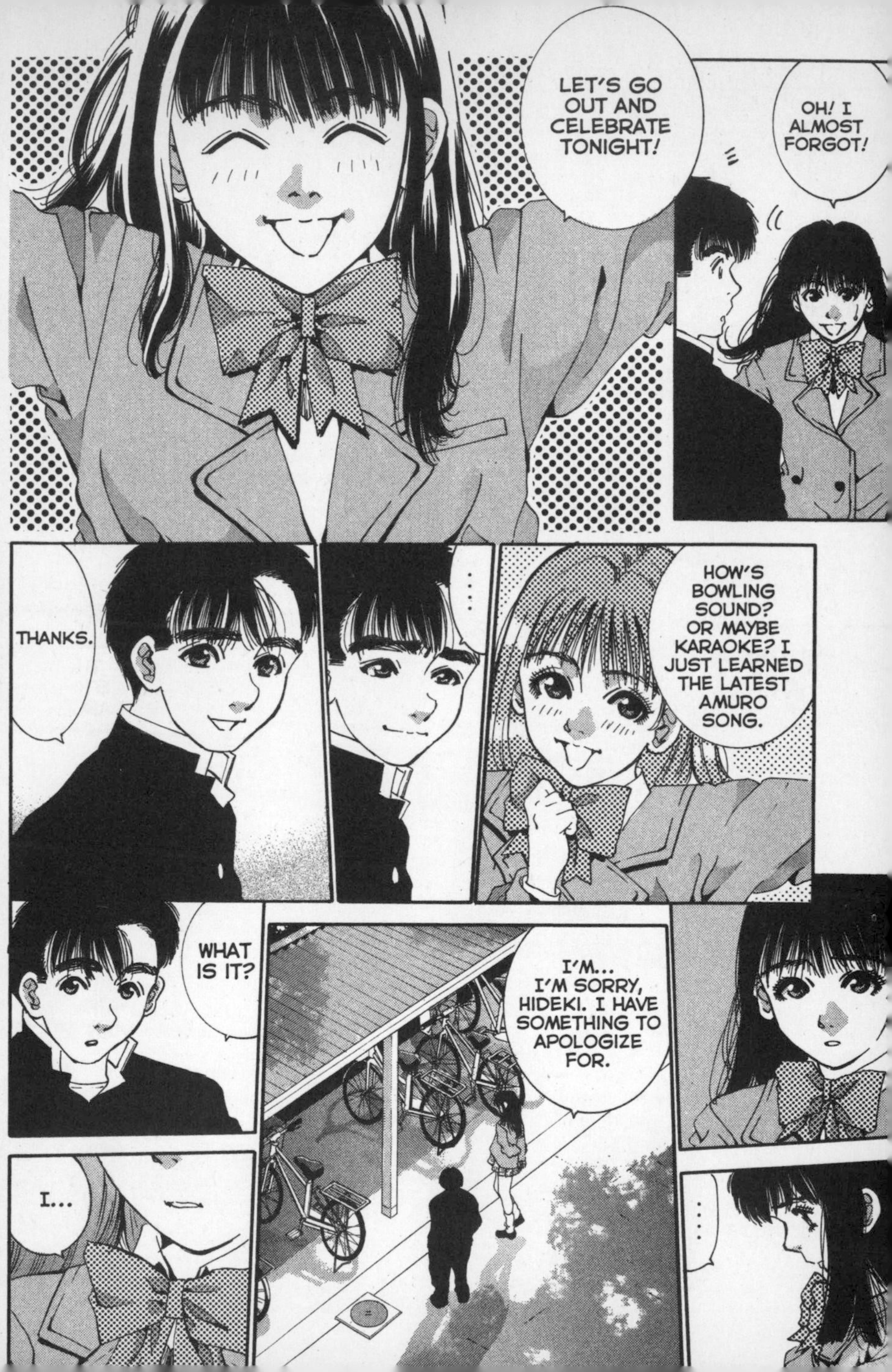

OH! I ALMOST FORGOT!
LET'S GO OUT AND CELEBRATE TONIGHT!
HOW'S BOWLING SOUND? OR MAYBE KARAOKE? I JUST LEARNED THE LATEST AMURO SONG.
....
THANKS.
....
I'M... I'M SORRY, HIDEKI. I HAVE SOMETHING TO APOLOGIZE FOR.
WHAT IS IT?
I...

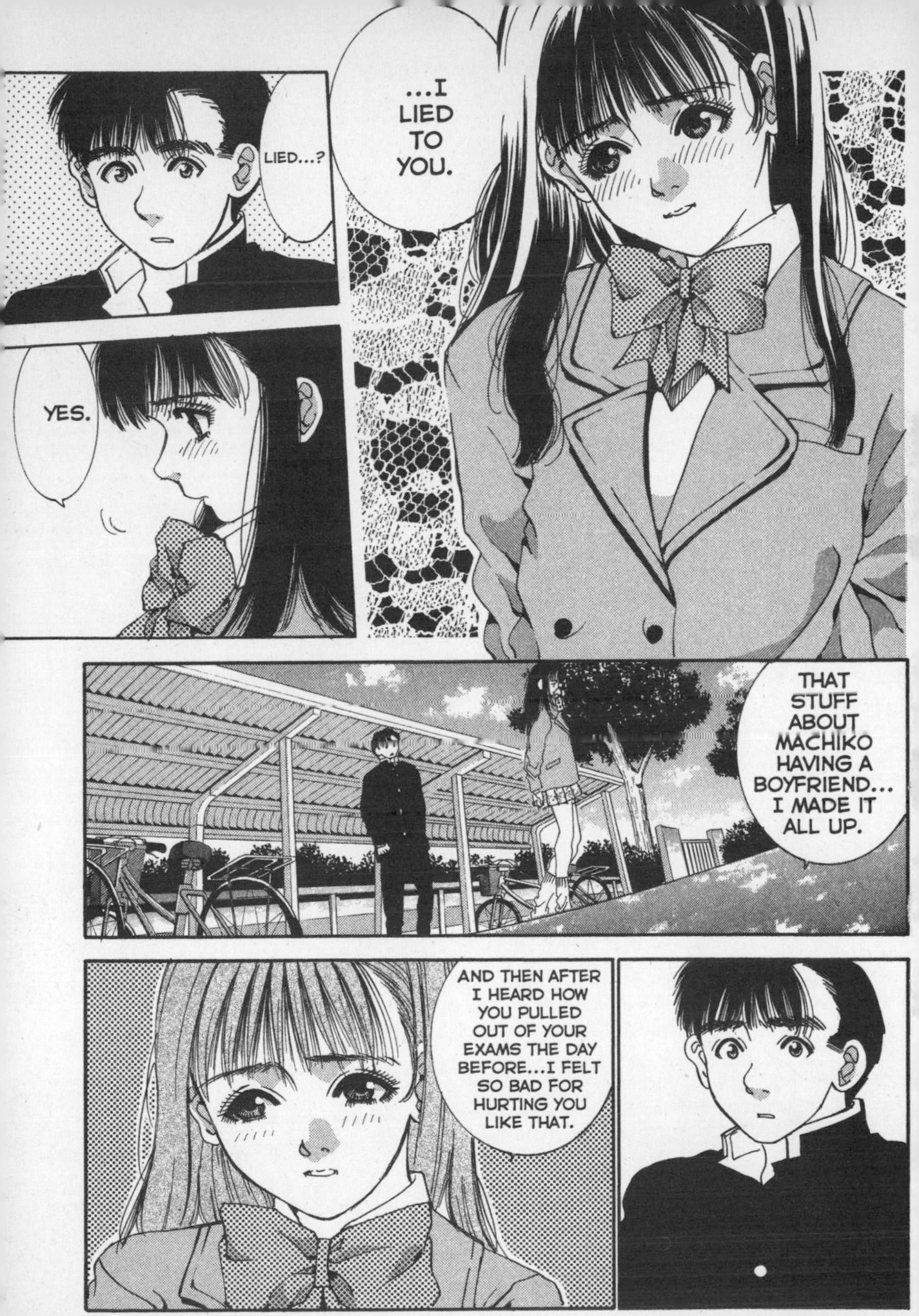
...I LIED TO YOU.
LIED...?
YES.
THAT STUFF ABOUT MACHIKO HAVING A BOYFRIEND... I MADE IT ALL UP.
AND THEN AFTER I HEARD HOW YOU PULLED OUT OF YOUR EXAMS THE DAY BEFORE...I FELT SO BAD FOR HURTING YOU LIKE THAT.

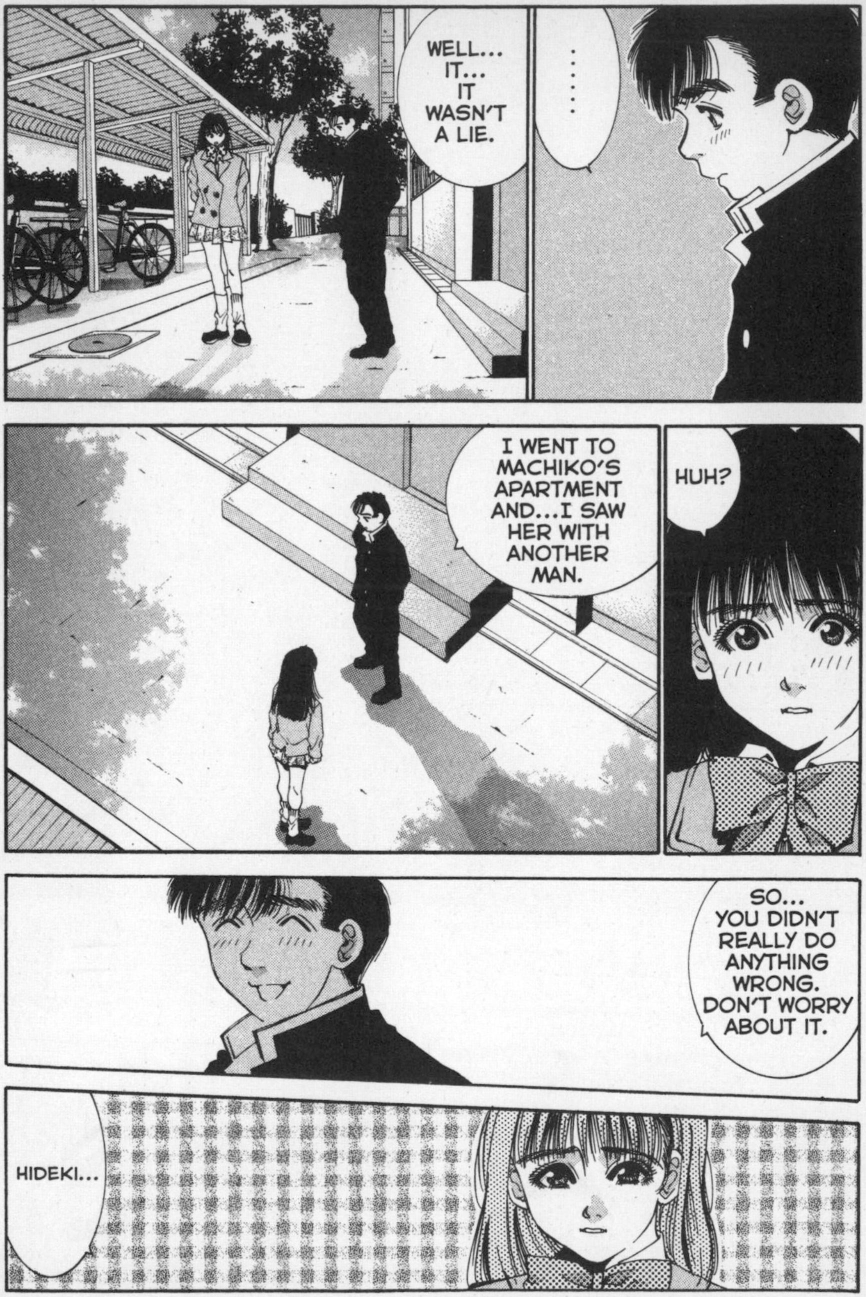
......
WELL... IT... IT WASN'T A LIE.
HUH?
I WENT TO MACHIKO'S APARTMENT AND...I SAW HER WITH ANOTHER MAN.
SO... YOU DIDN'T REALLY DO ANYTHING WRONG. DON'T WORRY ABOUT IT.
HIDEKI...

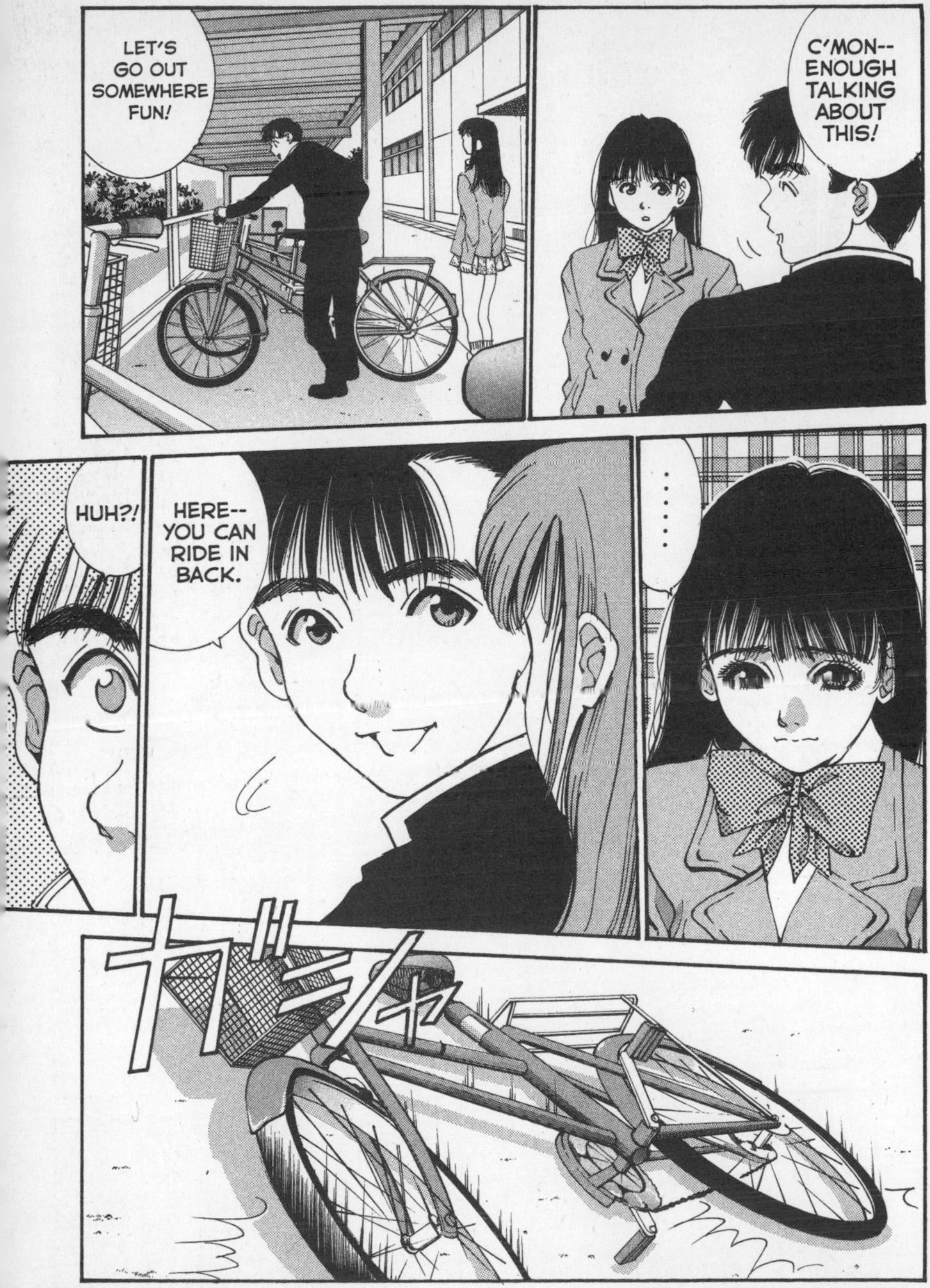

C'MON-- ENOUGH TALKING ABOUT THIS!
LET'S GO OUT SOMEWHERE FUN!
......
HERE-- YOU CAN RIDE IN BACK.
HUH?!

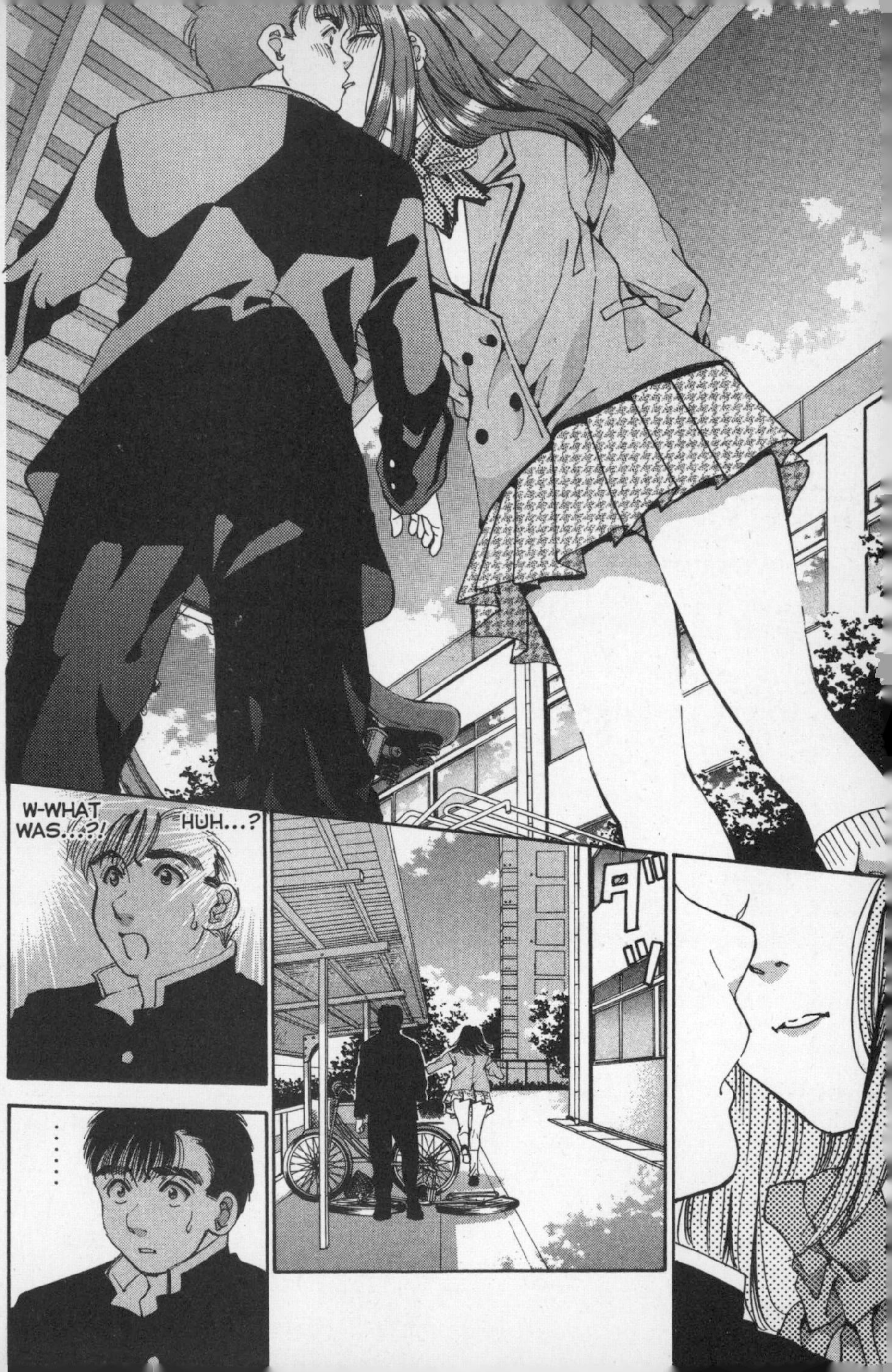
ダッ
HUH...?
W-WHAT WAS...?!
......

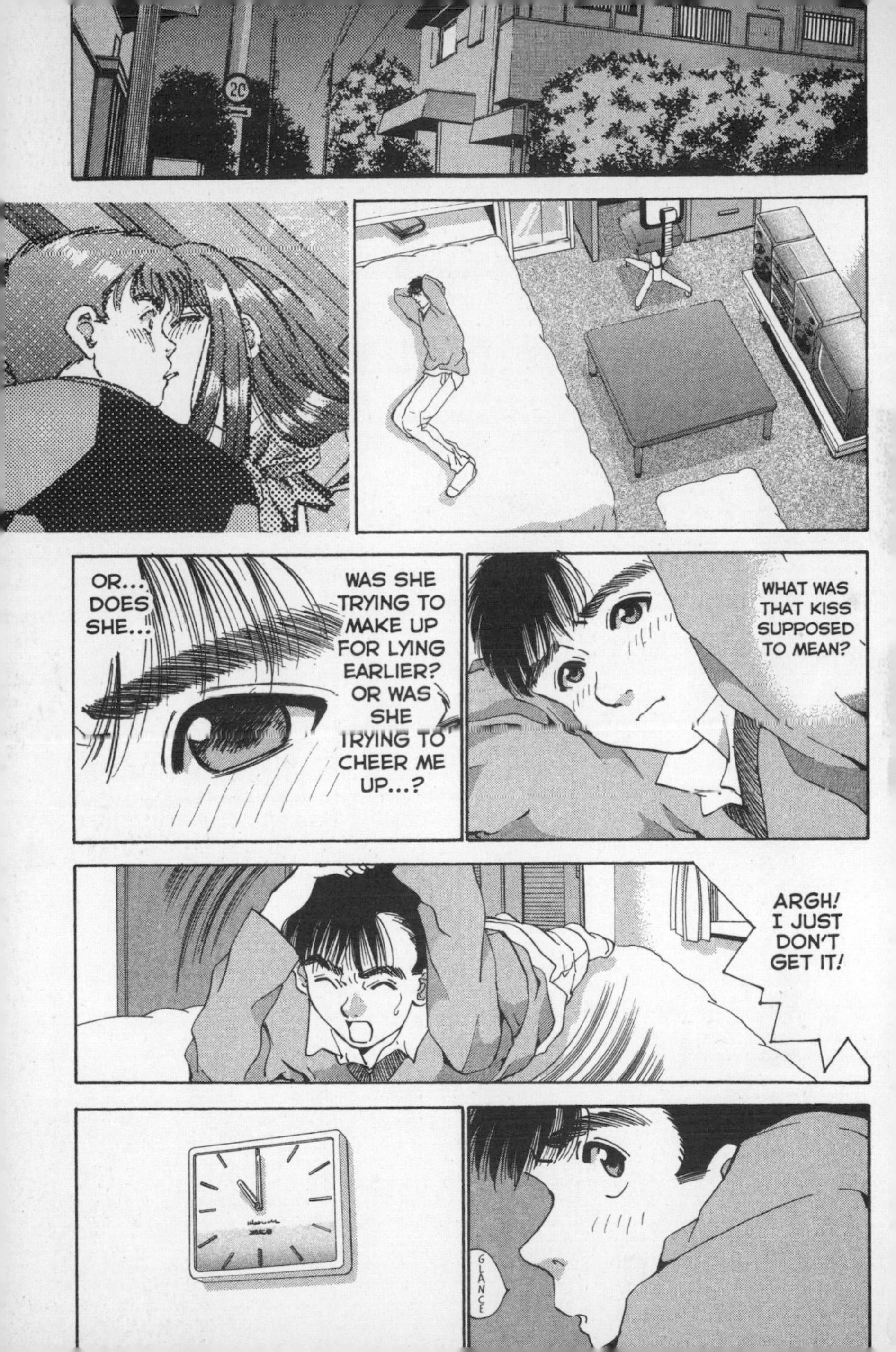
WHAT WAS THAT KISS SUPPOSED TO MEAN?
WAS SHE TRYING TO MAKE UP FOR LYING EARLIER? OR WAS SHE TRYING TO CHEER ME UP...?
OR... DOES SHE...
ARGH! I JUST DON'T GET IT!
GLANCE

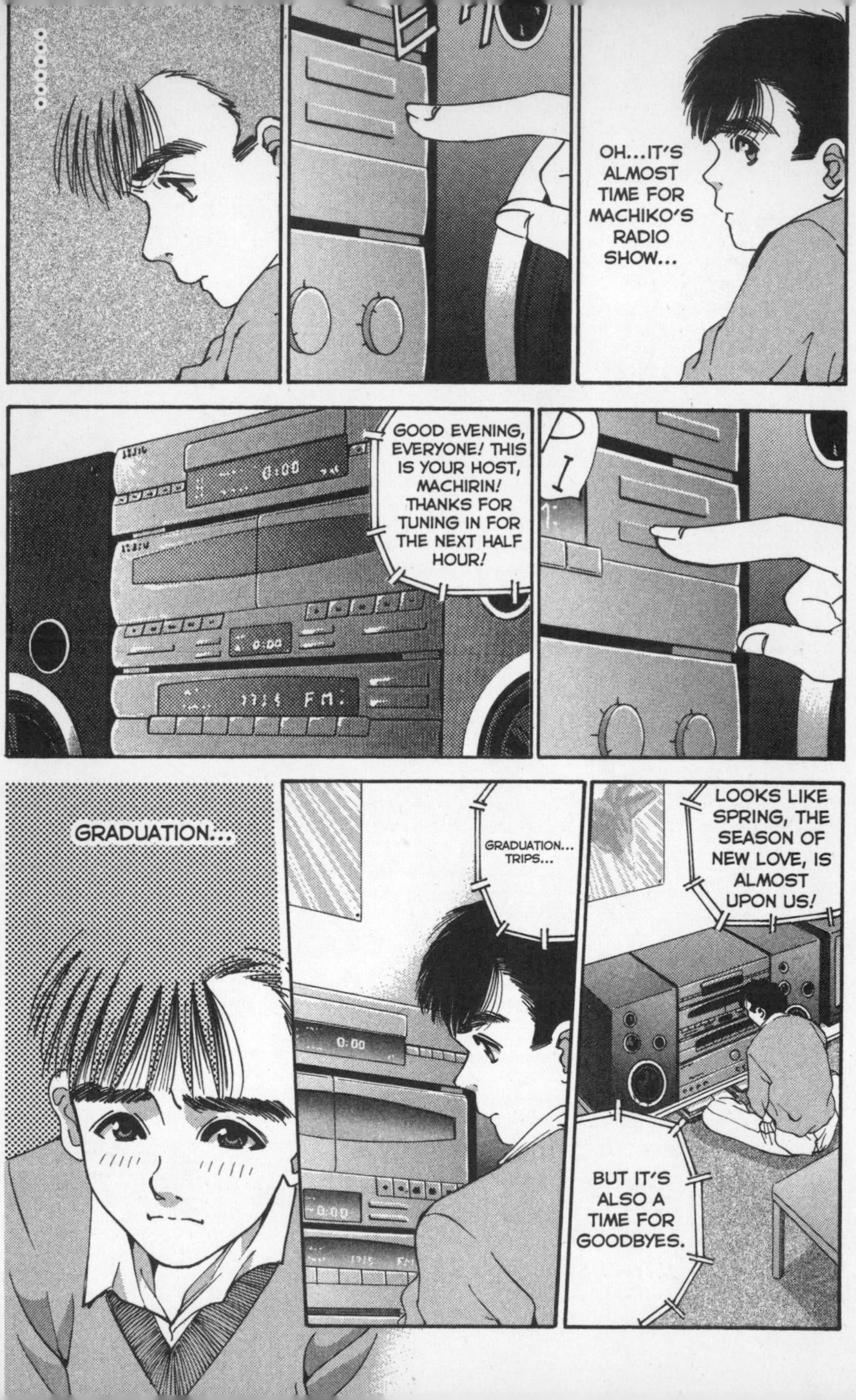

OH...IT'S ALMOST TIME FOR MACHIKO'S RADIO SHOW...
PI
GOOD EVENING, EVERYONE! THIS IS YOUR HOST, MACHIRIN! THANKS FOR TUNING IN FOR THE NEXT HALF HOUR!
LOOKS LIKE SPRING, THE SEASON OF NEW LOVE, IS ALMOST UPON US!
BUT IT'S ALSO A TIME FOR GOODBYES.
GRADUATION... TRIPS...
GRADUATION...

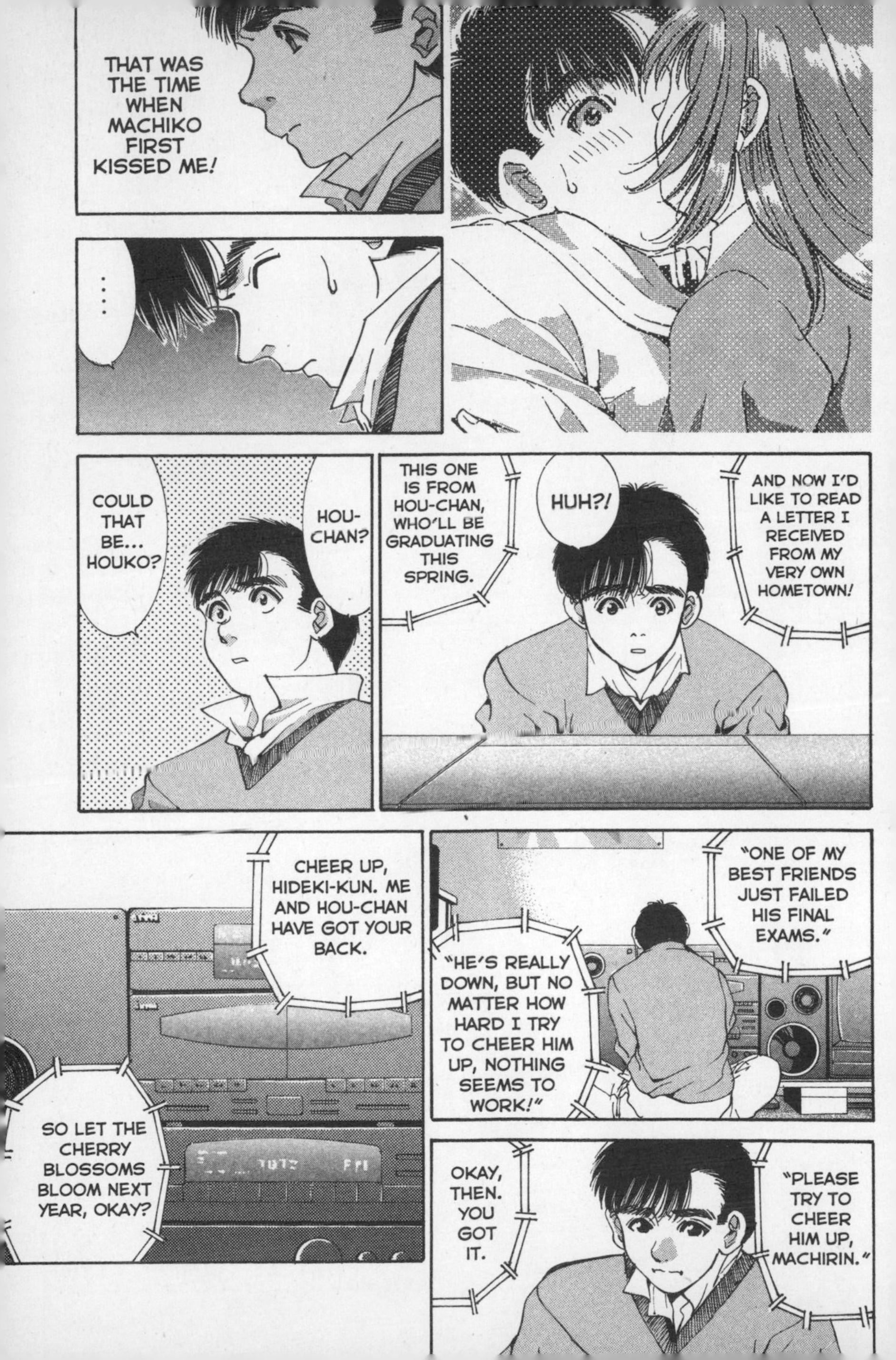
THAT WAS THE TIME WHEN MACHIKO FIRST KISSED ME!
.....
AND NOW I'D LIKE TO READ A LETTER I RECEIVED FROM MY VERY OWN HOMETOWN!
HUH?!
THIS ONE IS FROM HOU-CHAN, WHO'LL BE GRADUATING THIS SPRING.
HOU-CHAN?
COULD THAT BE... HOUKO?
"ONE OF MY BEST FRIENDS JUST FAILED HIS FINAL EXAMS."
"HE'S REALLY DOWN, BUT NO MATTER HOW HARD I TRY TO CHEER HIM UP, NOTHING SEEMS TO WORK!"
"PLEASE TRY TO CHEER HIM UP, MACHIRIN."
OKAY, THEN. YOU GOT IT.
CHEER UP, HIDEKI-KUN. ME AND HOU-CHAN HAVE GOT YOUR BACK.
SO LET THE CHERRY BLOSSOMS BLOOM NEXT YEAR, OKAY?

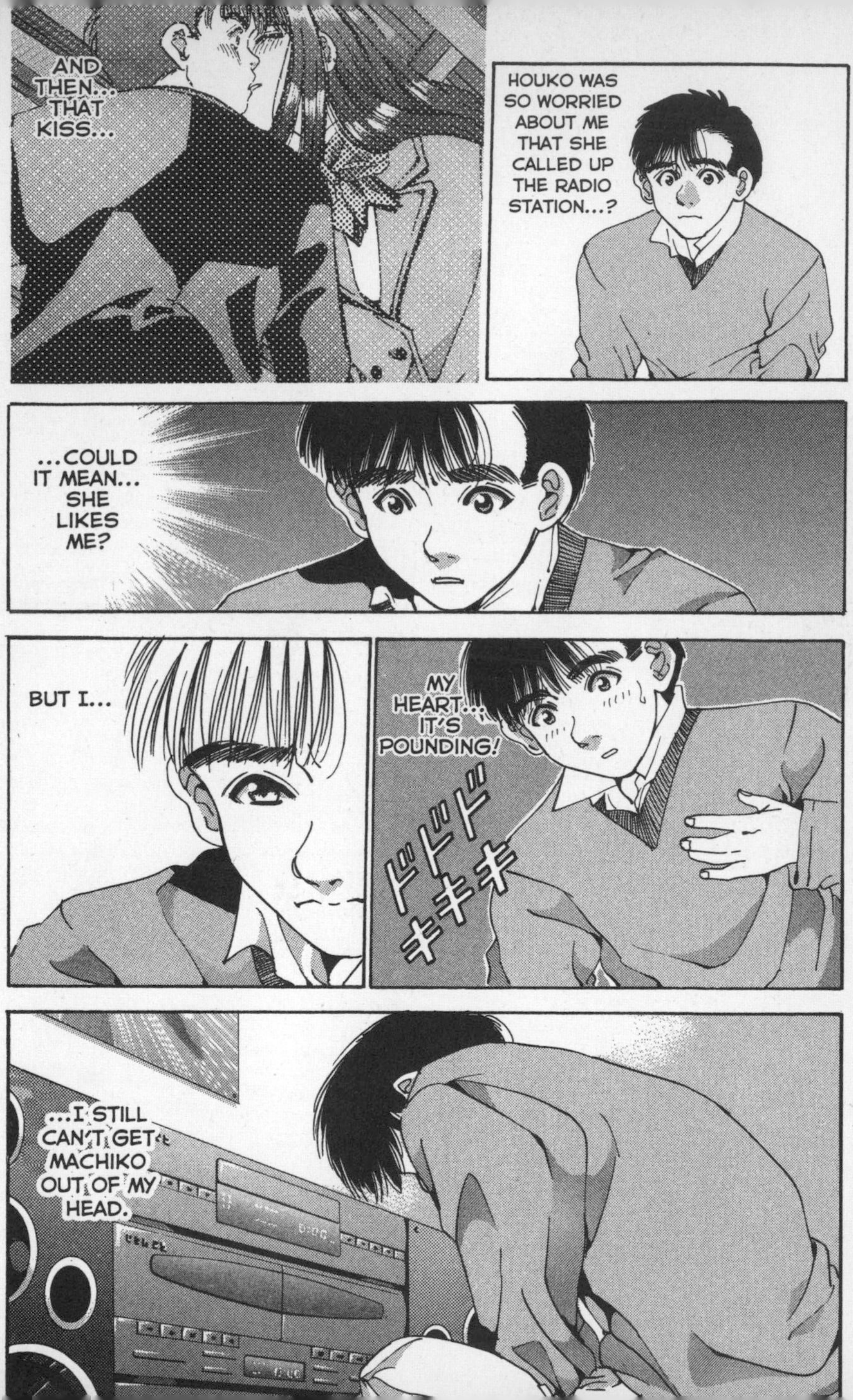
HOUKO WAS SO WORRIED ABOUT ME THAT SHE CALLED UP THE RADIO STATION...?
AND THEN... THAT KISS...
...COULD IT MEAN... SHE LIKES ME?
MY HEART... IT'S POUNDING!
ドキドキドキ
BUT I...
...I STILL CAN'T GET MACHIKO OUT OF MY HEAD.

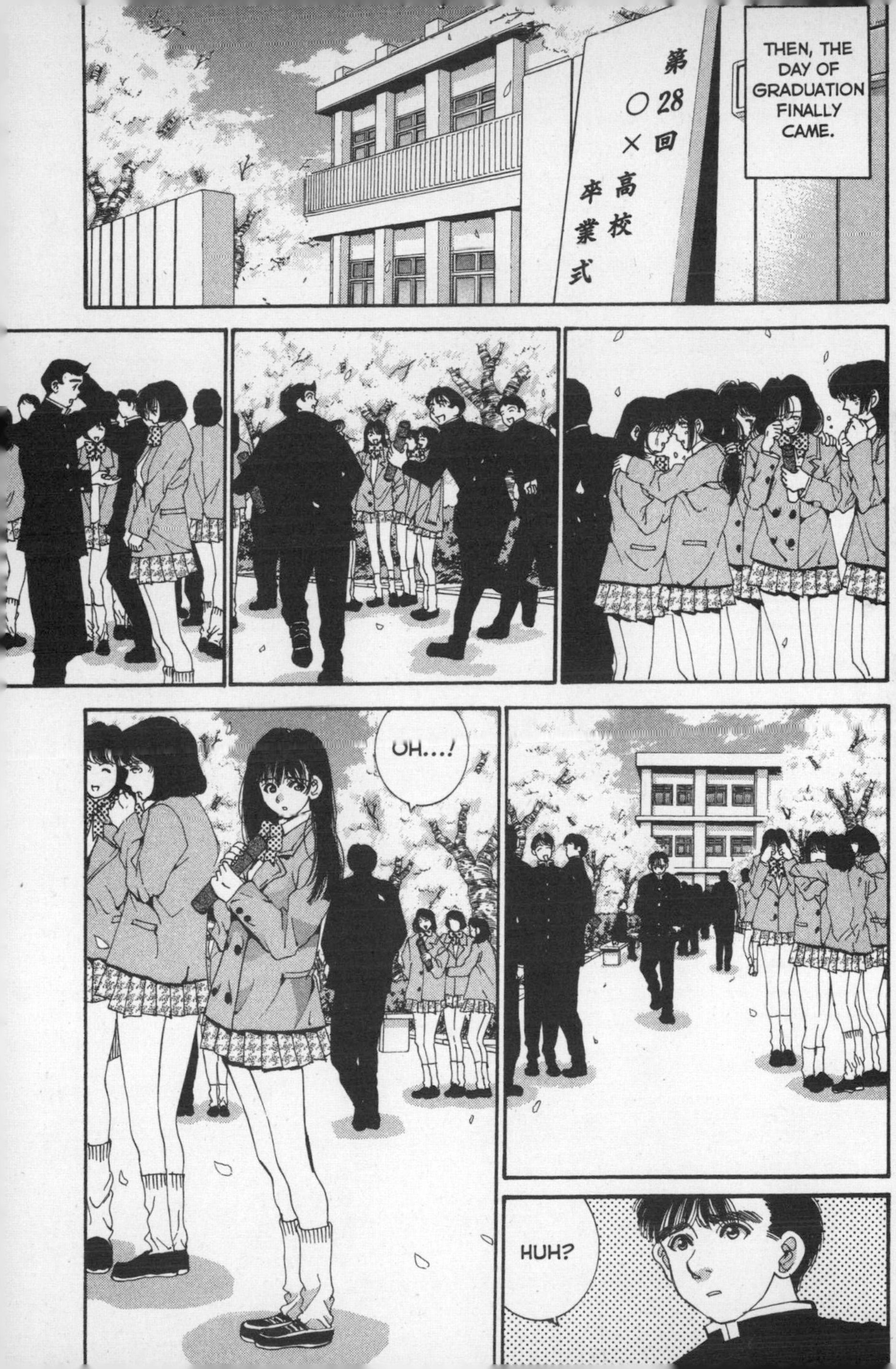
第28回○×高校卒業式
THEN, THE DAY OF GRADUATION FINALLY CAME.
HUH?
UH...!

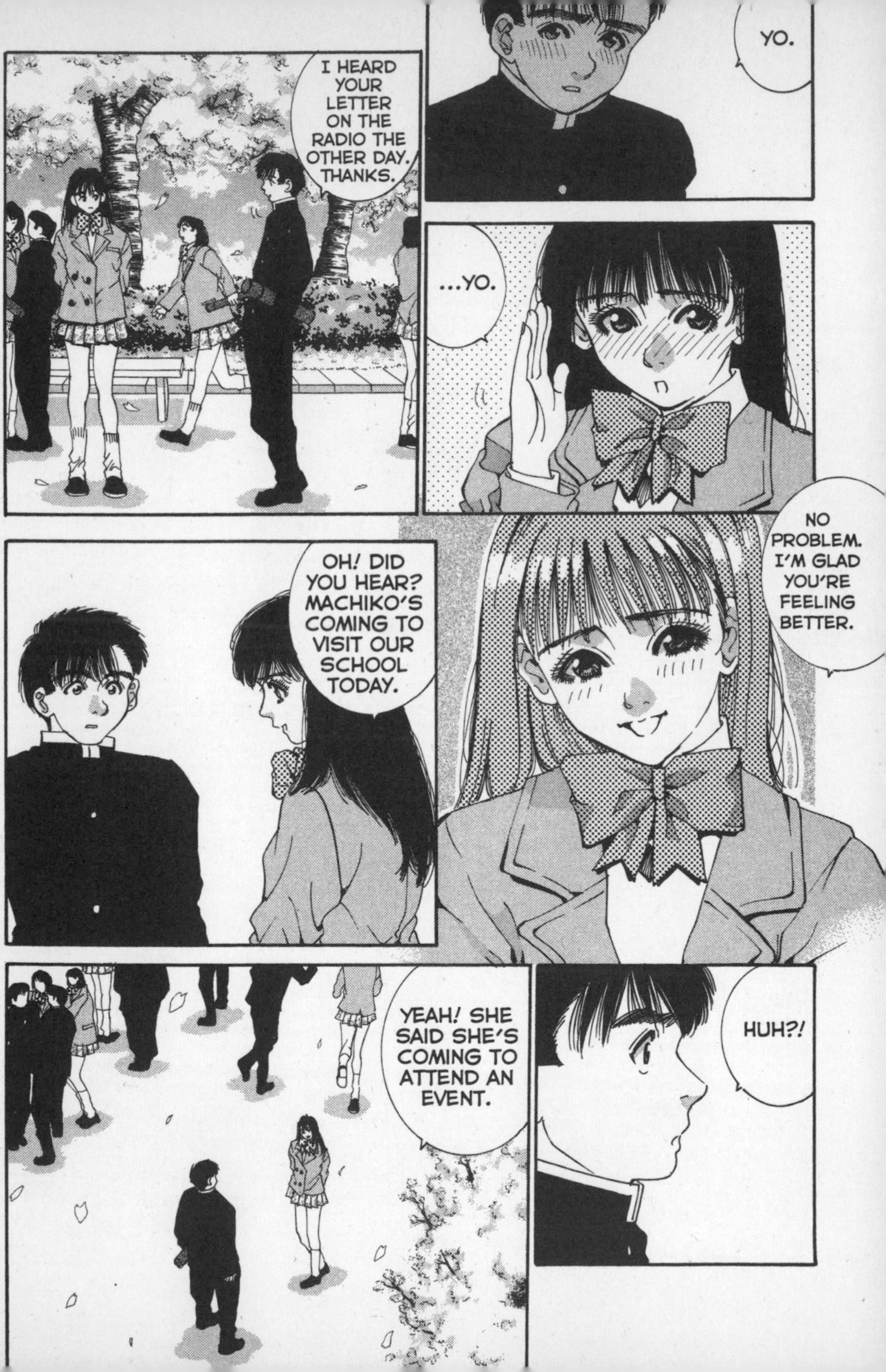
YO.
...YO.
I HEARD YOUR LETTER ON THE RADIO THE OTHER DAY. THANKS.
NO PROBLEM. I'M GLAD YOU'RE FEELING BETTER.
OH! DID YOU HEAR? MACHIKO'S COMING TO VISIT OUR SCHOOL TODAY.
HUH?!
YEAH! SHE SAID SHE'S COMING TO ATTEND AN EVENT.

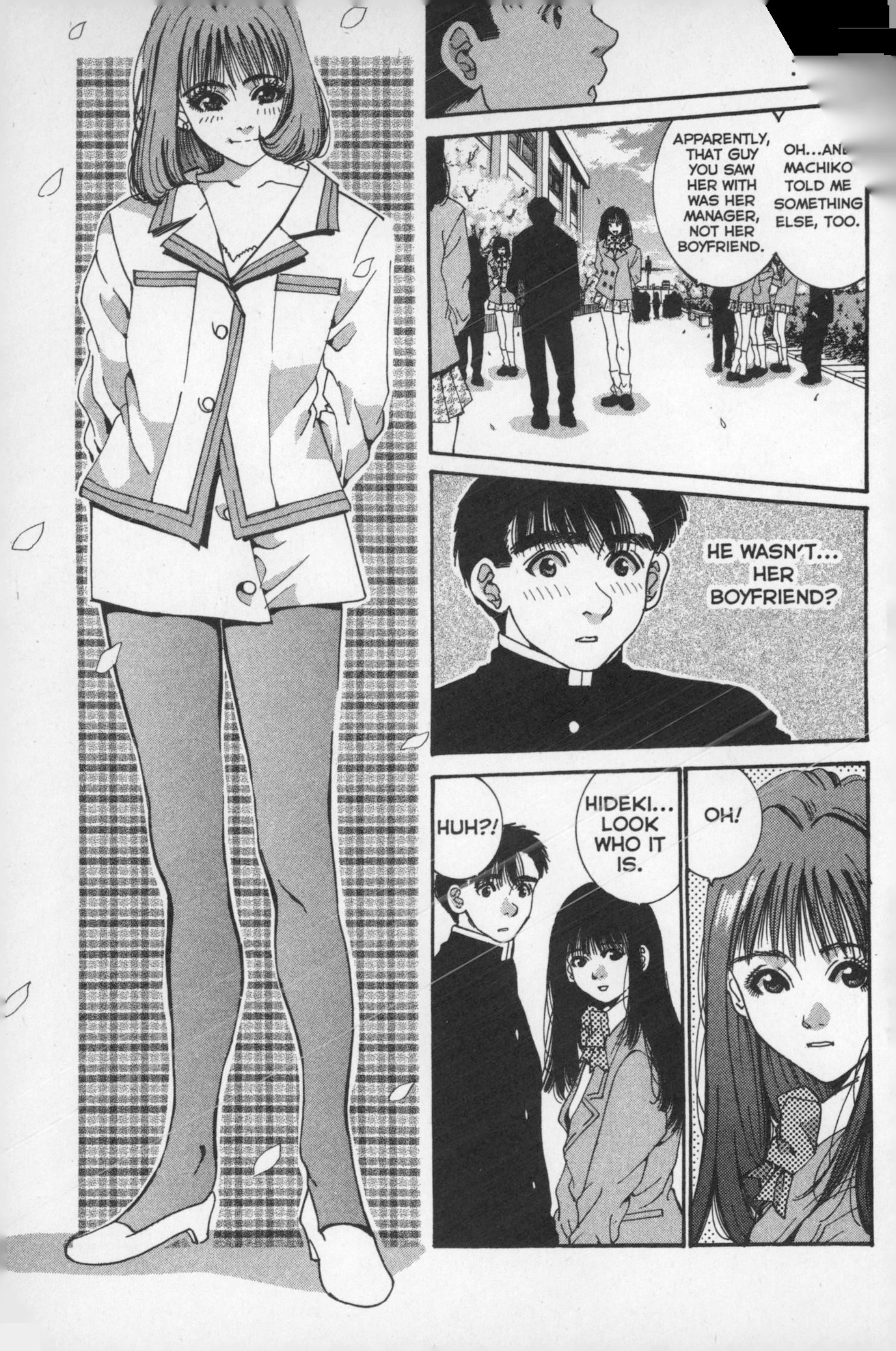
OH...AN
MACHIKO TOLD ME SOMETHING ELSE, TOO.
APPARENTLY, THAT GUY YOU SAW HER WITH WAS HER MANAGER, NOT HER BOYFRIEND.
HE WASN'T... HER BOYFRIEND?
OH!
HIDEKI... LOOK WHO IT IS.
HUH?!

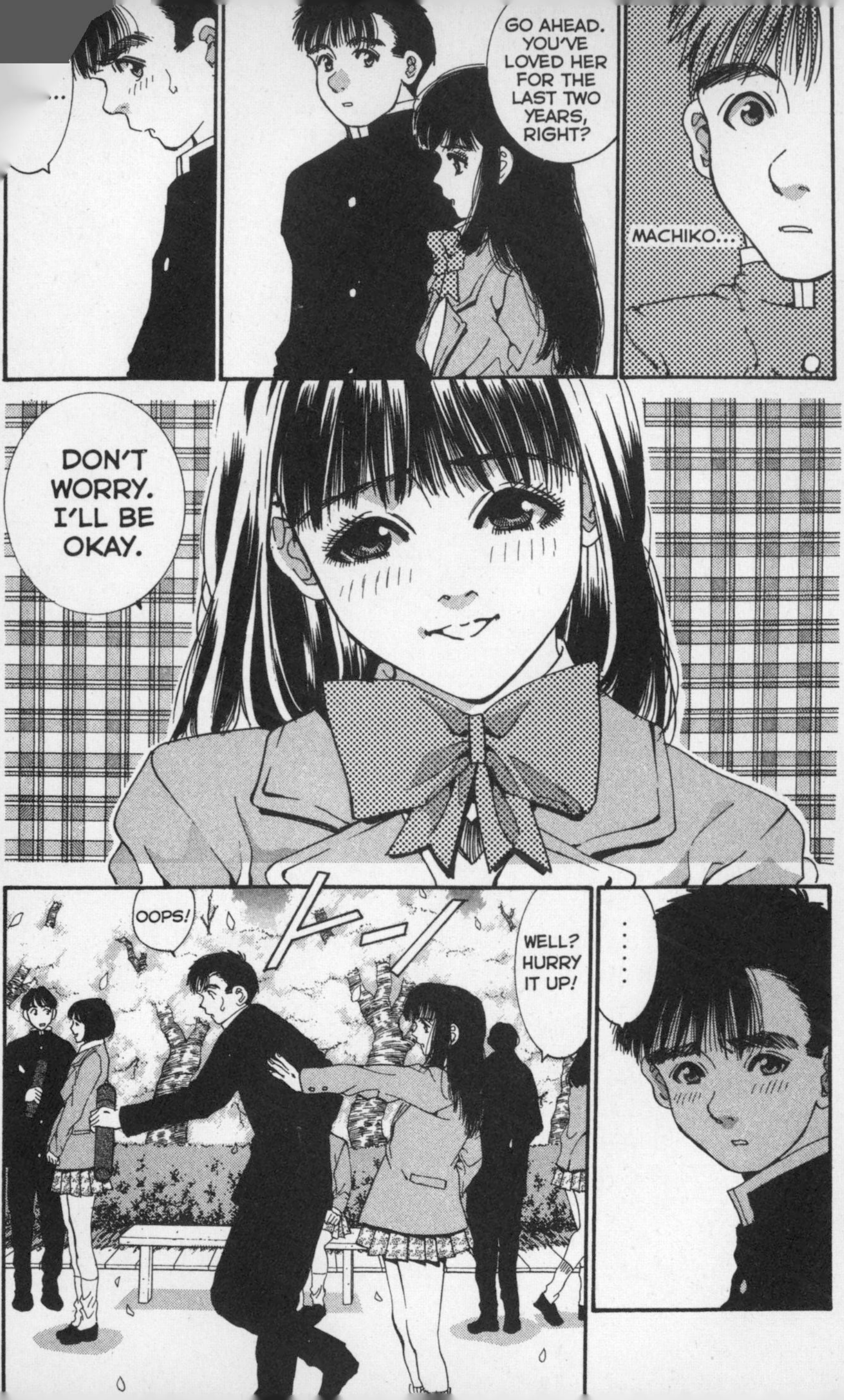
MACHIKO...
GO AHEAD. YOU'VE LOVED HER FOR THE LAST TWO YEARS, RIGHT?
...
DON'T WORRY. I'LL BE OKAY.
......
WELL? HURRY IT UP!
OOPS!

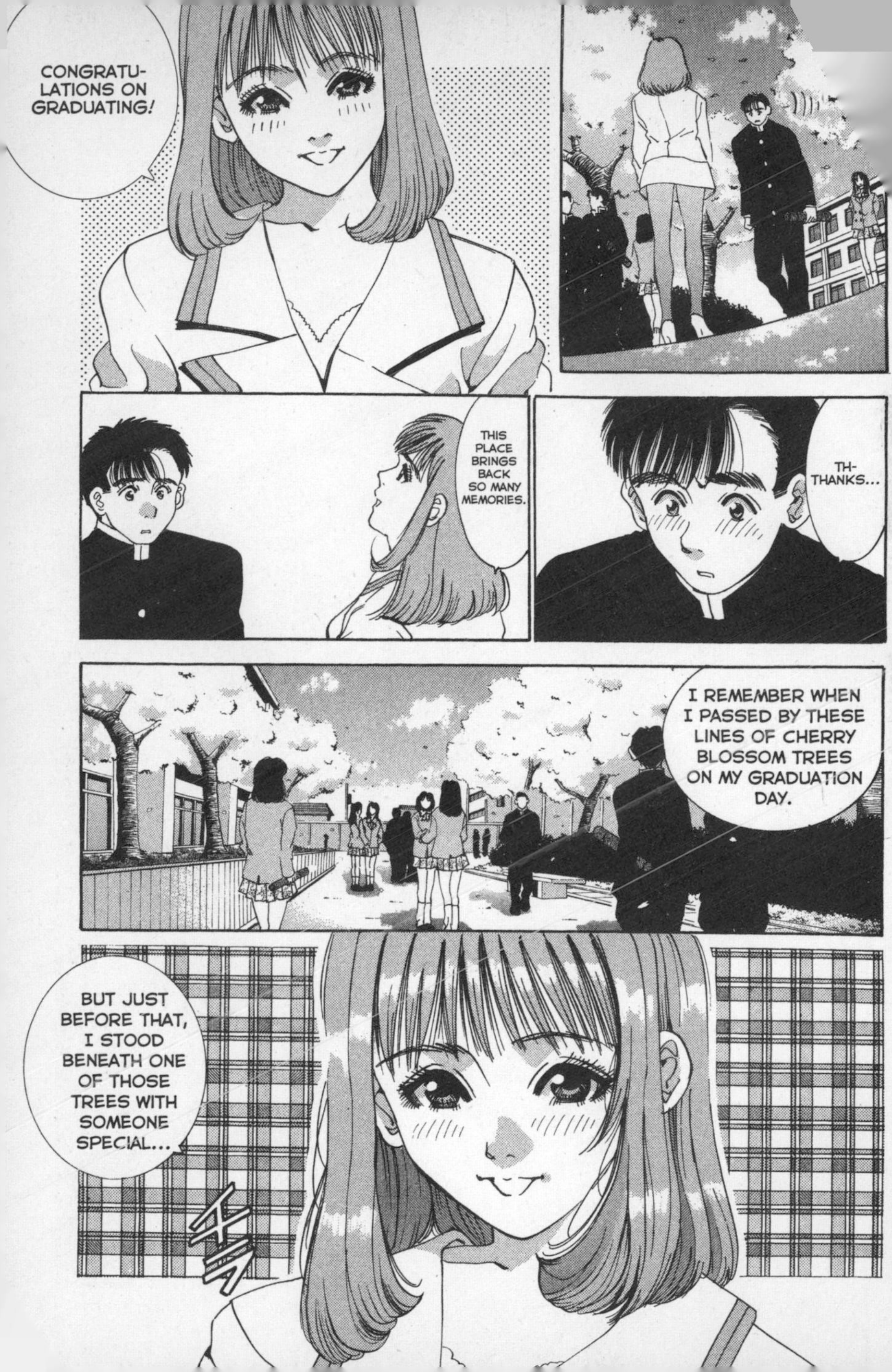
CONGRATULATIONS ON GRADUATING!
TH-THANKS...
THIS PLACE BRINGS BACK SO MANY MEMORIES.
I REMEMBER WHEN I PASSED BY THESE LINES OF CHERRY BLOSSOM TREES ON MY GRADUATION DAY.
BUT JUST BEFORE THAT, I STOOD BENEATH ONE OF THOSE TREES WITH SOMEONE SPECIAL...

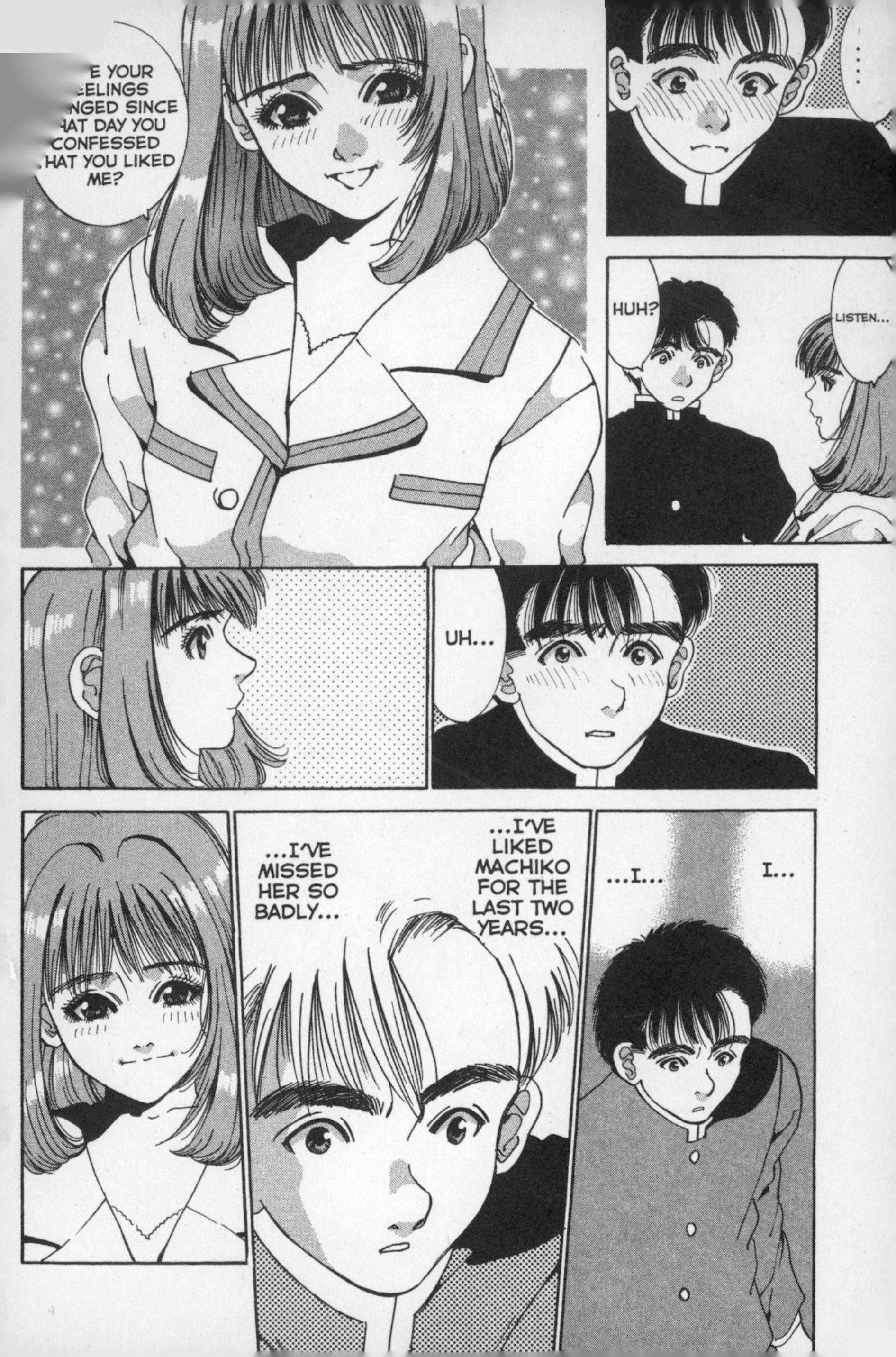

...
LISTEN...
HUH?
E YOUR EELINGS NGED SINCE HAT DAY YOU CONFESSED HAT YOU LIKED ME?
UH...
I...
...I...
...I'VE LIKED MACHIKO FOR THE LAST TWO YEARS...
...I'VE MISSED HER SO BADLY...

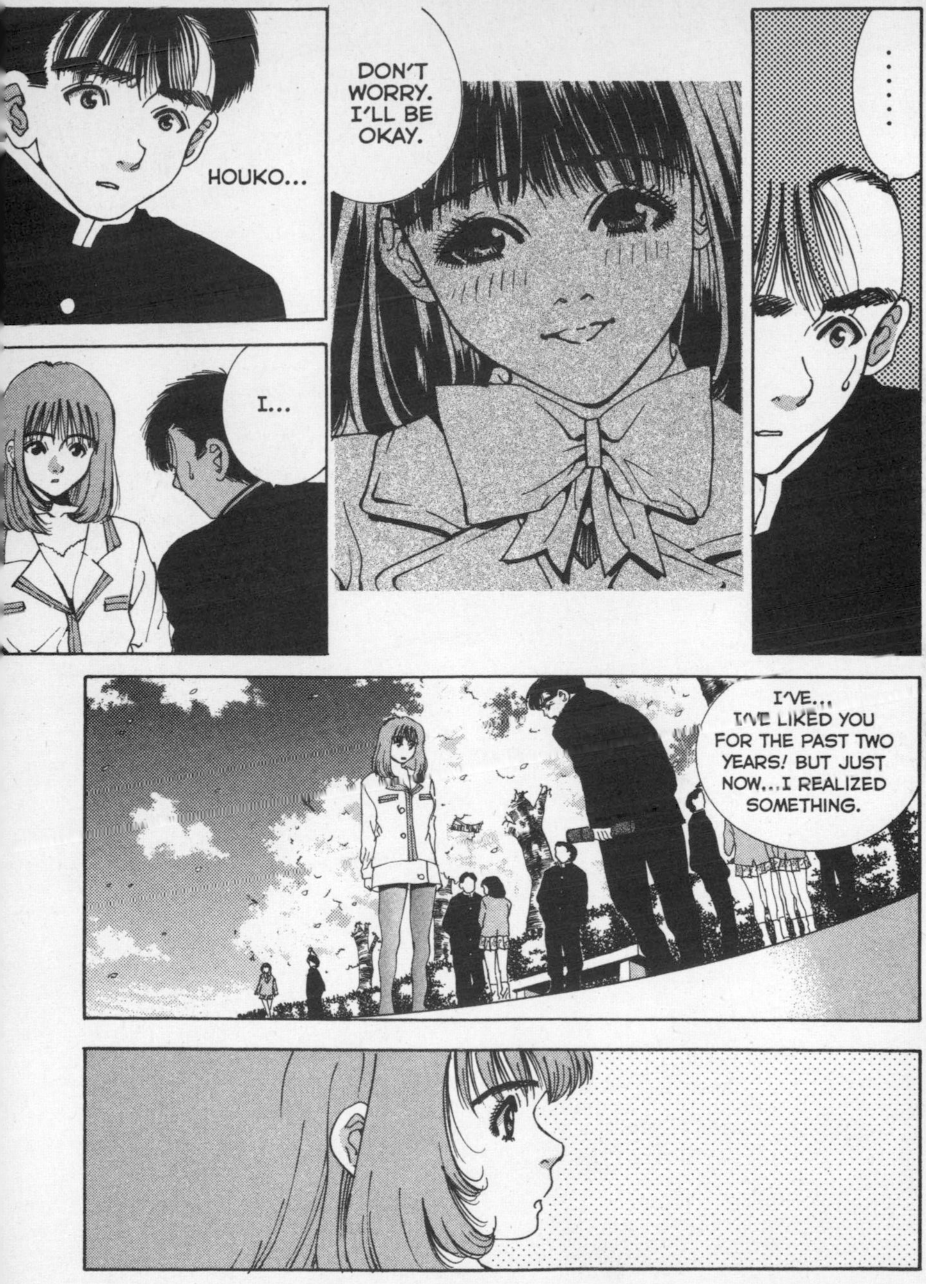
......
DON'T WORRY. I'LL BE OKAY.
HOUKO...
I...
I'VE... I'VE LIKED YOU FOR THE PAST TWO YEARS! BUT JUST NOW...I REALIZED SOMETHING.

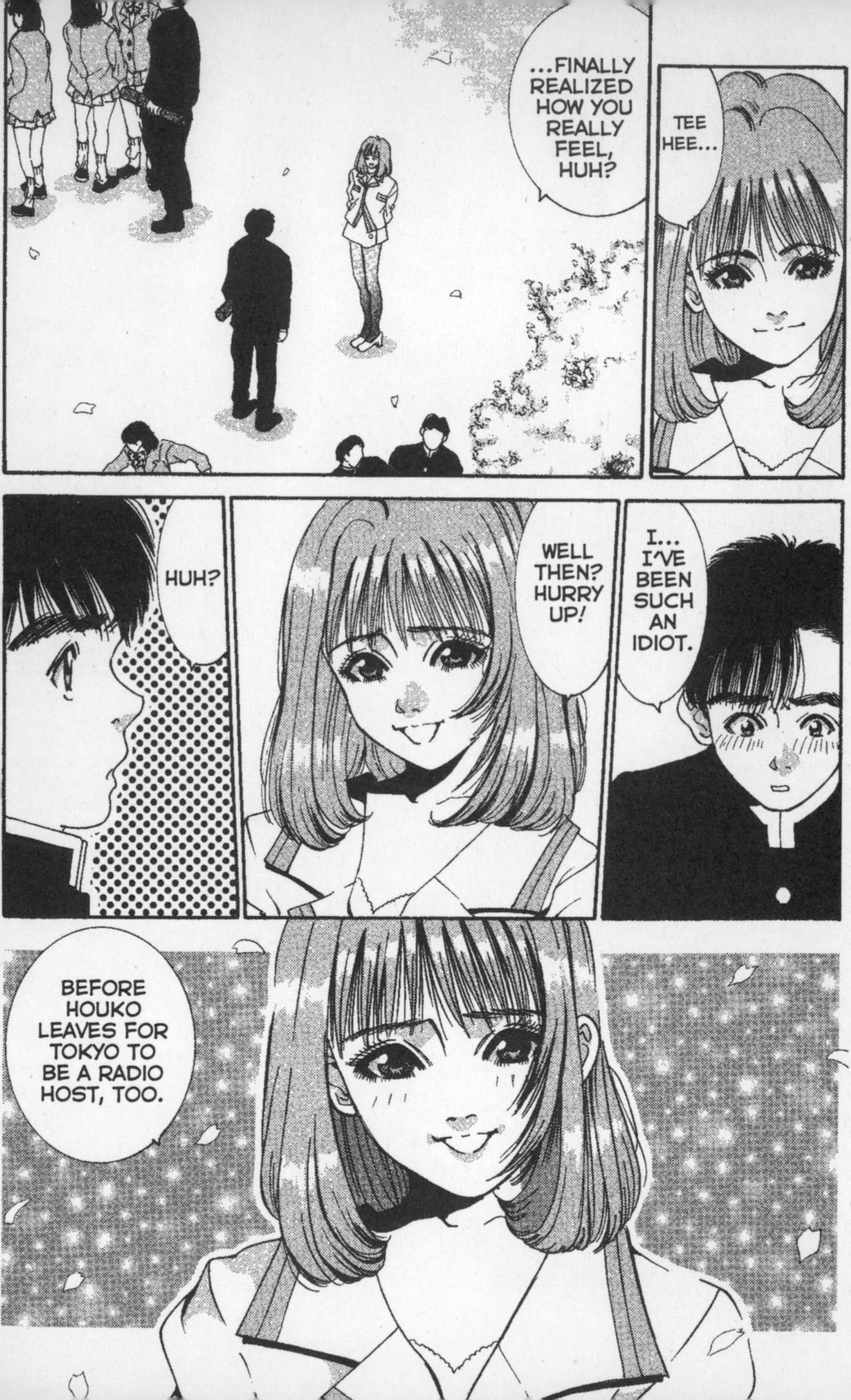
TEE HEE...
...FINALLY REALIZED HOW YOU REALLY FEEL, HUH?
I... I'VE BEEN SUCH AN IDIOT.
WELL THEN? HURRY UP!
HUH?
BEFORE HOUKO LEAVES FOR TOKYO TO BE A RADIO HOST, TOO.

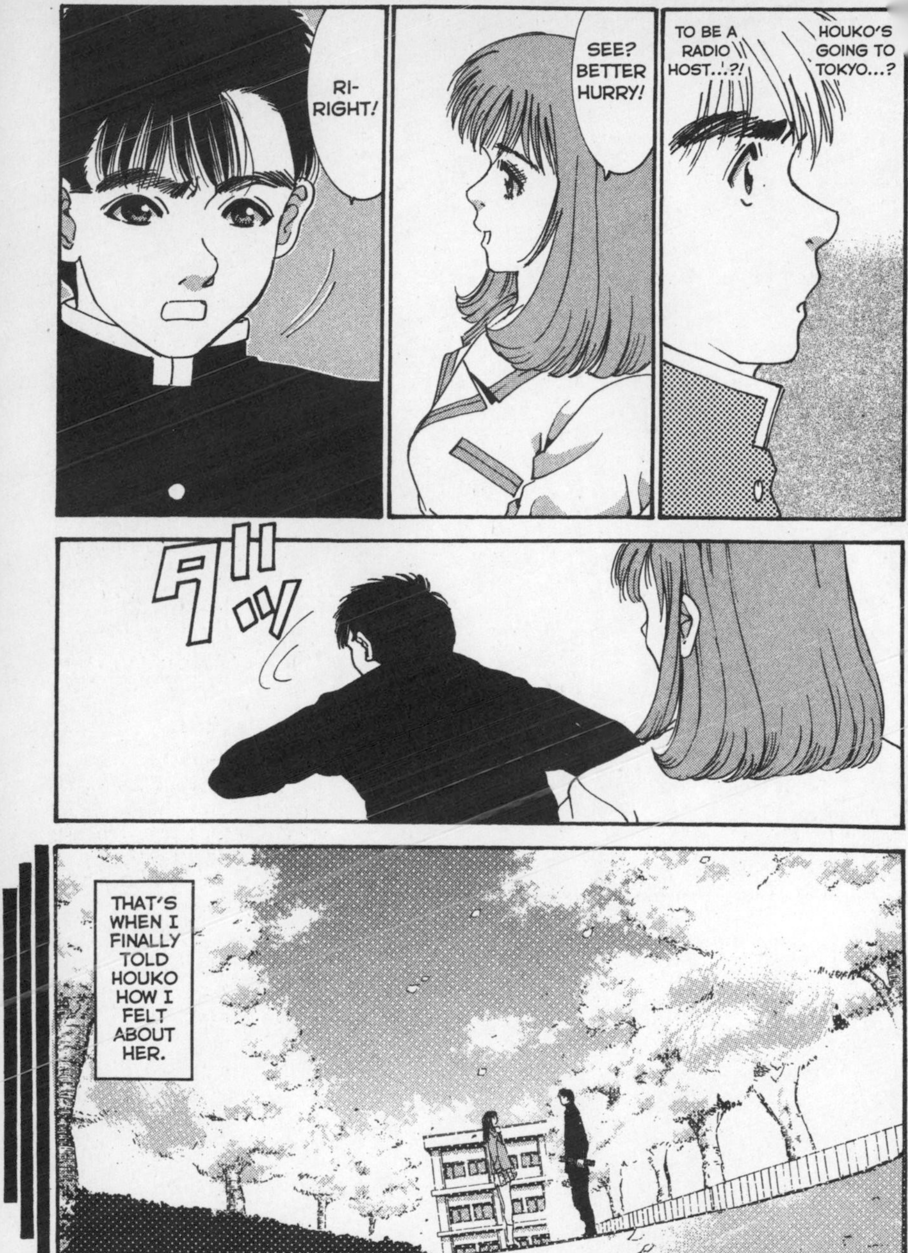
HOUKO'S GOING TO TOKYO...?
TO BE A RADIO HOST...!?!
SEE? BETTER HURRY!
RI- RIGHT!
ダッ
THAT'S WHEN I FINALLY TOLD HOUKO HOW I FELT ABOUT HER.

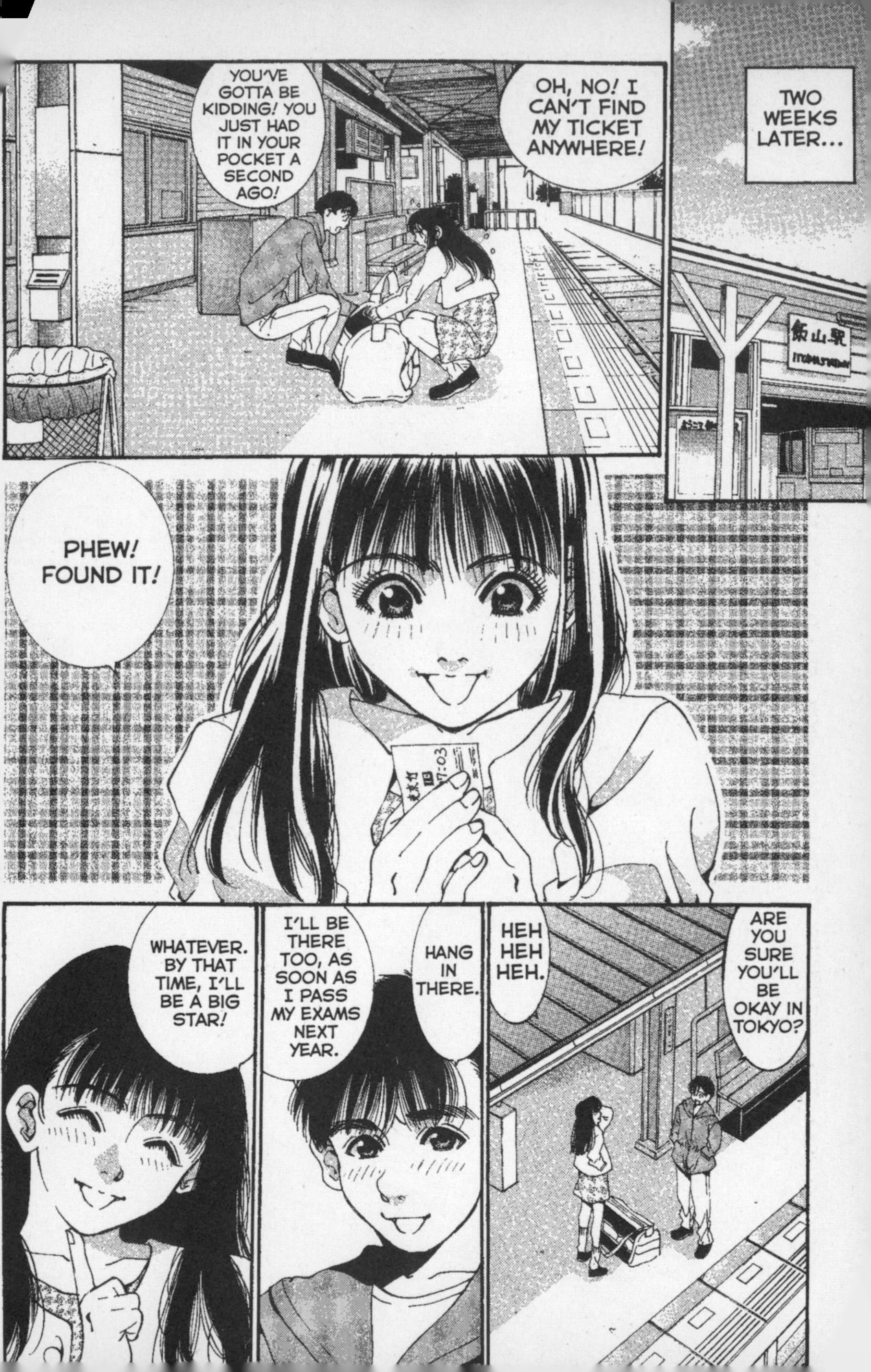
TWO WEEKS LATER...
飯山駅
OH, NO! I CAN'T FIND MY TICKET ANYWHERE!
YOU'VE GOTTA BE KIDDING! YOU JUST HAD IT IN YOUR POCKET A SECOND AGO!
PHEW! FOUND IT!
ARE YOU SURE YOU'LL BE OKAY IN TOKYO?
HEH HEH HEH.
HANG IN THERE.
I'LL BE THERE TOO, AS SOON AS I PASS MY EXAMS NEXT YEAR.
WHATEVER. BY THAT TIME, I'LL BE A BIG STAR!

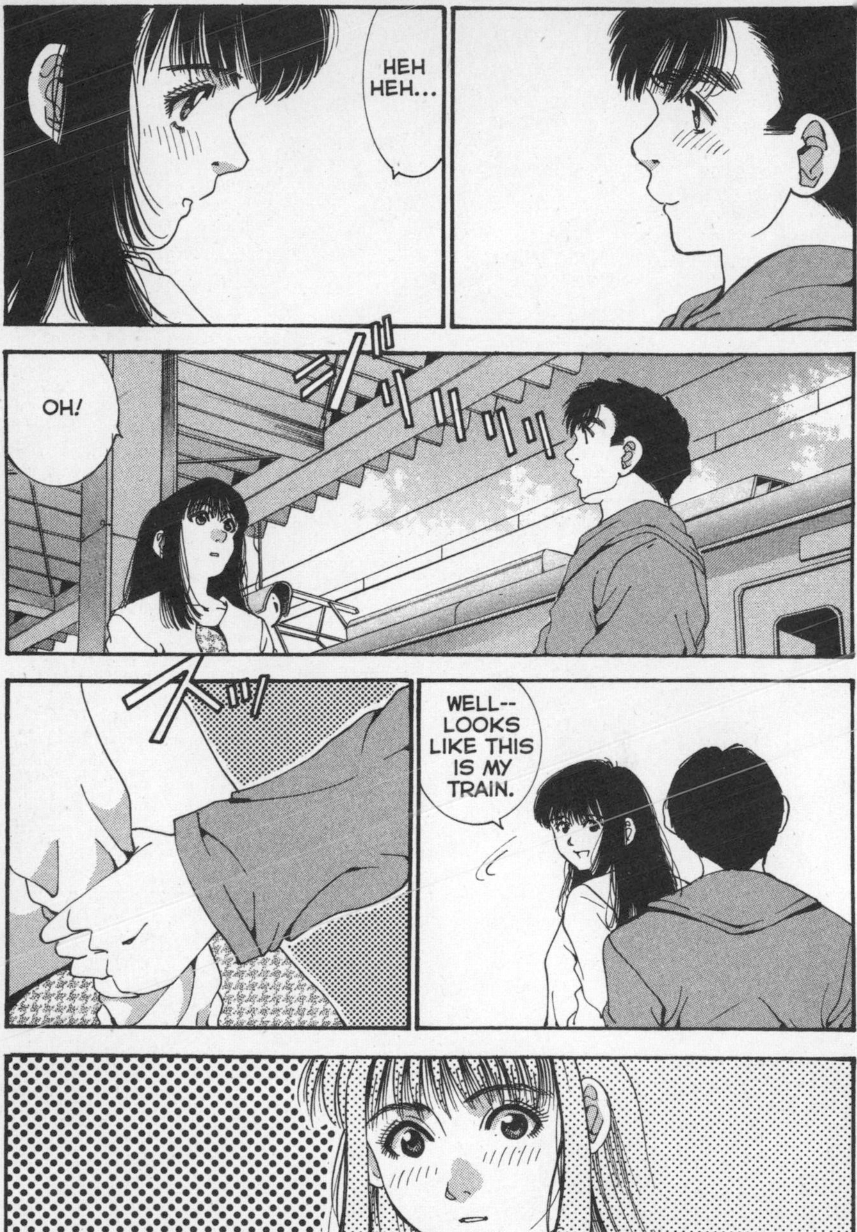
HEH HEH...
ジリリリリ
OH!
WELL-- LOOKS LIKE THIS IS MY TRAIN.
スッ

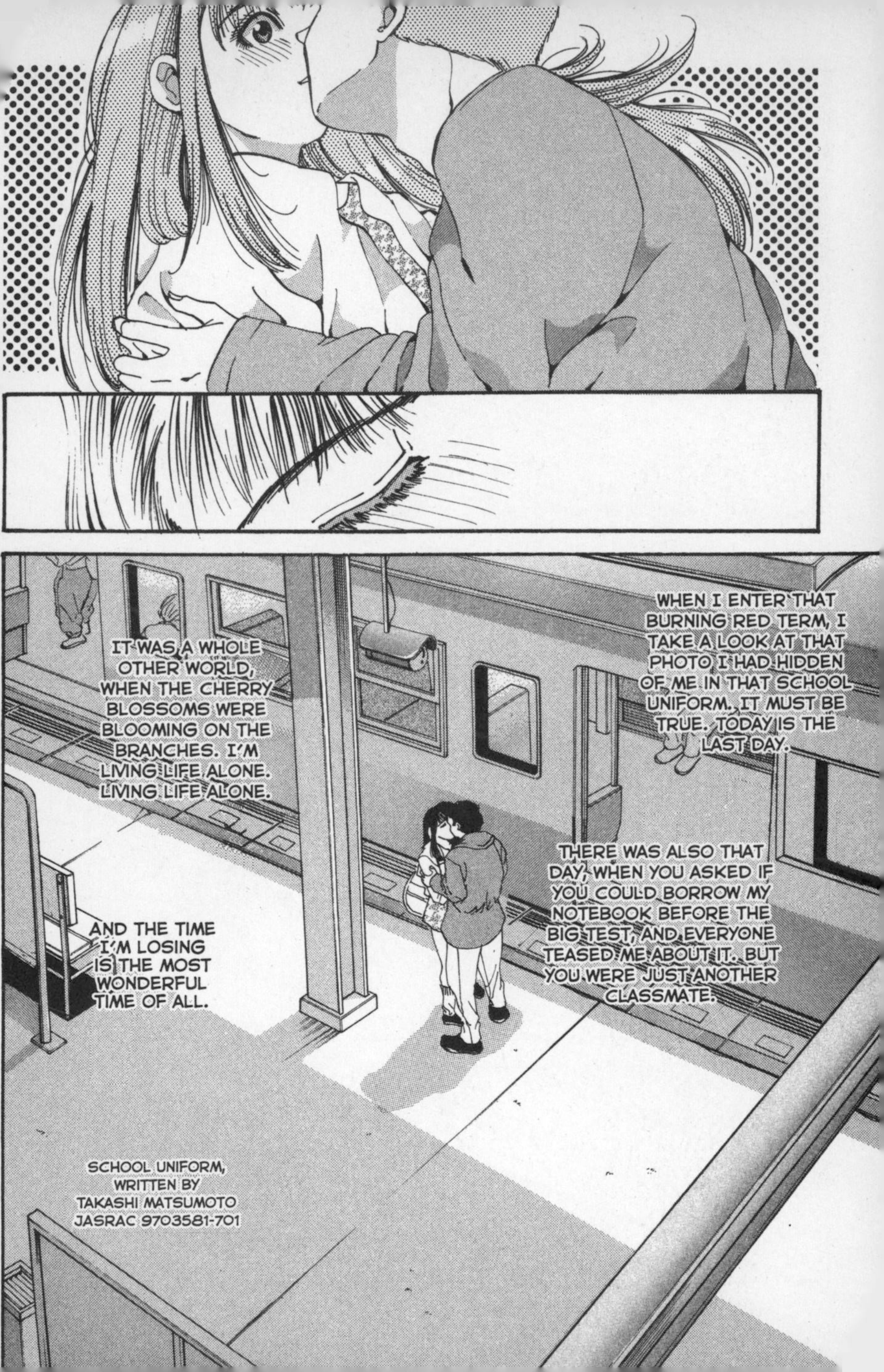
WHEN I ENTER THAT BURNING RED TERM, I TAKE A LOOK AT THAT PHOTO I HAD HIDDEN OF ME IN THAT SCHOOL UNIFORM. IT MUST BE TRUE. TODAY IS THE LAST DAY.
IT WAS A WHOLE OTHER WORLD, WHEN THE CHERRY BLOSSOMS WERE BLOOMING ON THE BRANCHES. I'M LIVING LIFE ALONE. LIVING LIFE ALONE.
THERE WAS ALSO THAT DAY, WHEN YOU ASKED IF YOU COULD BORROW MY NOTEBOOK BEFORE THE BIG TEST, AND EVERYONE TEASED ME ABOUT IT. BUT YOU WERE JUST ANOTHER CLASSMATE.
AND THE TIME I'M LOSING IS THE MOST WONDERFUL TIME OF ALL.
SCHOOL UNIFORM, WRITTEN BY TAKASHI MATSUMOTO JASRAC 9703581-701

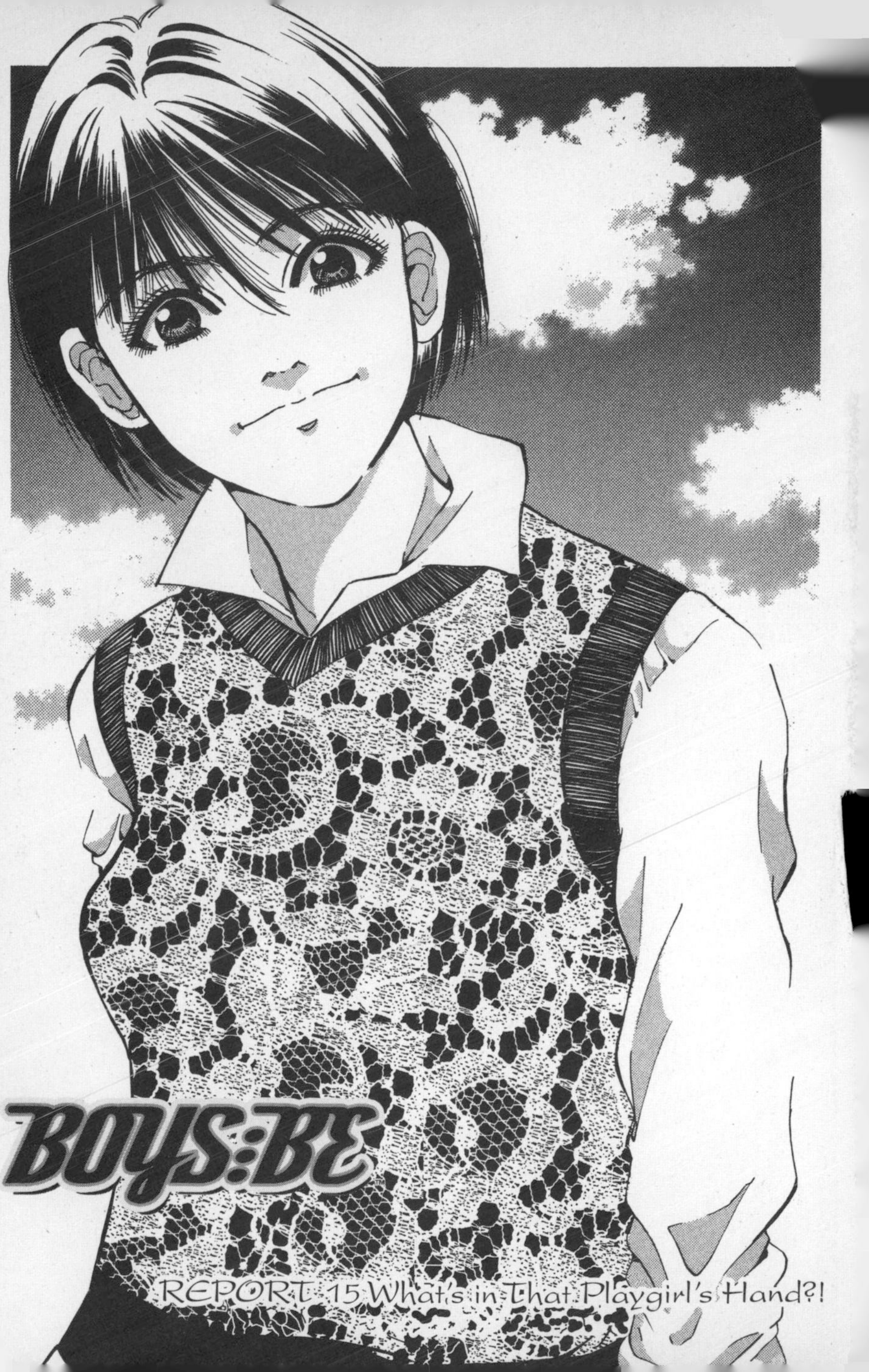
BOYS BE
REPORT 15 What's in That Playgirl's Hand?!

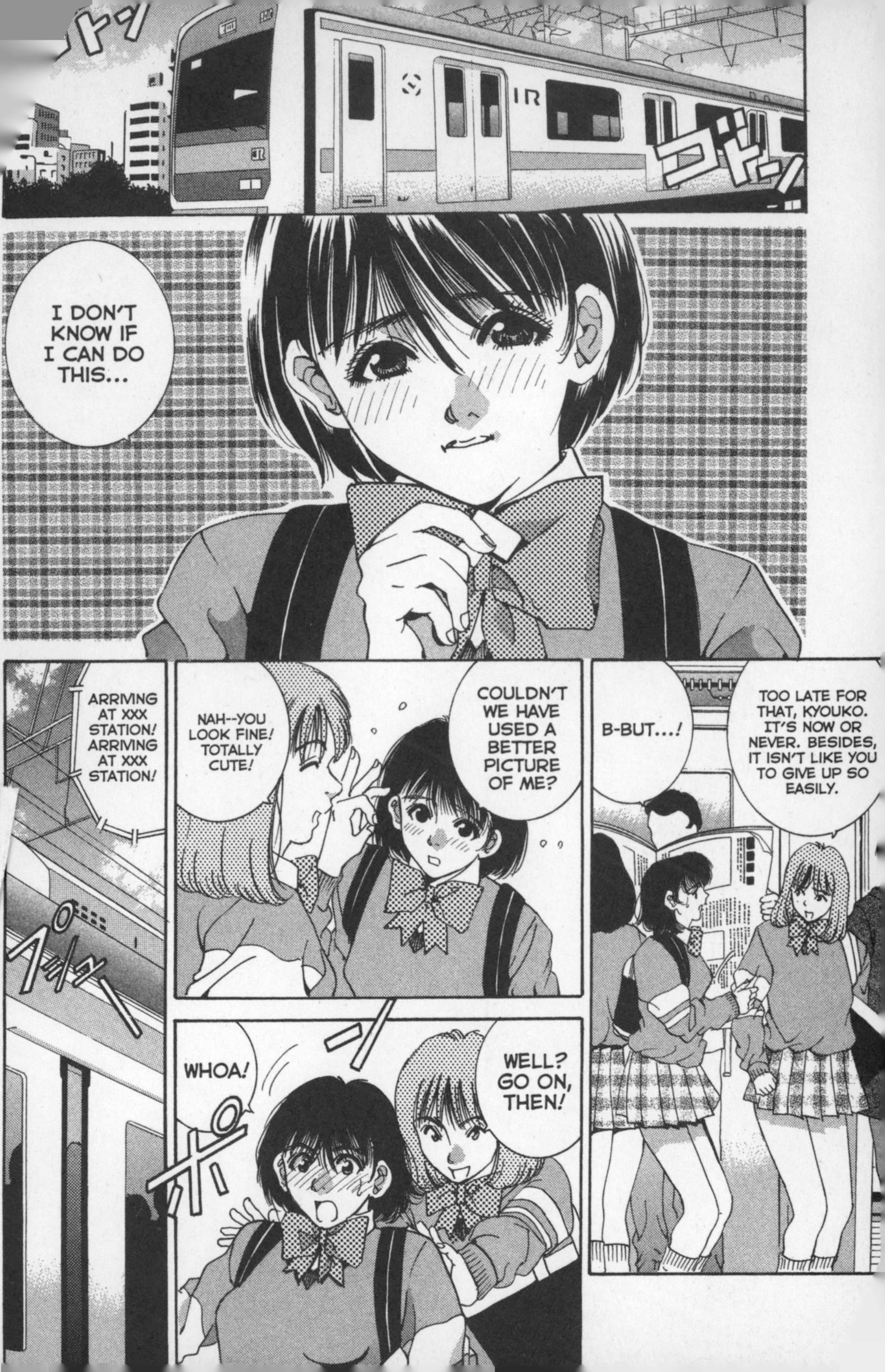
I DON'T KNOW IF I CAN DO THIS...
TOO LATE FOR THAT, KYOUKO. IT'S NOW OR NEVER. BESIDES, IT ISN'T LIKE YOU TO GIVE UP SO EASILY.
B-BUT...!
COULDN'T WE HAVE USED A BETTER PICTURE OF ME?
NAH--YOU LOOK FINE! TOTALLY CUTE!
WELL? GO ON, THEN!
WHOA!
ARRIVING AT XXX STATION! ARRIVING AT XXX STATION!

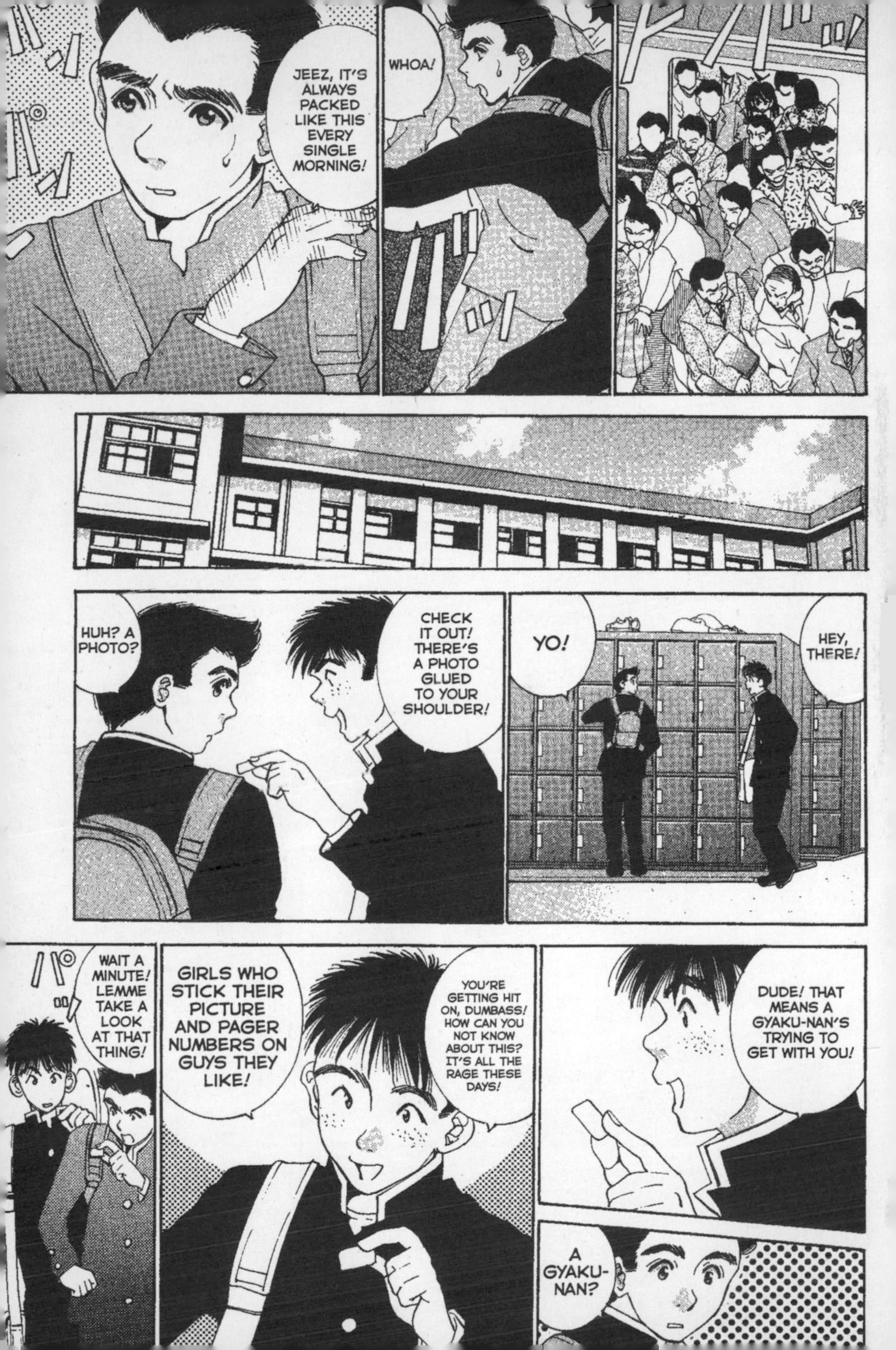
WHOA!
JEEZ, IT'S ALWAYS PACKED LIKE THIS EVERY SINGLE MORNING!
HEY, THERE!
YO!
CHECK IT OUT! THERE'S A PHOTO GLUED TO YOUR SHOULDER!
HUH? A PHOTO?
DUDE! THAT MEANS A GYAKU-NAN'S TRYING TO GET WITH YOU!
A GYAKU-NAN?
YOU'RE GETTING HIT ON, DUMBASS! HOW CAN YOU NOT KNOW ABOUT THIS? IT'S ALL THE RAGE THESE DAYS!
GIRLS WHO STICK THEIR PICTURE AND PAGER NUMBERS ON GUYS THEY LIKE!
WAIT A MINUTE! LEMME TAKE A LOOK AT THAT THING!

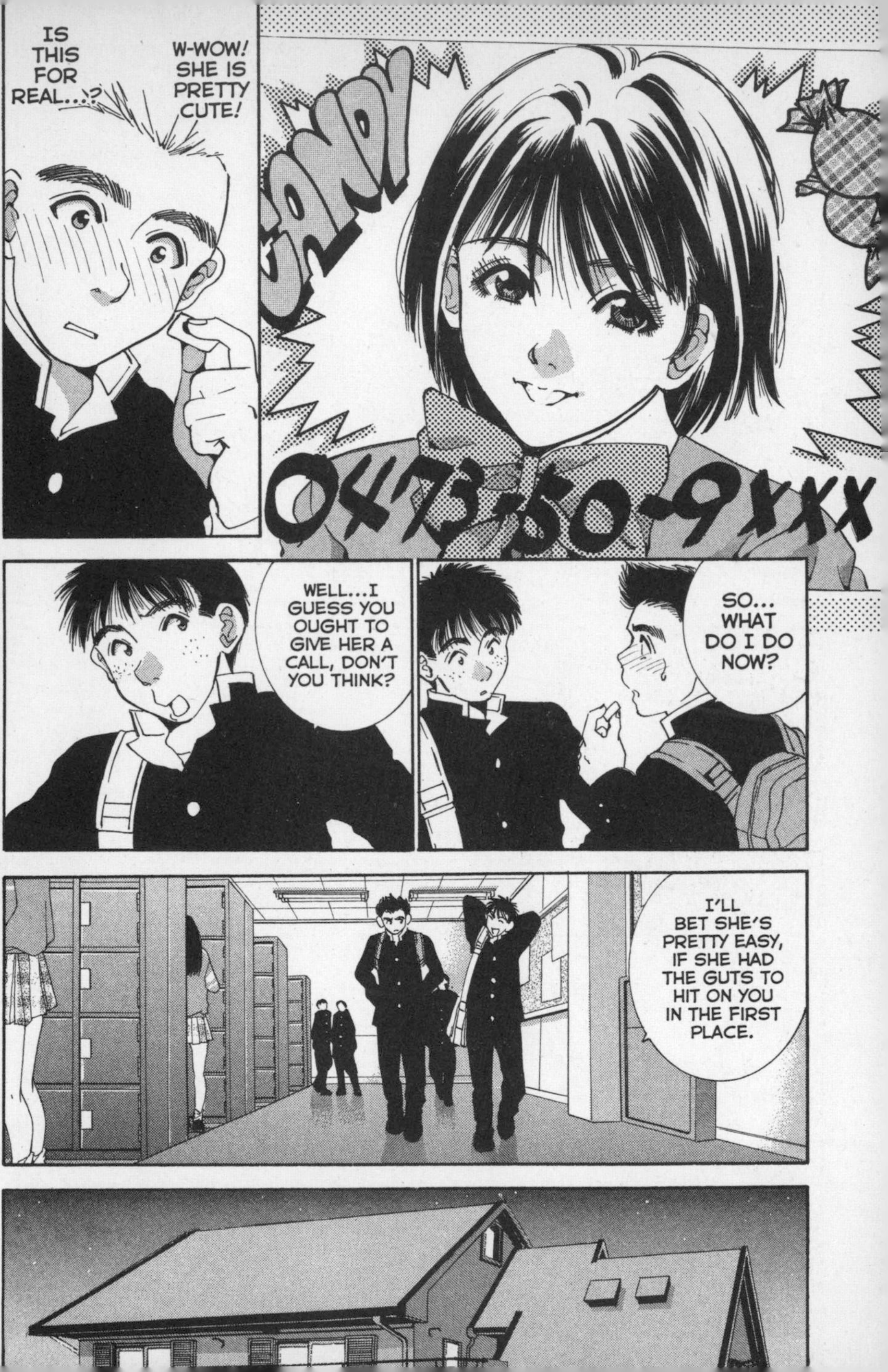
CANDY
0473-50-9XXX
W-WOW! SHE IS PRETTY CUTE!
IS THIS FOR REAL...?
SO... WHAT DO I DO NOW?
WELL...I GUESS YOU OUGHT TO GIVE HER A CALL, DON'T YOU THINK?
I'LL BET SHE'S PRETTY EASY, IF SHE HAD THE GUTS TO HIT ON YOU IN THE FIRST PLACE.

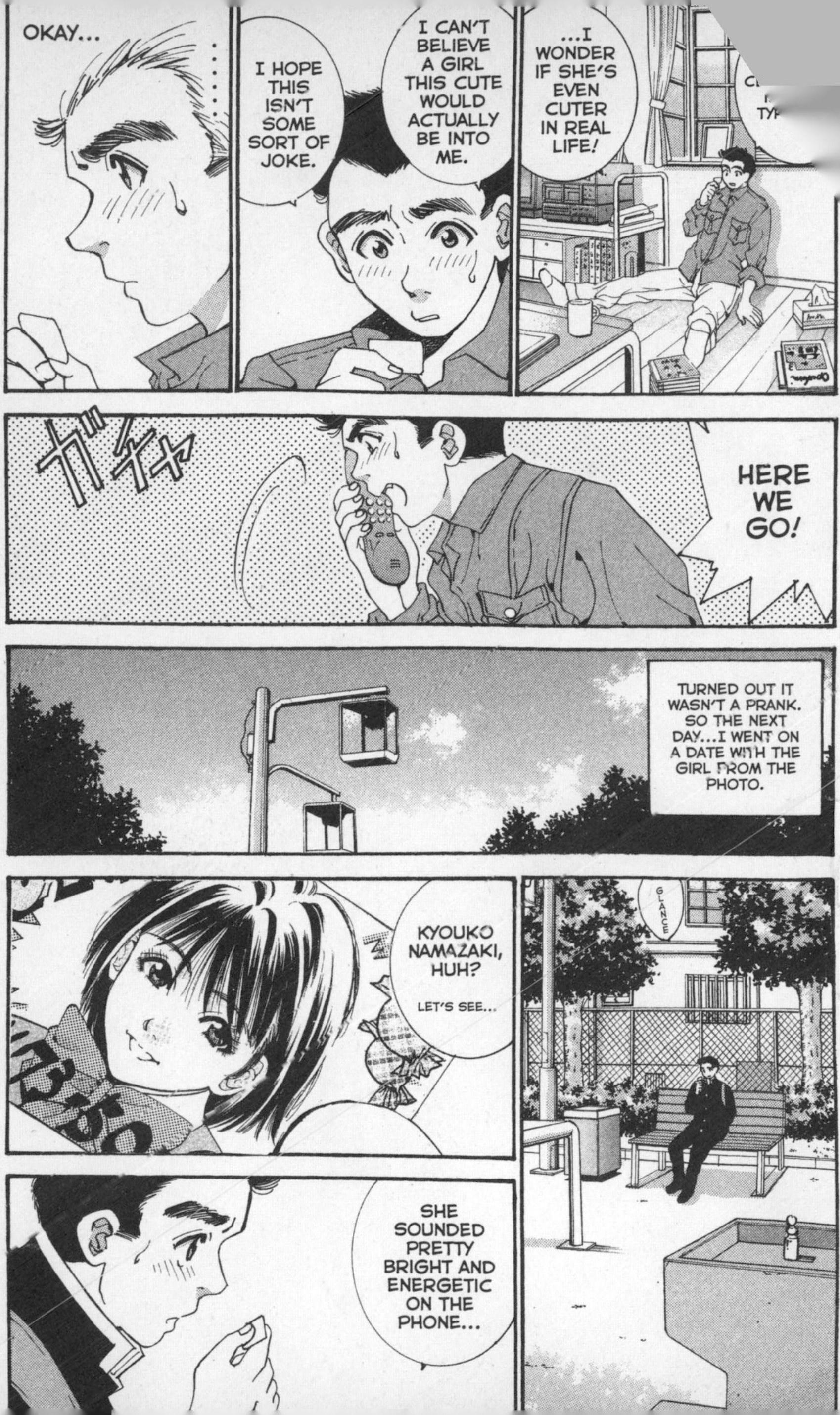
...I WONDER IF SHE'S EVEN CUTER IN REAL LIFE!
I CAN'T BELIEVE A GIRL THIS CUTE WOULD ACTUALLY BE INTO ME.
I HOPE THIS ISN'T SOME SORT OF JOKE.
OKAY...
HERE WE GO!
ガチャ
TURNED OUT IT WASN'T A PRANK. SO THE NEXT DAY...I WENT ON A DATE WITH THE GIRL FROM THE PHOTO.
GLANCE
KYOUKO NAMAZAKI, HUH?
LET'S SEE...
SHE SOUNDED PRETTY BRIGHT AND ENERGETIC ON THE PHONE...

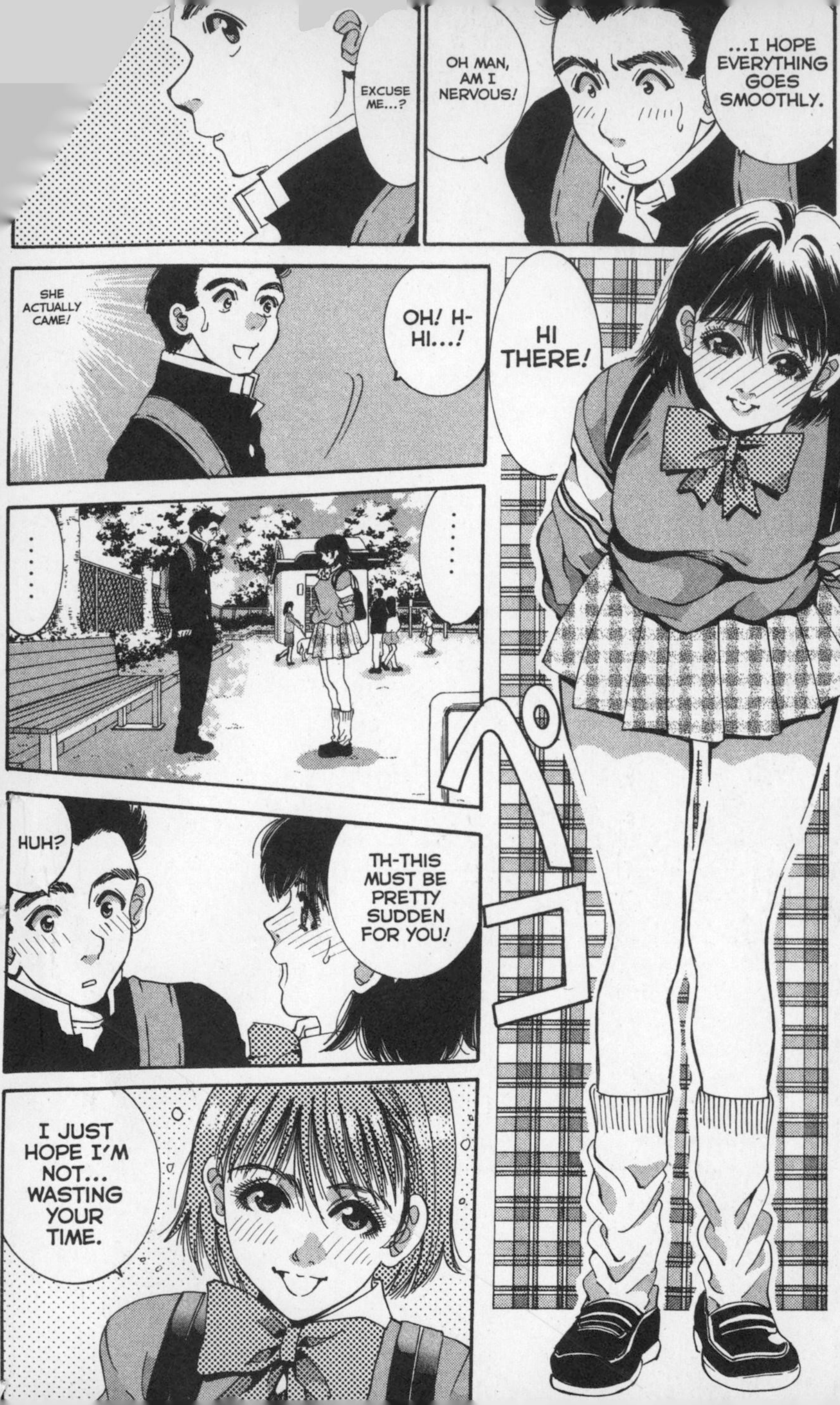

OH MAN, AM I NERVOUS!
...I HOPE EVERYTHING GOES SMOOTHLY.
EXCUSE ME...?
HI THERE!
ペコ
OH! H-HI...!
SHE ACTUALLY CAME!
......
......
TH-THIS MUST BE PRETTY SUDDEN FOR YOU!
HUH?
I JUST HOPE I'M NOT... WASTING YOUR TIME.

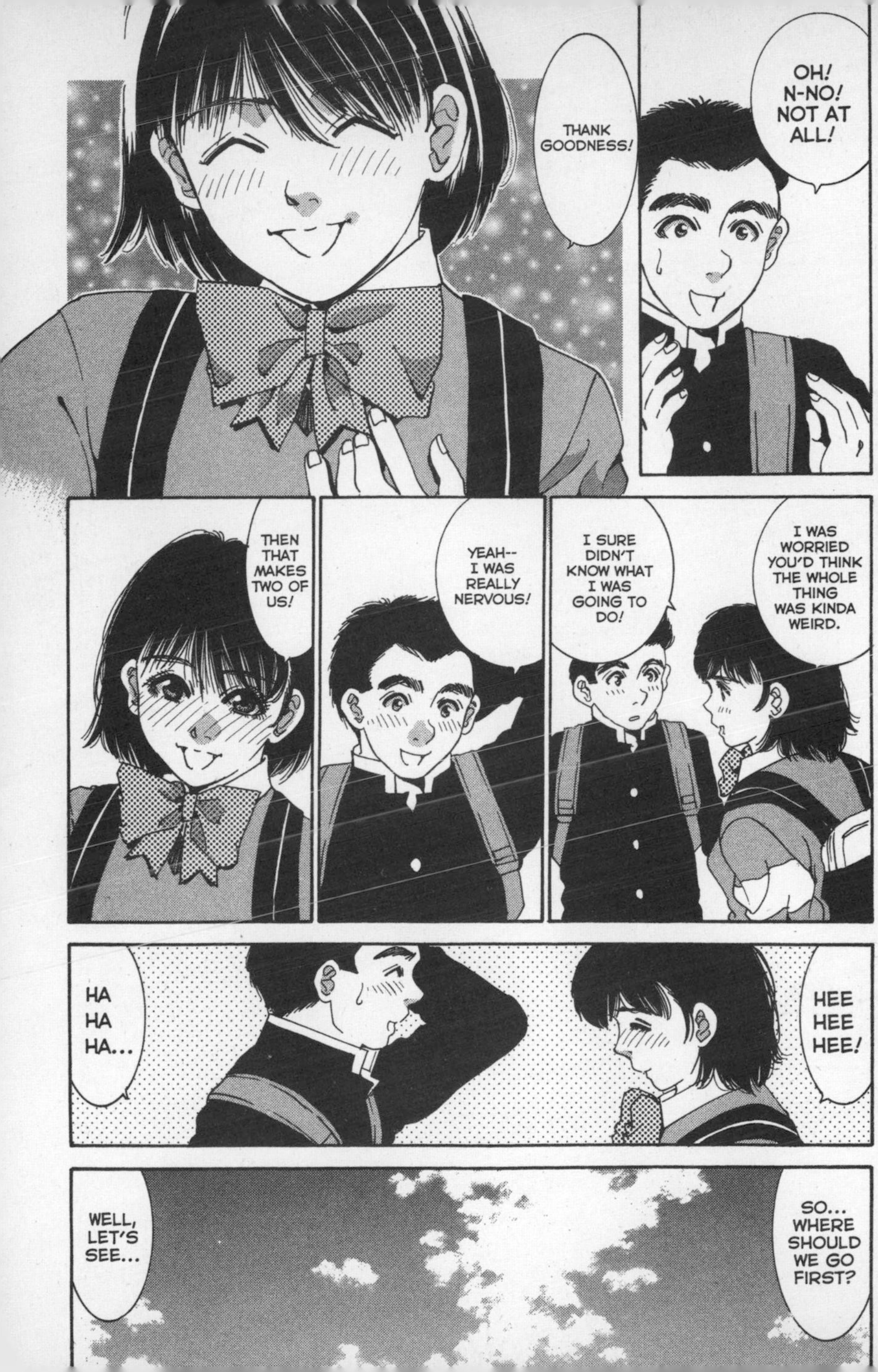
OH! N-NO! NOT AT ALL!
THANK GOODNESS!
I WAS WORRIED YOU'D THINK THE WHOLE THING WAS KINDA WEIRD.
I SURE DIDN'T KNOW WHAT I WAS GOING TO DO!
YEAH-- I WAS REALLY NERVOUS!
THEN THAT MAKES TWO OF US!
HEE HEE HEE!
HA HA HA...
SO... WHERE SHOULD WE GO FIRST?
WELL, LET'S SEE...

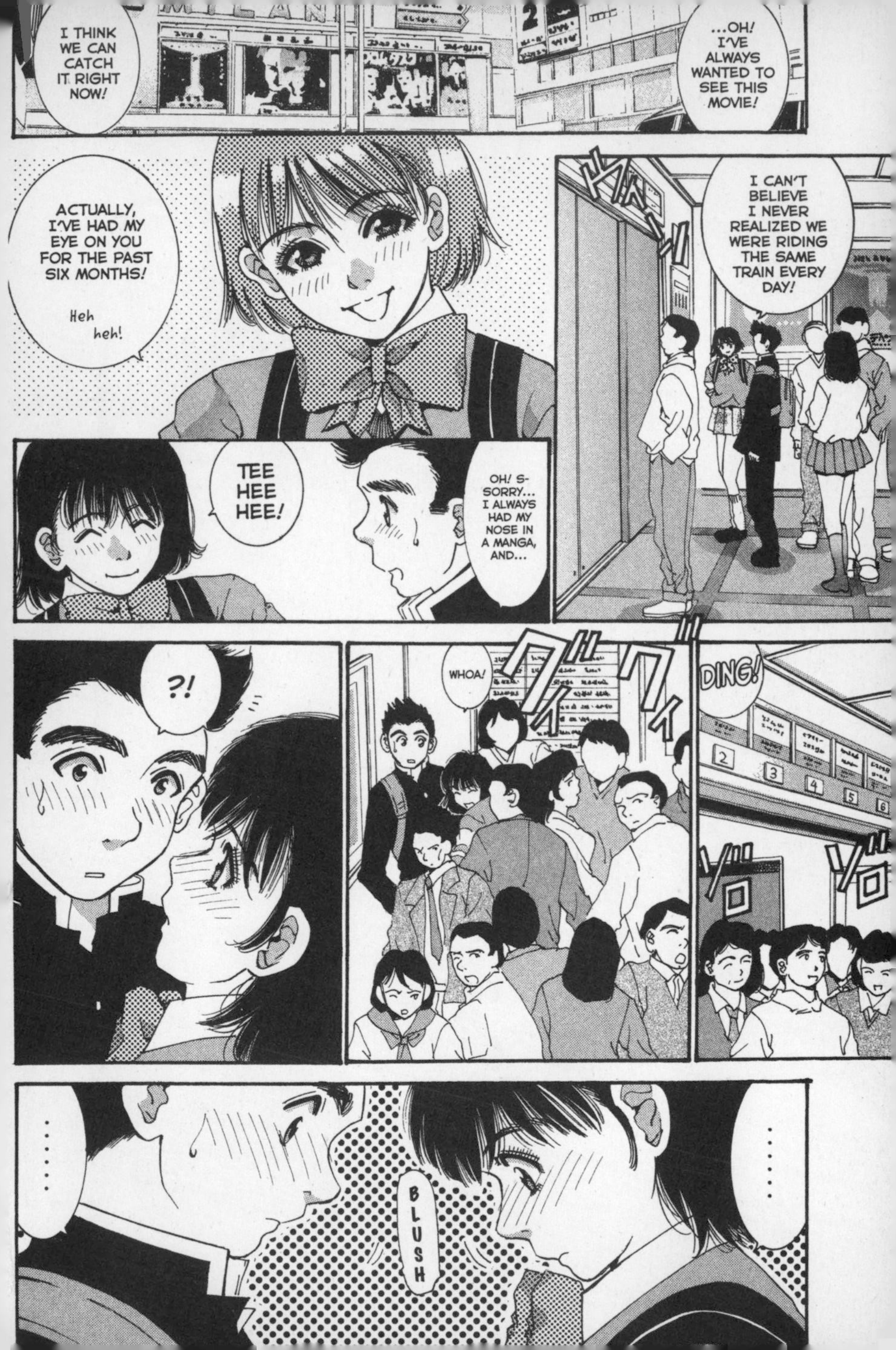
...OH! I'VE ALWAYS WANTED TO SEE THIS MOVIE!
I THINK WE CAN CATCH IT RIGHT NOW!
I CAN'T BELIEVE I NEVER REALIZED WE WERE RIDING THE SAME TRAIN EVERY DAY!
ACTUALLY, I'VE HAD MY EYE ON YOU FOR THE PAST SIX MONTHS!
Heh heh!
OH! S-SORRY... I ALWAYS HAD MY NOSE IN A MANGA, AND...
TEE HEE HEE!
DING!
WHOA!
?!
......
BLUSH
......

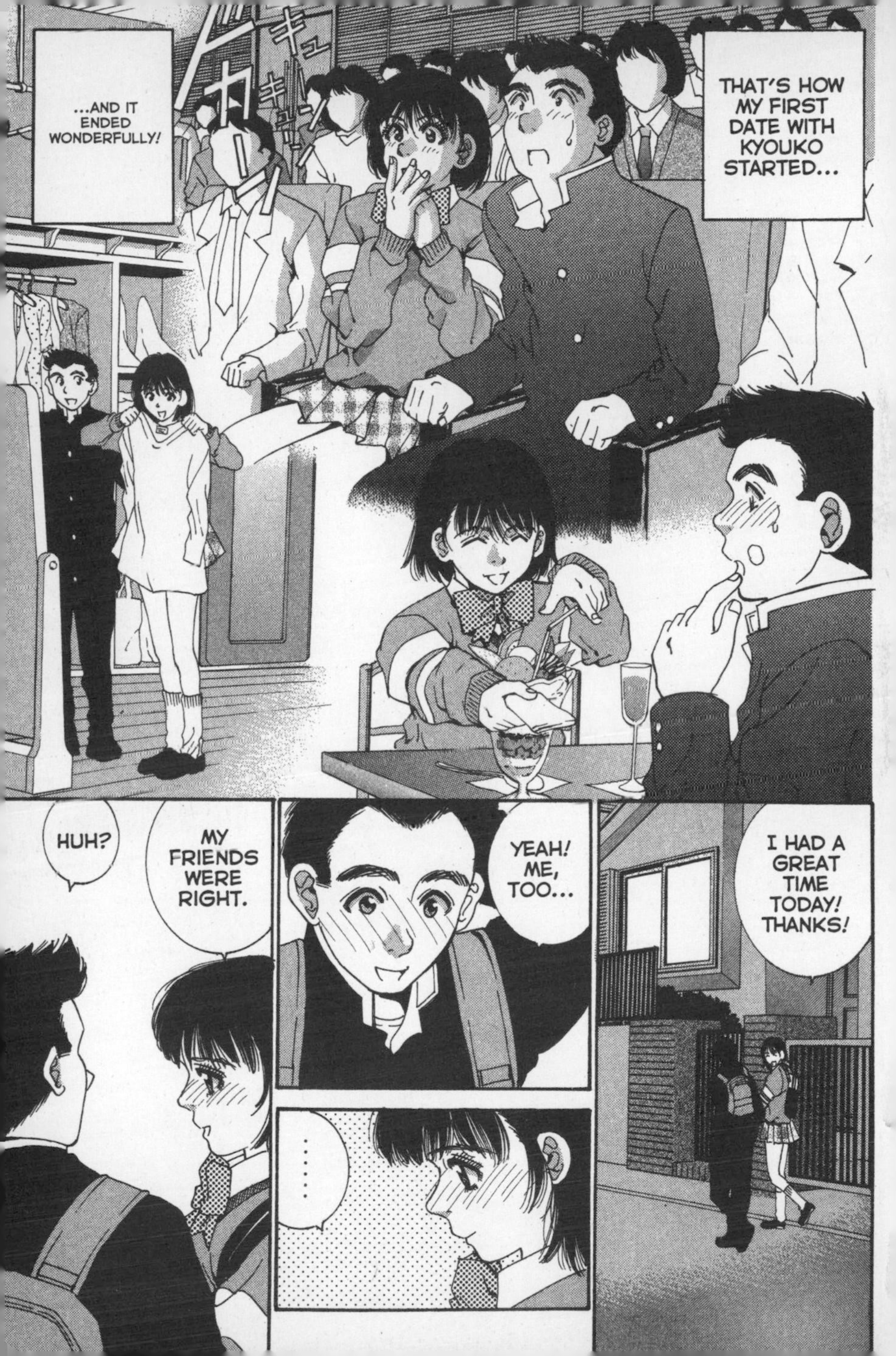
THAT'S HOW MY FIRST DATE WITH KYOUKO STARTED...
...AND IT ENDED WONDERFULLY!
I HAD A GREAT TIME TODAY! THANKS!
YEAH! ME, TOO...
......
MY FRIENDS WERE RIGHT.
HUH?

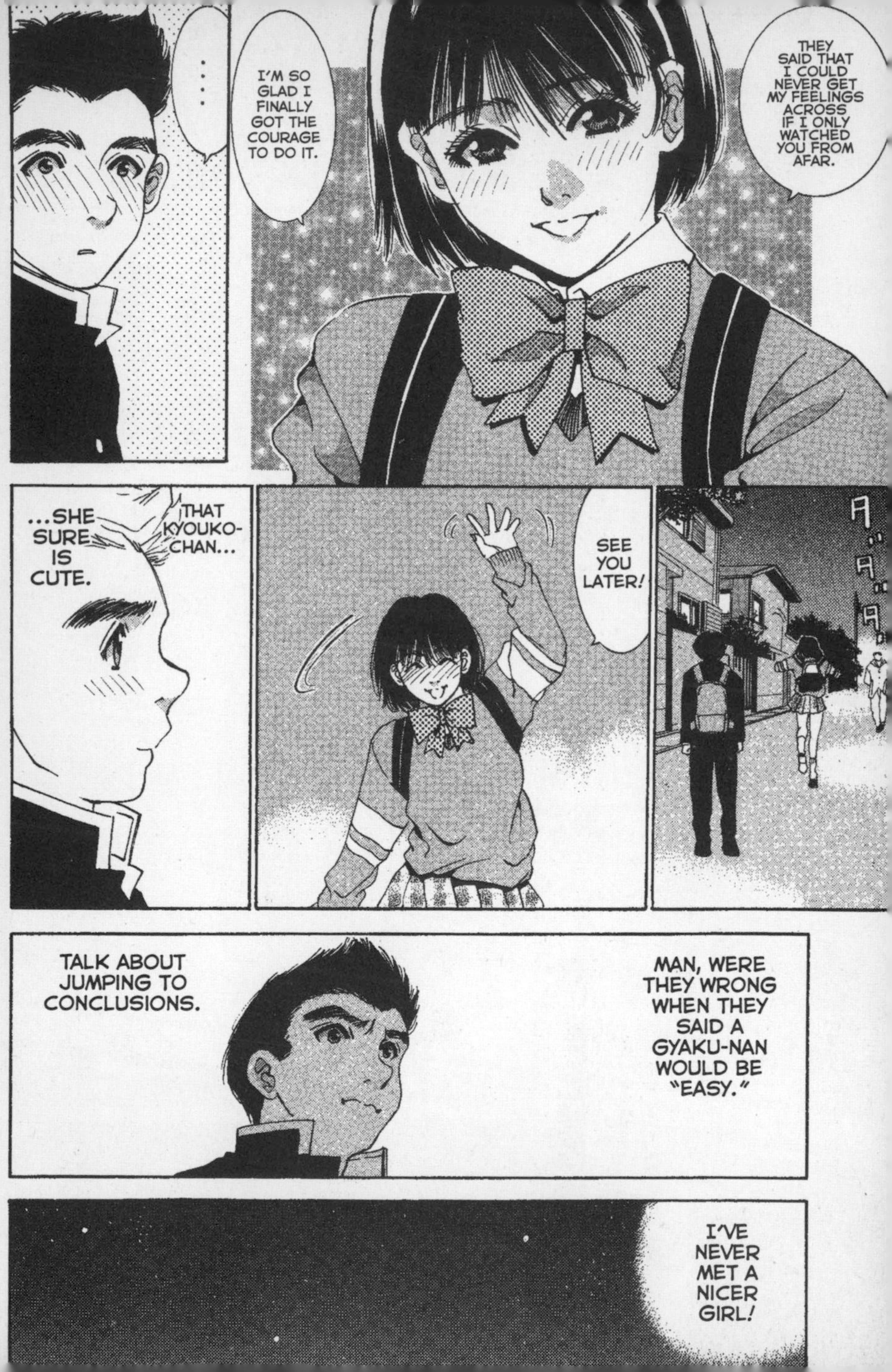
THEY SAID THAT I COULD NEVER GET MY FEELINGS ACROSS IF I ONLY WATCHED YOU FROM AFAR.
I'M SO GLAD I FINALLY GOT THE COURAGE TO DO IT.
....
SEE YOU LATER!
THAT KYOUKO-CHAN...
...SHE SURE IS CUTE.
MAN, WERE THEY WRONG WHEN THEY SAID A GYAKU-NAN WOULD BE "EASY."
TALK ABOUT JUMPING TO CONCLUSIONS.
I'VE NEVER MET A NICER GIRL!

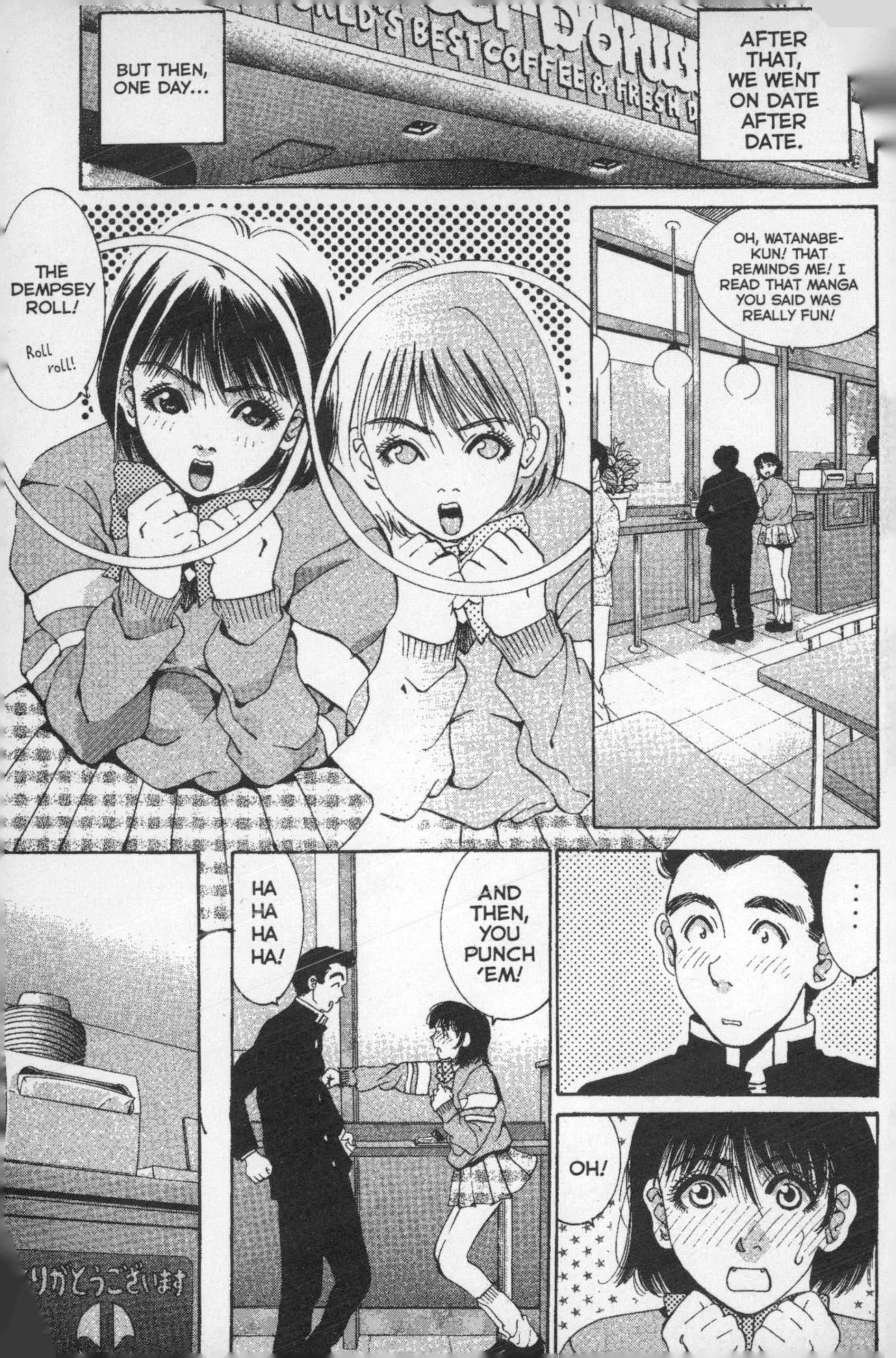
AFTER THAT, WE WENT ON DATE AFTER DATE.
BUT THEN, ONE DAY...
OH, WATANABE-KUN! THAT REMINDS ME! I READ THAT MANGA YOU SAID WAS REALLY FUN!
THE DEMPSEY ROLL!
Roll roll!
....
OH!
AND THEN, YOU PUNCH 'EM!
HA HA HA HA!

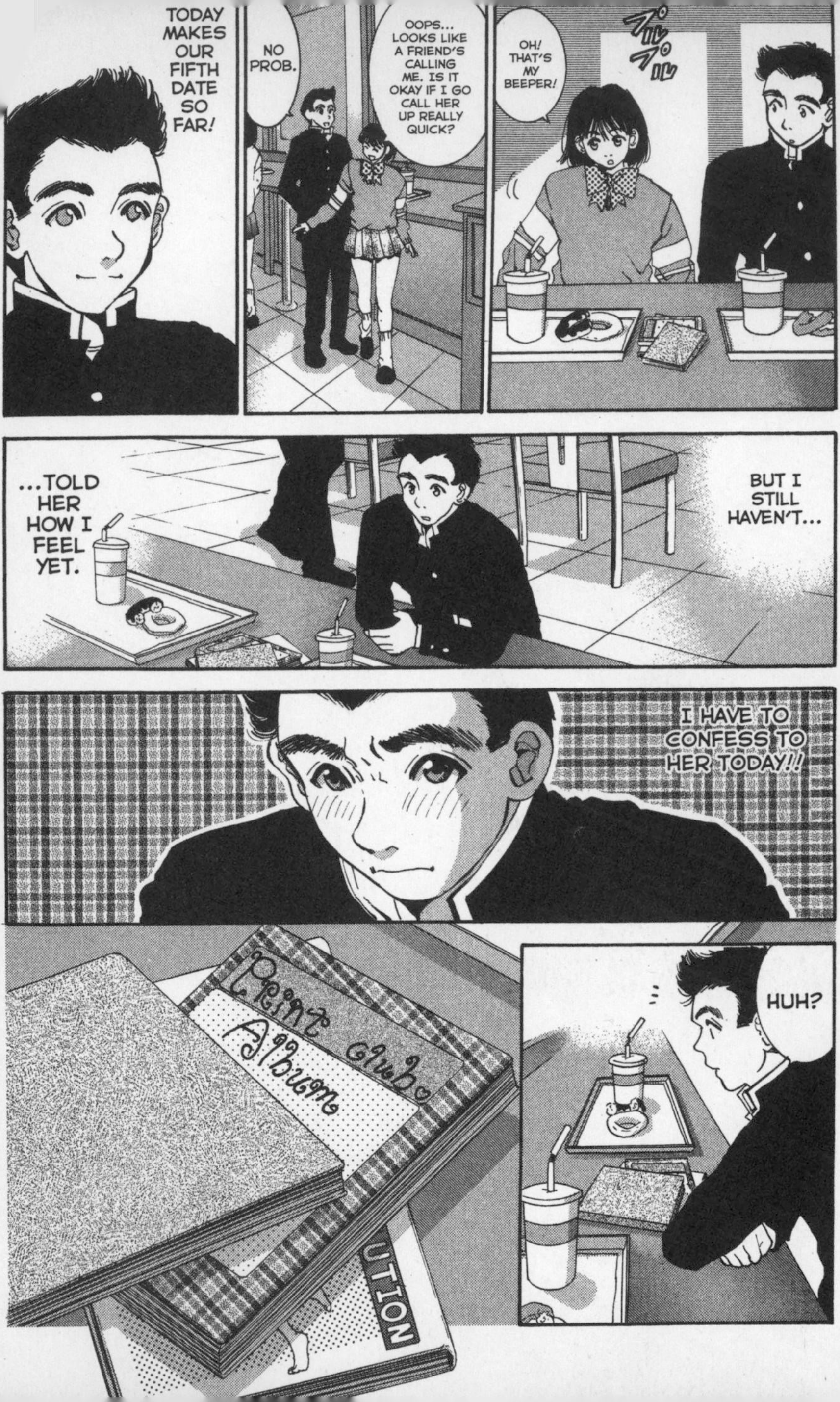

プルプル
OH! THAT'S MY BEEPER!
OOPS... LOOKS LIKE A FRIEND'S CALLING ME. IS IT OKAY IF I GO CALL HER UP REALLY QUICK?
NO PROB.
TODAY MAKES OUR FIFTH DATE SO FAR!
BUT I STILL HAVEN'T...
...TOLD HER HOW I FEEL YET.
I HAVE TO CONFESS TO HER TODAY!!
HUH?
Print club Album

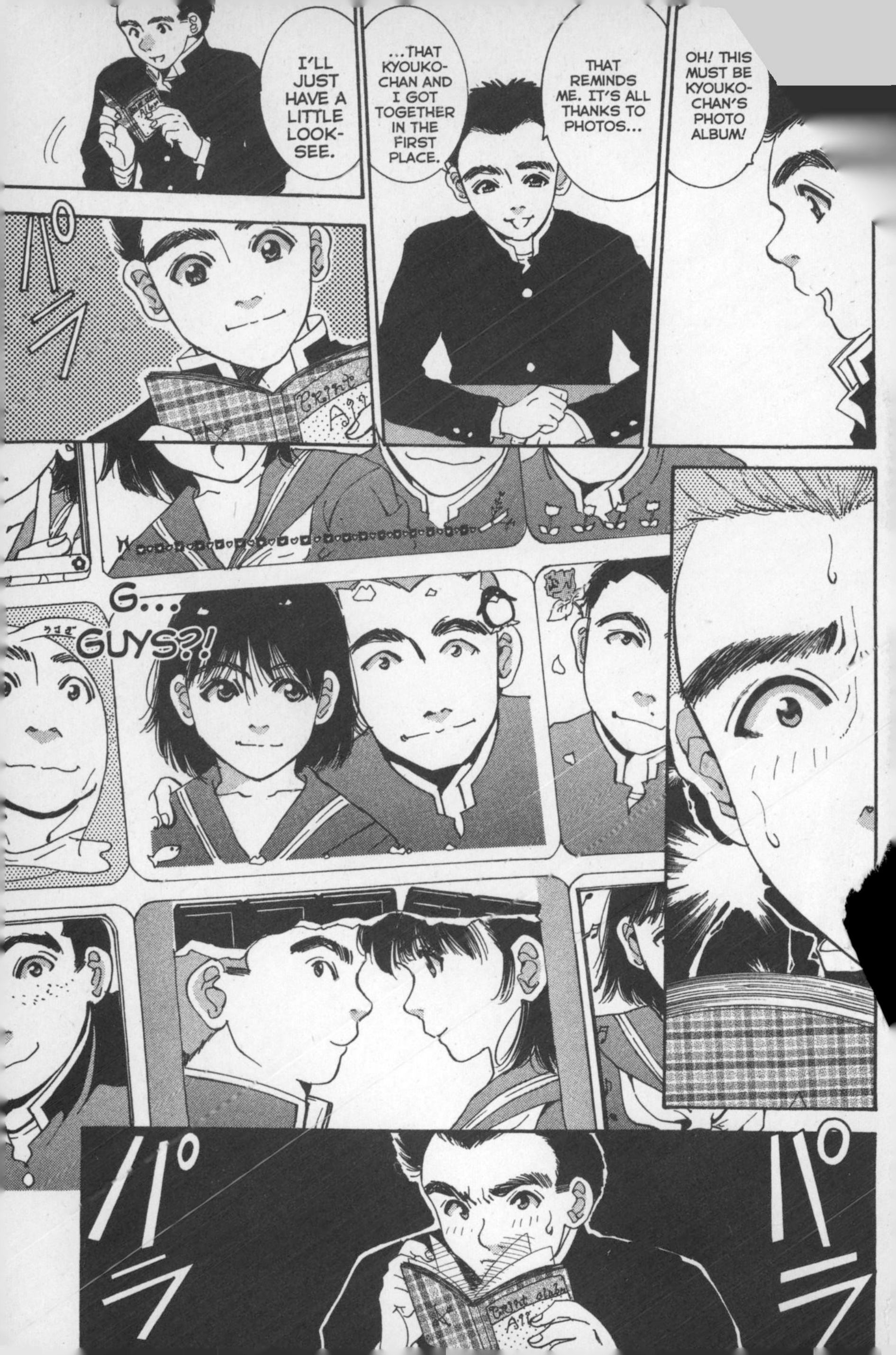
OH! THIS MUST BE KYOUKO-CHAN'S PHOTO ALBUM!
THAT REMINDS ME. IT'S ALL THANKS TO PHOTOS...
...THAT KYOUKO-CHAN AND I GOT TOGETHER IN THE FIRST PLACE.
I'LL JUST HAVE A LITTLE LOOK-SEE.
パラ
G... GUYS?!
パラ
パラ

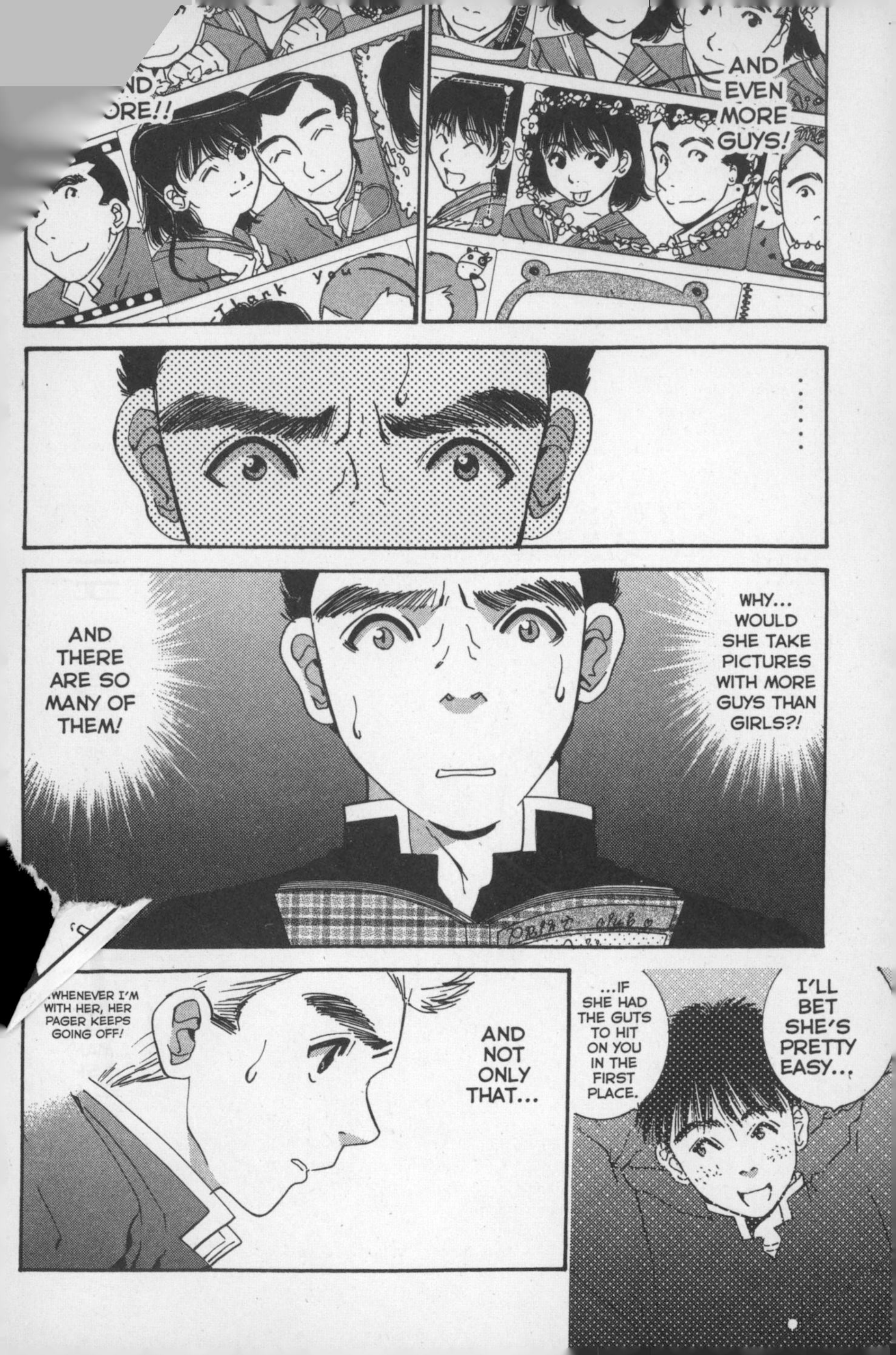
AND EVEN MORE GUYS!
ND ORE!!
WHY... WOULD SHE TAKE PICTURES WITH MORE GUYS THAN GIRLS?!
AND THERE ARE SO MANY OF THEM!
I'LL BET SHE'S PRETTY EASY...
...IF SHE HAD THE GUTS TO HIT ON YOU IN THE FIRST PLACE.
AND NOT ONLY THAT...
WHENEVER I'M WITH HER, HER PAGER KEEPS GOING OFF!

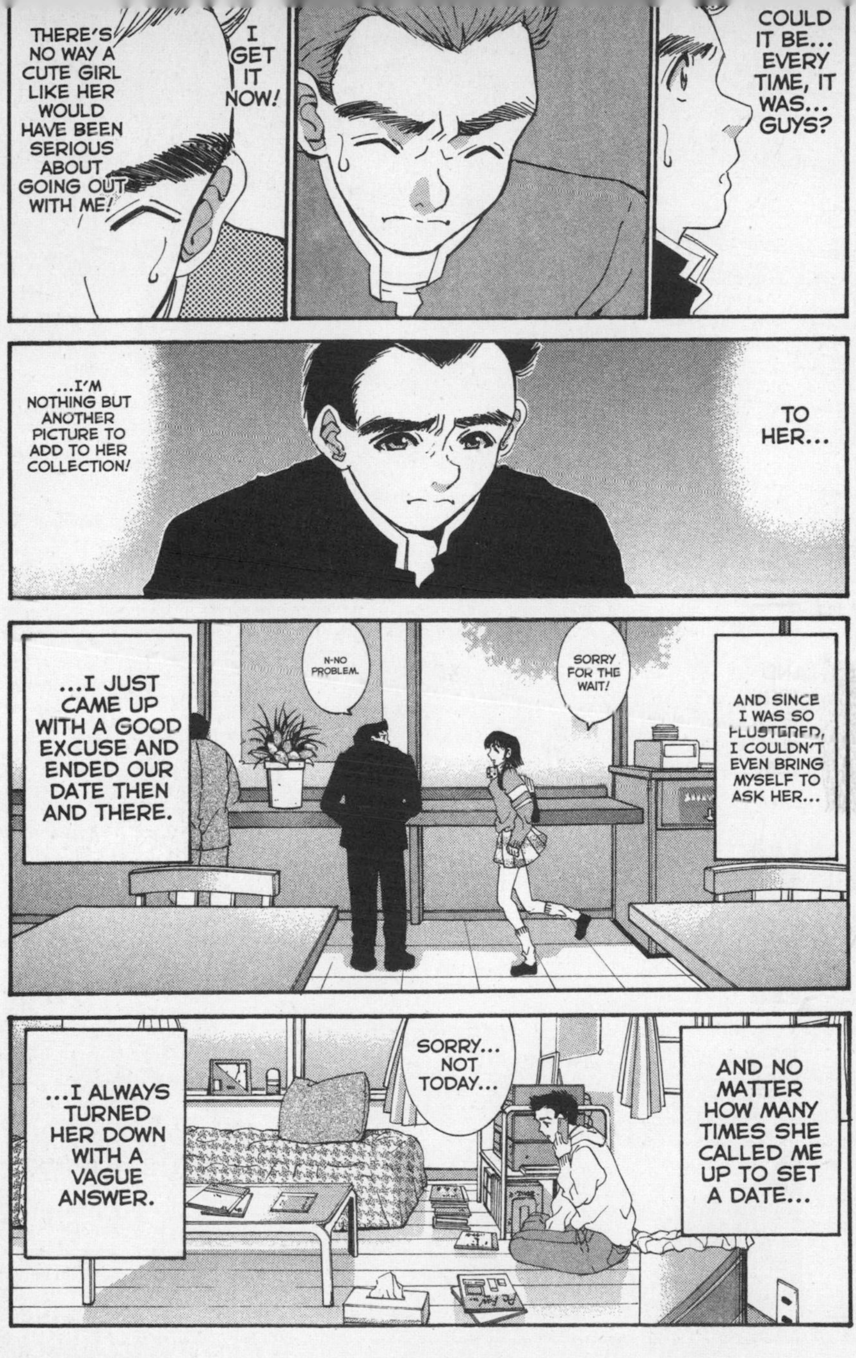
COULD IT BE... EVERY TIME, IT WAS... GUYS?
I GET IT NOW!
THERE'S NO WAY A CUTE GIRL LIKE HER WOULD HAVE BEEN SERIOUS ABOUT GOING OUT WITH ME!
TO HER...
...I'M NOTHING BUT ANOTHER PICTURE TO ADD TO HER COLLECTION!
AND SINCE I WAS SO FLUSTERED, I COULDN'T EVEN BRING MYSELF TO ASK HER...
SORRY FOR THE WAIT!
N-NO PROBLEM.
...I JUST CAME UP WITH A GOOD EXCUSE AND ENDED OUR DATE THEN AND THERE.
AND NO MATTER HOW MANY TIMES SHE CALLED ME UP TO SET A DATE...
SORRY... NOT TODAY...
...I ALWAYS TURNED HER DOWN WITH A VAGUE ANSWER.

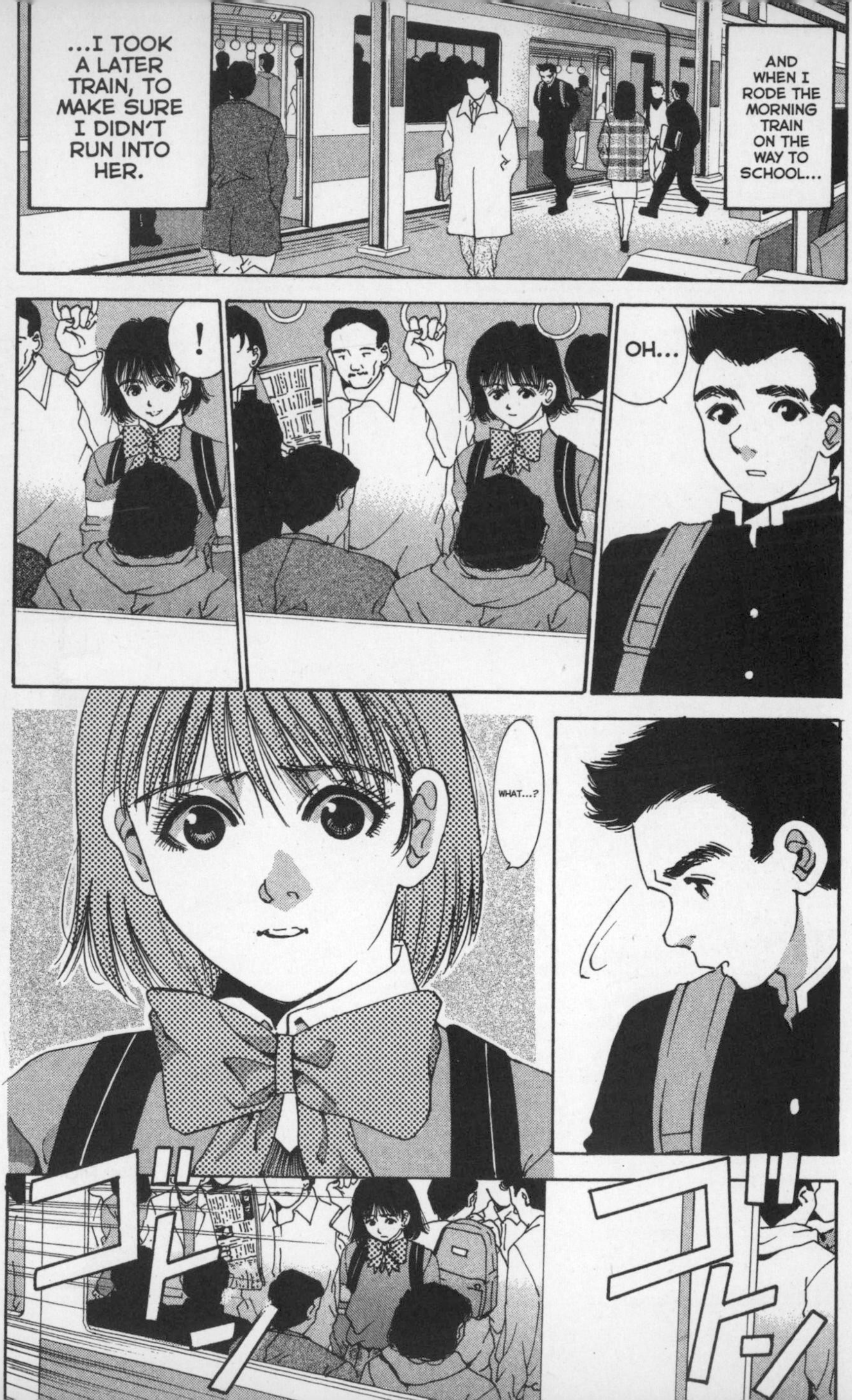
AND WHEN I RODE THE MORNING TRAIN ON THE WAY TO SCHOOL...
...I TOOK A LATER TRAIN, TO MAKE SURE I DIDN'T RUN INTO HER.
OH...
!
WHAT...?

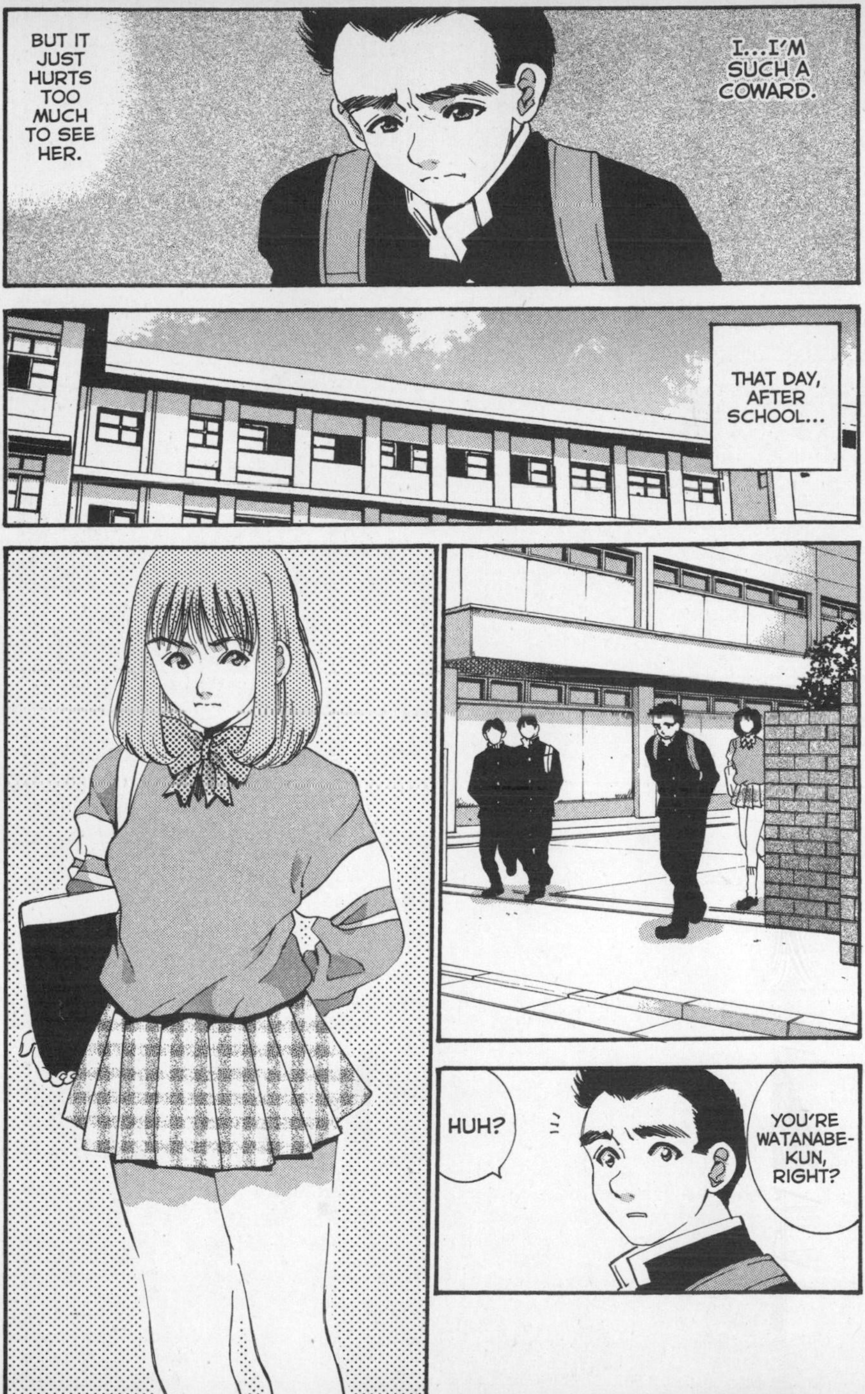
I...I'M SUCH A COWARD.
BUT IT JUST HURTS TOO MUCH TO SEE HER.
THAT DAY, AFTER SCHOOL...
YOU'RE WATANABE-KUN, RIGHT?
HUH?

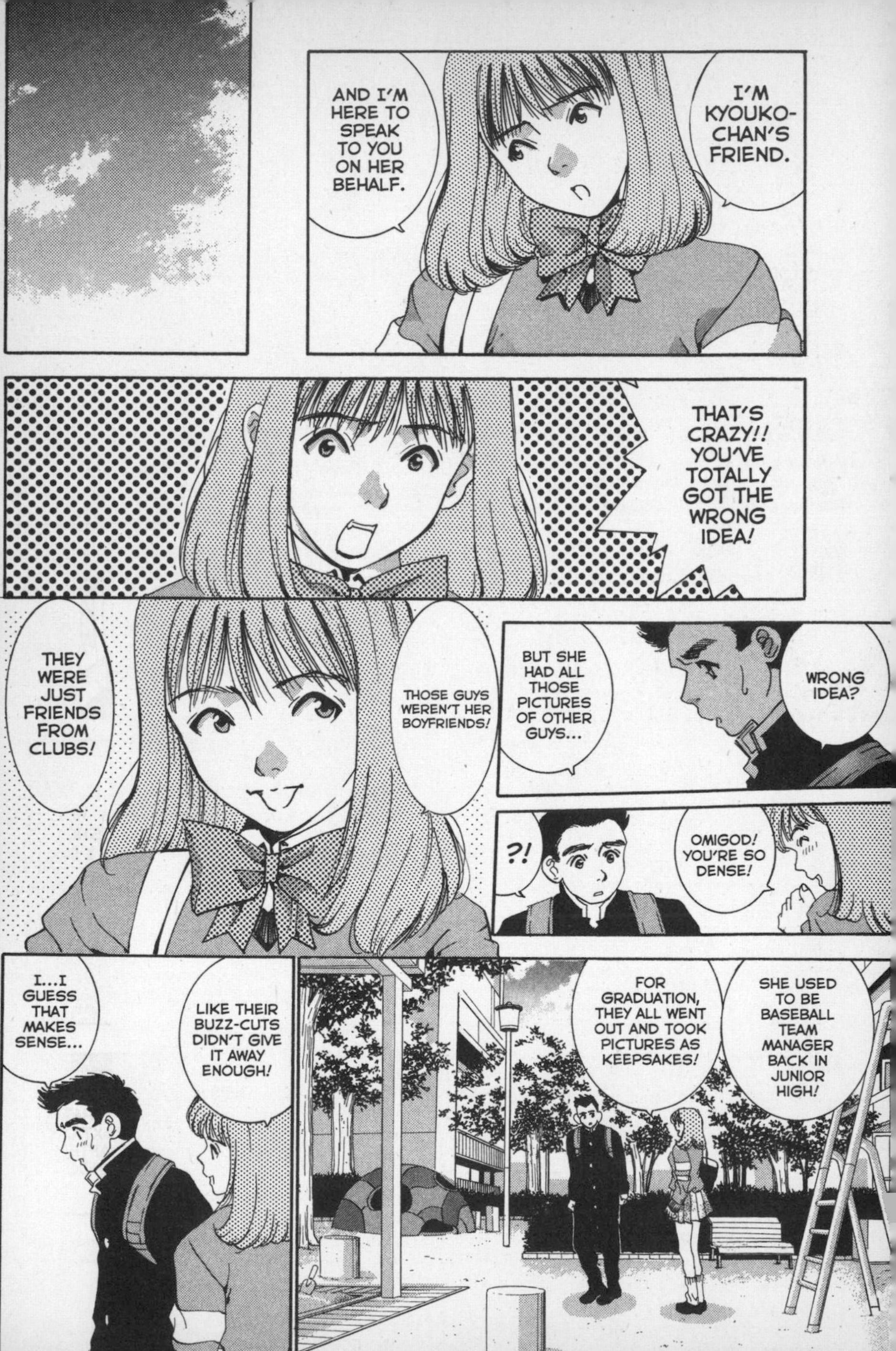
I'M KYOUKO-CHAN'S FRIEND.
AND I'M HERE TO SPEAK TO YOU ON HER BEHALF.
THAT'S CRAZY!! YOU'VE TOTALLY GOT THE WRONG IDEA!
WRONG IDEA?
BUT SHE HAD ALL THOSE PICTURES OF OTHER GUYS...
OMIGOD! YOU'RE SO DENSE!
?!
THOSE GUYS WEREN'T HER BOYFRIENDS!
THEY WERE JUST FRIENDS FROM CLUBS!
SHE USED TO BE BASEBALL TEAM MANAGER BACK IN JUNIOR HIGH!
FOR GRADUATION, THEY ALL WENT OUT AND TOOK PICTURES AS KEEPSAKES!
LIKE THEIR BUZZ-CUTS DIDN'T GIVE IT AWAY ENOUGH!
I...I GUESS THAT MAKES SENSE...

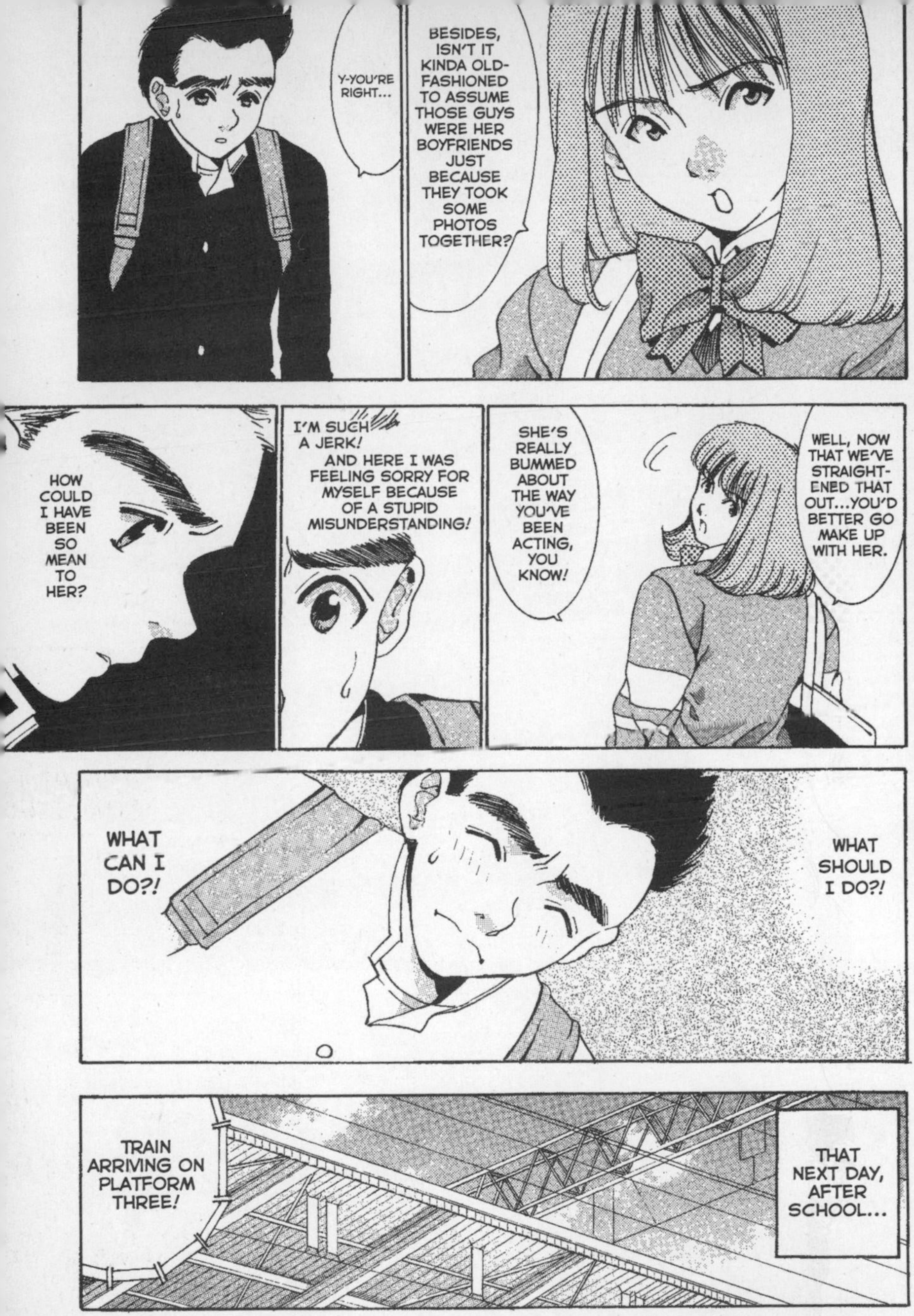
BESIDES, ISN'T IT KINDA OLD-FASHIONED TO ASSUME THOSE GUYS WERE HER BOYFRIENDS JUST BECAUSE THEY TOOK SOME PHOTOS TOGETHER?
Y-YOU'RE RIGHT...
WELL, NOW THAT WE'VE STRAIGHT-ENED THAT OUT...YOU'D BETTER GO MAKE UP WITH HER.
SHE'S REALLY BUMMED ABOUT THE WAY YOU'VE BEEN ACTING, YOU KNOW!
I'M SUCH A JERK! AND HERE I WAS FEELING SORRY FOR MYSELF BECAUSE OF A STUPID MISUNDERSTANDING!
HOW COULD I HAVE BEEN SO MEAN TO HER?
WHAT SHOULD I DO?!
WHAT CAN I DO?!
THAT NEXT DAY, AFTER SCHOOL...
TRAIN ARRIVING ON PLATFORM THREE!

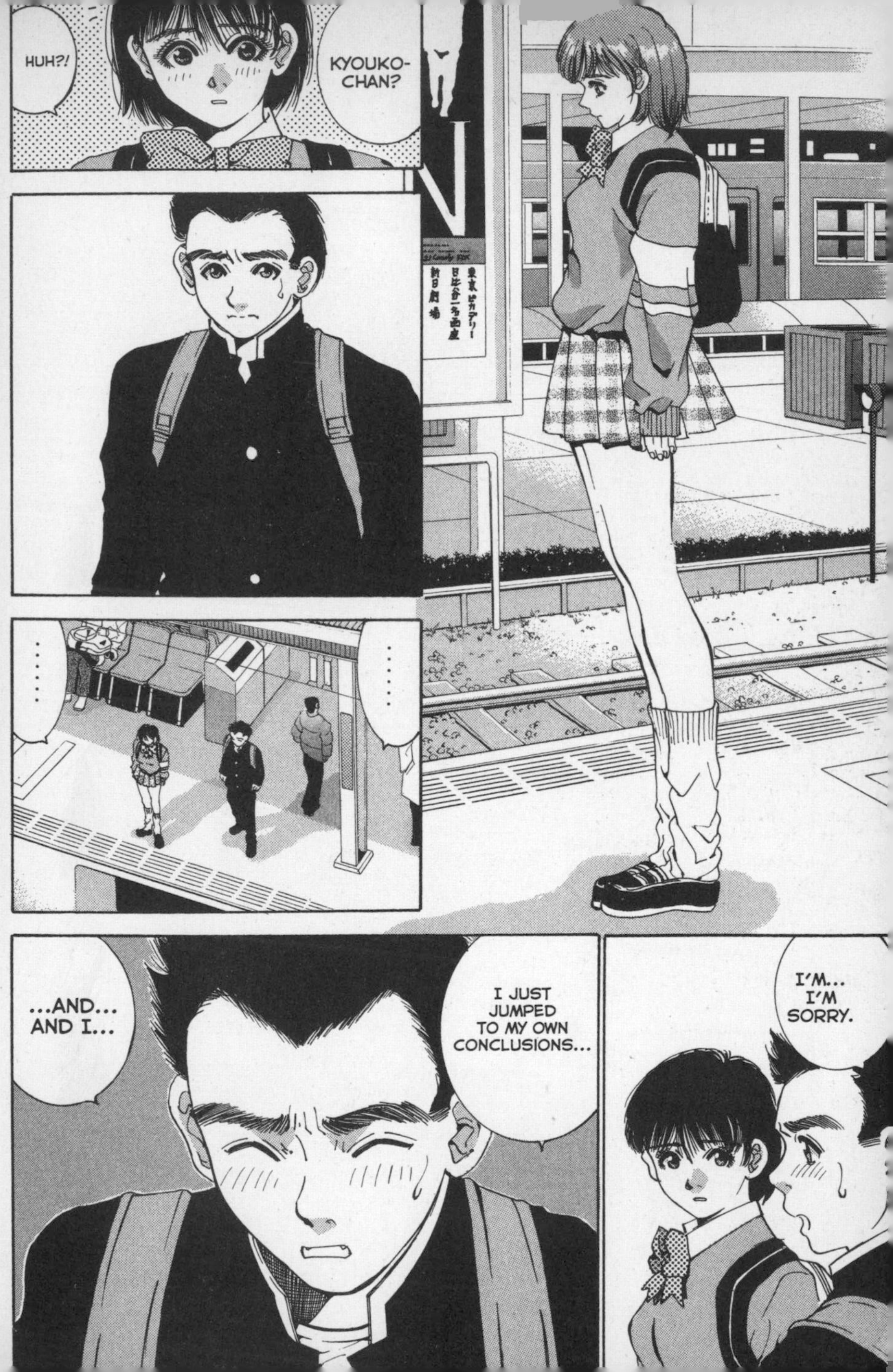
KYOUKO-CHAN?
HUH?!
......
......
I'M... I'M SORRY.
I JUST JUMPED TO MY OWN CONCLUSIONS...
...AND... AND I...

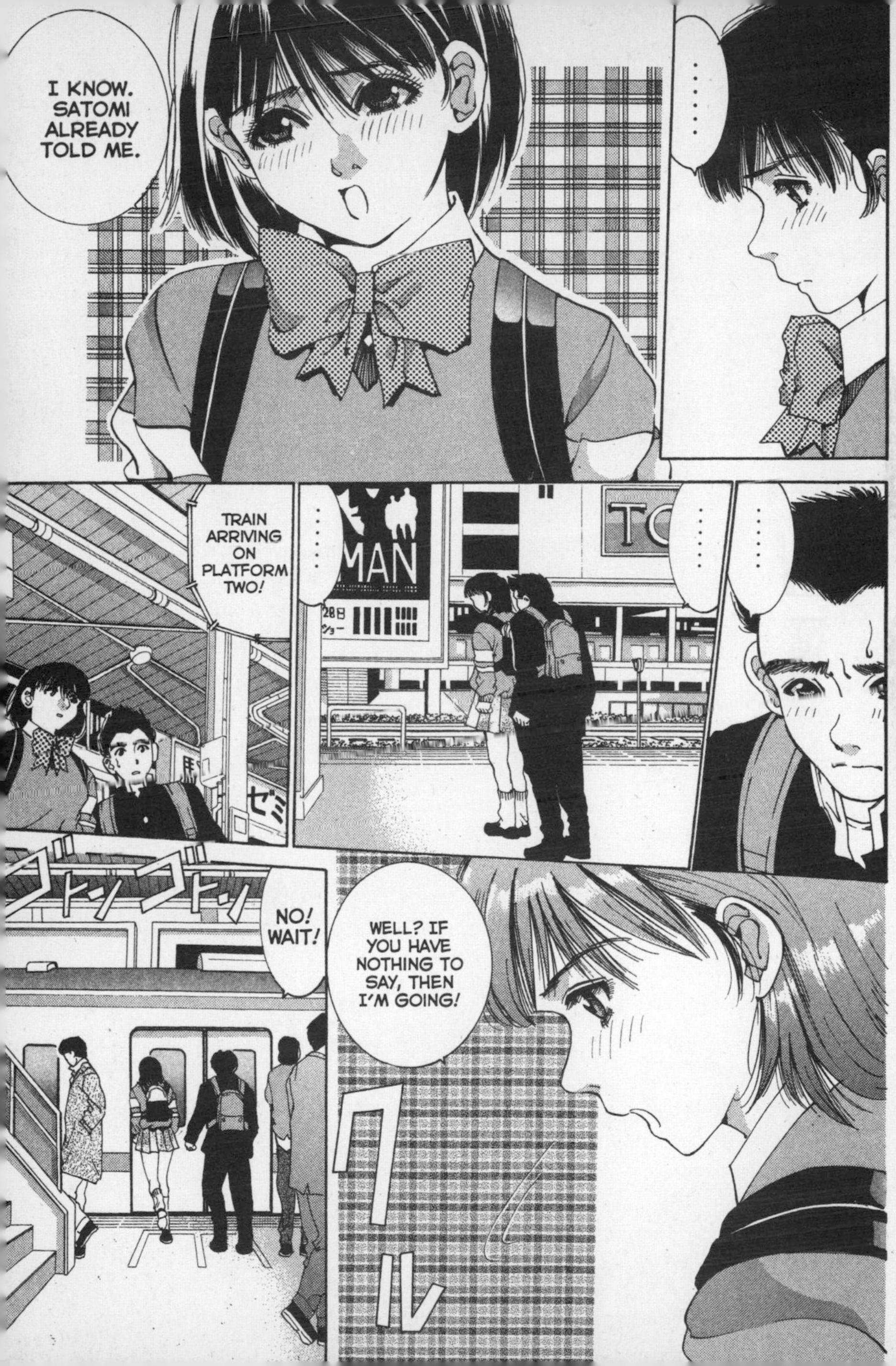
......
I KNOW. SATOMI ALREADY TOLD ME.
......
......
......
TRAIN ARRIVING ON PLATFORM TWO!
WELL? IF YOU HAVE NOTHING TO SAY, THEN I'M GOING!
NO! WAIT!

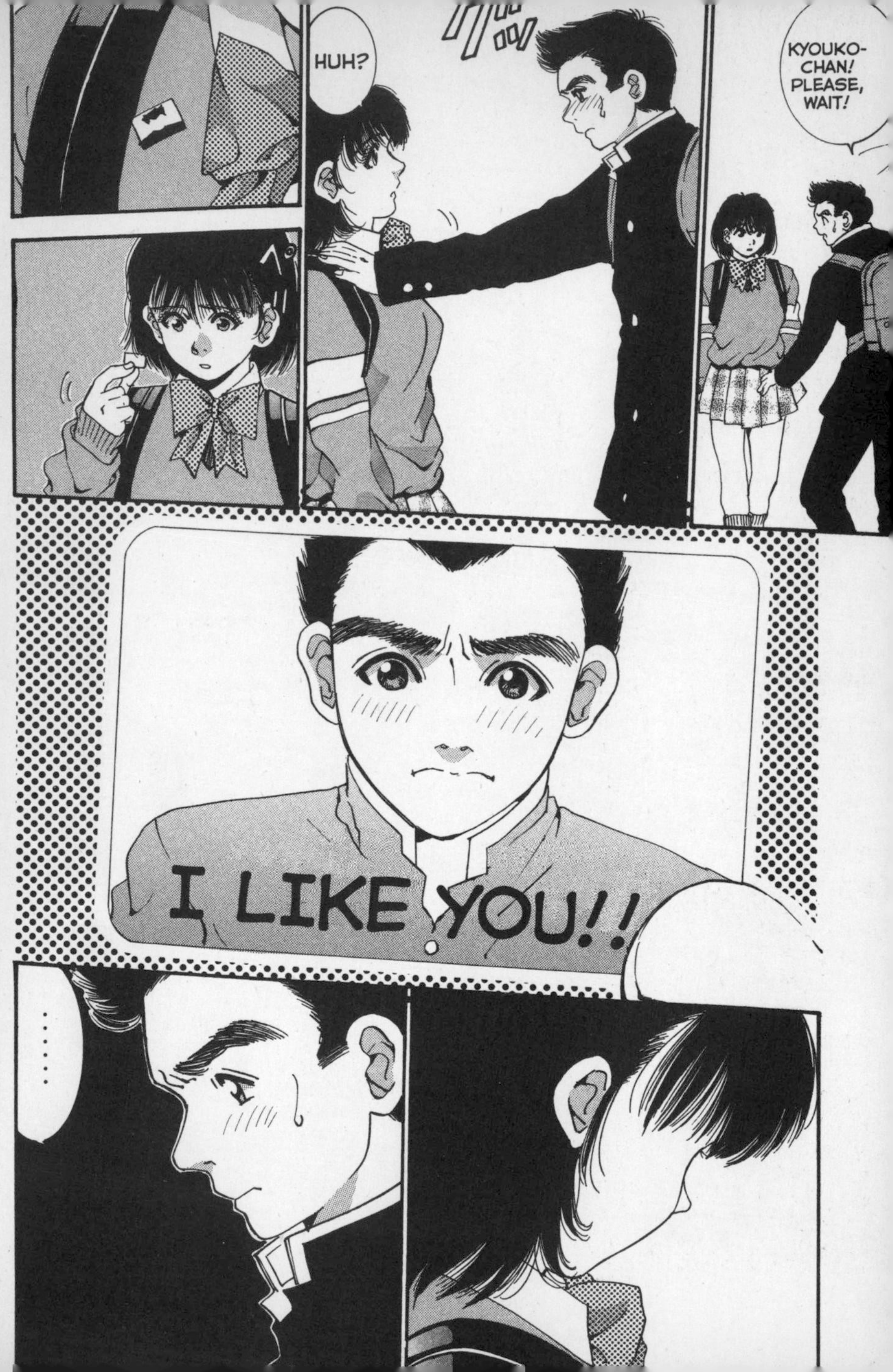
KYOUKO-CHAN! PLEASE, WAIT!
HUH?
I LIKE YOU!!
......

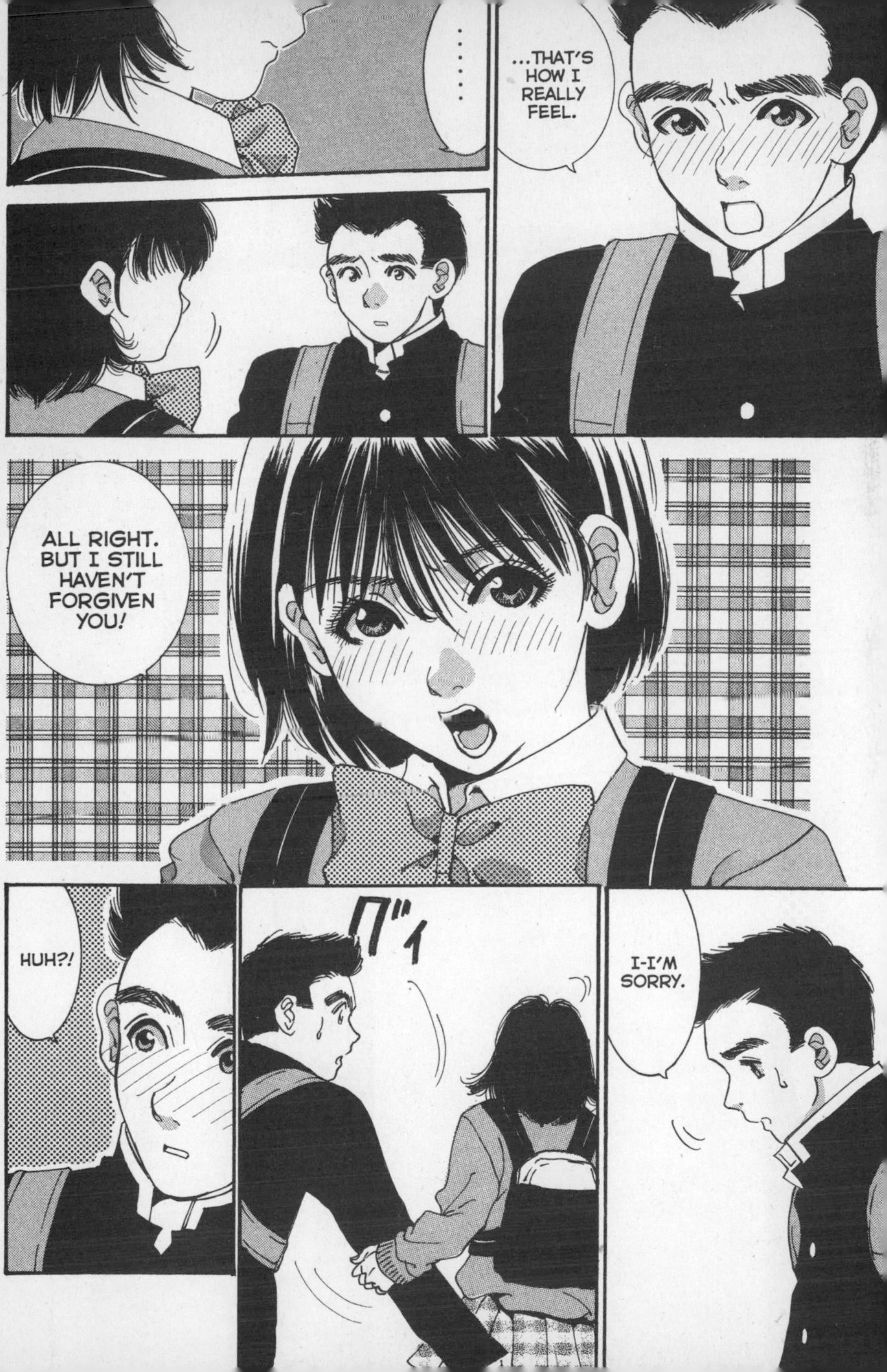
...THAT'S HOW I REALLY FEEL.
......
ALL RIGHT. BUT I STILL HAVEN'T FORGIVEN YOU!
I-I'M SORRY.
グイ
HUH?!

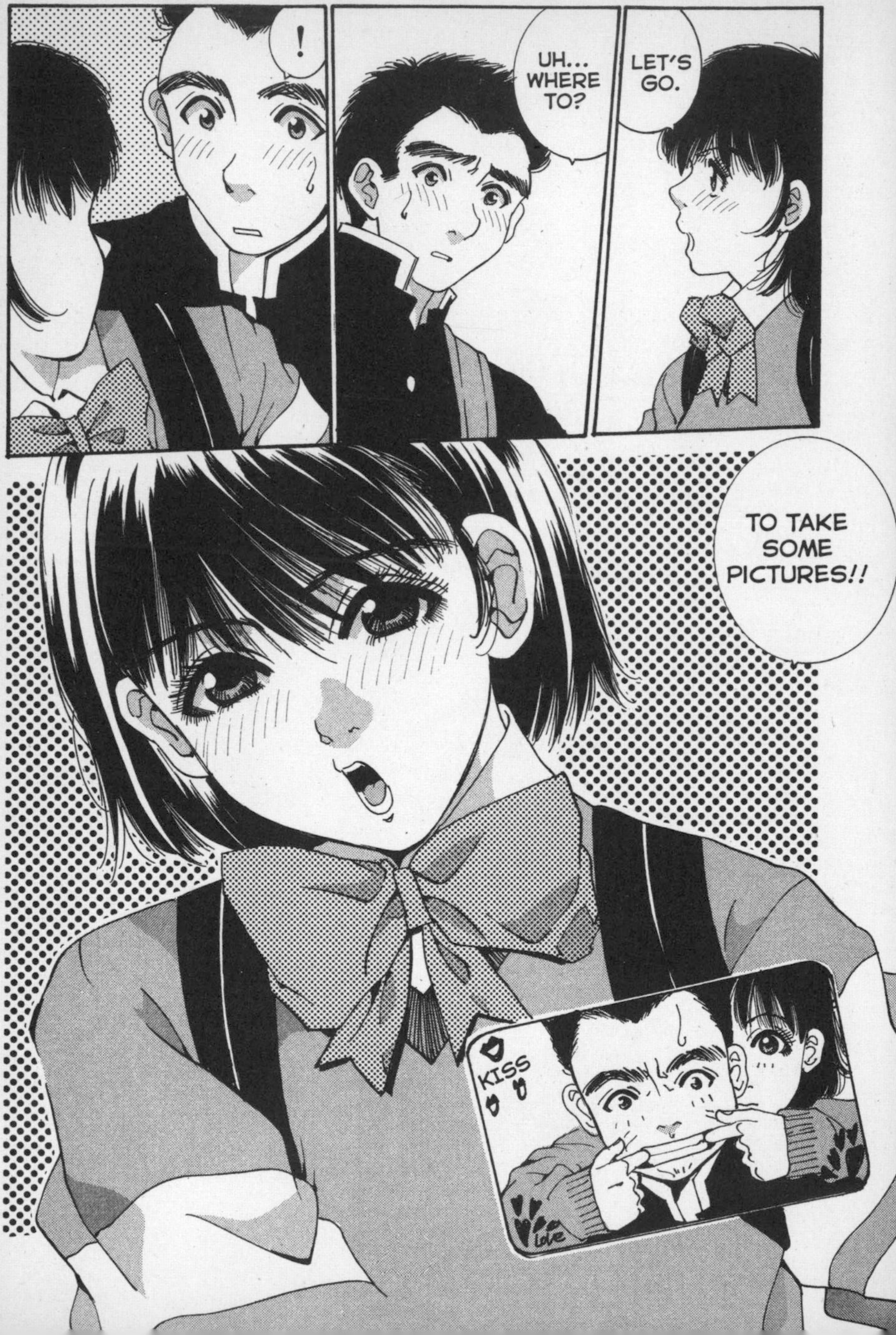
LET'S GO.
UH... WHERE TO?
!
TO TAKE SOME PICTURES!!
KISS
LOVE

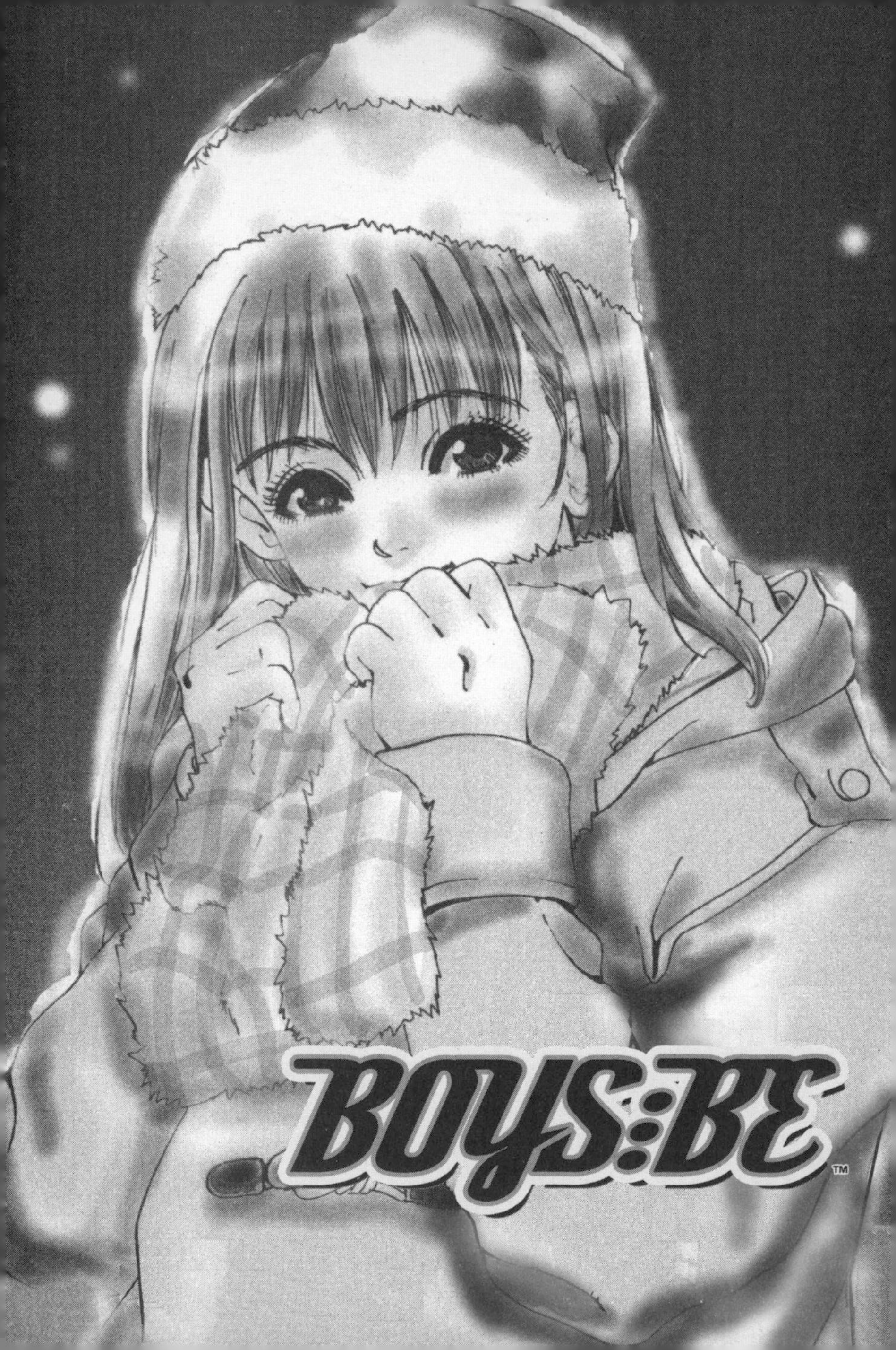
BOYS BE

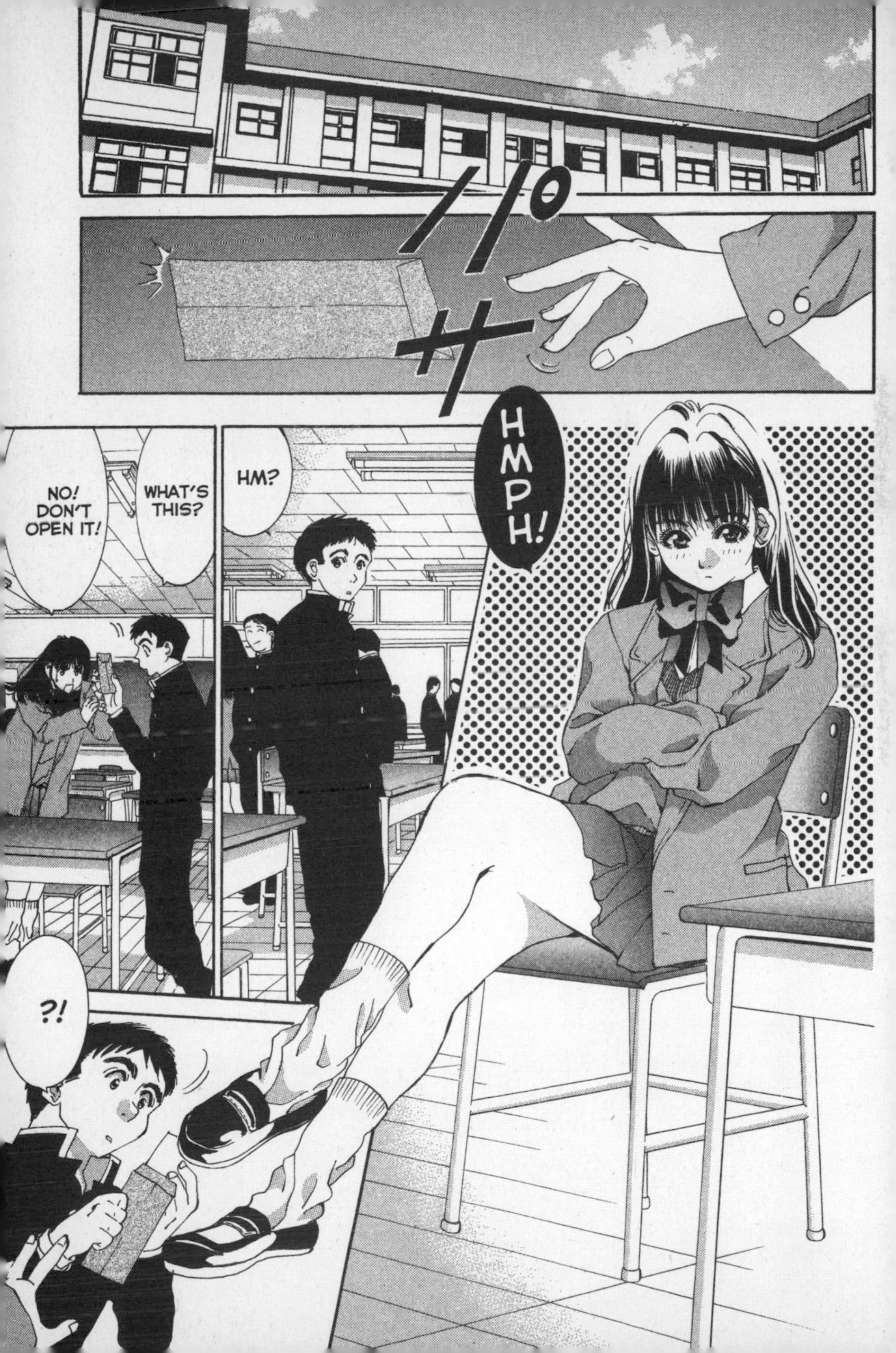
パサ
HMPH!
HM?
WHAT'S THIS?
NO! DON'T OPEN IT!
?!

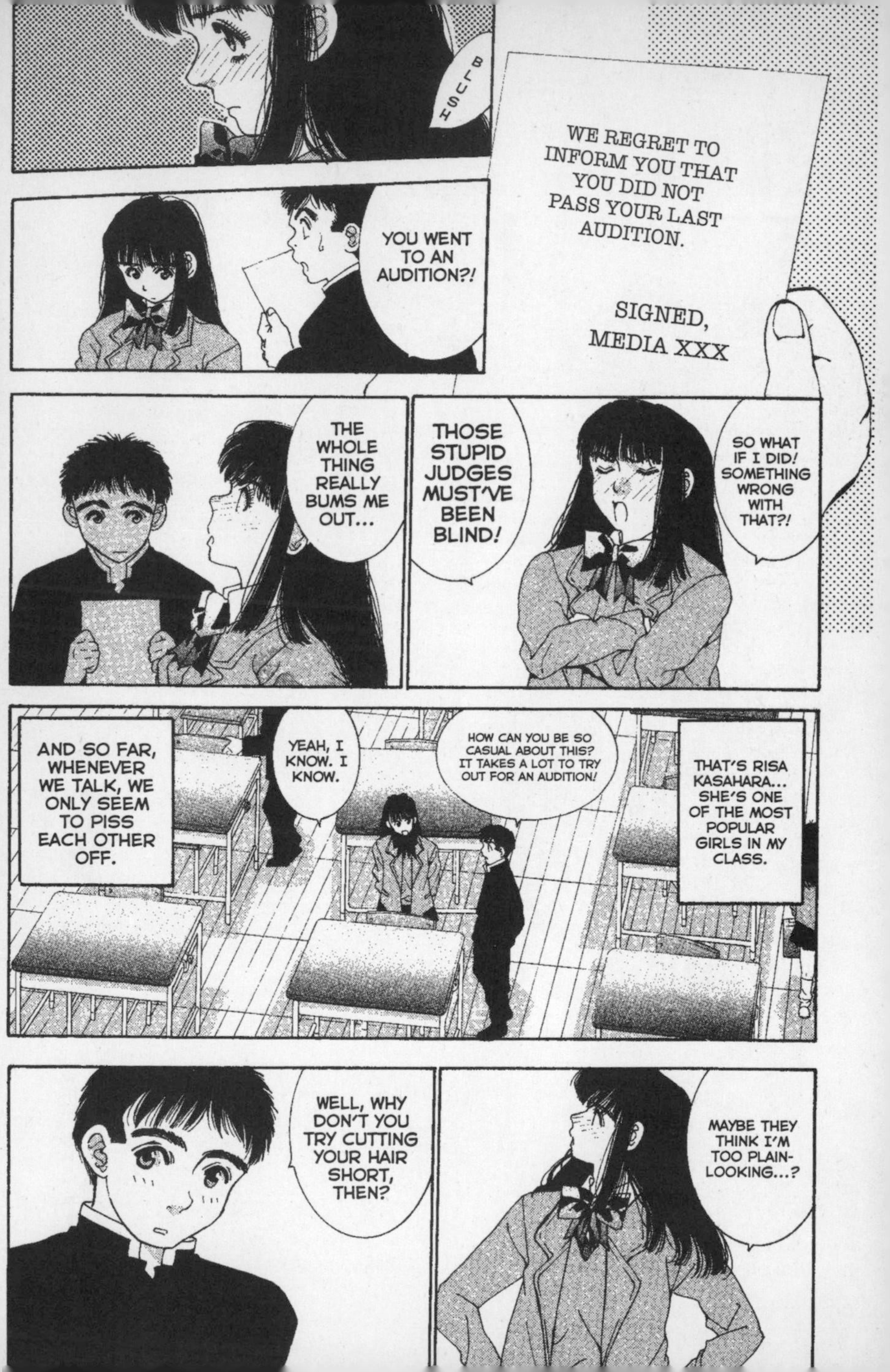
WE REGRET TO INFORM YOU THAT YOU DID NOT PASS YOUR LAST AUDITION.
SIGNED, MEDIA XXX
BLUSH
YOU WENT TO AN AUDITION?!
SO WHAT IF I DID! SOMETHING WRONG WITH THAT?!
THOSE STUPID JUDGES MUST'VE BEEN BLIND!
THE WHOLE THING REALLY BUMS ME OUT...
THAT'S RISA KASAHARA... SHE'S ONE OF THE MOST POPULAR GIRLS IN MY CLASS.
HOW CAN YOU BE SO CASUAL ABOUT THIS? IT TAKES A LOT TO TRY OUT FOR AN AUDITION!
YEAH, I KNOW. I KNOW.
AND SO FAR, WHENEVER WE TALK, WE ONLY SEEM TO PISS EACH OTHER OFF.
MAYBE THEY THINK I'M TOO PLAIN-LOOKING...?
WELL, WHY DON'T YOU TRY CUTTING YOUR HAIR SHORT, THEN?

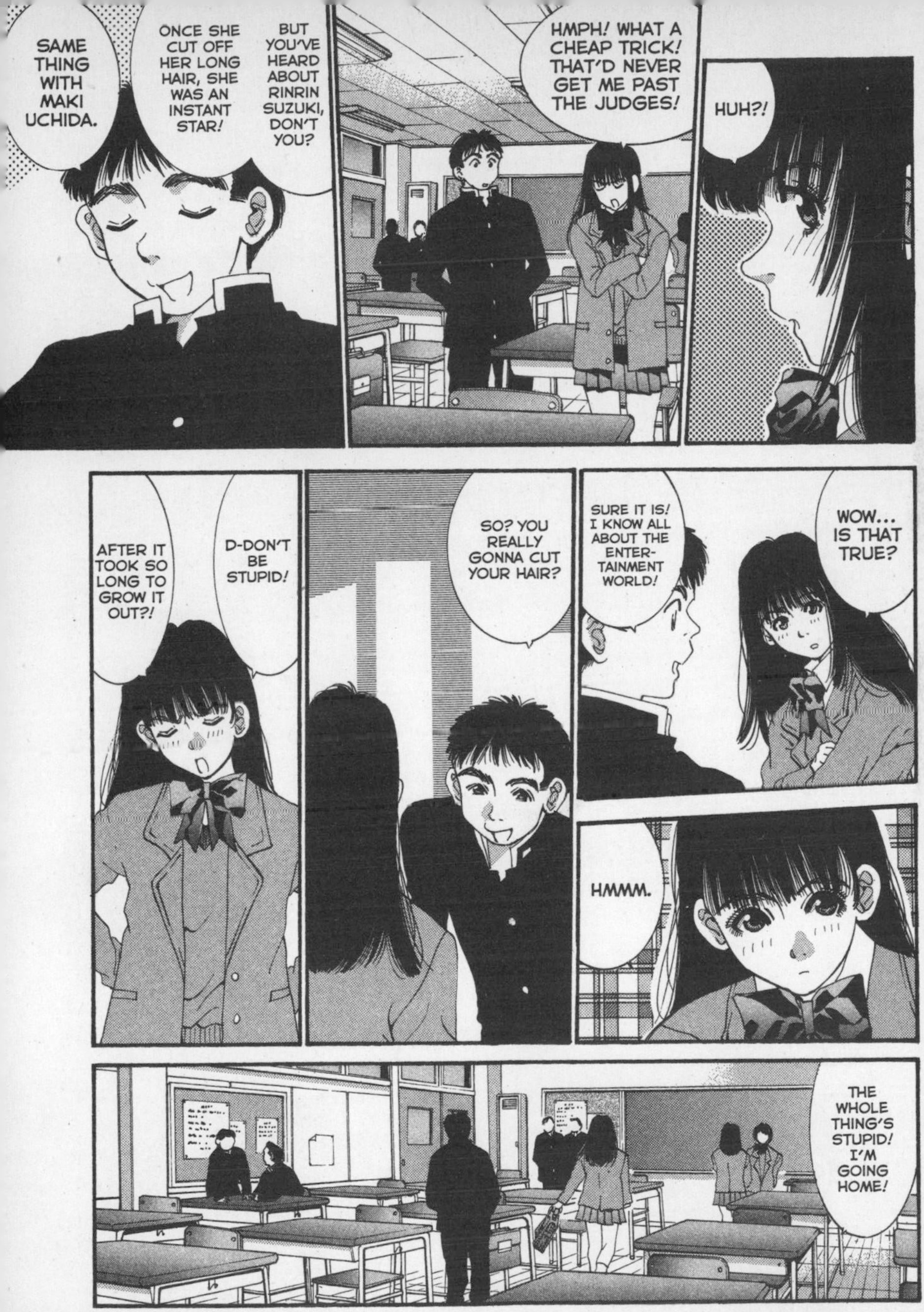
HUH?!
HMPH! WHAT A CHEAP TRICK! THAT'D NEVER GET ME PAST THE JUDGES!
BUT YOU'VE HEARD ABOUT RINRIN SUZUKI, DON'T YOU?
ONCE SHE CUT OFF HER LONG HAIR, SHE WAS AN INSTANT STAR!
SAME THING WITH MAKI UCHIDA.
WOW... IS THAT TRUE?
SURE IT IS! I KNOW ALL ABOUT THE ENTER-TAINMENT WORLD!
HMMM.
SO? YOU REALLY GONNA CUT YOUR HAIR?
D-DON'T BE STUPID!
AFTER IT TOOK SO LONG TO GROW IT OUT?!
THE WHOLE THING'S STUPID! I'M GOING HOME!

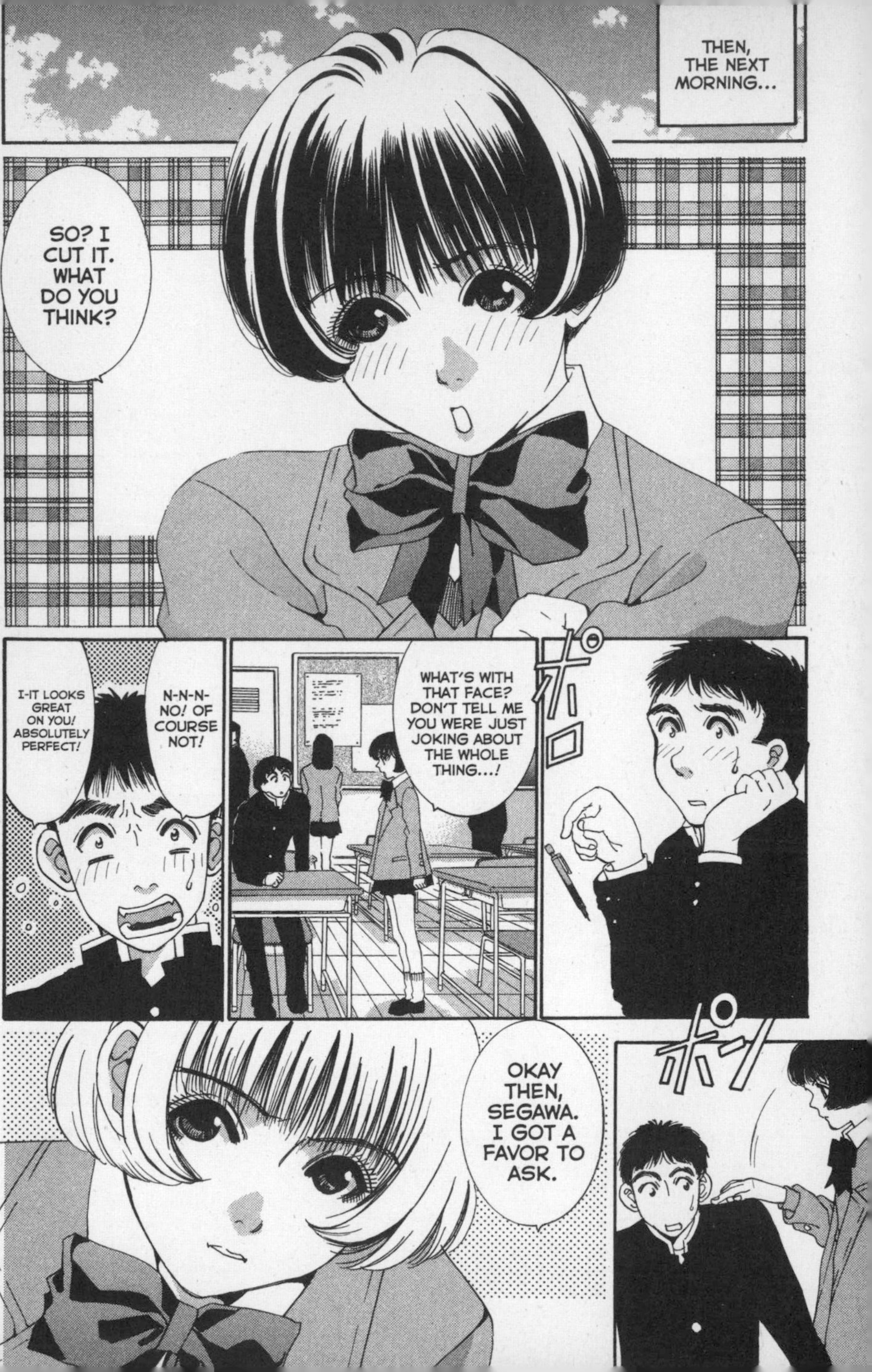
THEN, THE NEXT MORNING...
SO? I CUT IT. WHAT DO YOU THINK?
ポロ
WHAT'S WITH THAT FACE? DON'T TELL ME YOU WERE JUST JOKING ABOUT THE WHOLE THING...!
N-N-N-NO! OF COURSE NOT!
I-IT LOOKS GREAT ON YOU! ABSOLUTELY PERFECT!
ポン
OKAY THEN, SEGAWA. I GOT A FAVOR TO ASK.

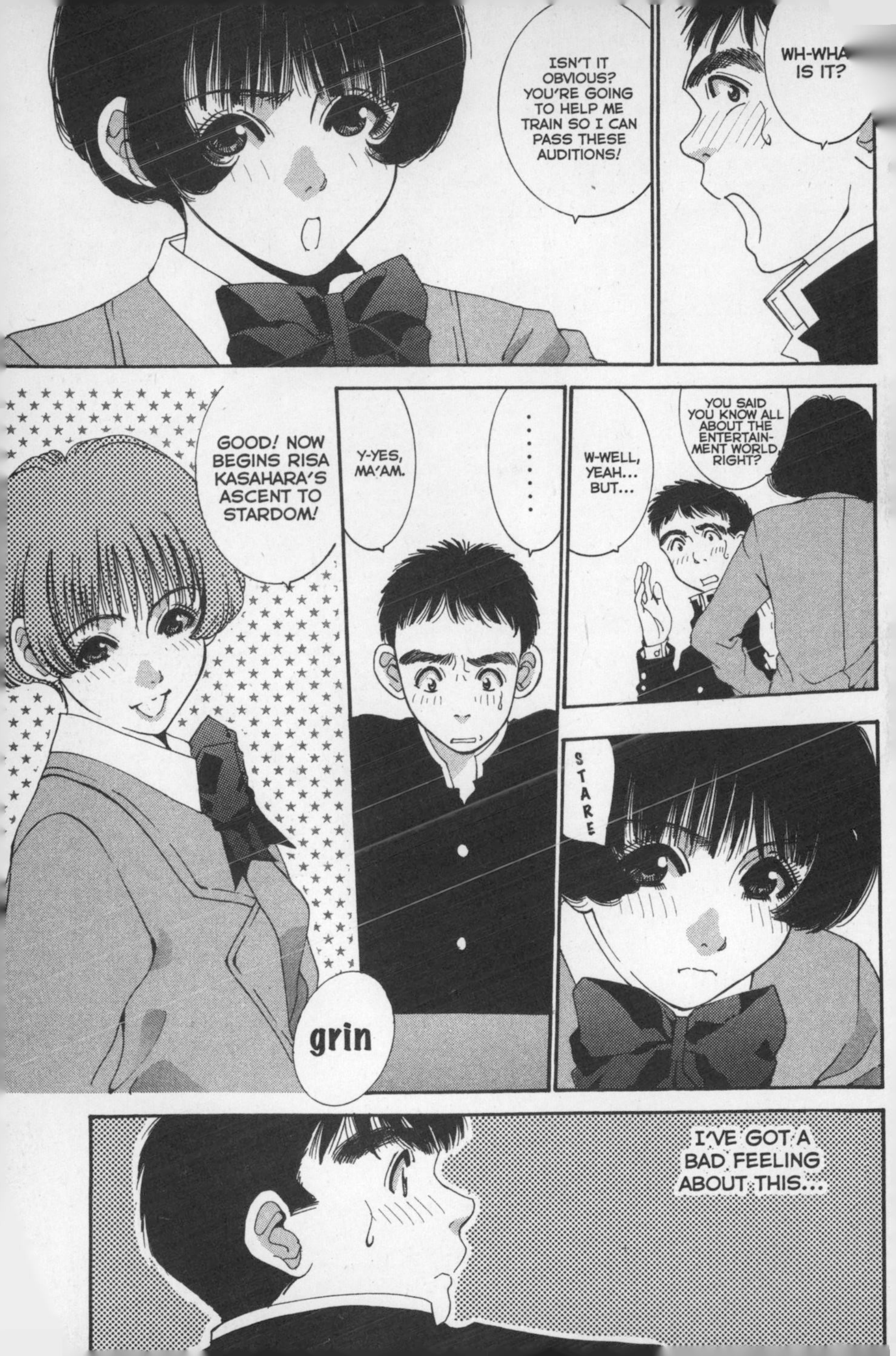
WH-WHA
IS IT?
ISN'T IT OBVIOUS? YOU'RE GOING TO HELP ME TRAIN SO I CAN PASS THESE AUDITIONS!
YOU SAID YOU KNOW ALL ABOUT THE ENTERTAIN-MENT WORLD, RIGHT?
W-WELL, YEAH... BUT...
STARE
....
Y-YES, MA'AM.
GOOD! NOW BEGINS RISA KASAHARA'S ASCENT TO STARDOM!
grin
I'VE GOT A BAD FEELING ABOUT THIS...

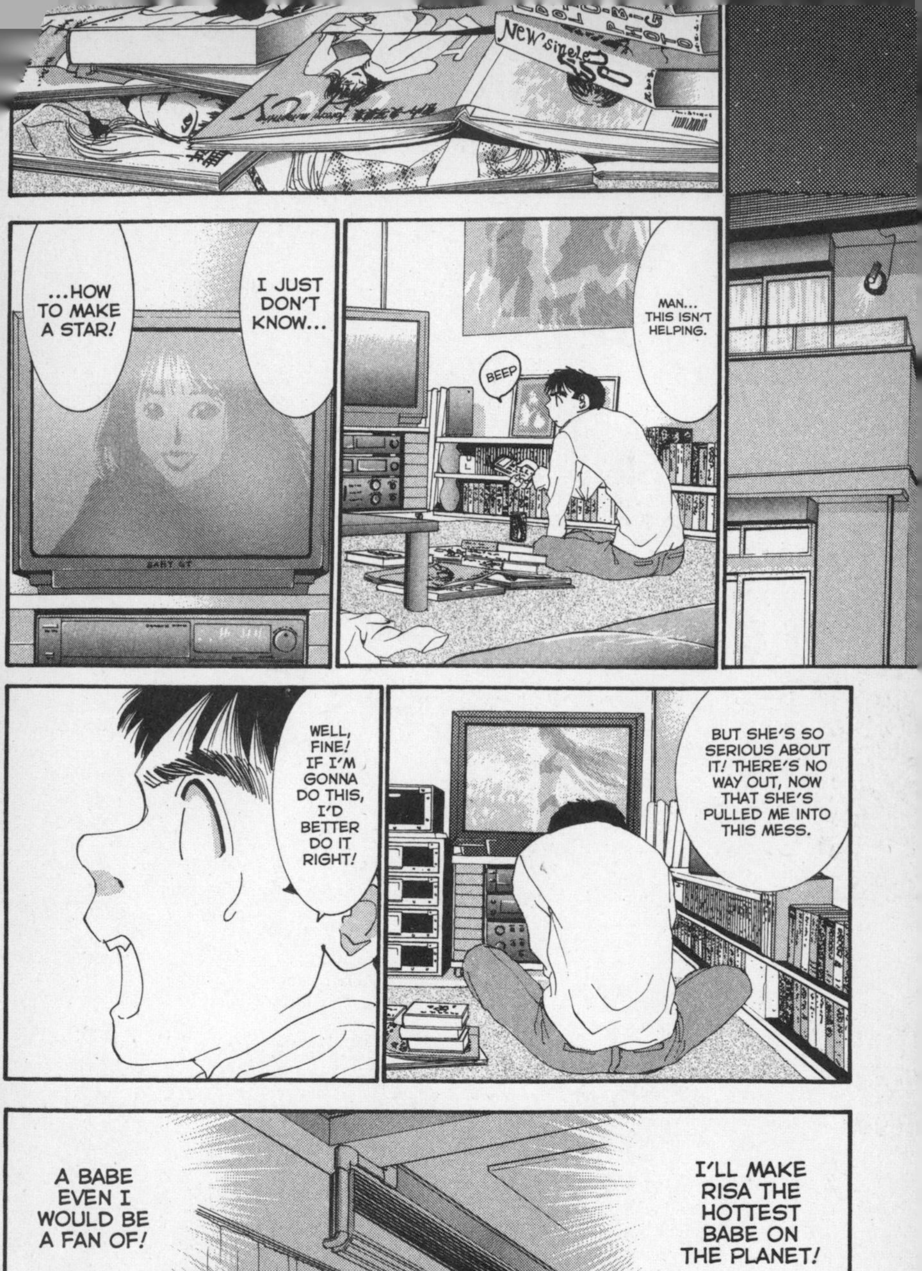
MAN... THIS ISN'T HELPING.
BEEP
I JUST DON'T KNOW...
...HOW TO MAKE A STAR!
BUT SHE'S SO SERIOUS ABOUT IT! THERE'S NO WAY OUT, NOW THAT SHE'S PULLED ME INTO THIS MESS.
WELL, FINE! IF I'M GONNA DO THIS, I'D BETTER DO IT RIGHT!
I'LL MAKE RISA THE HOTTEST BABE ON THE PLANET!
A BABE EVEN I WOULD BE A FAN OF!

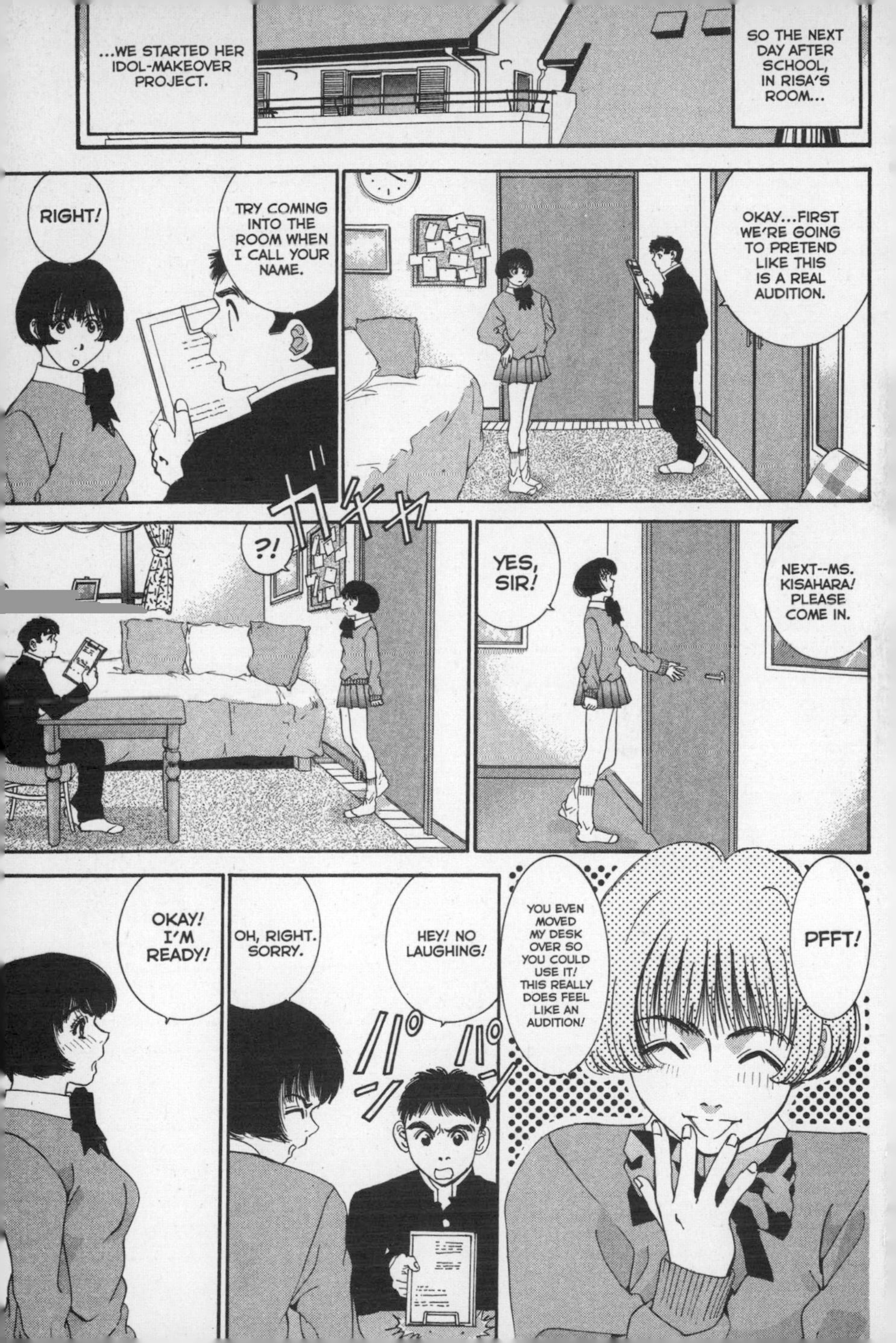
SO THE NEXT DAY AFTER SCHOOL, IN RISA'S ROOM...
...WE STARTED HER IDOL-MAKEOVER PROJECT.
OKAY...FIRST WE'RE GOING TO PRETEND LIKE THIS IS A REAL AUDITION.
TRY COMING INTO THE ROOM WHEN I CALL YOUR NAME.
RIGHT!
NEXT--MS. KISAHARA! PLEASE COME IN.
YES, SIR!
ガチャ
?!
PFFT!
YOU EVEN MOVED MY DESK OVER SO YOU COULD USE IT! THIS REALLY DOES FEEL LIKE AN AUDITION!
HEY! NO LAUGHING!
OH, RIGHT. SORRY.
OKAY! I'M READY!

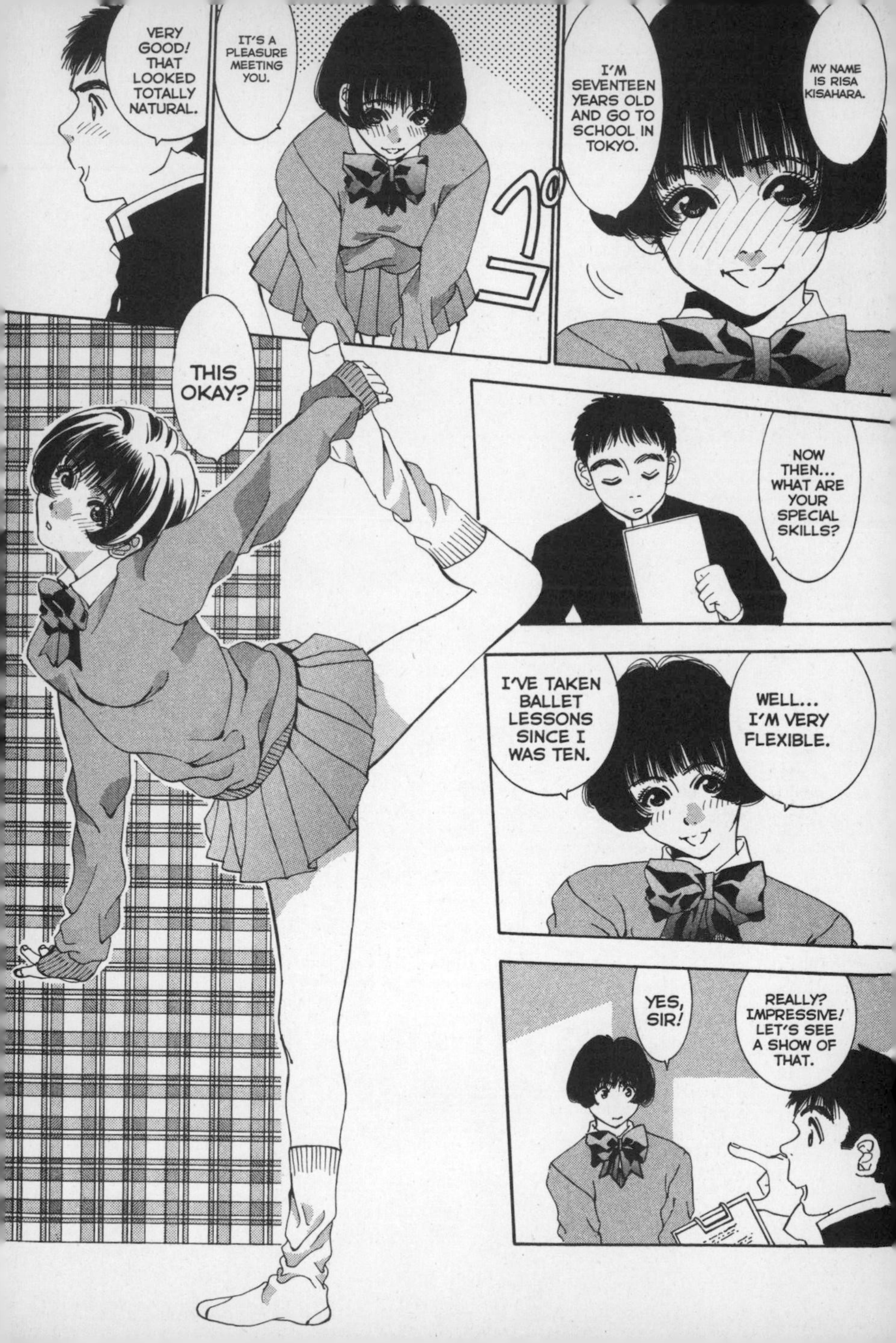
MY NAME IS RISA KISAHARA.
I'M SEVENTEEN YEARS OLD AND GO TO SCHOOL IN TOKYO.
IT'S A PLEASURE MEETING YOU.
VERY GOOD! THAT LOOKED TOTALLY NATURAL.
NOW THEN... WHAT ARE YOUR SPECIAL SKILLS?
WELL... I'M VERY FLEXIBLE.
I'VE TAKEN BALLET LESSONS SINCE I WAS TEN.
REALLY? IMPRESSIVE! LET'S SEE A SHOW OF THAT.
YES, SIR!
THIS OKAY?

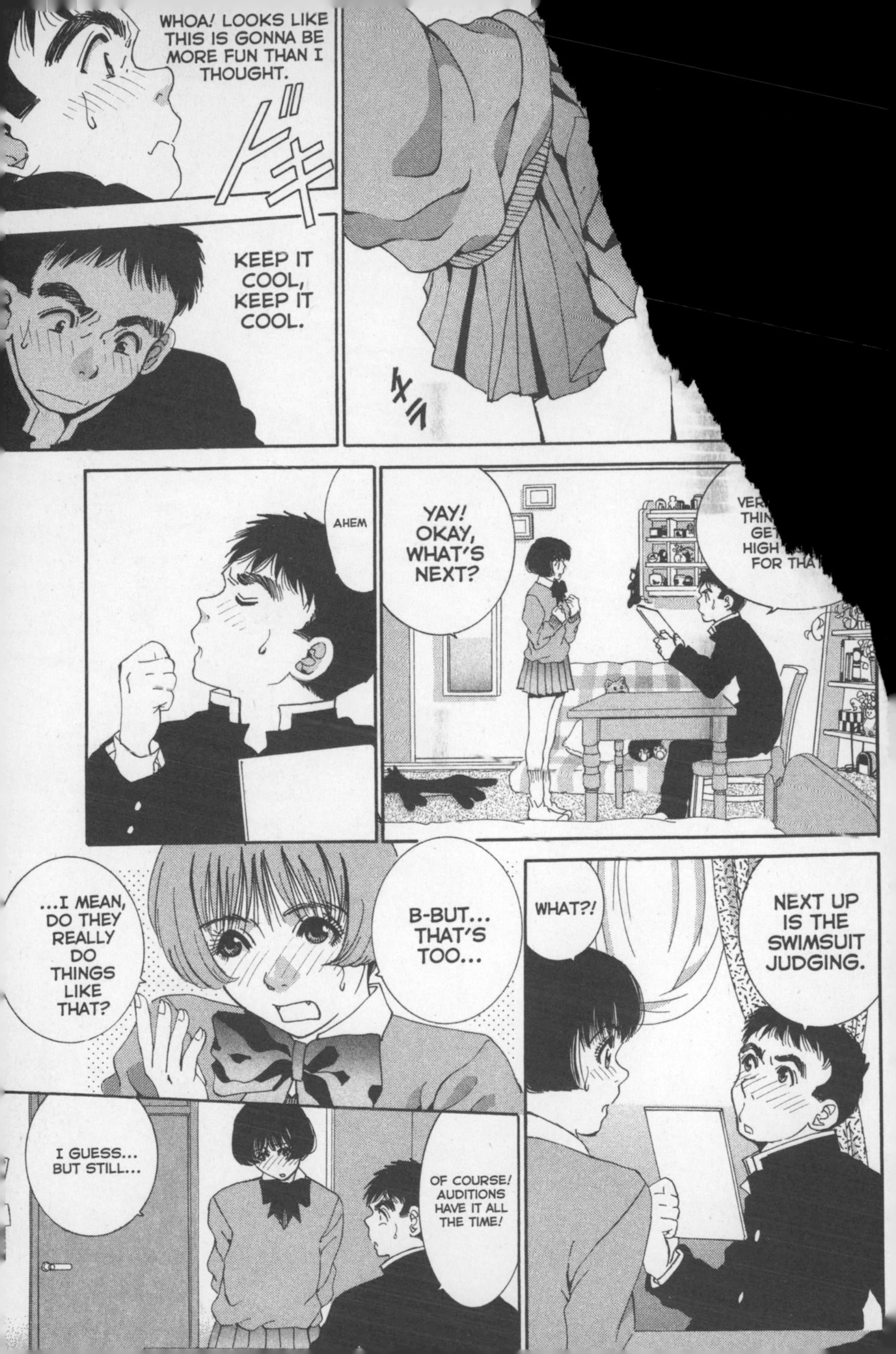

WHOA! LOOKS LIKE THIS IS GONNA BE MORE FUN THAN I THOUGHT.
ドキ
KEEP IT COOL, KEEP IT COOL.
YAY! OKAY, WHAT'S NEXT?
AHEM
NEXT UP IS THE SWIMSUIT JUDGING.
WHAT?!
B-BUT... THAT'S TOO...
...I MEAN, DO THEY REALLY DO THINGS LIKE THAT?
OF COURSE! AUDITIONS HAVE IT ALL THE TIME!
I GUESS... BUT STILL...

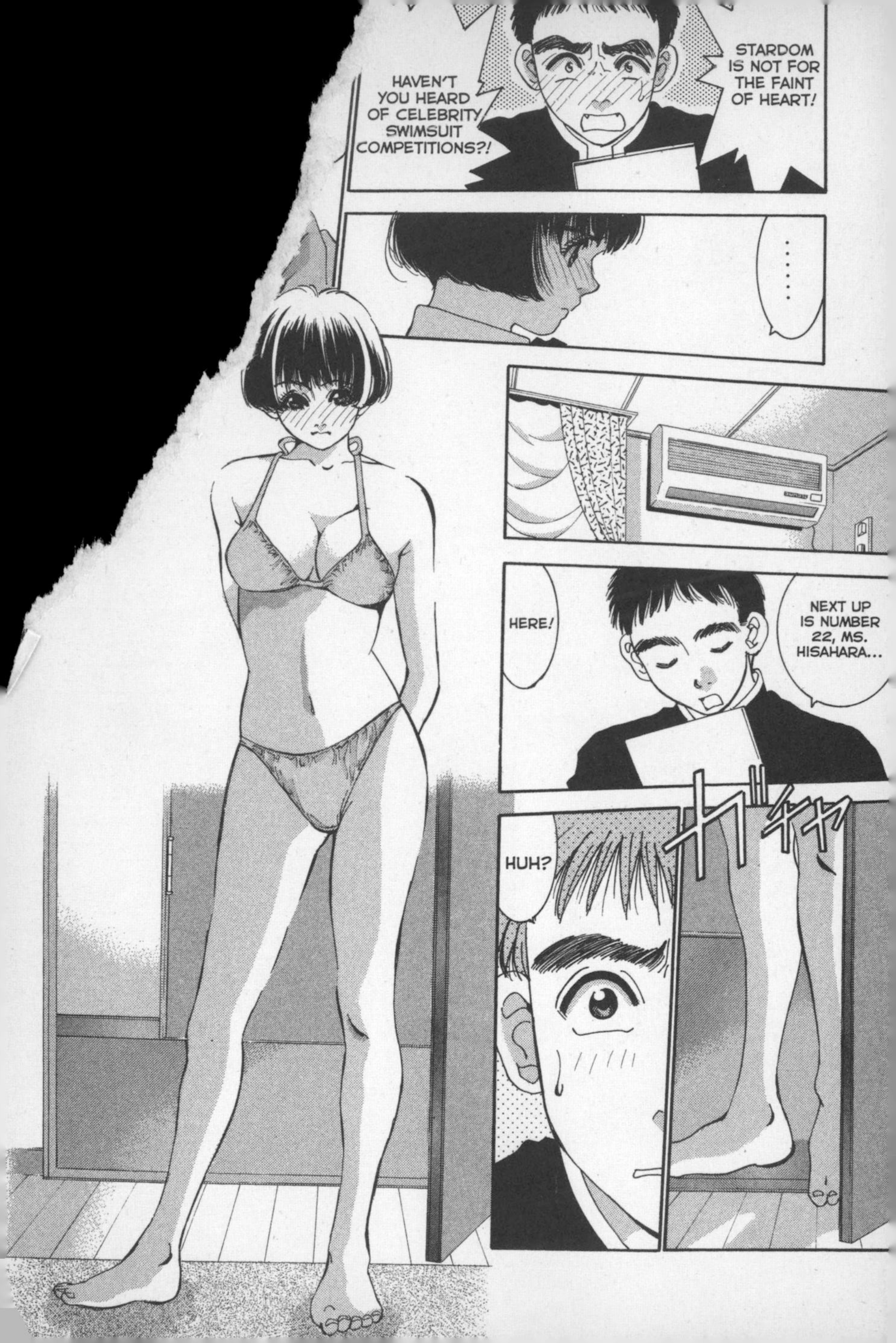
STARDOM IS NOT FOR THE FAINT OF HEART!
HAVEN'T YOU HEARD OF CELEBRITY SWIMSUIT COMPETITIONS?!
......
NEXT UP IS NUMBER 22, MS. HISAHARA...
HERE!
ガチャ
HUH?

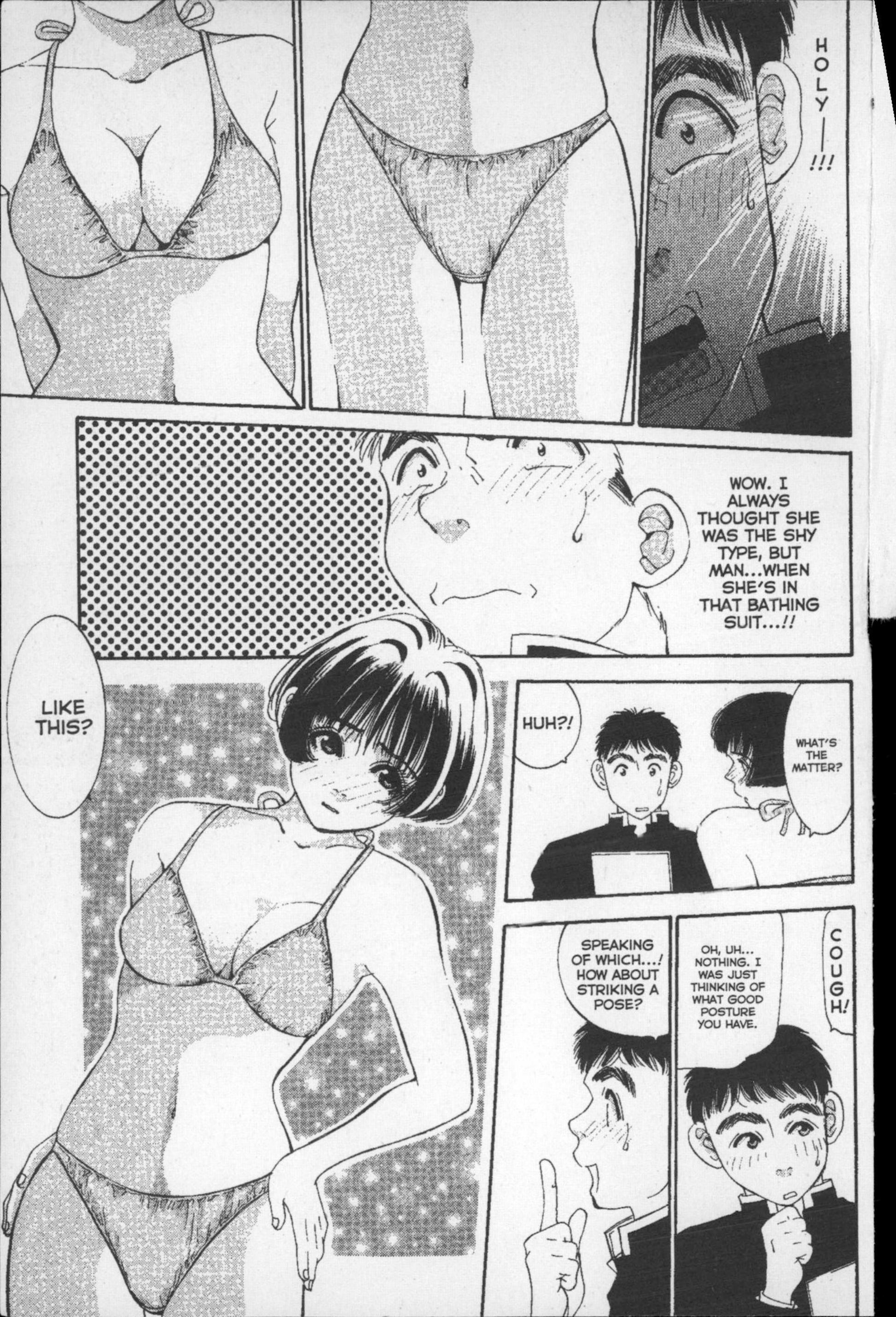
HOLY—!!!
WOW. I ALWAYS THOUGHT SHE WAS THE SHY TYPE, BUT MAN...WHEN SHE'S IN THAT BATHING SUIT...!!
WHAT'S THE MATTER?
HUH?!
COUGH!
OH, UH... NOTHING. I WAS JUST THINKING OF WHAT GOOD POSTURE YOU HAVE.
SPEAKING OF WHICH...! HOW ABOUT STRIKING A POSE?
LIKE THIS?

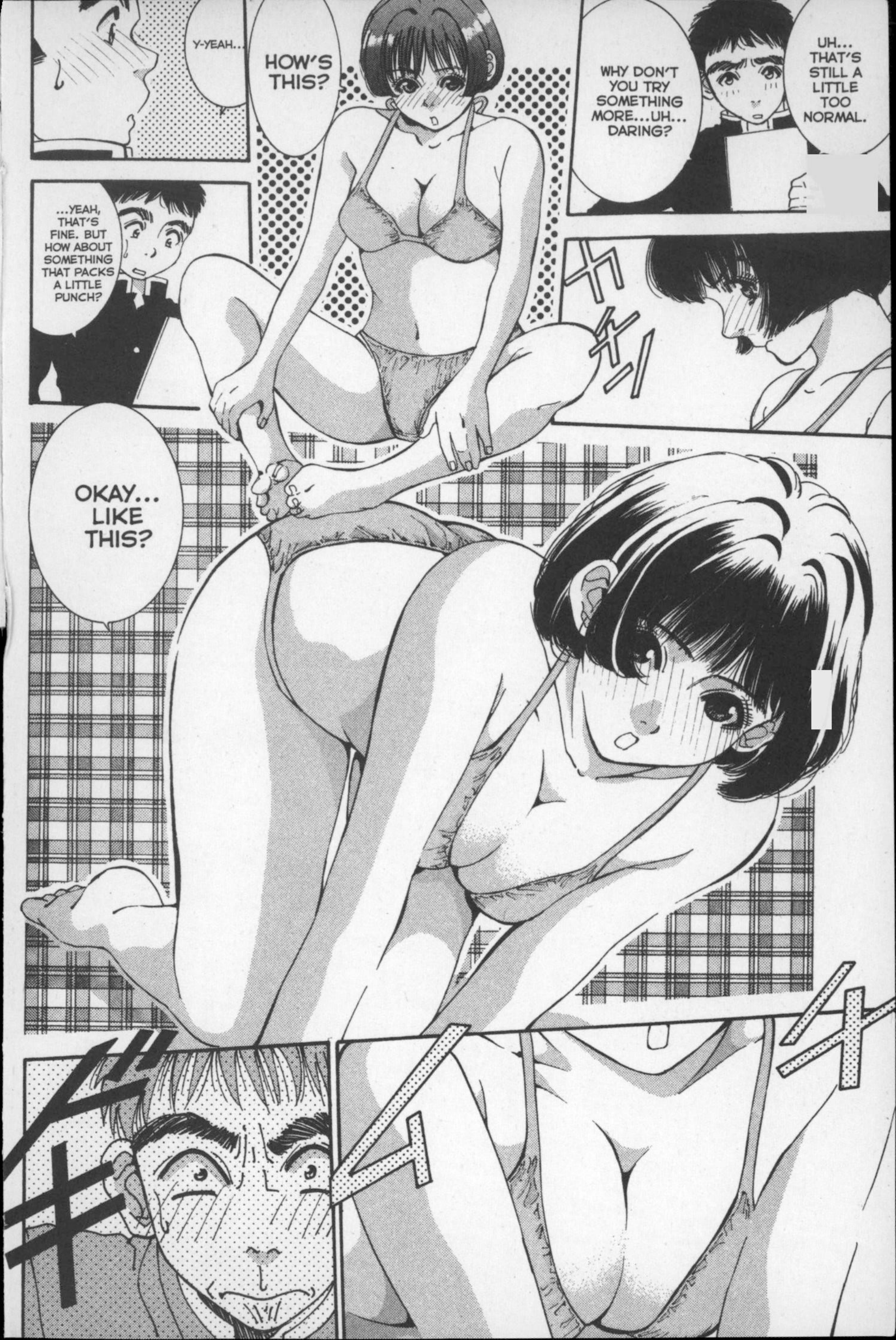
UH... THAT'S STILL A LITTLE TOO NORMAL.
WHY DON'T YOU TRY SOMETHING MORE...UH... DARING?
HOW'S THIS?
Y-YEAH...
...YEAH, THAT'S FINE. BUT HOW ABOUT SOMETHING THAT PACKS A LITTLE PUNCH?
OKAY... LIKE THIS?

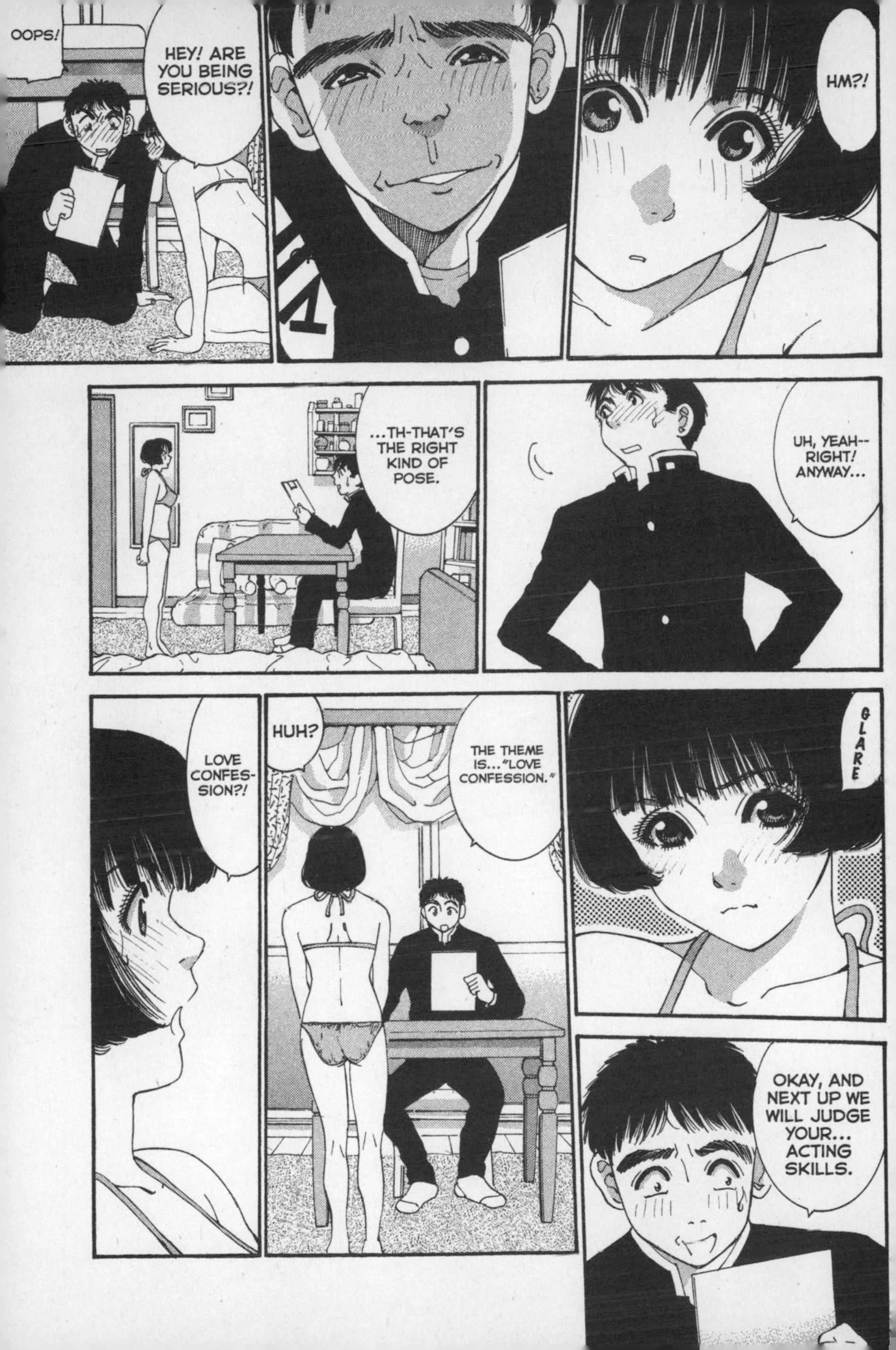
HM?!
HEY! ARE YOU BEING SERIOUS?!
OOPS!
UH, YEAH-- RIGHT! ANYWAY...
...TH-THAT'S THE RIGHT KIND OF POSE.
GLARE
OKAY, AND NEXT UP WE WILL JUDGE YOUR... ACTING SKILLS.
THE THEME IS..."LOVE CONFESSION."
HUH?
LOVE CONFESSION?!

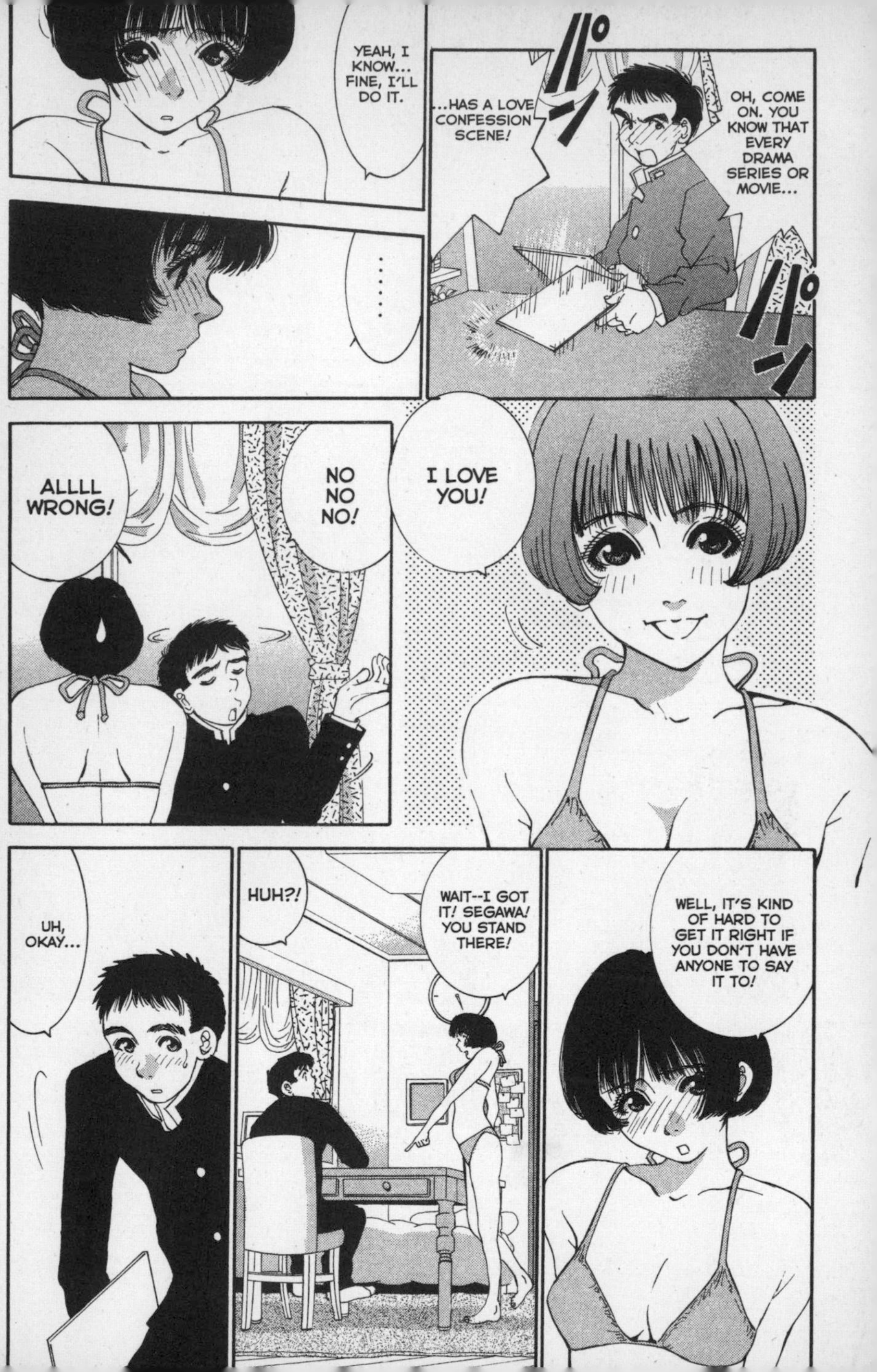

パン
OH, COME ON. YOU KNOW THAT EVERY DRAMA SERIES OR MOVIE...
...HAS A LOVE CONFESSION SCENE!
パン
YEAH, I KNOW... FINE, I'LL DO IT.
......
I LOVE YOU!
NO NO NO!
ALLLL WRONG!
WELL, IT'S KIND OF HARD TO GET IT RIGHT IF YOU DON'T HAVE ANYONE TO SAY IT TO!
WAIT--I GOT IT! SEGAWA! YOU STAND THERE!
HUH?!
UH, OKAY...

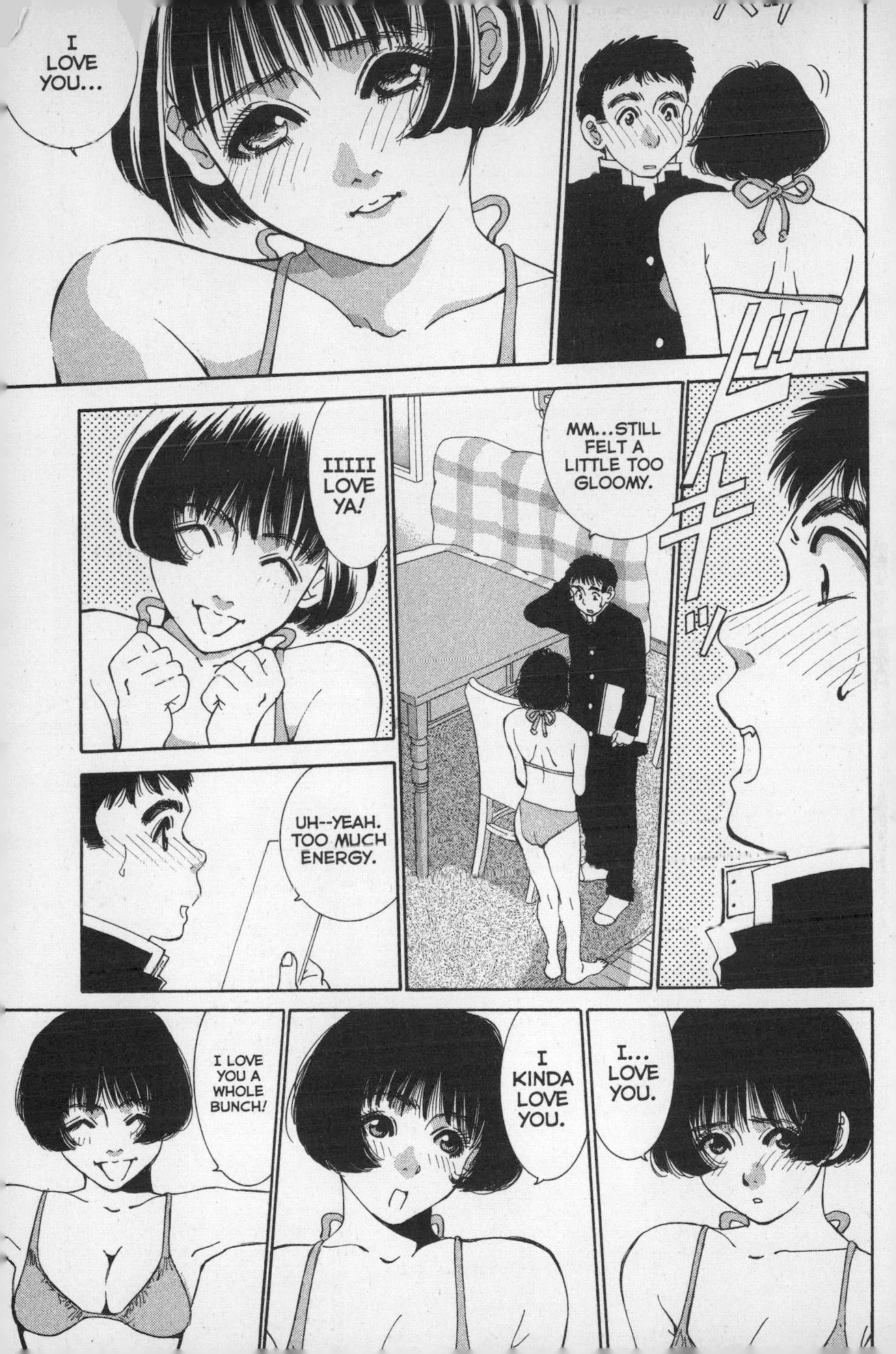
I LOVE YOU...
MM...STILL FELT A LITTLE TOO GLOOMY.
IIIII LOVE YA!
UH--YEAH. TOO MUCH ENERGY.
I... LOVE YOU.
I KINDA LOVE YOU.
I LOVE YOU A WHOLE BUNCH!

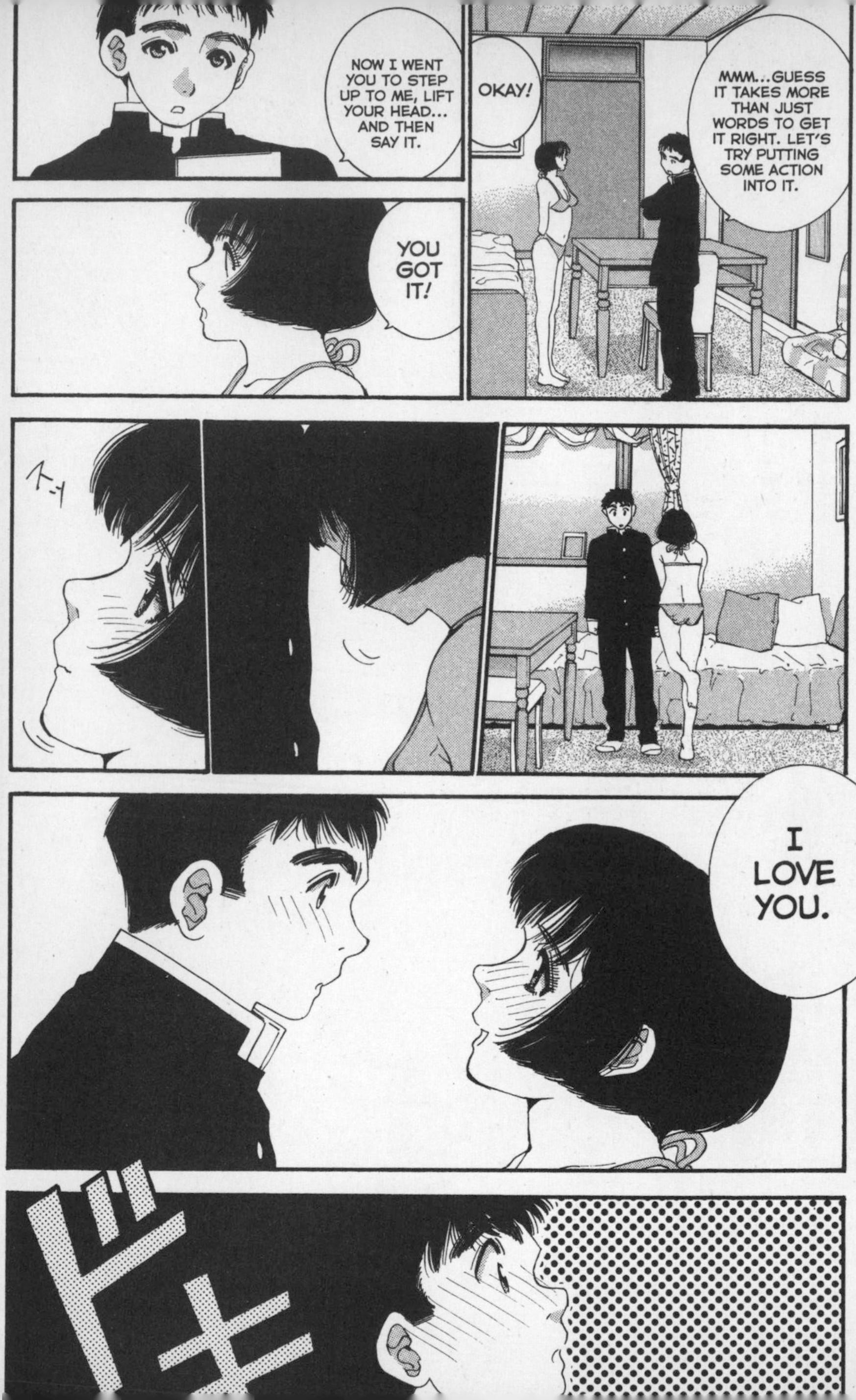
MMM...GUESS IT TAKES MORE THAN JUST WORDS TO GET IT RIGHT. LET'S TRY PUTTING SOME ACTION INTO IT.
OKAY!
NOW I WENT YOU TO STEP UP TO ME, LIFT YOUR HEAD... AND THEN SAY IT.
YOU GOT IT!
I LOVE YOU.
ドキ

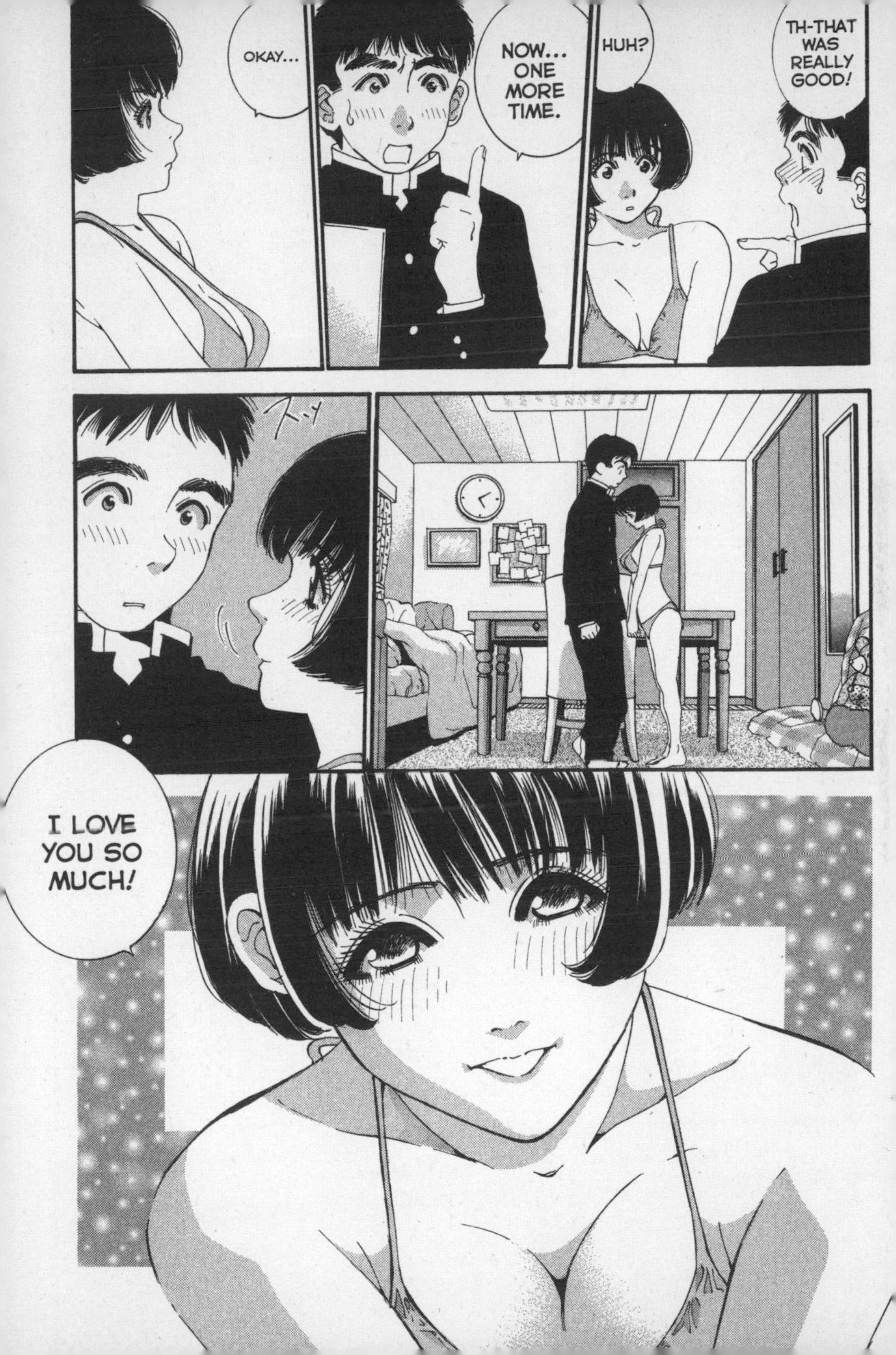
TH-THAT WAS REALLY GOOD!
HUH?
NOW... ONE MORE TIME.
OKAY...
I LOVE YOU SO MUCH!

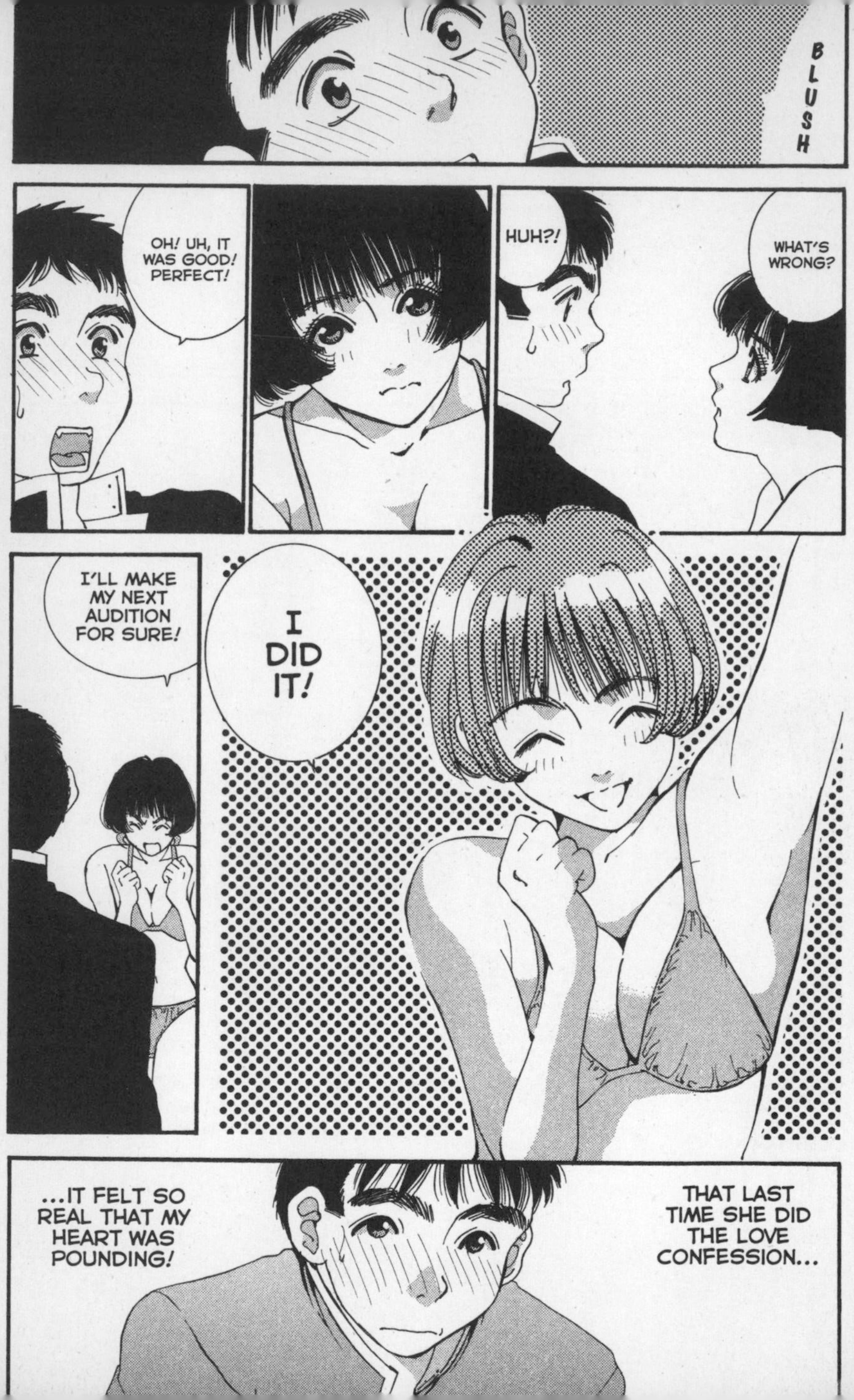
BLUSH
WHAT'S WRONG?
HUH?!
OH! UH, IT WAS GOOD! PERFECT!
I DID IT!
I'LL MAKE MY NEXT AUDITION FOR SURE!
THAT LAST TIME SHE DID THE LOVE CONFESSION...
...IT FELT SO REAL THAT MY HEART WAS POUNDING!

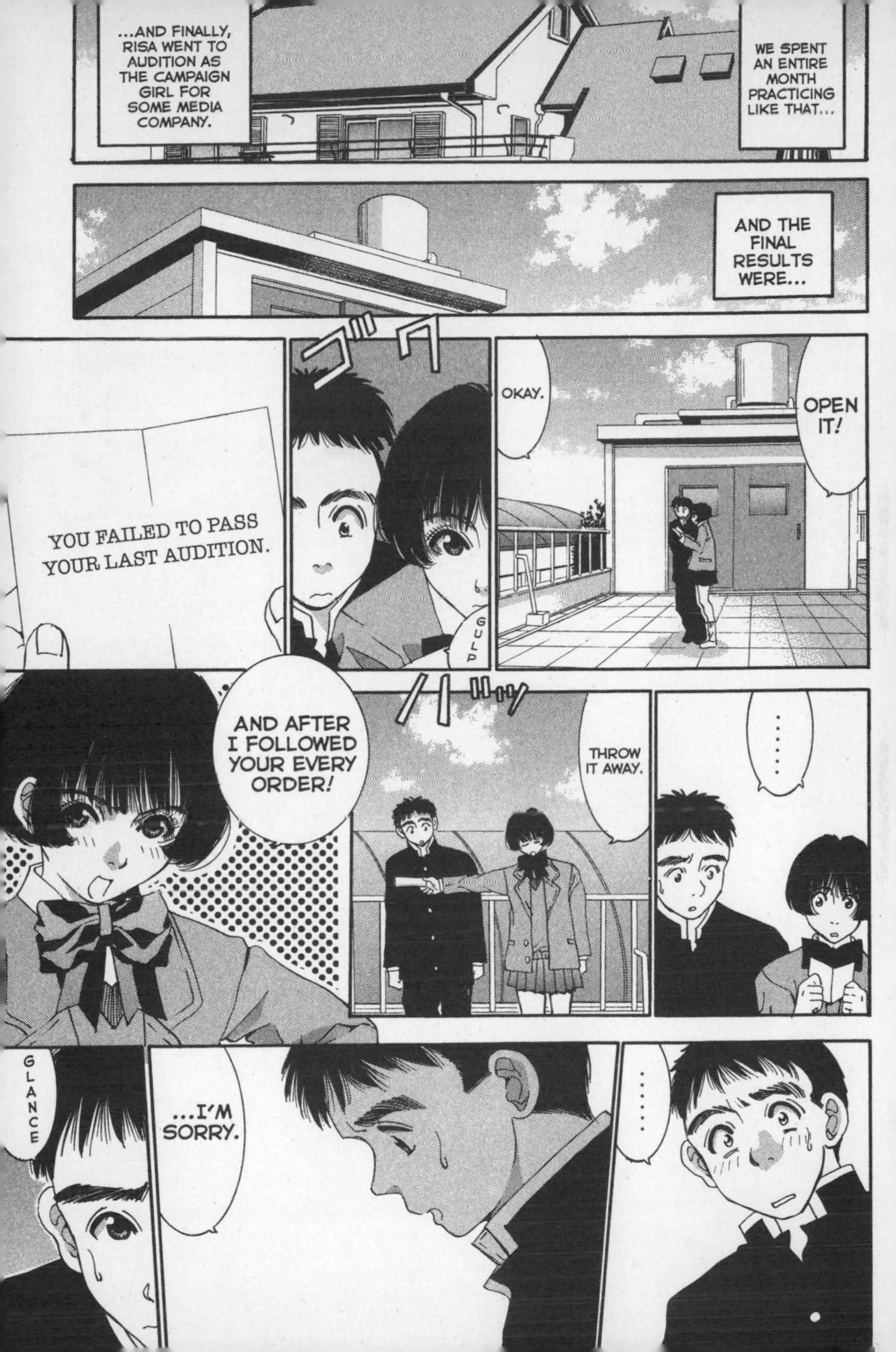
WE SPENT AN ENTIRE MONTH PRACTICING LIKE THAT...
...AND FINALLY, RISA WENT TO AUDITION AS THE CAMPAIGN GIRL FOR SOME MEDIA COMPANY.
AND THE FINAL RESULTS WERE...
OPEN IT!
OKAY.
GULP
YOU FAILED TO PASS YOUR LAST AUDITION.
......
THROW IT AWAY.
AND AFTER I FOLLOWED YOUR EVERY ORDER!
......
...I'M SORRY.
GLANCE

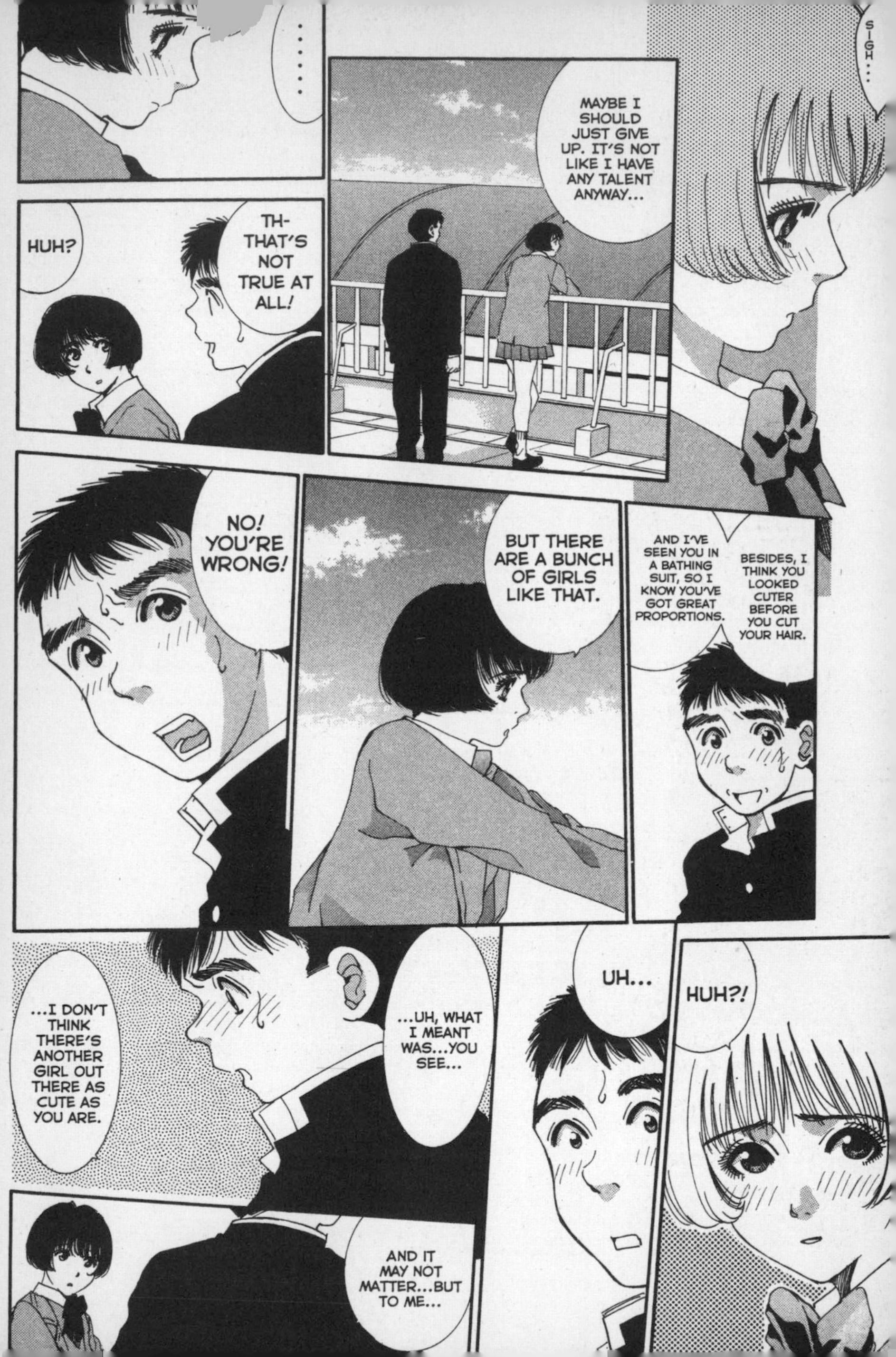
SIGH...
MAYBE I SHOULD JUST GIVE UP. IT'S NOT LIKE I HAVE ANY TALENT ANYWAY...
......
TH-THAT'S NOT TRUE AT ALL!
HUH?
BESIDES, I THINK YOU LOOKED CUTER BEFORE YOU CUT YOUR HAIR.
AND I'VE SEEN YOU IN A BATHING SUIT, SO I KNOW YOU'VE GOT GREAT PROPORTIONS.
BUT THERE ARE A BUNCH OF GIRLS LIKE THAT.
NO! YOU'RE WRONG!
HUH?!
UH...
...UH, WHAT I MEANT WAS...YOU SEE...
...I DON'T THINK THERE'S ANOTHER GIRL OUT THERE AS CUTE AS YOU ARE.
AND IT MAY NOT MATTER...BUT TO ME...

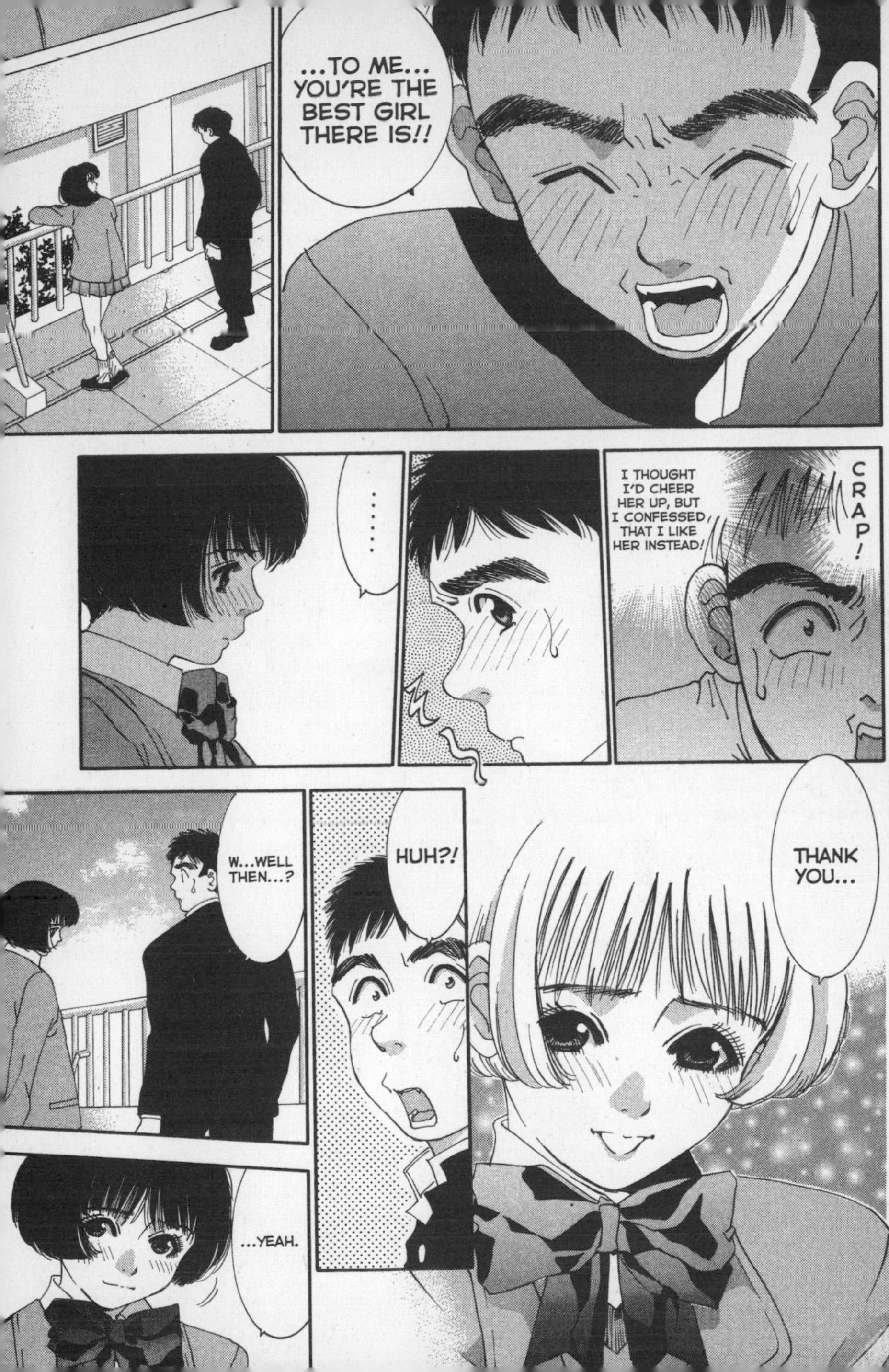
...TO ME... YOU'RE THE BEST GIRL THERE IS!!
CRAP!
I THOUGHT I'D CHEER HER UP, BUT I CONFESSED THAT I LIKE HER INSTEAD!
......
THANK YOU...
HUH?!
W...WELL THEN...?
...YEAH.

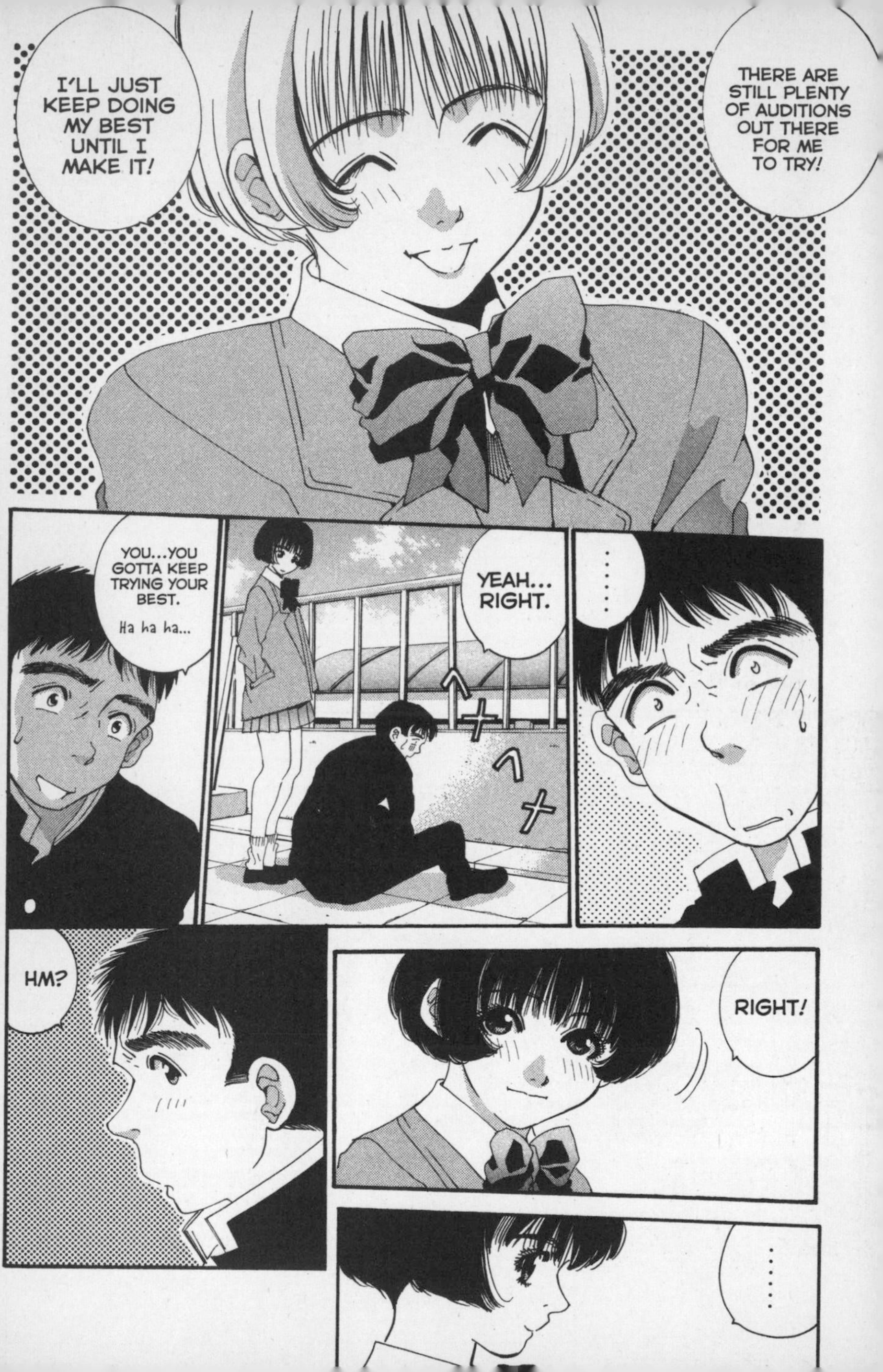
THERE ARE STILL PLENTY OF AUDITIONS OUT THERE FOR ME TO TRY!
I'LL JUST KEEP DOING MY BEST UNTIL I MAKE IT!
......
YEAH... RIGHT.
へナへナ
YOU...YOU GOTTA KEEP TRYING YOUR BEST.
Ha ha ha...
RIGHT!
......
HM?

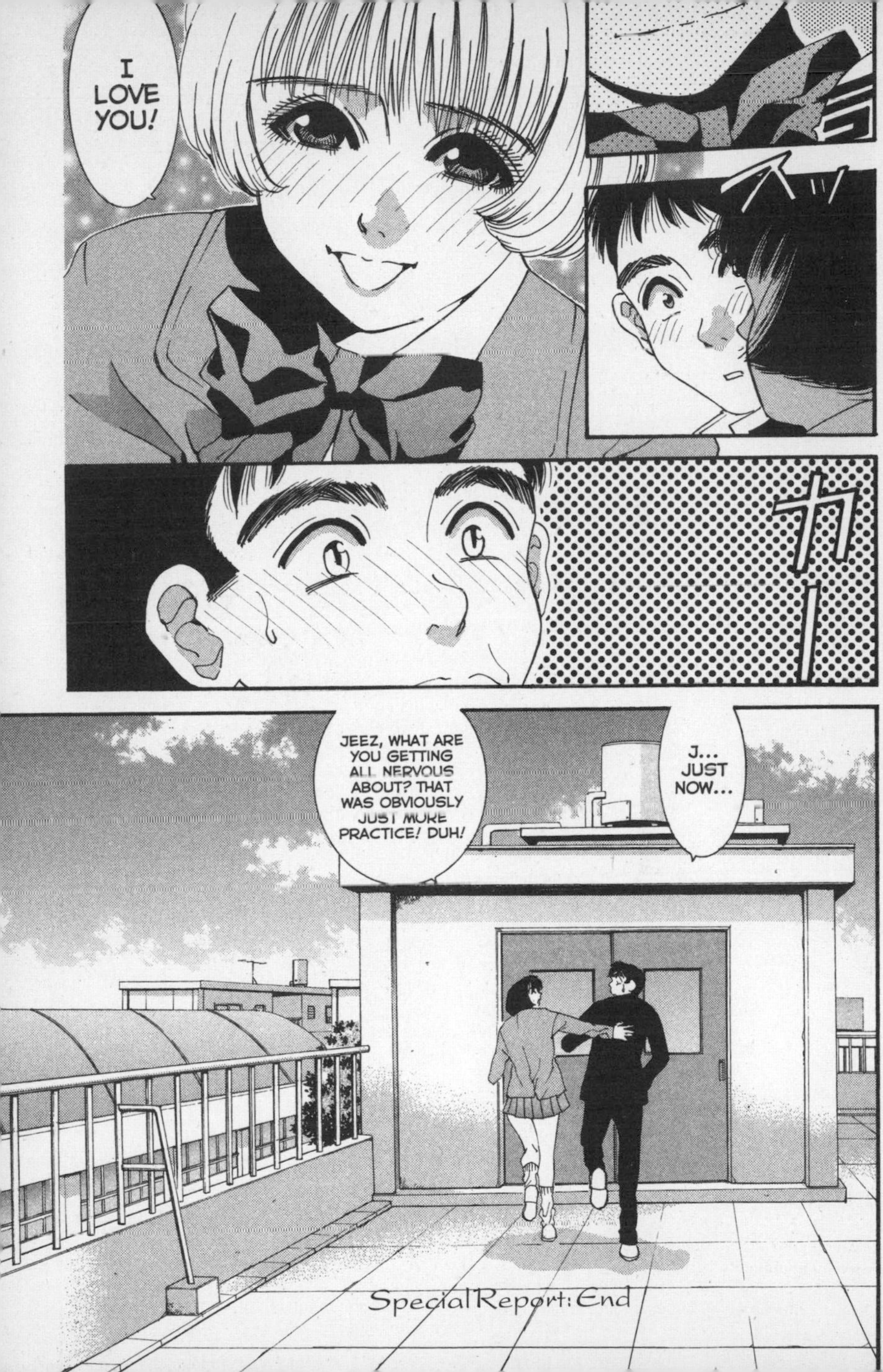
スッ
I LOVE YOU!
カー
J... JUST NOW...
JEEZ, WHAT ARE YOU GETTING ALL NERVOUS ABOUT? THAT WAS OBVIOUSLY JUST MORE PRACTICE! DUH!
Special Report: End

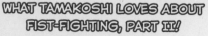

WHAT TAMAKOSHI LOVES ABOUT FIST-FIGHTING, PART II!

NOW, I'M SURE I SAID THIS IN THE LAST VOLUME, BUT I JUST LOOOOVE FIST-FIGHTING (FROM THE BOTTOM OF MY HEART)! AND IF YOU'RE LOOKING FOR SOME PROOF OF THAT, YOU CAN FIND IT IN THE "VIRTUAL FIGHTER 3" VIDEO GAME THAT I EVEN BRING TO WORK! YES, I ACTUALLY BOUGHT THE THING. THAT'S ABOUT THE ONLY REASON WHY I LOVE FIST-FIGHTING AND FIST-FIGHTING GAMES SO MUCH! AND WHEN THE MOMENT'S WORK IS OVER, WE ALL SIT DOWN FOR A GOOD OLD VIRTUAL TOURNAMENT! IN THE TOURNAMENT WE MADE, WE ALL GET A CHANCE TO TRY OUR SKILLS AGAINST EVERYONE ELSE. THE ONLY PROBLEM IS THAT WE START SYMPATHIZING SO MUCH WITH THE GAME CHARACTERS THAT A LOT OF ARGUMENTS OFTEN BREAK OUT...BUT AT LEAST EVERYONE ENJOYS PLAYING THE GAME!!

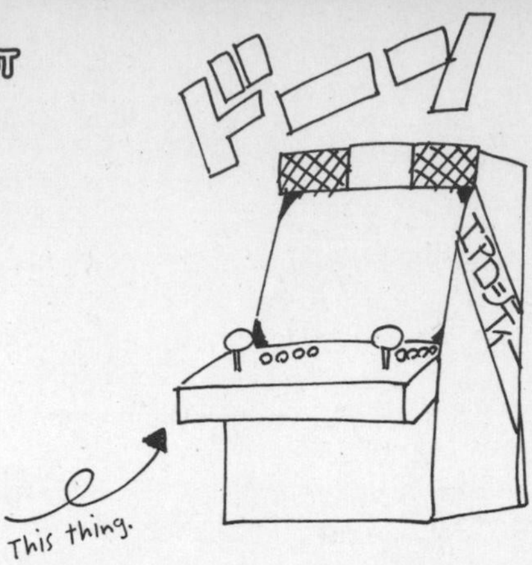
This thing.

PLUS, MY NAME IN THE RING IS..."MONKEY BALL"!

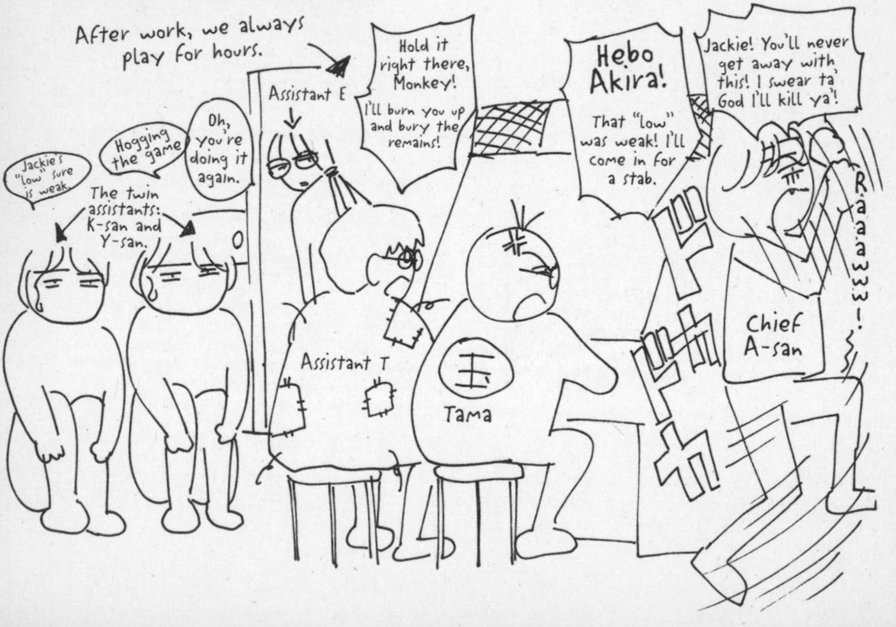
Jackie! You'll never get away with this! I swear ta' God I'll kill ya'!
Raaaww!
Chief A-san
Hebo Akira!
That "low" was weak! I'll come in for a stab.
Tama
Hold it right there, Monkey!
I'll burn you up and bury the remains!
Assistant E
Assistant T
After work, we always play for hours.
Oh, you're doing it again.
Hogging the game
The twin assistants: K-san and Y-san.
Jackie's "low" sure is weak.

Next Time in BOYS BE

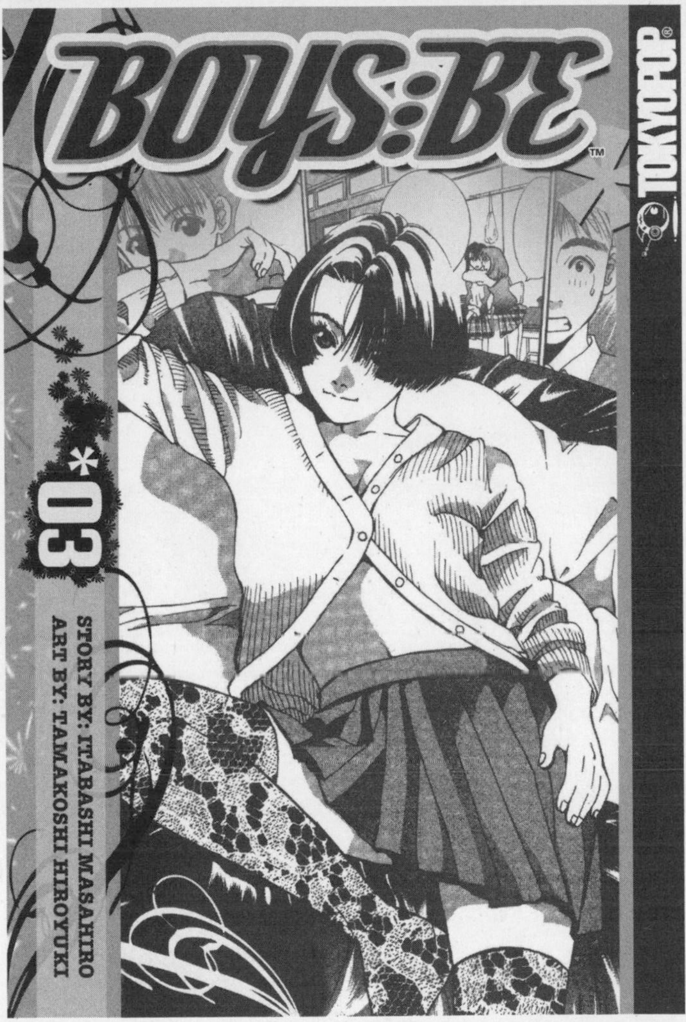
BOYS:BE™
TOKYOPOP®
*03
STORY BY: ITABASHI MASAHIRO
ART BY: TAMAKOSHI HIROYUKI

Young men and women starting relationships face tons of challenges: Testosterone-driven young boys idealizing their fantasy girl, getting over a first crush, lying and misunderstanding...there are many lessons to be learned in the game of love, and you'll find all the rules inside this volume of Boys Be...!

Twin Talk: A Guy's Guide to Girls
By Kathy and Chrissy Schilling

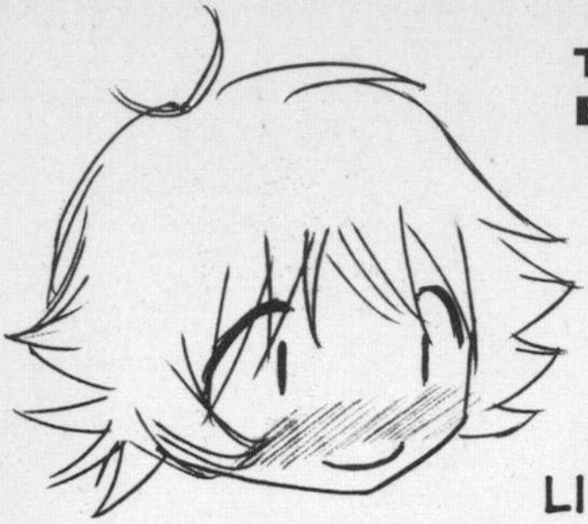

OKAY, FOR STARTERS: TWO THUMBS WAY UP TO OUR MAIN GIRL FOR TAKING THE INITIATIVE LIKE THAT AND ASKING HER CRUSH OUT. THIS STORY'S GOT TOP-QUALITY "GIRL POWER" GOING ON.

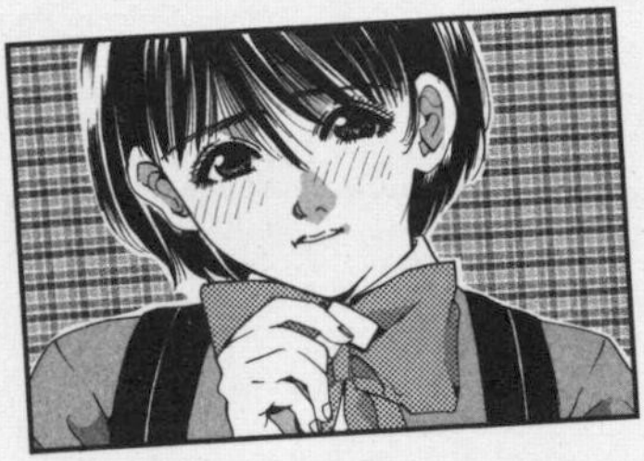

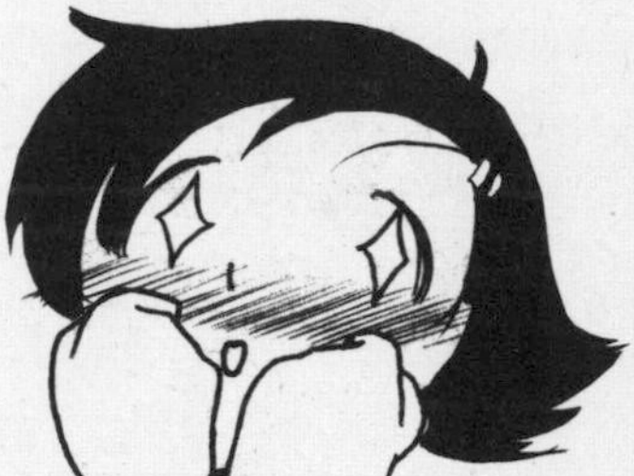

HELLO, IT'S ALL ABOUT THE PURIKURA! TOTALLY FASHIONABLE, CUTE, AND AS OUR MAIN CHARACTER DEMONSTRATED, A UNIQUE WAY TO LEAVE QUITE AN IMPRESSION ON A GUY...

RIGHT...MORE IMPORTANT TO POINT OUT, THOUGH: WATANABE'S BEHAVIOR AFTER FINDING THE PURIKURA SCRAPBOOK WAS NOT SO IMPRESSIVE. JUMPING TO MAD CONCLUSIONS ABOUT KYOUKO...? I MEAN, YOU COULD DO THE GIRL A FAVOR AND JUST ASK HER DIRECTLY WHAT THE STORY IS.

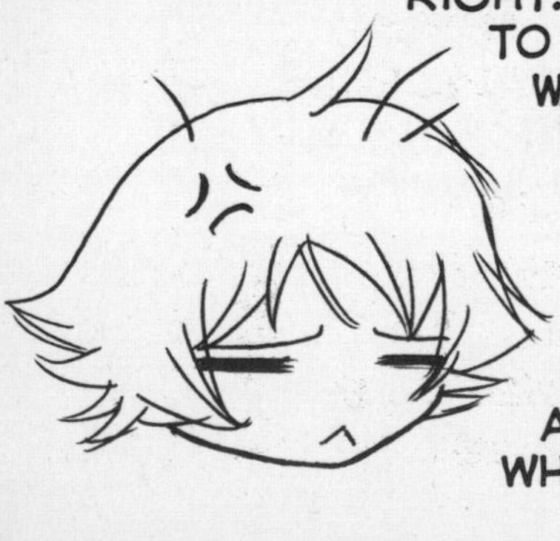

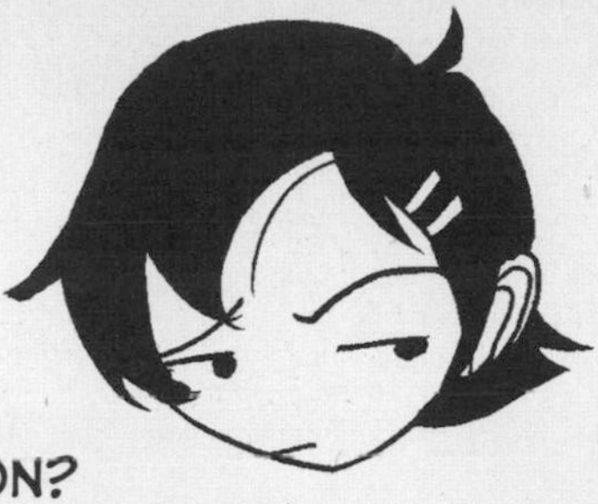

OH YEAH, FOR SURE. GOOD POINT. AND I MEAN, REALLY, AFTER DATING THE SWEET GIRL FOR A COUPLE OF WEEKS, HOW COULD HE TAKE HER FOR SOME KIND OF SL*T AFTER ONE LOOK AT HER PHOTO COLLECTION? SIMPLY UNCOOL ASSUMPTION GOING ON.

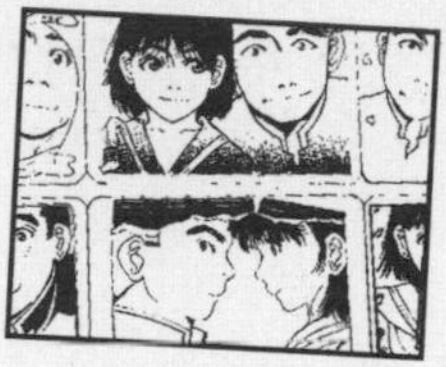

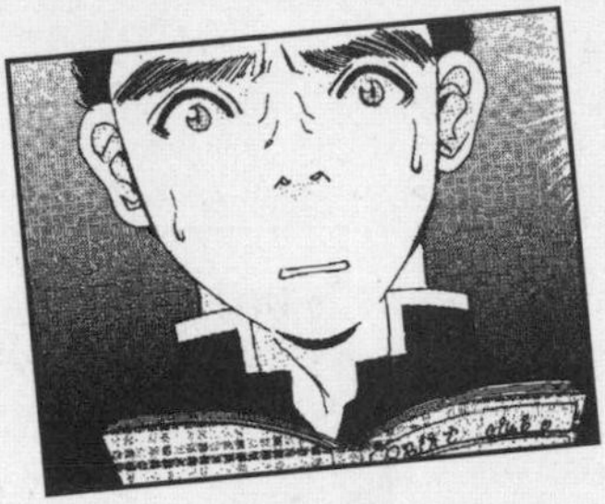

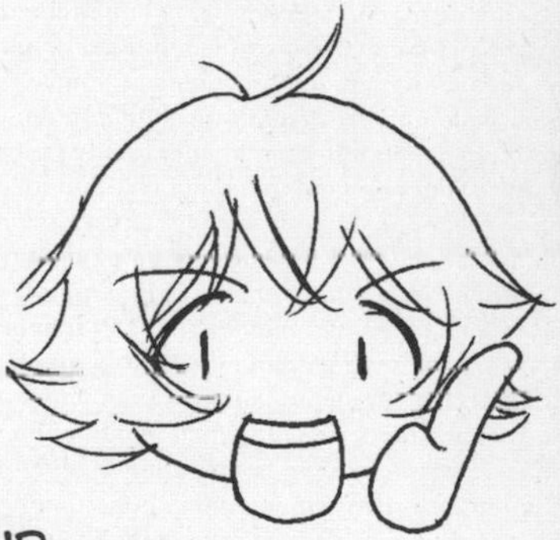

EXACTLY. SO IN SHORT: GUYS, IF YOU'VE GOT A BIT OF SUSPICION GOING ON WITH YOUR GIRL, DON'T JUST BOIL ABOUT IT AND THEN BLOW UP ON HER. GET ALL THE FACTS DOWN BEFORE YOU DUMP A TOTALLY FINE GIRL...LIKE KYOUKO.

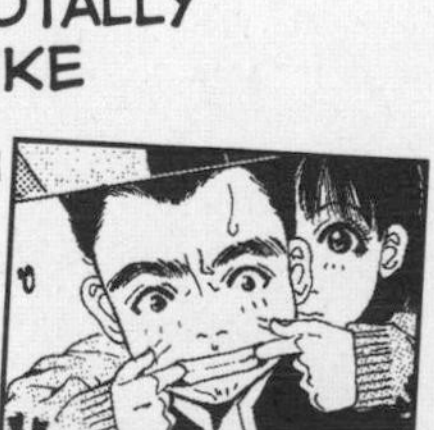

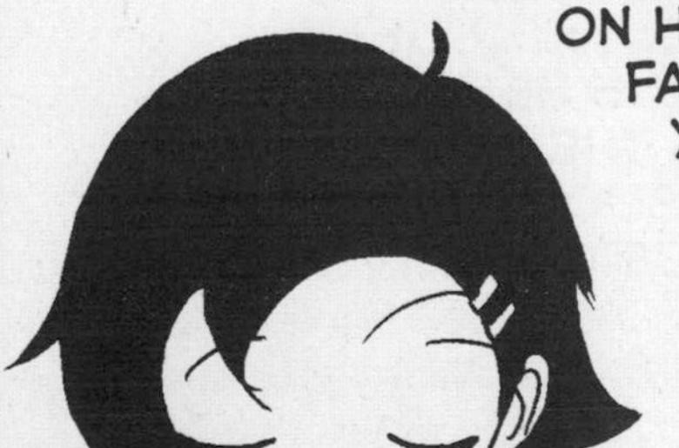

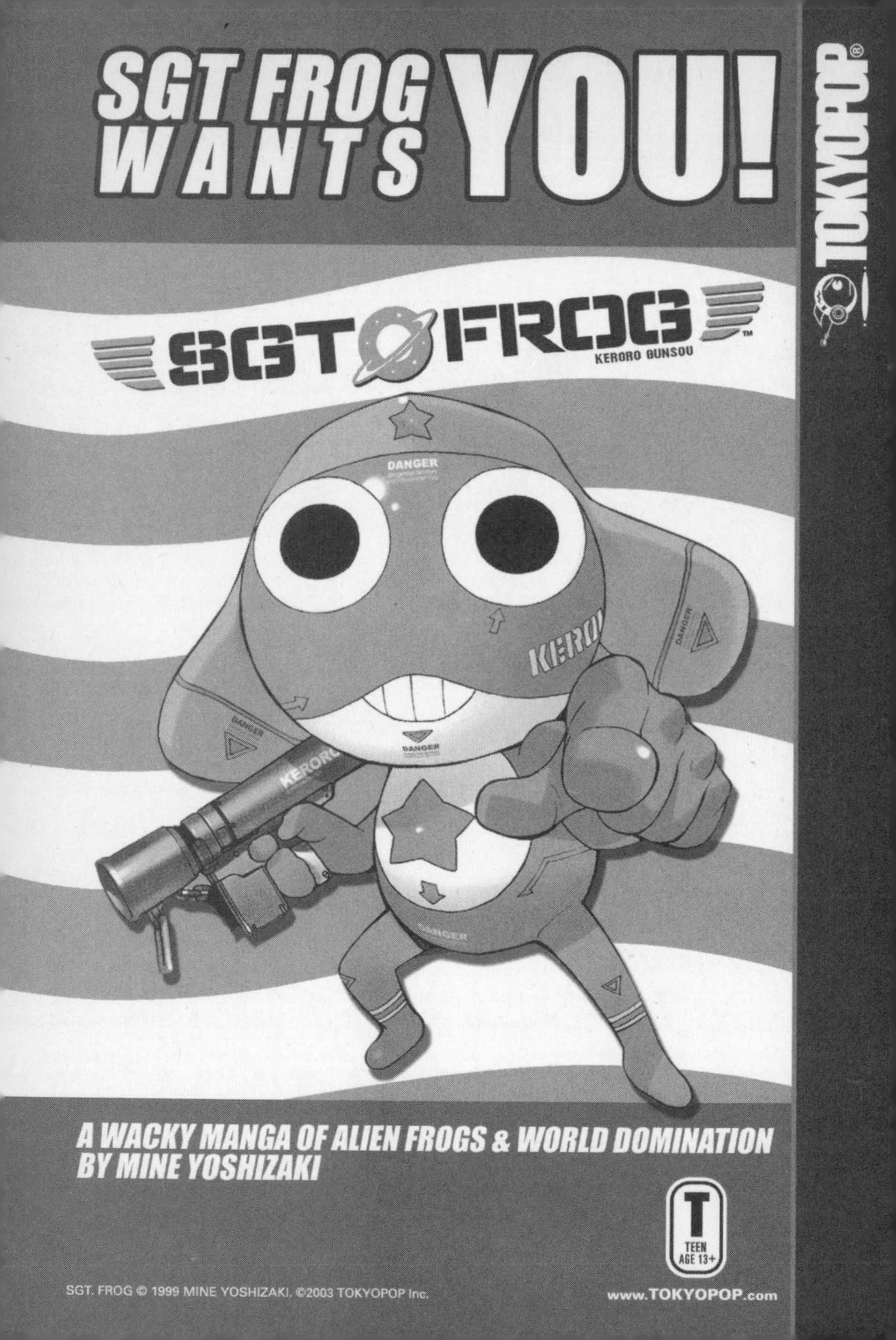
SGT FROG WANTS YOU!
TOKYOPOP®
SGT FROG™
KERORO GUNSOU
DANGER
KERORO
A WACKY MANGA OF ALIEN FROGS & WORLD DOMINATION
BY MINE YOSHIZAKI
T
TEEN AGE 13+
SGT. FROG © 1999 MINE YOSHIZAKI. ©2003 TOKYOPOP Inc.
www.TOKYOPOP.com

ALSO AVAILABLE FROM TOKYOPOP®

ALSO AVAILABLE FROM ☺TOKYOPOP®

MANGA

.HACK//LEGEND OF THE TWILIGHT
@LARGE
ABENOBASHI: MAGICAL SHOPPING ARCADE
A.I. LOVE YOU
AI YORI AOSHI
ALICHINO
ANGELIC LAYER
ARM OF KANNON
BABY BIRTH
BATTLE ROYALE
BATTLE VIXENS
BOYS BE...
BRAIN POWERED
BRIGADOON
B'TX
CANDIDATE FOR GODDESS, THE
CARDCAPTOR SAKURA
CARDCAPTOR SAKURA - MASTER OF THE CLOW
CHOBITS
CHRONICLES OF THE CURSED SWORD
CLAMP SCHOOL DETECTIVES
CLOVER
COMIC PARTY
CONFIDENTIAL CONFESSIONS
CORRECTOR YUI
COWBOY BEBOP
COWBOY BEBOP: SHOOTING STAR
CRAZY LOVE STORY
CRESCENT MOON
CROSS
CULDCEPT
CYBORG 009
D•N•ANGEL
DEARS
DEMON DIARY
DEMON ORORON, THE
DEUS VITAE
DIABOLO
DIGIMON
DIGIMON TAMERS
DIGIMON ZERO TWO
DOLL
DRAGON HUNTER
DRAGON KNIGHTS
DRAGON VOICE
DREAM SAGA
DUKLYON: CLAMP SCHOOL DEFENDERS
EERIE QUEERIE!
ERICA SAKURAZAWA: COLLECTED WORKS
ET CETERA
ETERNITY
EVIL'S RETURN
FAERIES' LANDING
FAKE
FLCL
FLOWER OF THE DEEP SLEEP
FORBIDDEN DANCE
FRUITS BASKET

G GUNDAM
GATEKEEPERS
GETBACKERS
GIRL GOT GAME
GRAVITATION
GTO
GUNDAM SEED ASTRAY
GUNDAM WING
GUNDAM WING: BATTLEFIELD OF PACIFISTS
GUNDAM WING: ENDLESS WALTZ
GUNDAM WING: THE LAST OUTPOST (G-UNIT)
HANDS OFF!
HAPPY MANIA
HARLEM BEAT
HYPER RUNE
I.N.V.U.
IMMORTAL RAIN
INITIAL D
INSTANT TEEN: JUST ADD NUTS
ISLAND
JING: KING OF BANDITS
JING: KING OF BANDITS - TWILIGHT TALES
JULINE
KARE KANO
KILL ME, KISS ME
KINDAICHI CASE FILES, THE
KING OF HELL
KODOCHA: SANA'S STAGE
LAMENT OF THE LAMB
LEGAL DRUG
LEGEND OF CHUN HYANG, THE
LES BIJOUX
LOVE HINA
LOVE OR MONEY
LUPIN III
LUPIN III: WORLD'S MOST WANTED
MAGIC KNIGHT RAYEARTH I
MAGIC KNIGHT RAYEARTH II
MAHOROMATIC: AUTOMATIC MAIDEN
MAN OF MANY FACES
MARMALADE BOY
MARS
MARS: HORSE WITH NO NAME
MINK
MIRACLE GIRLS
MIYUKI-CHAN IN WONDERLAND
MODEL
MOURYOU KIDEN: LEGEND OF THE NYMPH
NECK AND NECK
ONE
ONE I LOVE, THE
PARADISE KISS
PARASYTE
PASSION FRUIT
PEACH FUZZ
PEACH GIRL
PEACH GIRL: CHANGE OF HEART
PET SHOP OF HORRORS
PITA-TEN
PLANET LADDER

09.

STOP!

This is the back of the book.
You wouldn't want to spoil a great ending!

This book is printed "manga-style," in the authentic Japanese right-to-left format. Since none of the artwork has been flipped or altered, readers get to experience the story just as the creator intended. You've been asking for it, so TOKYOPOP® delivered: authentic, hot-off-the-press, and far more fun!

DIRECTIONS

If this is your first time reading manga-style, here's a quick guide to help you understand how it works.

It's easy... just start in the top right panel and follow the numbers. Have fun, and look for more 100% authentic manga from TOKYOPOP®!